MW00799649

13TH FLOOR ELEVATORS

A Visual History

by

PAUL DRUMMOND

Edited by

MARK IOSIFESCU and
JOHAN KUGELBERG

Assistant Editor:

JON SAVAGE

Anthology Editions
New York

First published in the United States of America in 2020 by Anthology Editions

87 Guernsey Street
Brooklyn, NY 11222

anthologyeditions.com

Foreword by Lenny Kaye
Introduction by Jon Savage

Art Director: Bryan Cipolla
Cover and Interior Design: Alex Tults
Cover Photograph: Bob Simmons

Proofreaders: Chris Peterson and Grace Srinivasiah

First Edition
Second Printing
ARC 031

ISBN: 978-1-944860-11-0
Library of Congress Control Number: 2019953028

For ROKY ERICKSON
July 15, 1947 – May 31, 2019

CONTENTS

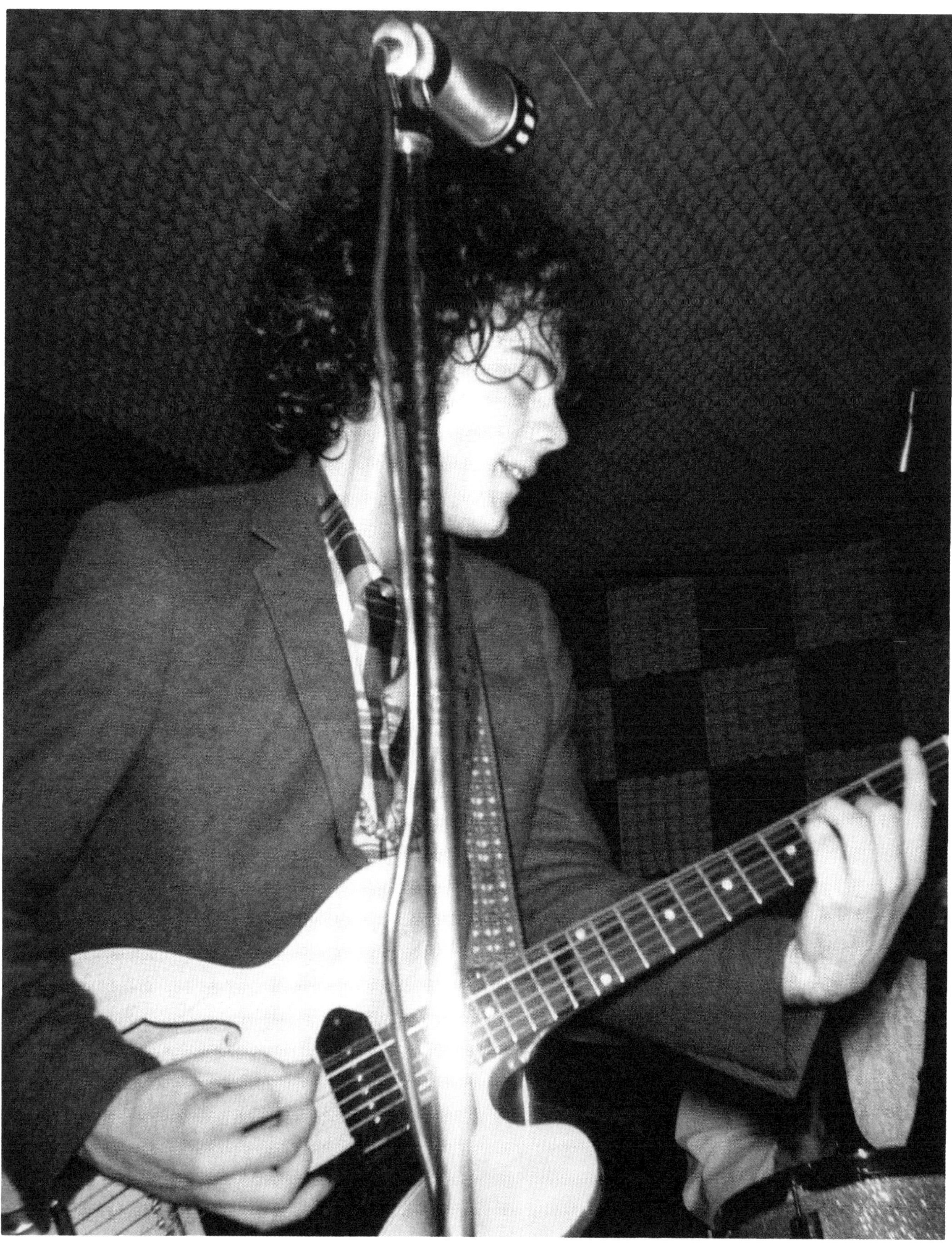

Above: Roky Erickson at the Holiday Inn Club, in New Braunfels, Texas's Landa Park, February 11, 1967.

I HAD TO TELL YOU
Preface by Paul Drummond

The label "legend" is too often applied to notable musicians. However, in Roky Erickson's case, it's undeniably valid. Roky's musical career defied conventional wisdom; in fact, from the outset, he had to defy the authorities just to be heard. He was the ultimate rebel outsider.

There are musicians who have suffered—and then there's Roky, who was forced to battle his inner demons while contending with the pharmacopoeia of substances he ingested, whether in pursuit of enlightenment or as part of a brutal medical regimen at a maximum-security unit for the criminally insane.

As the lead singer of the 13th Floor Elevators, Roky created the new musical genre of psychedelic rock before circumstances ejected him from the scene. Later, he returned at the advent of punk to add his voice to the cacophony, never complaining about his fate or the lost years, instead conjuring a colorful array of demons and gremlins to sing about.

However, there again followed years in the wilderness, until, at the start of the twenty-first century, like a revenant—Roky returned. Once again, he did it with good humor. As he told me, he felt like he had something left to say. And for the last thirteen years, he successfully toured the globe, delighting fans who had never dared dream they'd get to experience his music live.

He joined the list of famous failures who are now considered inspirational geniuses. Just read the obituaries following his death in the international mainstream media.

For me, documenting Roky's story has been a twenty-year journey that is finally over. Mostly, I'll miss the experience of just hanging out: Roky had the ability to transform the smallest pleasure into infinite fun.

Hopefully I have made a small contribution to helping Roky perpetuate his musical legacy for future generations. Thanks, Roky, for making me understand Gurdjieff and "the Work." As you explained to me in 1999: "I won't worry about it, it's gonna come, you know: when these things we have been talking about will come together and form a whole that you'll be able to know."

Goodbye. You're greatly missed.

Above: The 13th Floor Elevators at the Holiday Inn Club, in New Braunfels, Texas's Landa Park, February 11, 1967.

FOREWORD
Lenny Kaye

Though their first album was called *The Psychedelic Sounds of . . .*, it was the 13th Floor Elevators themselves who were the true psychedelia: ingesting LSD on a daily basis, haunted by law enforcement in their native Texas, their molecular structure transformed, mutated, leading them into uncharted waters of psychosis and spiritual illumination, be they negative, positive, or some madness in between.

No other band from the geologic layer of what I archaeologized in the *Nuggets* compilation as the First Psychedelic Era lived their dream and nightmare like the Elevators: Tommy Hall metaphysically charted a pathway to higher consciousness, chakra by chakra; Stacy Sutherland tended to the music and guitaring; Roky Erickson offered himself as self-sacrifice and resurrection. Bass players and drummers came and went, but the third-eye pyramid of Hall–Sutherland–Erickson persisted through a pairing of classic albums (the second was *Easter Everywhere*), grasping at the ineffable, the godhead within this music we call garage rock, and then made way for those who would take inspiration from them.

The Elevators' mid-sixties arc resonates in parabolic waves, like the "Reverberation" they celebrated, the "Roller Coaster" they rode, the "Slip Inside This House" that was their crash pad. The primal scream that opens "You're Gonna Miss Me" is a plea into the black hole of the universe, hoping for divine meaning and absolution. With the hypnotic threnody of Tommy's jug, Stacy's Lone Star licks, and Roky's savant vocalizing, they created the most outré and outrageous music to missionary position the high hopes and incipient lunacy that would be the legacy of summer's love. That it would end badly was a given, a gift, and their glory—that we now celebrate and levitate.

Above: The band at the Catacombs club in Houston, December 1966.

INTRODUCTION
Jon Savage

It's the sixteenth of March, 1966. KAZZ-FM is live broadcasting a show by the 13th Floor Elevators from the New Orleans Club in Austin. In external reality, the war in Vietnam is escalating and the number-one record in the country—for the second week—is that dreary military call to arms "The Ballad of the Green Berets," by Staff Sergeant Barry Sadler. At number one on the album charts is a whole album's worth of militaria by the very same Sadler. Clearly, the country is in a martial mood, swinging behind the war in a way that it never will again.

But the Elevators are diving deep within their own world. Since their formation only four months previous, in December 1965, they have been moving far and fast, and are accelerating to warp speed. Their first single, released on the local Contact label, is nearing the KAZZ-FM chart even as it is banned on competitor KNOW. At the same time, they are under the cosh after a serious pot bust at the end of January, which has them confined to the state of Texas on $1,000 bond until the case goes to grand jury.

External reality has declared an extreme hostility, but the Elevators' momentum is barely dented. In February 1966, they record ten more songs for a putative first album. Their first date at the New Orleans Club that month has drawn ecstatic praise from writer and booster Jim Langdon: "'Psychedelic Rock' was showing its effect on the wildly enthusiastic audience. The place was so jammed one could hardly move . . . no one has ever heard anything quite like the sound they put out, anywhere."

One month later, the group is white-hot in front of a capacity audience of around 600 people: "The place is packed tonight and there's lots of action going on on the floor," says MC Rim Kelly, introducing the group on radio. The first song is the mid-paced "Monkey Island"—a sharp comment on having to live in Texas with the rednecks and the police: "Well there's one thing about these monkeys, baby / They don't know I'm around / But that's pretty good 'cause if they knew / They'll probably come and put me down."

But it's on "Roller Coaster" that they really begin to turn on the heat. "Roller Coaster" takes you through the LSD experience. It begins slowly. The musicians are fighting to restrain themselves, and then at the lyric "You've got to open up your mind and let everything come through"—they accelerate so quickly that it makes your stomach drop. "Come on," Roky Erickson yells, as the band whoops and Stacy Sutherland takes off on a vertiginous lead guitar run: "You've got to let it happen to you."

The musicians are tripping, and so is the audience, whether on psychedelic drugs or the simple excitement and passion that the group produces. It builds to an absolute peak on the third song that remains in the public arena, a cover of that garage band staple, Van Morrison and Them's "Gloria"—soon to be a US top ten by the Shadows of Knight. As a club band, the Elevators still have to bow to that go-go imperative—dance tunes for teen punters—but their version shows why that era is coming to an end.

Suddenly, after nearly eight minutes, they stop on a dime. The audience whoops and hollers. The MC comes back in.

It sounds like he's got a contact high: "The 13th Floor Elevators, playing a song called 'Gloria'—one that they don't like to quit playing, and of course nobody here likes for them to quit playing, it just kinda keeps going, keeps going and keeps going and keeps going." In his own scrambled way, Kelly is trying to make sense of something extraordinary that you can still hear through the distortion and tape hiss. The electricity is such that it transmits with the feedback into an intangible third force: the sound of communal ecstasy.

In keeping with the Elevators' occluded career, this incredible document was not widely heard until 2009, when, thanks to the scholarship and persistence of Paul Drummond, the first comprehensive collection of their work was finally released, in the *Sign of the 3 Eyed Men* box set. In the intervening forty-three years, all manner of legends and myths had grown up around the group; partly because their career was so short and so ill-starred, more so because they embodied the possibilities of the sixties at their highest.

This was deliberate from the very start. The Elevators were young musicians programmed to promote their quasi-religious LSD use: indeed, they would sing, write, and record under the influence. Operating almost like a hermetic sect, they existed outside the music industry and media mainstreams: apart from a brief stay in California, they were confined to Texas for the duration. Not much pop media there. Apart from a couple of lip-synced television slots, there is no moving footage of the group. There are, also, almost no contemporary interviews.

Psychedelic drugs were the Elevators' rocket fuel, propelling them higher and furthur than any other group of that period—except perhaps the Syd Barrett Pink Floyd or the Skip Spence Moby Grape. There was a wildness to them that you can still hear in the recordings: a high whistling sound that is the gateway into the higher-key consciousness that they wished to communicate. They didn't hold anything back, hurling themselves into the void with each show, with each recording—with no thought of the exhaustion that it might bring.

Above all, the Elevators were a product of their moment in that they thought, like many others at the time, that LSD could change the world. It was all so new: nothing like this—the nexus of mass communication, truly popular music with radical messages, bohemian clothes and attitudes, a whole new way of being beaming straight into your mind through Top 40 radio and TV—had ever happened before.

The story of the 13th Floor Elevators is classic cautionary tale. Psychedelic drugs took them very high very fast. Orbiting at warp speed within their own universe, they completed two stages of their revolutionary plan. But they were attempting something very ambitious—a complete rewiring of the human brain, language and perception—with an unstable compound and within a very hostile climate. The dangers, from outside and inside, were real. They enacted Huxley's psychedelic duality of Heaven and Hell—in that order.

But their journey still occasions wonder and awe. For so many years, it was hardly told. Here it is, in pictures and words. This is the way, step inside.

▲

THE ELEVATORS were an intense hybrid of the British R&B groups—Them, the Who, the Kinks, the Yardbirds, the Rolling Stones—and their Texan heritage. Present always in their sound, particularly in Stacy Sutherland's ringing, clear guitar tones, was the haunting influence of Buddy Holly. They began just at that moment when American pop music regained its confidence after the onslaught from the UK—developing under increasing pressure as the Vietnam War escalated.

The dominant forces in the group were eighteen-year-old singer Roky Erickson, possessed of an unearthly shriek, and Tommy Hall—the older, manipulative drug dealer, jug player, and acid intellectual. Super-talented lead guitarist Stacy Sutherland mediated between the two, providing the arrangements and the musicianship. At bottom, they rode on John Ike Walton's explosive rimshots and driving cymbal work. The result was a mutated R&B that twisted and turned in sudden builds, harsh peaks, and shafts of pure liquid distance: LSD made sound.

By the beginning of 1966, the LSD genie was out of the bottle. Synthesized in 1942, LSD had its first use in psy-ops and deep psychiatry: thoughtful adherents had warned about this potent agent spreading from the laboratory into the populace and, by the mid-sixties, their worst predictions had come true. By 1966, culture leaders such as the Beatles, the Rolling Stones, and Bob Dylan had all been exposed to the drug, and were beginning to translate its effects and its language into hit records.

The two groups who openly proselytized LSD in the United States were polar opposites in their methodology. Timothy Leary and Richard Alpert set up the Castalia Foundation in a New York State mansion: seeking a quasi-religious program, they emphasized set and setting, quiet, and spiritual input. Ken Kesey's Merry Pranksters took the chaotic route: deliberately putting themselves and others into unpredictable situations. Holding large parties called Acid Tests, they exhibited a kind of machismo: one of their handbills read "Can YOU pass the Acid Test?"

Using the tools at hand—a rock band—Tommy Hall sought a third way. The Elevators would be living embodiments of the LSD experience: the idea was that they should get used to "playing the acid"—transmitting the synaesthetic effects of the drug and therefore making the audience high, dissolving the boundaries between the people up onstage and those in the crowd to fuse a new kind of enlightened entity. No other group was doing this in early 1966: others might have sung coded songs about tripping, but a whole program? They wouldn't have dared.

The Elevators were a kick-ass rock band, and as they played, the acid added to both the excitement and the harshness of their live shows and recordings. Reissued on the Texan label International Artists in May/June, their first single slowly became a hit, reaching a peak of #55 on October 8, after eight weeks in the top 100. Not only did it dovetail with the developing market for psychedelic pop songs, it also slotted the band into the fresh wave of hard rocking American groups. "Punks," or "garage bands," they'd later be called, but they were prominent in the top 100 during that week: at #3, ? and the Mysterians ("96 Tears"); at #9, Count Five ("Psychotic Reaction"); at #43, Love ("7 & 7 Is," perhaps the wildest record ever to feature in the Billboard charts); and, at #50, the Standells ("Dirty Water"). This was the return of the repressed: the earthy, basic but kinetic vein of American pop music that had been temporary silenced by the unprecedented success of the Beatles. "Rockers," they were called at the time, because that's what they were.

By that time, the Elevators had moved out to California: having escaped a serious penalty from the January 1966 bust, they were seeking relief from their oppressive home state. Having come to the notice of the authorities and gotten away with it by the skin of their teeth, the group was a prime target for the cops, particularly since they refused to moderate their illegal drug use. It wasn't as though they were home free anyway: two of the group were on strict probation, and the shadow of the Vietnam War draft loomed.

In contrast to the Grateful Dead or Jefferson Airplane, the Elevators had an extensive knowledge of blues, soul, and the more experimental British groups; they had cut their teeth in beach bars and teen clubs, where you had to make people dance. They played hard and fast, with a very strong bottom line thanks to new bassist Ronnie Leatherman and John Ike Walton's ferocious snare and cymbal work. Plus, they did what others merely talked about: they recorded and played on LSD, and they held it together while emanating the message.

This is music of extraordinary power. Even the chauvinistic San Franciscan media were forced to recognize the group's quality. Reviewing a show on October 16, 1966 (which featured the Dead, Big Brother, Quicksilver, and Country Joe and the Fish—the cream of the Haight crop), Greg Shaw wrote: "The most interesting group musically was the 13th Floor Elevators. They are a really freaky group. They look strange, they sound strange, and they are all good musicians, doing original material . . . The songs they do are new and different."

Meanwhile, LSD consciousness was spreading into the mainstream. On Tuesday, September 20, Timothy Leary inaugurated the League for Spiritual Discovery in front of 2,000 people at the Village Theater in New York. He had, according to the *New York Post*, "announced the founding of the 'religion' on Monday, saying that its followers 'seek to find the divinity within us' through the use of LSD, peyote and marijuana." The word "psychedelic" was beginning to spread into radio, advertising, and film.

That day, the Elevators were back in Houston to record a follow-up to their hit. Three days later, on the twenty-third—the day that the Rolling Stones released their ultimate freak-out 45, "Have You Seen Your Mother Baby, Standing in the Shadow?"—the Elevators had the promo day from hell.

They began their day at 6:00 a.m. when, as Paul Drummond writes, "they boarded a ferry circling Alcatraz Island to play a KFRC Radio poll winner's party at 7:00 a.m. They then flew to Encino, near LA, to mime 'You're Gonna Miss Me' poolside at Dick Clark's house for his national TV show *Where the Action Is*. Next, they played Bill Quarry's 'Teens 'n Twenties' dance at the Rollarena in San Leandro, followed by another undocumented gig in San Rafael." This would have been an insane schedule even if most of the group weren't tripping.

The *Where the Action Is* footage presents a bizarre spectacle: the sight of the country's furthest-out psychedelic group, dressed down in work clothes, miming their big record poolside behind a line of carefully-selected, frantically frugging Californian beauties. Boys in the audience act stoned, but the group patently is. Stacy Sutherland is stock-still and menacing, his only sign of movement one leg pumping, while Roky Erickson stands crab-wise before erupting in full-body screams and shrieks. Clearly, the Elevators were not quite teen TV naturals.

The Elevators—in particular Tommy Hall—were not messing around. They were determined to spread the LSD gospel in any way that they could. This was made crystal clear on the release of their first album, *The Psychedelic Sounds of the 13th Floor Elevators*, which occurred in late November 1966, making it one of the very first albums to carry that explicit message: it was just pipped to the post by the Deep's *Psychedelic Moods*, although Capitol had released Lawrence Schiller's documentary album *LSD* in late summer.

The album's original running order—starting with "You Don't Know," that critique of false consciousness, and ending with the swooning exhalations of "Kingdom of Heaven"—makes total sense as a trip guide. It begins in the world outside—false and hostile—then takes you deep into what it is to take a trip: the excitement, the pure exhilaration, the fear, the psychological blockages that are thrown up and how to overcome them ("Splash 1," "Don't Fall Down") in order to reach a place of peace and sanity. Feeling is paramount, expressed in pure sound.

International Artists changed the running order to place the hit at the top—as was done with most albums of the day—but even so, the message comes through, all the more because the playing, despite the duress under which it was recorded, is sympathetic, tight, and disciplined. There are no fifteen-minute freak-outs or lame blues covers, no straying beats or rambling exegeses. Everything is focused—the group is well drilled from playing constantly—and yet the LSD breaks through, in sudden shafts of liquid guitar, ghostly harmonies, eldritch shrieks, and otherworldly noises.

Heaven is thus reconciled with Hell—in an extremely accurate forty-or-so-minute distillation of the LSD experience. If it had been released on a major label, with proper promotional support, the album would probably have made major waves; it's certainly far superior to *Jefferson Airplane Takes Off*, the first Grateful Dead album, or most other early "psychedelic" artifacts. Yet at the time, it disappeared, almost without notice: the only contemporary review was in a local underground paper that criticized the poor sound and the general shoddiness of the package.

The musicians didn't help themselves. After spending the autumn in San Francisco, the group came back to Austin in disarray. The aftermath of the court case meant that the Elevators were still under surveillance, and both Tommy Hall and Stacy Sutherland remained on probation, but there were no tours, as had been vaguely promised, on the East Coast or in Europe. Having come roaring out of the gate as true pioneers, they were marooned as the psychedelic culture spread around the Western world.

After the second single, "Reverberation," stalled, that was it for the Elevators as a hit group, and after a disastrous February showcase at the Houston Music Theatre—where Stacy Sutherland had the mother and father of all bad trips and was unable to play—that was the end of the group as a guaranteed killer live act. The chaos, both external and internal, was getting to everyone. Roky Erickson was beginning to show signs of psychological disturbance, while Sutherland had severe doubts about the wisdom of their constant LSD diet.

With the new rhythm section of Danny Galindo and Danny Thomas, they started rehearsing material for a second album, which they began recording on eight track at Andrus Studio in Houston at the end of August 1967. It would be tempting to state that the Summer of Love had passed them by, but in the end they delivered the most fully realized psychedelic statement of that year or any year.

On *Easter Everywhere*, everything is carefully thought through. The beautiful yellow-on-gold cover makes it absolutely clear: this is a positive, clear-light statement. This is amplified by the image on the back cover, taken from a tantric art book, of a guru emanating force down the chakras through the third eye.

"Slip Inside This House" is Tommy Hall's grand statement, a dizzying tour through world religions and spiritual disciplines. It's a synthesis of all that has been learned from prolonged explorations in the outer reaches of the psyche: the measured, if not stately nature of its tempo and Erickson's careful, patient vocal—enhanced by Sutherland's simple, brief, but truly transcendent guitar solo—is a world away from the chaos of "Roller Coaster." It points to the hard work that must follow in order to translate the psychedelic flash into spiritual practice.

Compared to the wild momentum of *Psychedelic Sounds*, *Easter Everywhere* is thoughtful and measured, yet no less otherworldly. The break has happened: now how to make sense of this experience, how to integrate it into everyday life? The album is the Elevators' masterpiece. A half century after its release, it still stands at the very pinnacle of the higher-key documents released during that time of ferment. Inside the ten songs was a clear message on how to go beyond the initial phase of the psychedelic experience into something that could work over a lifetime—a parallel to those early LSD heads who turned their back on drugs and devoted themselves to prolonged spiritual discipline. The tragedy was that the Elevators could not, or would not, enact its message.

And, in the short term, it fell on deaf ears. Released in November 1967, *Easter Everywhere* suffered from a shoddy mixing and mastering process: the cover, while striking, was poorly printed and soiled very easily. Despite its getting a special-merit pick in *Billboard*, International Artists arranged very little promotion—a TV appearance, and the group's first collective press appearance, in a local underground magazine called *Mother*—which, together with poor distribution, sealed the album's fate. *Easter Everywhere* dropped into a hole of indifference and obscurity.

Its appearance coincided with the death of the hippie dream, at least for those in the know. In San Francisco, the incubator of the culture, the Diggers held a mock funeral to announce the end of this experiment in October 1967. By this time, the Haight was overrun by runaways and bad drugs—speed, downers, heroin. As fake psych like the Strawberry Alarm Clock's *Incense and Peppermints* went to the top of the charts, the high-minded—or at least exploratory—ideas of the early adepts were on their way to being replaced by squalid poly-drug abuse.

For the Elevators, after the pinnacle was the fall.

The group would never be as cohesive again. After a few desultory live dates, Stacy Sutherland went into the studio early in 1968 to begin the third album. This time, things would be different: less Hall-dominated, simpler musical textures. After several sessions, which resulted in six pretty much completed songs, the whole project went on hold when Roky Erickson suffered a major breakdown in April. A vain attempt by Tommy Hall to relaunch the group in San Francisco left Sutherland stuck in Texas, unable to travel under the terms of his probation.

The rest was disintegration. Tommy Hall's ideas got more and more dogmatic and difficult to realize, his tightly structured vision dissolving into spirals of chaos: he left for San Francisco and resumed his old métier of drug dealing. Sutherland began to take heroin and was busted at the end of 1968, and in October 1969, the law caught up with Erickson, when he was sentenced to indefinite detainment in Rusk State Hospital. For the next few years, almost every member of the Elevators had severe problems with the authorities, mental health issues, and the draft: Ronnie Leatherman was sent to Vietnam for two years.

It was as though they were cursed. Perhaps it was inherent in the name—the unlucky script contained in the number thirteen. Perhaps it was to do with the Icarus syndrome: they flew so high that the fall was vertiginous. No doubt it was also to do with personal dynamics. Whatever the cause, it was over. It had taken four years, but the Elevators' white light/white heat program had dissolved into the chaos and hopelessness of the time. They had, more than any other group, sought to open the doors of perception. Now those doors were slammed shut.

▲

IN 1972, Lenny Kaye issued *Nuggets*, a double album that, through twenty-seven tracks, deep-mined the fertile mid-sixties—"a changeling era which dashed by so fast that nobody knew much of what to make of it while it was around." In prime position, at the end of side two, was "You're Gonna Miss Me." In his notes,

Kaye observed that the Elevators "seemed to take the hallucinogenic experience to heart in a way not touched on before or since." Kaye conceived of the compilation as a manifesto: the twenty-seven groups featured—bar one or two exceptions—summarized a genre and an aesthetic sorely needed in the face of a "hardened and formalized" rock scene: "the name that has been unofficially coined for them—'punk rock'—seems particularly fitting in this case, for if nothing else they personified the berserk pleasure that comes from being onstage outrageous, the relentless middle finger drive and determination only offered by rock 'n' roll at its finest."

In his review of *Nuggets* for *Rolling Stone*, a magazine that had ignored the Elevators in their time, Greg Shaw picked the group as a "standout": "'You're Gonna Miss Me' . . . is an inadequate but well-chosen example of their sound, a weird mixture of Buddy Holly, Rolling Stones, falsetto screams and jug-blown popping sounds. Not only were they punks, they were mystic punks with album covers full of third eyes and songs about reincarnation. They were one of the strangest groups in the history of rock 'n' roll, and well worth a full-scale reissue of their own."

Thanks to *Nuggets*, the Elevators were presented afresh: so few people had heard or seen them at the time that it was as though they were a new group—with the added attraction of a great backstory.

In 1975, Roky Erickson resumed a recording career with the scorching lo-fi single "Two Headed Dog," produced by Doug Sahm. The Elevators and he had shared a bill with Sahm's Sir Douglas Quintet in San Francisco during the band's California stint, and Erickson made an unscheduled appearance with him in Los Angeles that July.

The cult just kept expanding. In 1974 and 1975, Television regularly played a wild cover of "Fire Engine" during their sets at CBGB: the song fit in the brief period when, as Patti Smith wrote, "they play pissed off, psychotic reaction. They play like they got a knife fight in the alley after the set." During 1976, London's Rock On was selling bootleg reissue copies of the first single by the Spades, Roky's pre-Elevators band: this was one of the records that Malcolm McLaren had on the jukebox in the Sex shop where John Lydon first auditioned for the Sex Pistols.

During 1977, Erickson released two new 45s: the *Mine, Mine, Mind* EP (including a rerecording of "Two Headed Dog" and "I Have Always Been Here Before"), on the Sponge label out of France, and "Bermuda," on Virgin in the UK. These continued the storyline into the present. Turning necessity into a virtue, the fact that Erickson's new records were released on small, independent labels over the next few years tied him into the underground, do-it-yourself nature of punk in its widest sense.

In July 1977, I wrote a long article for *Sounds* about Roky and the Elevators, cobbled together from existing sources: "Among the recent half-joking talk about a Psychedelic Revival," I wrote, "there's a tiny grain of truth: 1977 has seen, apart from everything else, two extraordinary singles by supposedly 'burnt-out' acid cult cases—'Beautiful Stars,' by Sky Sunlight and the New Seeds, and 'Bermuda' by Roky Erickson. To the ever-present dementia has been added a solid '77 rock base: still on the edge, further maybe, but TIGHTER, 1967 through a finer mesh."

The week after this piece appeared, I was approached by a fellow writer who castigated me, saying, "You can't write about psychedelia while you're writing about punk; it's completely contradictory." He was informed, in no uncertain terms, that he didn't know anything: for me, there was no gap between the Elevators and the Sex Pistols in 1977, particularly after I'd just traded in a whole pile of bad punk singles for a copy of *Psychedelic Sounds*. Both, in their different ways, had a spirit that made the whole world new.

And at the same time, there was an irresistible "decline and fall" rock myth, such as was being enacted in front of our eyes in Britain during 1977: "If you wanted to, you could see the Elevators' story as the paradigm of the acid band, or, even further, any group of people who publicly live too fast, too free, too open for society's comfort (like the Pistols now). The euphoria gave way to a nightmare reality: they flew higher—fell harder . . . now all that remains is for someone to release the original Elevators albums, NOW. So they can work their power."

The years 1977 and early 1978 also saw the distribution in the UK of records by Chrome, the Residents, Devo, and Pere Ubu that restated the dark psych theme—as David Thomas told Cleveland's

Plain Dealer in 1975. "We're putting out the hits of the next psychedelic era." In April 1978, Roky Erickson did a long interview for KSAN radio in San Francisco, putting him in the late-night "Outcastes" punk slot filled at other times by the Sex Pistols, Devo, the Cramps, the Dead Boys, Iggy Pop, and others. He stole the show.

In 1978, Radar Records issued the first two Elevators albums and "You're Gonna Miss Me" for the first time in the UK: label head Andrew Lauder was a longtime psych head and fan who understood the group's allure. That year I visited Los Angeles and America for the first time. One of my tasks, arranged by Andrew, was to interview the band's promoter Lelan Rogers in Century City, where he would talk on the record about International Artists and the Elevators. Rogers was both charming and at pains to tell the story as best he could. The resultant interview was printed in a *Radar* pamphlet titled "Howdy from Texas," released to coincide with the Elevators and Red Krayola issues, along with a Mayo Thompson interview and a reprint of the *Mother* article from 1968. It also found its way onto the inner sleeve of *Epitaph for a Legend*, an International Artists double album that appeared out of nowhere in 1980, and included material from across the artist roster, particularly both sides of the Spades single, a clip from the KSAN interview, and unreleased Elevators songs like "Wait for My Love" and "Right Track Now." No info, though.

Epitaph for a Legend felt like a bootleg even though it wasn't, and it set the tone for the group's releases in the eighties and nineties: a deluge of bootlegs. At that point, it seemed that the Elevators' achievement would dissipate in a morass of catalogue raids and poor digital mastering.

It was only after Paul Drummond's 2007 biography *Eye Mind*, the product of eight years' research and writing, that the full story was told: and the deeper you went, the more extraordinary it got. Drummond also researched and compiled 2009's ten-CD *Sign of the 3 Eyed Men* box, with full remasters, outtakes, and proper recording data—a labor of love that, in lifting the veil of poor sound that has obscured the group's music for the last four-and-a-half decades, only amplifies how great the Elevators were and are.

Words, music, visuals. The book in your hands is the final part of the trilogy.

Above: Austin, 1965. The domed Texas State Capitol, built in 1888, appears at center, flanked on the right by the tower at the University of Texas. These two buildings represent the conflicting ideologies at the heart of this story: the old guard versus the avant-garde.

CAST OF CHARACTERS

WALT ANDRUS: Houston producer who worked with the Elevators from their first sessions through *Easter Everywhere*.

JOHNDAVID BARTLETT: Austin musician signed to International Artists.

GORDON BYNUM: Record producer who first scouted the Elevators in January 1966, offering them their first recordings on his newly created Contact label.

STEPHANIE CHERNIKOWSKI: Friend of the band from their earliest Austin days.

JOHN CLEVELAND: University of Texas art student enlisted to bring Tommy Hall's designs to life, as seen on John Ike Walton's painted drum head and the legendary cover art for *Psychedelic Sounds*.

DUKE DAVIS: Bassist on the band's third album, *Bull of the Woods*.

FRANK DAVIS: Engineer on *Easter Everywhere*.

BILL DILLARD: Houston lawyer and partner in the International Artists label.

DONNIE ERICKSON: Roky's younger brother.

EVELYN ERICKSON: Roky's mother.

MIKEL ERICKSON: Roky's younger brother.

ROGER ERICKSON: Roky's father.

ROKY ERICKSON: Maverick rebel and face of the 13th Floor Elevators: founding member, lead singer, songwriter, and rhythm guitarist.

SUMNER ERICKSON: Roky's youngest brother.

DANNY GALINDO: Austin musician who took over Elevators bass duties from Ronnie, playing with the band from April to December 1967, notably on *Easter Everywhere*.

CPT. HARVEY GANN: Head of Austin Vice and Narcotics, 1955–1984.

JOHNNY GATHINGS: Stacy's close friend from boyhood; hung out with the band in Texas and during their California sojourn.

LT. BURT GERDING: Surveillance officer for the Austin police; member of Captain Gann's vice squad in the late 1960s.

NOBLE GINTHER, JR.: Houston lawyer and partner in International Artists.

CLEMENTINE HALL: Wife of Tommy Hall and key collaborator who not only named the band but also co-wrote lyrics. Most wonderful person you've never met.

JAMES (TOMMY) HALL: The Elevators' Svengali founding member and LSD evangelist who, as lyricist (and electric jug player), tried to put the "acid into the music."

JAMES HARRELL: Singer/songwriter with the Lost and Found, another International Artists signee.

CHET HELMS: Austin scene veteran turned key San Francisco concert promoter.

DR. HARRY HERMON: Austrian-born Austin psychiatrist known as "Crazy Harry" who notoriously prescribed LSD, marijuana, and peyote to patients at the height of the repressive Texan 1960s.

JOHN HOWARD: Junior partner at the law firm of Simons, Cunningham, and Coleman and critical participant in the effort to get Roky released from Rusk State Hospital in 1972.

LYNN HOWELL: Austinite, friend, and documentarian of the Elevators saga.

DON HYDE: Co-owner of the Vulcan Gas Company, Austin's answer to San Francisco's psychedelic ballrooms.

JACK JACKSON (JAXON): University of Texas *Ranger* staffer, UT "Ghetto" fixture, and pioneer of underground comix.

LAURIE JONES: Stacy's girlfriend during the Elevators' ascent.

JOSEPH KAHN: Young writer who fell under the Elevators' spell during his time at Harvard; upon graduation in 1971, he sought out the band members for interviews—including Roky, then locked up at Rusk.

JOHN KEARNEY: Boyhood friend of Roky and drummer for the Spades.

GEORGE KINNEY: Roky's classmate, husband of Dana Morris, and lead singer of the Golden Dawn.

JIM LANGDON: *Austin Statesman* columnist whose "Nightbeat" column covered the rise of the Spades, the Elevators, and Austin's psychedelic culture.

RONNIE LEATHERMAN: Stacy's school friend and high school bandmate; became the Elevators' second bassist in the "classic" live lineup, then rejoined for the final LP.

JERRY LIGHTFOOT: Friend of the band who became a mainstay of the Houston blues scene.

SANDY LOCKETT: Self-appointed acoustical engineer from the band's first gig; later promoter with the Electric Grandmother and Vulcan Gas Company.

LESTER J. MARTIN: Recording studio owner and founding partner in International Artists.

JACK McCLELLAN: Lawyer for the Waltons, frequently called upon to extricate the band from legal entanglements.

TERRY MOORE: Roky's high school friend.

CECIL MORRIS: The Elevators' roadie and occasional onstage collaborator.

DANA MORRIS: Roky's girlfriend and eventual wife, as well as the mother of his son, Jegar.

TARY OWENS: Key player in the university "Ghetto" bohemian scene; would become a notable Texas musician and folklorist.

CHARLIE PRICHARD: Austin musician known as "Fat Charlie"; played guitar in the band Conqueroo and was the inspiration for the character "Fat Freddy" in the *Fabulous Furry Freak Brothers* comic.

LELAN ROGERS: The brother of country star Kenny Rogers; record promoter turned band wrangler on behalf of International Artists.

GILBERT SHELTON: University of Texas *Ranger* staffer, art director of the Vulcan Gas Company, and key player in the development of underground comix.

BOB SIMMONS: UT student and participating bystander who photographed the band in their earliest incarnation.

KENDALL (KEN) SKINNER: Houston record business hustler who formed the label International Artists.

RAYWARD POWELL ST. JOHN: Known as Powell, was an early instigator of underground culture in Austin as performer, songwriter, and artist; wrote for and performed with Janis Joplin, and despite not being an actual band member, wrote several of the Elevators' most significant songs.

JIM STALAROW: The band's (self-appointed) first manager.

BOB SULLIVAN: Recording engineer at Sumet Sound Studios in Dallas, where the Elevators recorded *Psychedelic Sounds*.

BEAU SUTHERLAND: Stacy's brother.

SIBYL SUTHERLAND: Stacy's mother.

STACY SUTHERLAND: Founding member of the Elevators, lead guitarist, songwriter, singer, and undisputed architect of the band's sound.

PAUL TENNISON: Houston guitarist recruited by Stacy in August 1969 to replace a hospitalized Roky on vocals.

DANNY THOMAS: The Elevators' second drummer, having been recruited by Stacy in summer 1967 to play on *Easter Everywhere*.

BENNY THURMAN: Fiddle player in the pre-Elevators band the Lingsmen and first bassist for the Elevators themselves—even though he had to be taught the instrument by Ronnie Leatherman, his eventual replacement.

STEVE TOLIN: Ace promoter for the Elevators' California gigs who soon went to work for Dick Clark Productions.

EMMA WALTON: John Ike's mother and the band's first financial backer.

JOHN IKE WALTON: Founding member and first drummer of the Elevators.

WILLIAM WARNER: Photographer who began documenting the band as a high school student in early 1967.

RUSSELL WHEELOCK: Photographer who documented the *Easter Everywhere* recording sessions.

HOUSTON WHITE: Member of Austin's Electric Grandmother promotion group, performer of the Jomo Disaster light show, and cofounder of the Vulcan Gas Company.

INTERVIEW CREDITS

Oral history edited from interviews conducted by Paul Drummond from 1999 to 2019, unless noted below.

1973 or K Joseph Kahn interviews: Roky, 1973; Tommy Hall, 1975; Ronnie Leatherman, 1973; John McClellan, 1973; Stacy Sutherland, 1973 and 1974; John Ike Walton, 1973; Emma Walton, 1973

1975 *Not Fade Away*, 1975: Doug Hanners, Kirby McDaniel, Joe Nick Patoski

1977 Stacy Sutherland and Danny Thomas circa 1977: Conducted by unidentified University of Texas students

AB Andrew Brown

AC *The Austin Chronicle*, 2004

AV Allan Vorda

JS Jon Savage, 1980

KUT KUT-FM, 1985: Larry Monroe

M *Mother*, 1967

MF Max Fredrikson

RNR *It's Only Rock 'n' Roll*, 1979: Clyde Kimsey

THE 13TH FLOOR ELEVATORS

I

YOU'RE GONNA MISS ME

Prehistory

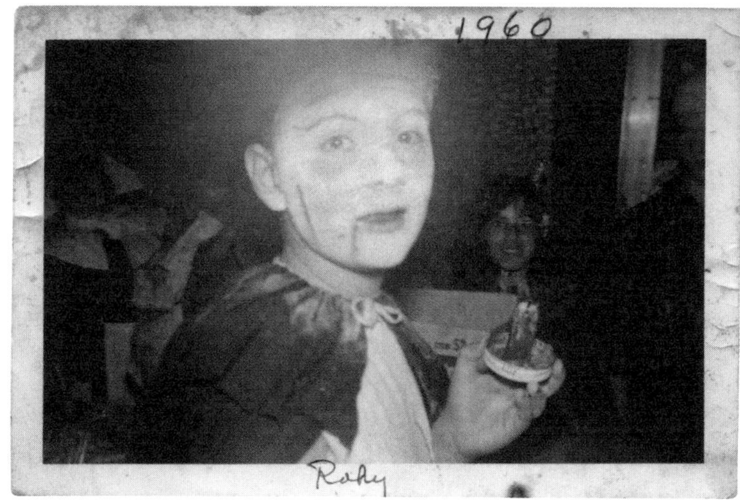

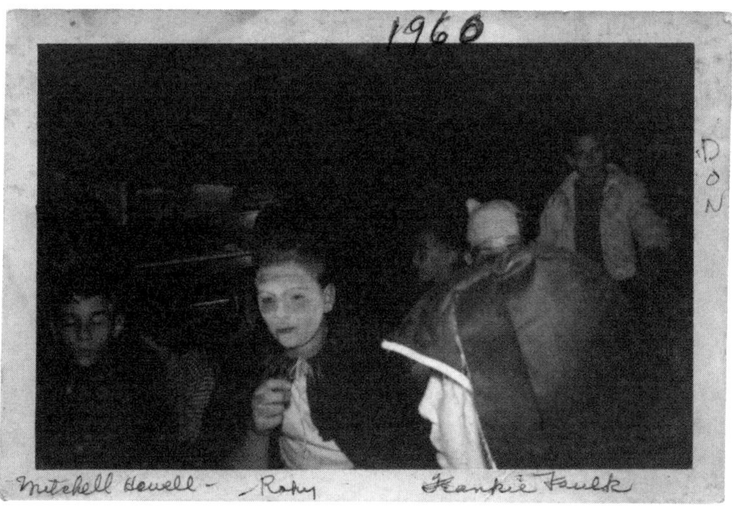

Top left: Roky Erickson, father Roger, brother Mikel, and mother Evelyn, 1950.

Top right: Roky with father Roger circa 1951.

Center left: Austin Civic Theater production of *Alice in Wonderland*, circa 1958. Melissa Winn as Alice, Cindy Winn as the March Hare, Dana Womack as the Dormouse, and Roky as the Mad Hatter.

Center right: Roky, Halloween 1960.

Bottom right: Mitchell Howell, Roky, Frankie Faulk, Donnie Erickson, Halloween 1960.

Austin is a city of divides running from north to south, bisected geographically by the Colorado River. The authoritarian and academic heart of the city is in the north, while shady suburbs occupy the south; the affluent have long resided in the west and the poor in the east. Basic amenities, such as electricity and water, were once afforded to African-Americans only if they complied with the dictum of segregation and resided on the east side. While today, urban gentrification has replaced explicitly racist division, the privately-policed West Lake Hills in the southwest remain predominately white, affluent, and middle-aged. Meanwhile, the city's downtown has changed beyond recognition as Austin continues to be razed to the ground and rebuilt skyward. Perhaps because of its allegedly "oppressive" reputation, Texas has, historically, been a breeding ground for "don't fence me in" rebels.

Roger Kynard Erickson was born on July 15, 1947, at the Nightingale Hospital in Dallas. He was immediately renamed "Ro-Ky," a near-acronym of his parents' names: the first two letters of his father's name with the first two letters of Evelyn's maiden name, Kynard. Said his father, Roger: "I didn't want him to be 'Junior,' because I detested those."

> EVELYN ERICKSON: He was a straight kid—I'd taken him to church with me every day since he was five. Sang in the choir. I couldn't leave them at home unsupervised with their father. When he was taking piano at seven years old, he wrote two songs—one was about a frog, the other was about thunder. He wrote it all out, including notation.

> ROKY: When I was four or five years old, before I could read, my mother had me take piano lessons from a neighbor called Alma Jean Ward. I also remember when I was about eight or ten years old that she took lessons on how to play the guitar. Then she would run home and teach my brothers and I how to play the two or three chords she had learned.

Like Roky, James Thomas Hall was also named after his father, but known as Tommy. He was born on September 21, 1942, at the hospital inside England Air Force Base, near Alexandria, Louisiana.

> TOMMY: I was raised in Memphis, the world of Null-A, non-Aristotelian reasoning.

His father, Colonel James Tidwell Hall, was a military doctor who had served during World War II in France at the American Hospital of Paris. Tommy's mother, Margaret Perkins, known as "Perky," was a nurse, and his maternal grandmother was a full-blooded Native American. Tommy lived on the outskirts of Memphis, amid the best of both city and rural life. He attended Caldwell-Guthrie High School in North Memphis from 1948 to 1953. When he was in high school, his parents divorced; this put significant financial strain on Tommy's mother, who continued to raise him in Memphis, while his father moved to Lubbock, Texas, and started a new family.

TOMMY (*1973*): I got taught classical music when I was little. They just brought me right up into the upper class, just how they trained me. They just designed me. My parents divorced and I used to visit my father in Texas. I automatically had an interest because he has money. I had to be super groovy to be my father's son. He was an ear, nose, and throat specialist with a big clinic in Lubbock. He had a heated swimming pool and knew all the big Texas politicians. Living with him was like living in another world. I had to be cool, you know—just shut up.

Tommy's early love of science fiction developed into an interest in psychology, which in turn led him to the work of Hegel and Nietzsche. While expanding his inquiring mind, Tommy developed an unfazed sense of amusement when people were unreceptive to his views. Later, his claim of a 180 IQ would be the only validation given in support of his ideas.

Stacy Sutherland was born on May 28, 1946, at the Santa Rosa Hospital in San Antonio. His parents, George Charles, Jr. (known as G. C.) and Sibyl Sutherland, owned two ranches—one in Center Point, the other on the Kerrville/Fredericksburg border—and a house on West Water Street near the center of Kerrville.

While G. C. was Baptist, Sibyl was Mormon, and G. C.'s ancestors had been among the 150 Mormon colonists to arrive in Texas, only to be excommunicated shortly after. Religion would loom large in Stacy's life. Once Sibyl found him lying on the earth, trying "to get closer to God."

SIBYL SUTHERLAND: He said, "I know this book [the Bible] is true, but I can't live by it; it's too strict." And I said, "Nobody can live by it without the help of the Lord." He always had scripture open, lying on the windowsills, and when he found something that troubled him, he'd say, "What does this mean?" I tried to tell him that half the world didn't know what this stuff meant.

STACY (*K*): When I was a kid in church they told me, "The Kingdom of Heaven is within you." I just took that point-blank to be true.

SIBYL SUTHERLAND: [Stacy's] Daddy gave him his first gun when he was seven, and I just threw an all-out fit. I just couldn't imagine anybody in their right mind giving a kid of seven a gun! But I had one all my life and that's what you do—you learn and teach them. One day he came home dragging a rattlesnake that he'd shot and killed—that picture made half the magazines in Texas.

Opposite top left: Tommy Hall, Memphis, Tennessee, 1946.

Opposite top right: Tommy, Memphis Zoo, 1958.

Opposite bottom: Peter, Tommy, and Carolyn Hall, circa Easter 1963. A few months later, Tommy would take LSD for the first time.

MEMPHIS ZOO
1958
JULY
MEMPHIS
ZOOLOGICAL
GARDEN
MEMPHIS
ZOOLOGICAL
GARDEN

When Stacy was nine, he requested a guitar for Christmas and begged his mother for lessons at Alamo Music in San Antonio.

> SIBYL SUTHERLAND: He said, "This isn't what I want to learn. I don't want this ABC stuff." I said, "Well, what is it you want?" He said, "I want to learn progression." I said, "Well, what is progression?" He said, "It's where each musician does his own thing."

John Ike Walton was born on November 27, 1942, in Beeville, Texas. He spent much of his childhood on the coast in Port Aransas until oil was struck on land to which his "wildcatter" father owned the profitable mining rights. In 1950, the Waltons moved to Kerrville and built a sprawling house on Fairview Drive. He joined the school band as a drummer and threw together what he could find into a makeshift drum kit. Realizing he was serious, his mother, Emma, took him to San Antonio to buy his first kit, a pearl-finish Ludwig set with Zildjian cymbals. Since Kerrville wasn't the heart of rock 'n' roll, John Ike's first foray into live music was sitting in with a country band, Fiddlin' Phil Trimble and the Rhythm Ranch Hands.

> JOHN IKE: I didn't know hardly anything, but they were desperate for a drummer, and I had a set of drums. So even though I was fifteen or sixteen years old then, they started teaching me how to play.

Ronald Maxwell Leatherman's father was a local painter and decorator in Kerrville, where Ronnie was born on January 31, 1948, while his mother was secretary at the local Baptist church. Ronnie started playing ukulele at an early age, and later took trumpet lessons. When he saw Stacy performing with his band, the Signatures, at Tivy High School, he realized what he wanted to do. When the Signatures split and lead singer Max Range formed a new band, Ronnie turned up at a rehearsal and announced, "I'll be your bass player." Ronnie discovered John Ike via a mutual interest in motorbikes and hotrod racing, and when he got a call to play with Dennis Crow—an old country singer—he found John Ike sitting in on drums.

Ronnie would miss the opportunity to become the Elevators' original bass player solely because he didn't graduate from high school in time. That role would instead go to Benny Thurman—whom Ronnie ended up teaching.

> BENNY: I'm the Benny of the bunch. I was born in '43, February 20, right at the cusp of Pisces. Well, I went to the Baptist church and everybody assumed I was a Christian. When I was about fifteen, I really felt—I don't know if they doped me, or I felt the pull, but I walked the aisle and dedicated my life to Jesus, but I couldn't make it work for me. I couldn't make God fit into my life . . . [Musically] I was getting really tired of Vivaldi and Brahms in the practice rooms four hours a day. And all those stuffy people and the orchestra. They very seldom smile.

Opposite: Photos from a Sutherland family album: at **top right**, Stacy with friend Johnny Gathings; at **bottom left**, eight-year-old Stacy with the five-foot-long rattlesnake he's just shot and killed (this picture appeared in *The Kerrville Times* of April 14, 1955, under the headline "Big Rattler").

▲ **DESPITE THE LACK** of vocational opportunity, Evelyn did everything she could to nurture Roky's natural talent as a performer. From an early age, he was entered into every costume parade, talent contest, and school play, and from 1951 he got used to being regularly featured in the *Austin Statesman* newspaper, costumed at some event or other.

Roky was enrolled at Austin's Civic Children's Theater School from an early age, and appeared in several productions between 1958 and 1965 at the Playhouse on West Fifth. These included roles as the Mad Hatter in *Alice and Wonderland*, Sonny in *Cat on a Hot Tin Roof*, and Injun Joe in a dramatization of *Tom Sawyer*. Breaking down the barrier between actor and audience has a long tradition in the theater, and when Roky appeared in *Tom Sawyer* in July 1965, he spontaneously decided to liven up his role.

> JOHN KEARNEY: Roky was always an actor. I remember [seeing] him play Injun Joe. When Roky came out everyone went, "Wow, here's someone who's into the part." And when he chases Tom and his girlfriend, Roky—instead of chasing them round the stage—ran and jumped off the stage and into the front row of kids, screaming and howling. Really, all he wanted to do was entertain.

In 1961, Roky began checking out the city's homegrown folk artists, like Carolyn Hester, at local beatnik cafes. Hester hosted a local TV show but commanded Roky's attention as she'd recorded with Bob Dylan, whose first recordings were as a session player on her eponymous LP for Columbia.

> GEORGE KINNEY: [Roky and I] had the whole image of the bad guys, made our reputations as the militants, played guitar, smoked cigarettes—our teachers hated us. We skipped school one day and got a bottle of vodka and went out to see a friend of ours, Mack Rawl. He was one of the early guys who introduced us to the folk scene in Austin, the Red Lion and the well-known beatnik places, where you'd have espresso coffee and listen to folk music. Roky and I met Townes Van Zandt through Mack Rawl. It was kind of how the university people and us met each other. Roky played and sang some then. He wasn't really writing his own songs, he was mainly singing Bob Dylan songs and Peter, Paul and Mary—folk music.

On May 27, 1963, Bob Dylan released *The Freewheelin' Bob Dylan* just as Roky finished his first year at Travis High. Roky packed his guitar and, along with his brother Donnie, took the bus to New York.

> ROKY: We just went up to New York and stayed with John Henry Faulk. He was a Texas writer, a friend of the family, and he said if we came to New York we could stay at his place. They had folk singers in the Village, where we were hanging out.

The Christmas Dance

Top left: Roky's Porter Junior High School yearbook photos, 1960.

Top middle: Ronald Leatherman circa 1952, Kerrville, Texas.

Top right: John Ike Walton, Kerrville, Texas.

Center left: Roky and date at the Travis High Christmas Dance, 1963. Printed in Roky's 1964 Travis High School "Rebel Roundup" yearbook.

Center right: Roky with swimmer and film star Esther Williams at a Dallas swimming pool convention, 1958.

Bottom right: Benny Thurman (with violin), McCallum High School Orchestra, Austin, Texas.

Above: Childhood paintings by Roky.

DONNIE ERICKSON: I was so scared to be up there—thought some green stuff was going to come out the ground—but Roky wasn't. We were playing in Greenwich Village and Roky borrowed some guy's guitar and was doing Bob Dylan, and people just drew around him.

JOHN KEARNEY (*AB*): Travis High School had a talent show. The Spades were the top bill. Much to everyone's surprise—no one expected it—they say, "OK, the next act is Roky Erickson and Joe Bierbower." Roky has this horrible old Sears amp and a very cheap electric guitar, and both of them look like they have been dragged through the mud for years. The amp rattles, but it doesn't matter—when Roky hits his singing and then blows into his harmonica, it just electrified everybody, including me! Roky just blew everyone away.

In 1964, not long after the talent show, Roky composed his most famous and enduring song, "You're Gonna Miss Me." Although his high school sweethearts have dreamt the lyrics were about them, Roky has done his best to avoid divulging his impetus for writing it.

ROKY: I didn't understand "You're Gonna Miss Me." I wrote it, though, and understood it [then]. But then, I didn't understand it. Like, "You must leave now," Bob Dylan writes in "[It's All Over Now,] Baby Blue"—I think that's the same reason I wrote "You're Gonna Miss Me." 'Cuz he said, "There's one place you must leave, because someone's gonna bust you."

His family, meanwhile, imagined the song to be about them.

EVELYN ERICKSON: Four sons took a lot of energy out of me—trying to keep up with teenagers and babies at the same time. You know how you're gonna miss somebody when they leave. The first time [Roky left]? Probably about fourteen. Where to? Friends, musicians . . . learn music without paying for it . . . he was a really good student till he hit junior high.

Meanwhile Roky's father was descending into monosyllabic alcoholism, rarely speaking to his family. Per Donnie: "Roky coined the phrase, 'Dad's an alcoholic and Mom's a neurotic.'"

MIKEL ERICKSON: [Roger] was a good architect and he was making money. They always had parties, and they always had a stocked bar, and drank a lot. Then one day my mother just decided she wasn't going to drink anymore. My mother was a heavy spender; she loved dressing the part. When we went to conventions, she'd spend thousands. Dad pretty much stayed in the office, and we'd see Dad for an hour or two and my mother would have a list—bad, good, bad—and it was his job to go punish [us]. He was an alcoholic workaholic.

Top: Halloween 1963: Roky, Grandmother Kynard, and Evelyn.

Center: Roky in the family's Arthur Lane living room.

Bottom: The Ericksons at home (left to right: Mikel, Evelyn, Roger, Roky, Donnie, Ben). Note Evelyn's abstract paintings on the wall, still there today, representing each of her five sons.

In 1964, Roky left the family home on Arthur Lane and got a cramped subterranean apartment at 404 East 18th Street.

TERRY MOORE: I met Roky in the tenth grade. There was a grocery store where we were able to buy beer without an ID, and we'd go drink a couple of beers before school. I was having trouble with my girlfriend, and this was a school day, so I drove over to Roky's and of course he was still in bed. And he answered the door all groggy-eyed and I said, "Hey man, I got some beer and wanna get drunk." He said, "Put that away and come on back here, I've got something better." He got out his little half a pipe—didn't have the stem on it—and loaded it up with pot. I'd never smoked pot before. We proceeded to fire it up and I got paranoid—I've got to get back to school. At this point he wasn't coming to school at all, and there were rumors all around about Roky smoking pot, and at this time in the midsixties, smoking pot was akin to shooting heroin. There were whispers about Roky being a drug addict.

▲

JOHNNY GATHINGS: I MET Stacy in the second grade. I didn't have a father and it was a father-son day, and he took me home with him to that ranch out there, and it developed to being best friends. He was popular but a loner. He played basketball until I think they caught him smoking a cigarette. We didn't drink or smoke pot until after high school.

It was a chance meeting in 1963 between John Ike Walton and Stacy Sutherland that sowed the initial seeds of the band that evolved into the 13th Floor Elevators. Drive-ins and parking lots were still the center of every teenager's social universe, and one night outside the Grove Restaurant, twenty-year-old John Ike's display of banjo skills was shown up by seventeen-year-old Stacy's guitar playing.

JOHN IKE: I was sitting in the back of a pickup playing my banjo, and he came by with his guitar. The next day we met again—I saw him by the sports center, and he had twelve tubes of glue and no models. He says, "Hey man, do you want to go sniff some glue?" and I said, "No, think I'm going to pass." The sports shop's proprietor told the police about Stacy buying so much glue and not buying any models—Stacy got wind of it and asked me if I turned him in to the law, which was ridiculous!

SIBYL SUTHERLAND: [Stacy] had a motorcycle that John Ike helped him fix up, but we never knew until he got four tickets in two weeks. His daddy paid the first one and told him, "I've never been in any trouble and there's no reason for it. I'm paying this one, and any trouble you get yourself in after this, you get yourself out of, because I won't be there." That's what marked him as a troublemaker with the police, and from that time on they rode him, bug hunting, every time he was in town. We began having arguments—he'd stay out late at night, and I'd say there wasn't anything good happening after twelve o'clock. But he didn't even come alive till then! And finally, when he was eighteen, I said, "If you're not going to abide by one rule of this household, maybe you need to get out there and find your own way," and he said, "I'll just do that and show you I can." And off he went.

It wasn't until meeting Johnny Bush—drummer with the Texas Top Hands—that John Ike found his musical style, and country remained his staple genre until he witnessed one of rock 'n' roll's genuine stars: Jerry Lee Lewis.

JOHN IKE: Jerry Lee Lewis came to Bandera in 1961 and I got to play on the same bill. I watched his drummer [Gene Crisman]—he was a big influence on me. He played hard. He was the first drummer I'd ever seen who really played hard and fast, and did not let up. He was sixteen years old.

Although he was a multi-instrumentalist, it was the drums that suited John Ike's personality the most—his lanky stature facilitated his drumming technique perfectly; his long reach allowed him to thrash the "bell" in the center of the ride cymbal as a trademark sound. He also had a custom size-thirteen drum pedal made for his huge feet. In 1962, after flunking out of college his sophomore year, John Ike toured Texas as the drummer for Sun recording artist Sleepy LaBeef.

▲ **TOMMY ENROLLED** at the University of Texas in August 1961 as a chemical engineering major, with a minor in psychology. Eager to make friends, he joined the student Republican society.

TARY OWENS: He used to hang out at the Chuck Wagon, but he was considered uncool. He was very into folk music, but he was different from all the rest of us. Whereas politically we were very left-wing, Tommy Hall was very right-wing. He was a member of the Young Americans for Freedom, a super-right-wing organization. That bothered me about him from the very beginning. His arrogance was really hard to put up with.

CLEMENTINE: I met Tommy in the Chuck Wagon. He was bearded and very arrogant and I instantly disliked him, and continued to dislike him for a full year. There was something about the way he just sat there and was really smug that bothered me. Other people were turning into hippies, and he was not loving and warm. He walked around in Bermuda shorts with white gym socks—a really unattractive cat. He stood out in his unattractiveness.

Top: Stacy's first musical outing on the Tivy High School stage, 1961. Previously the Travelers Three, with Stacy on guitar, the band became the Travelers Four (left to right: Stacy, Ollie Brooker, Carlton White, Kathy Bartell).

Center left: The Traditions, Stacy's high school rock 'n' roll band; Kerrville, Texas, circa 1961 (left to right: Stacy, Bob Schmerbeck, Eddie Flores, Bobby Sanchez, Randy Jackson).

Center right: John Ike Walton performing with Garland Arnold, Southwest Texas College, 1963.

Bottom right: Benny in the US Marine Corps, "A" Company, 1st Battalion, 2nd Infantry Training Regiment. Camp Pendleton, California, May 10, 1963.

ENTERTAINMENT ACTION!

MAX RANGE
BOBBY SANCHEZ
BOBBY HUNTER
RANDY JACKSON
STACY SUTHERLAND

THE TRADITIONS

Will Be Entertaining <u>*YOU*</u> *at–*

"Mad Dog's" Bar
RT 1 Freeport, Tex.
"The place where friends meet."
Mrs. R. A. Hunter: manager

(We mix 'em under The Bar)

FOR ENGAGEMENTS CONTACT: MARVIN E. TAYLOR, 108 HERZOG, KERRVILLE, TEXAS, Phone CL 7-4338 or CL 7-6610

Tommy was befriended by a student from Laredo, Texas, named Rayward Powell St. John. Known as Powell, he was integral in every form of counter-cultural development on and off campus, and he inadvertently became Tommy's introduction to the bohemian world with which he wanted to ingratiate himself.

> POWELL ST. JOHN: Folk music was a big deal. One of my friends, Stephanie Chernikowski, started a club at the student union, but there were no dues. It was set up just to come with your instrument and play, or if you had something to sing, raise your hand and just do it, and people would join in if they knew the tune. In that context, I formed a group, the Waller Creek Boys, with a guitar player, Lanny Wiggins, and Janis Joplin. As a part of everyone coming there on Wednesday nights, Tommy Hall appeared. I think he was attempting the mandolin, and not particularly successfully. And so that was how Tommy got into the jug . . . Tommy was a drug pioneer, and he and I had that in common. He and I never talked politics, but we were both Dylan fans, and the only time that I ever realized what his politics might be, was when *The Freewheelin' Bob Dylan* came out, where he did a number of social protest songs. Tommy just hated it.

While the Chuck Wagon, UT's student union canteen, provided an essential meeting place for kindred spirits, it was still part of the university—carved outside the entrance was the ominous phrase "The Eyes of Texas Are Upon You," which, while supposedly a statement of encouragement, sounded to the bohemians like a veiled threat. Although Janis Joplin once produced a bag of marijuana there, this was more for shock value, since there was no way it could be smoked on school property; deviant behavior had to take place off campus.

It was the assortment of bars, clubs, and drive-ins opposite UT on the Guadalupe drag that provided the setting for underground Austin's evolution. A few blocks north of UT, at 2808 Guadalupe, is Dirty Martin's drive-in. Having opened in 1926 as a basic burger and milkshake joint—it's still there today—it was also a popular late-night hangout. This was where, in the spring of '65, an unsuspecting Benny Thurman, fresh out of the Marines, was putting on a show playing his fiddle when he was spotted by Stacy and John Ike. Somewhat reluctantly, Benny would become the first bassist with the Elevators.

> JOHN IKE: I met Benny at Dirty Martin's drive-in, where they have carhops. He was out in the parking lot, and Stacy and I got out of my car, because we saw him with a violin. Well, I had my banjo and Stacy had his guitar—we had just blown into Austin, and I think Stacy was trying to score a lid of weed. We started playing in the parking lot.

> BENNY: I was in the Marines for life—but it didn't work out that way. I got out for sleepwalking, because I had a sleep

Opposite: Rare poster for a Traditions performance at Randy Jackson's mother's bar.

dysfunction and I couldn't tell my dreams from reality. I had a rough time. I was going to the drive-in all the time. One night I was alone playing fiddle and John Ike and Stacy came up with a five-string. They were cracking the egg, so to speak. I had failed in the Marines, I had failed in college, and I'd had my fill. We were searching for some way to make money off the talents that were left to us.

Dirty's was also essential for its supplying of beer to the student "Ghetto" across the street. In sharp architectural contrast to its neighbors—the perfectly white Zeta Psi Fraternity House and Zeta Tau Alpha sorority houses—the Ghetto was a complex of dilapidated WWII barracks converted into student apartments, home to Austin's bohemian fringe since the 1950s. Powell lived at the Ghetto from 1962 to 1964 and could be found in the yard most nights drinking beer and playing music while Janis Joplin sang old Bessie Smith renditions. Another important Ghetto resident was John Clay—notable for writing his own songs, which he performed on his banjo.

Tommy soon vacated the student dorms and moved into a property at 905 Shoal Cliff Court. The place was surrounded by frat houses but, more important, was only a few blocks from Dirty's and the Ghetto. It was here that Tommy learned to temper his rhetoric in order to be accepted.

TOMMY: When I saw Janis on the street, she came up and hugged me. That was like a sign that I had been finally accepted at the Ghetto. The problem was that I had nothing to say—everything canceled out, you know? The politics wasn't the same, and you had to be careful what you said.

While Tommy was at UT, the staff of the university's humor magazine, the *Texas Ranger*, included Gilbert Shelton, Jack Jackson, and Bob Simmons. Jackson wasn't even a UT student; he worked in the Texas State Capitol Building planning department. However, in 1964, under the pseudonym "Jaxon," he produced *God Nose*, now regarded as among the first of the underground comix. He used the Capitol Building print room after hours to run 1,000 copies, which he sold for a dollar apiece to UT students. Jaxon, along with Shelton, would later cofound the legendary Rip-Off Press.

GILBERT SHELTON: The *Texas Ranger* developed a social scene of its own, probably from the money earned from on-campus newsstand sales, which was always spent on a big monthly party. They were probably not much different from fraternity/sorority parties, with everyone drinking a lot of alcohol, except that our club had both male and female members. Later, when people started smoking marijuana, it sort of ruined this social scene, because pot smokers were too paranoid to assemble in large groups and didn't want to make a lot of noise.

After hours, the *Ranger* parties often transferred to the Ghetto.

CLEMENTINE (*K*): It was incredible [in the Ghetto]—everyone would sit around drinking beer and telling silly jokes, and then each one would tell the others how famous he or she was going to be. Janis was going to be a famous singer. Powell was going to be a famous artist or musician. Tommy was going to be a famous poet. Chet Helms was going to be a great entrepreneur.

In fact, not only did Chet Helms became one of the most important counterculture instigators of the sixties, he was also responsible for bringing Janis Joplin to international stardom. In San Francisco, Helms established the Family Dog Productions at the Avalon Ballroom, and persuaded Janis Joplin to leave Austin in May 1966, shortly after she'd reportedly entertained the idea of joining the Elevators as a singer. Jaxon soon joined Chet at the Avalon, where he set up the psychedelic poster department. When the Vulcan Gas Company, Austin's first dedicated rock venue, opened in 1967, Gilbert Shelton designed a series of psychedelic posters for the venue that are now regarded as being some of the finest examples of the genre. His Fabulous Furry Freaks Brothers, based on characters from the Vulcan and others, became favorites of the international underground comic press. Powell escaped to Mexico before finding success in San Francisco with the band Mother Earth. Janis and the Elevators both recorded versions of his songs.

CHET HELMS: I was going to go back to California one of these days. We were all enamored of the Beat Generation, and SF was the whole mecca of the Beat thing. I was a math major [at UT] but within three weeks of enrolling, they gave me the opportunity to be in a liberal arts honors program. I was part of a circle that met on Thursdays in the student union [the Chuck Wagon]. It collected people interested in folk music—it was a hootenanny kind of thing. It wasn't really set up with a stage—people kind of sat around on these hassocks, and they traded off what people played. Well, there wasn't too much happening, quite honestly . . . Other than my roommate, I was the first person that I know that ever took [peyote]. He was a student in the anthropology department and had gone on a summer project where they participated in peyote rituals. He brought a couple of plants home and ate them. He had an interesting trip that didn't leave him crazy, so we all tried it.

TARY OWENS: [Peyote] was hard to get it down; you're physically ill, you throw up. The Indians say this is a purging of evil spirits from your body. If we'd have stuck with peyote, we would have been alright and none of this other stuff would have happened, because peyote made you so ill, it wasn't something you'd abuse. Somebody turned Tommy Hall on, and he could not keep his mouth shut. As soon as Tommy started taking peyote and smoking pot, he was a proselytizer and a dealer.

He wanted to tell the world about it. I didn't trust him; it all made me very nervous. The police had raided [Tommy's house] the Mansion and made a big splash in the paper—"Beatnik Pad Raided." It was very uncomfortable for me, living in the same building with him. At that time, one joint would get you twenty years—it was very scary.

CPT. HARVEY GANN: In 1955, you could name the drug addicts. I only had four men on the vice squad and maybe two on narcotics, [but] pretty soon you had 150 and it kept multiplying. [Marijuana] was a felony. If you got caught with a recognizable and weighable amount, you could get penitentiary time, anything from two to five [years]. Anywhere up to life, if you were a second-time offender.

LT. BURT GERDING: Oh, the Ghetto—it was a bunch of hippies, it was back to the Jack Kerouac crowd . . . mescaline—which was peyote cactus—grows wild all over west Texas, and marijuana, any identifiable amount, was two to ten years for a felony. You had this mixture of legal and illegal. But they were as opposed to heroin and hard drugs as anybody else.

STEPHANIE CHERNIKOWSKI: It was before you could get manufactured LSD. The reason Tommy was into it was that morning glories were allegedly the source of LSD. He'd grind them up and feed them to you in a milkshake. I remember him cooking down peyote into a tea. All of it was nauseating. Peyote is one of the vilest things you'll encounter, but he had all the chemistry down pat. I think it was all experimental at that point. Scoring it was not what it was about. Nobody ever asked me for a dime—I was always given everything. I knew him well and I never scored from him. Anything he gave me, he gave me because he felt I deserved enlightenment.

TARY OWENS: I remember the first time that Clementine took peyote. The first time is quite often very frightening, and with Clementine it triggered a lot of things from her past that were very frightening to her. The wondrous thing about peyote, though, is that once you've faced your demons . . . there's this

Opposite top left: Bob Simmons pictured prior to his move to Austin at Cascia Hall prep school in Tulsa, Oklahoma, 1959.

Opposite top right: Rayward Powell St. John. Simmons: "I took this in the Chuck Wagon at UT. It was the hangout for all the campus lefty BoHos and smarty troublemaker types."

Opposite center left: *Ranger* staffers Gilbert Shelton and Lieuen Adkins, 1964.

Opposite center right: Clementine Tausch, 1963.

Opposite bottom left: Janis Joplin, shot by Bob Simmons in her Austin days. Simmons: "The photo is from a performance Janis did at the 11th Door, a club run by Bill Simonson, who later built Mother Blues in Dallas. I think he got busted for pot there and took a Texas-sized fall, yet Austin has almost totally forgotten him."

Opposite bottom right: Jaxon, 1966, photographed by Bob Simmons. Simmons: "Jaxon, then Jack Jackson. 1966 at his studio/apartment on Brazos Street with his painting entitled 'Hi Mom.' It was this period when he and his pals were deep into exploring the mysteries of the peyote experience. Revelations were all around us."

HI
MOM

wondrous feeling of oneness with the universe with hallucinations, both with eyes closed and with eyes open, that is indescribably beautiful. For Clementine, after a really rough time with it, where she thought she was going to die, she started having a wonderful experience. Somewhere after this, she started seeing Tommy.

CLEMENTINE: I think the reason I fell madly in love with Tommy is that when he stopped being so unattractive he looked so good in comparison, and it blew my mind. He got into Edwardian suits, and the first time he washed his hair and didn't plaster it back with grease, he was stunning.

GEORGE KINNEY: In Austin, they didn't take Tommy that seriously. They should have. Even the old Austin hippies—Tommy was way too far-out for them. Tommy made you feel uncomfortable. And Texas is really like that too. You've got some strange combinations—the redneck hippies and guns are involved. These guys were raised killing things—and when they saw the light above that, they came from a stronger position because they'd already been through the whole blood-and-guts Vietnam thing and still went to the next level. I'm a pretty liberal thinker; my philosophy includes higher levels of existence as a reality. But I have guns, I go hunting; I still think we could be under attack at any time.

There's a lot of conjecture over who was responsible for introducing LSD to Austin and when, but two names have predominated. The first is Billy Lee Brammer, one of Lyndon B. Johnson's former speechwriters. Brammer wrote a novel, *The Gay Place*, published in 1961, that exposed the workings of the Johnson state government. While on the East Coast, Brammer was able to procure vials of Sandoz LSD-25, which he introduced to the Austin scene. The other contender is New York hipster Rick Lloyd. Lloyd's exploits could likewise fill a book: everything from crashing through a plate glass window while conducting an armed robbery to decapitating a circus elephant by driving under a low bridge. Since Tommy recently divulged that he never knew his contact's name but that he was introduced to LSD by "a carny type," it may have been via Lloyd.

For Tommy, the difference between home-synthesized mescaline and laboratory LSD was mindblowing, and he soon acquired the nickname "Turn-On Tommy" from his enthusiastic proselytizing. He didn't have a clear direction or medium for expressing these ideas, however, until Sunday, February 9, 1964, when Tommy and Clementine invited Stephanie Chernikowski to a dinner party in honor of the Beatles' appearance on *The Ed Sullivan Show*. They also indulged in LSD.

CLEMENTINE: We often held dinners and acid trips for good friends when we knew of special performers appearing on TV, such as the Beatles on *Ed Sullivan*. I'll never forget it—because

By Tommy Hall
Illustrated by Pat Brown

BATHROOM DANDY

If you have a bunch of leftover cornmeal muffins, saw them in half (dia. 2¾ in.), sew them (54) together with a 3 in. silver coated needle (with eye—a 3 in. silver coated needle without an eye cannot be used because there is no place to put the thread) and high test (15–30 lbs.) black (or beige—neither will clash) thread, and paint with flour base muffin paint to make a nice bathmat.

Finding it hard to keep your cast iron skillet from rusting after washing? This common household hazard can be avoided by rubbing the skillet gingerly with one to two teaspoons (depending on the size or depth of skillet—use three teaspoons for a cast iron dutch oven or deepfat fryer) of light weight (10–30 gauge) motor oil. The kind that pours free and easy at 30° F. and does not boil away at 200° F. will keep your skillet greasy and good all the time.

WASH AND WORM

Rid your dog of fleas and paint by rubbing turpentine into his coat (the hair will come out nice and glossy)—also good for worms.

SORE SAVES SHOE SOLES

Nailing wood to the bottom of your family's shoes saves on shoe repair bills.

TOOTHBRUSH TIP

An old toothbrush will help you reach those troublesome "hard to get" spots on the family car like under the carburetor and fuel pump or in the back of the headlight.

Mom, surprise Dad in the morning by gluing a quart jar on the dashboard and placing a pretty rose or colorful pansy in it before he goes to work. It certainly does make a person feel good to ride to work with a pansy on his dashboard.

Those destructive summer moths can be stopped from ruining your clothes by keeping your woolens in the refrigerator.

ROACH NO MORE

Placing several pieces of raw meat in your yard and porch rids the kitchen of roaches.

12 APRIL 1964

FAMILY FUNSIES

Take advantage of those Grass fires in your community—they can be a family sport.

One may avoid scorching leftover biscuits and toast by reheating them in an electric blanket

Lots of money can be saved with this idea:

Materials needed:

(1) The most inexpensive 16 foot plank of walnut (¾ x 11½ in.) you can find. (Helpful note: a junk store specializing in walnut lumber might have a 16 foot plank of walnut (¾ x 11½ in.)

(2) A saw—preferably a 3 foot cold tempered saw for heavy duty work, try a hardware store, or see Hints from Hairy, Vol. 13, No. 6 (February) of Good Mothers Everyday Diary, page 89, column 6, Hints from Hairy No. 3—for a saw of this type (3 foot cold tempered saw for heavy duty work, mentioned above).

(3) An Uncle Jack O' Mite Dandy Knife (Helpful note: Cracker Jacks box).

(4) A (6" x 8" x 16") receptacle (Helpful note: a receptacle (6" x 8" x 16") can be made by cutting the sides of a soap box—with the Uncle Jack O' Mite Dandy cut 6" along a line (previously measured) and then cut at a 90° angle, for 8" along a line (previously measured) then a 6" line at same angle and then 8" again. It is best if you end up at the point at which you started. You now have one side of your receptacle. Make one more the same size, two 6" x 16" and two 8" x 16". Paste the sides together with a paste made of flour and water (Helpful note: adding catsup to the paste from flour and water will help you blend in the paste with the color of the receptacle and eliminate the unsightly clash of white and red on an earth color, such as brown).

(5) Cut board into small pieces, then, with the Uncle Jack O' Mite Dandy Knife, gingerly carve into two-inch-long slivers—be sure to catch the carvings in the handy receptacle mentioned above. This hint will save you a fortune in toothpicks.

(6) You can fit your toothpicks into your decor by leaving them overnight in a bowl of catsup (red), mustard (yellow), Worcestershire sauce (brown), left-over Guacamole salad (green), or Curacao (blue).

(7) Surprise your guests by flavoring your toothpicks with toothpaste (Helpful note: boil toothpicks in a pureé of toothpaste or tooth powder and mouthwash, a charming variety can be achieved by verying the flavors). The bubbles produce a delightful treat to the mouth.

Here's a delightful stunt: If you have a lot of left-over sawdust and woodchips in your receptacle (see above), place them in the garage to keep it cool and dry.

TEXAS RANGER 13

GOD NOSE

ADULT COMIX

Top: "Hints from Hairy," Tommy Hall's contribution to the April 1964 *Texas Ranger* magazine, illustrated by Pat Brown.

Bottom: First edition of Jaxon's *God Nose*, 1964.

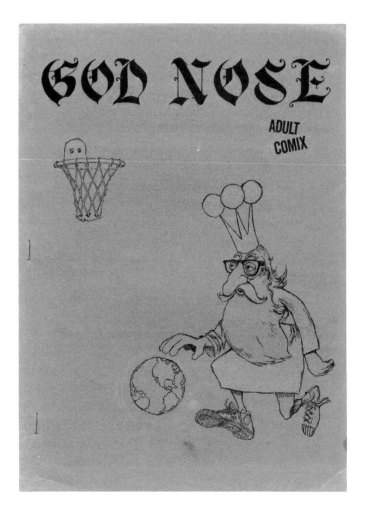

all of us were thunderstruck. I remember vividly many things that night. We had wonderful camaraderie and Stephanie was one of our favorite people. Tommy was a wonderful and generous host.

STEPHANIE CHERNIKOWSKI: Tommy turned me on to the Beatles. I remember watching them on *Ed Sullivan* at his house. He said, "You've got to come see these people, man, you gotta come see 'em."

CLEMENTINE: So, we're sitting there, and we've just had our mind blown by the Beatles, and Tommy holds up these cocktail-type napkins that said "The Dairy Queen Years: 1940–1964," and he says "Yes! We've just left the Dairy Queen Years!" We were so tickled by Tommy showing us that napkin, because it was all so true, everything [had been] so plastic.

Now, however, it seemed that era of blandness was over. Realizing that this new age of music could provide the perfect medium for his ideas, it was then that Tommy declared his new concept: a means of fusing his message with music in the form of "psychedelic rock."

CLEMENTINE: Around this time Tommy was writing poetry, and it was definitely psychedelic poetry—he's not capable of writing any other kind. It was definitely spiritual, because he was turning on all the time. He didn't know how to get that out to the public, other than rock music. You can't do a psychedelic thing with country and western, or classical, or Hawaiian music. Rock was the best medium.

▲

JOHNNY GATHINGS: WE HAD peyote in Kerrville. This guy had a cactus ranch, the Davis House. It was on Travis Street, right around the corner from where I lived. I bought 300 pods for three dollars, one cent a pod. One time we were at Stacy's mother's house and we'd eaten peyote, and I was at the fireplace playing my guitar, and the fire came out of the fireplace and into my guitar—and here comes Stacy outta the back bedroom with a rubber devil's mask on going, "Argghhh!" Scared the hell outta me. We smoked pot big-time. We got it from Austin. There was a guy, Gilbert Shelton—we used to go to his house and get peyote in caps.

STACY (*K*): Well, dig this: I met Tommy the first time when I was in high school and we wanted to buy some weed, and, like, it was about five people in Austin from the university and we were going to make several exchanges. We were over there and I ran into him at the Shamrock Bar, and we stood there and talked awhile, you know, and that was it—I never saw him [again]. And, like, a year or so later, we ran into him on the beach one day, and just got talking.

Stacy and John Ike were in Austin with the intention of playing bars to raise money for plane tickets for a planned emigration to Australia when they met Benny, who instead instigated a trip to Mexico. Broke upon their return, they headed to Port Aransas, on Texas's Gulf Coast, to find summer jobs. At a burger stand, they engaged in random conversation with a Mr. Plumley, the owner of the Dunes beach club, who desperately needed a band to entice the surfers off the beach and into his club. At $75 per week each plus lodgings, the offer was too good to pass up, and they lied and told him they were the perfect band. Panicked by the immediate start, they returned to Kerrville, ostensibly to collect their (nonexistent) instruments. Max Range, the singer from Stacy's high school bands, was available, but bassist Ronnie Leatherman wasn't due to graduate high school until the end of May, so Benny agreed to play bass. John Ike successfully convinced his mother to invest in his "business venture" and bought everyone instruments: Stacy a Gemini #2 Rickenbacker guitar, Benny a Fender Jazz Bass, and, for himself, a Rogers "Swiv-o-matic" drum kit.

A basic set of cover songs—the Surfaris' "Wipe Out," Beach Boys, classic R&B, rock 'n' roll, and British beat—was agreed upon but not rehearsed. Stacy named the band the Lingsmen, meaning, as Benny would explain, "Crazy. 'Ling' is 'crazy' in Chinese." Soon, Benny renamed everything they owned to match: the Lings-mobile, the Ling-shack, etc.

But when it came to their first performance, the band was in for a shock.

Advertisement for the Lingsmen at Maison Rouge from the *Corpus Christi Caller-Times* (Corpus Christi, Texas), October 26, 1965.

STACY (*K*): So we plugged in at our first show, and we're all nervous; we hadn't played together. Max is up there, and Benny says, "Hey man! I have to tell you something!" I'm going [*whispering*] "What? What?" He said, "I never played a lick of bass in my life." I freaked out. [But] he started watching me, and he hit the same frets I was hitting.

JOHN IKE: Benny had a show: he would break out his fiddle and play "Orange Blossom Special," and people would dance real crazy and wild out there. We'd start off real slow and then we'd play it real fast. He was an incredible violinist.

BENNY: We played Bo Diddley, "Wipe Out"—three-chord progressions. "You Really Got Me"—the Kinks . . . We had our minds completely blown; the wind would blow in all kinds of pills for one-night stands. And there were a lot of senators' daughters . . . Stacy, he had a hard, black soul, but he had a good dream. He was a barbiturate addict—downers. Had to have something to hold him down. So, that's why he kept getting into trouble; you're not going to find them on the streets, and he was hurt worst of any of us, chemically, because he couldn't get his drugs. You probably have to be a registered nurse working

1964 single by Max Range and the Penetrators, featuring Ronnie Leatherman on bass.

for a doctor to get the barbiturates that he was hooked on, or a doctor's daughter [as Stacy's high school girlfriend was]. He was, like, constantly trying to hold his brakes on.

JOHN IKE: We met [Tommy] in a filling station—he had kinda long hair and Beatle boots. So we knocked each other off as heads. I wasn't even a head—that was the first time I even smoked any dope. First we drank a bottle of [codeine cough syrup] Romilar, then started smoking some Acapulco Gold, and I was ripped beyond belief, man: I was hallucinating, houses were turning into monsters and walking across the land. We went to this stand called "Custer's Last Stand," but I don't remember being able to talk, and they asked us if we were from Russia because we were talking like "Wah, wah, wah," and they couldn't understand us . . . The cops came up, but Clementine said, "What's wrong, officers? We're a family and we're camped here." And they left us alone. If they'd rolled down the window and smelled the Acapulco Gold, we'd still be in prison.

STACY (*K*): Everybody knew we were turning on. We had two cops on Benny and I. Well, he and I used to go up there [to the Gunnery] every morning, man, and we'd sit up there, and you can see the whole island, and the pigs would drive up and they knew we were up there smoking. It would piss them off. And if they came up there we'd stash it in the sand. They'd walk all around checking in the sand and we'd ask them what they were looking for. It was a big sport, in a way.

As the summer drew to a close and their audiences dwindled, the band desperately needed a new gig, new digs, and, most pressingly, a new singer; Max, having had enough of his bandmates' antics, had walked. During their search, the Lingsmen encountered Tony Joe White, the groundbreaking songwriter and swamp rock pioneer, and invited him to the Dunes. Although Tony Joe sat in with the Lingsmen, his inclusion wouldn't last; a recently discovered letter from Stacy's then-girlfriend Laurie Jones suggests, however, that the Lingsmen and Tony Joe recorded a demo in Port Aransas, likely for the local J-Beck label: "*I'm so sorry that everything isn't working out with Tony and the record. Please send me a dub copy if you get it in the near future.*"

BENNY: Tony Joe had it down; he was really practiced. All of us went and listened and sat around and picked with him.

Opposite top left: The Lingsmen at the Dunes Club in Port Aransas, summer 1965.

Opposite center left: Left to right: Max Range, John Ike, Stacy, and Benny on Port Aransas Beach.

Opposite top and center right: Benny, Stacy, and John Ike at Club Malibu, Mexico, early summer 1965.

Opposite bottom left: The first of Benny's handwritten captions to the above photos: *"Played music for them The Mexicans of Viacouya Sinadad [sic]. From 60 miles + Hot summer, dry winds. Salt, Winds, Gusts 10mph. Sand hot dunes. Fried breaded red snapper French Fries."*

Opposite bottom middle: *"First time up together, First Highmen, Jesus is the light behind the girl. I have never seen God but I have seen his son through a mirror."*

Opposite bottom right: *"Okay lock up the fiddle, banjo and guitars and let's have a beer, citra or Canada Dry? Got too high on Benny's red hearts, upper barbiturates. Stacy had had it before and said "yuck". I went up and Stacy went down."*

#1

Played Music
for them.
THE
MEXICANS
of
Viacouya
Sinadad
Mexico
From: 60miles +
HOT summer dry
Salt Wind gusts 10-15mph
Sand Hot dunes

Fried Breaded
Red Snapper
French Frys

#3 Cock 4 + 2 in Rear
Check Beer level on bottle
FIRST 3 highmen
English OVAL (size)
Then 1 more highmen person.
GIRL
And then
there
were
4 persons Dig.
Jesus is
The light
behind the
GIRL.
FIRST
Time
up
Together.
and on and
on
Yellow
11
Cobb.
15 milly
can
I
have
another
from
The two in the rear of pic.
5 6 7 8 9 10 11 12
I have never
seen God but
I have seen
his son through
A mirror.
merck
cory reflections
paint of glass
Back of glass
mirror
J.C.'s
Image to
you
your
self.
Yes
Yes
3
yes
from Tendy
Kaughbough
and
Jerry
Levine
D.M.
CLAN TO CLEAN
TOLETO
Yes
CLEAR
Class Clear Jet

#2 3 Check Level of Beer
in Bennys bottle
Turnaround below line

Got too high
on Benny's
red ♥ hearts
upper barbital
Swiss London FAE
Song
Song
Small bit
of white left
Send one red
arrow in.
Yes Sir,
Master
STACY AND HAD IT
before sbo
Stacy
went
down
TO
HEAVEN
And
We
Are
Both
there
He's
in
me.
I went
up
Lets have a yuck
beer or CITRA
Canada dry?
Something.
OK. Lock
up the fiddle bango
and Guitars
and lets. get nice

But he was a very religious-type person; he was just like Elvis when he wasn't misbehaving.

JOHN IKE: Tony Joe's a "redneck"—he doesn't smoke dope, he's strictly into music. And I should have stayed with him. We left Tony in Corpus Christi and that's the last we heard of him until "Polk Salad Annie" [his #8 single from 1969, later covered by Elvis] came out.

▲ **WHEN THE SINGER** of Austin's Spades quit the band to get married and settle down, Roky was asked to replace him; there was no other contender for the job.

JOHN KEARNEY: The Spades had a reputation, as they'd been playing enough high school dances that people knew who they were. The bread and butter were the fraternity parties. During the summer, you starved.

When the band performed at the KOKE Radio "Battle of the Bands" event at Austin's cavernous Municipal Auditorium, there were no stage monitors—unable to hear what one another were playing, the Spades lost the competition to the Babycakes.

JOHN KEARNEY: It had to have been the worst performance given by the Spades, except Roky: he continued to do that 120 percent, blasting performance. Roky's performance was so electrifying, no one noticed that we didn't know what the hell we were doing. After that, our bookings tripled.

The Spades' manager, Gary McCaskill, booked the band regular club dates in Austin at venues such as the Jade Room and Le Lollypop. While the Jade Room was an old school beer joint, Le Lollypop was Austin's first discotheque, complete with go-go girls, and had a regular late Sunday afternoon slot for teen bands.

JOHN KEARNEY: The Jade Room was a view into the pre–go-go era: dark place, low light, the smell that old clubs have, something like an old pool hall: spilt beer, heavy smoke, but not unpleasant. The Friday night house band was called the Rhythm Kings; they'd been there forever. I don't know how Gary McCaskill got hooked up with [club owner] Marjorie Funk, except one day he woke up and decided to do his job.

TARY OWENS (*AV*): [*The Austin Statesman* writer] Jim Langdon, in the course of his [regular column] "Nightbeat" research, was going to the clubs, and had gone to the Jade Room and heard Roky and the Spades. He was totally blown away by this kid who could sing like James Brown, like Chuck Berry; he could do absolutely anything. He said, "You've got to come hear him."

Opposite: The Spades performing at Le Lollypop. At **top right**, left to right: Ernie Culley, Roky, John Kearney, John Eli, and John Shropshire. At **center left**, Roky sandwiched between go-go girls Jacki Kellendorf and Patty Badillo.

The Spades

So I went down there and heard him, and I was blown away by how immensely talented he was.

Jim Langdon's "Nightbeat" column, *The Austin Statesman*, October 29, 1965:

One of the good turnouts at any Austin club Thursday Night was at the Jade Room, where ROKY ERICKSON and the Spades enjoyed one of their best crowds at the club to date. Every time I catch the group, my feeling that Roky is one of the most exciting young singers to play in this area is reaffirmed.

Earlier in the month, Langdon had addressed the equally pressing matter of the Spades' singer's hair. From October 7, 1965:

Roky Erickson packed 'em in with the Spades, but his Beatle haircut didn't fare so well with Travis High. The exciting young combo—in modern rock 'n' roll vein—are now accompanied by Go Go Girls. Incidentally, while Roky seems to be pleasing Jade Room customers, he hasn't fared so well with officials at Travis High School. They said his Beatles-styled haircut would have to go or else. The "or else" means that Roky is now trying to finish his high school education by attending night school. It can't but strike me as peculiar that the length of a person's hair, (or color of their eyes for that matter) should have anything to do with that individual's academic standing in school. Pity poor Samson had he tried to get through Travis School without a haircut.

TERRY MOORE: He didn't get kicked out for long hair; Roky just quit coming! He just dropped out of school.

ROKY: Oh, I had long hair, and I just decided I didn't want to be in school anymore, and I asked my father if I could quit and he said yes. I just didn't like it—for some reason it was getting on my nerves. Something about it was really bothering me.

EVELYN ERICKSON: About two weeks before he was meant to graduate he got kicked out of school. He got his GED later [in prison]. Well, nobody had long hair then.

DONNIE ERICKSON: Oh, he was the most popular guy around. He was a poster child for long hair.

In early November, when President Lyndon Johnson scheduled a visit to Roky's family church, St. David's, Roky and John Kearney were singled out in the congregation by the Secret Service and asked to leave. Evelyn blamed her son's hair again.

Back in April, the Spades had released a relatively anodyne 45 to demonstrate their abilities and secure further gigs. Now that they had a dynamic new lead singer, they decided to showcase him and record two of his songs; on November 7, they headed to Texas 'N' Tanner Studios in San Antonio to record "You're Gonna Miss Me" b/w "We Sell Soul."

JOHN KEARNEY: The studio was the size of a hotel room with one mic—I had to move the drums closer or further away to get the balance right, and Roky would have to stand closer or further away. I was high as a kite; it was exciting. We were young, and at that point considered ourselves musical veterans. I don't think we played the song more than two or three times.

The launch party for the new Spades single was almost certainly November 24 at the Jade Room. Tary had alerted the UT bohemian elite to Roky and the Spades. Tommy was among those who heard the rumors and, knowing of the Lingsmen's difficulty finding a new singer, he suggested they check out Roky.

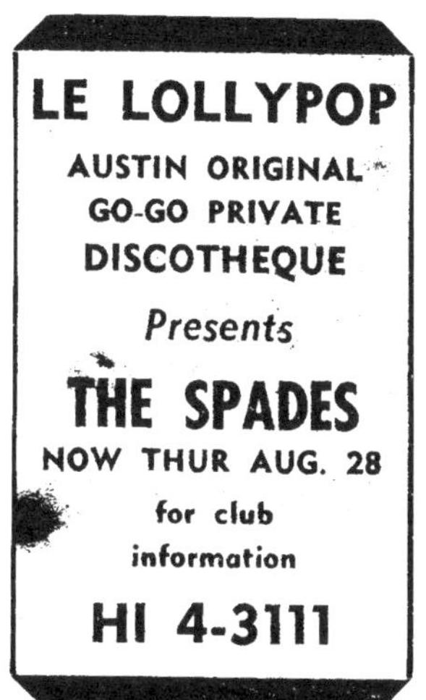

Advertisement for the Spades at Le Lollypop from the August 25, 1965 *Austin Statesman*.

TARY OWENS (*AV*): I told Tommy about Roky. I've thought about why so many times over the years—it's maybe the worst thing I did in my life. He met us down at the club. During the break I introduced them. I had second thoughts, as soon as I introduced him to Roky, that this might not be a good thing. Tommy was a manipulator and, frankly, I never trusted him. He thought drugs were the key to the universe . . . It affected Roky the most, but there wasn't a single person in that band who wasn't physically and/or mentally damaged by what happened.

JOHN KEARNEY: I can see it in my mind. You noticed [the Lingsmen] right off. It was evident from the moment they walked in the barroom door that this was a whole different element. Their dress was not mod or pop—it was hip. Benny stood out, because he was very tall and wore an earring. The only people who did that at the time were merchant marines; it meant something then. And they looked like musicians: Stacy, I remember, had a goatee. Their hair was longer. Beards were common, but the long hair—you were taking your chances. It was pretty radical stuff. Clementine was tall and beautiful and smiling. The night was a point of confluence where so many things came together.

ROKY (*1975*): I was playing with the Spades at the Jade Room, and all of a sudden, these four cats came in, and it was like they had auras around their heads, because you noticed them. Like, they came in and sat down, and I said, "I wonder who they are?" And then they came up and said, "Listen, man, we're with a group called the Lingsmen. And what we want to do is put together a big group."

CLEMENTINE: We knew that the Spades were OK, but not terribly good. But we knew that Roky was something very exceptional. Roky joined us—he came and sat with us, the first time Tommy and I saw him. Roky was very like a child. And Tommy's always looking for someone receptive to his ideas—who better than a child? So they were very fond of each other from the beginning.

The Spades' original 1965 release of "You're Gonna Miss Me"—recorded November 7, mastered November 18, and launched at the Jade Room on, most likely, Wednesday, November 24.

STACY (*K*): Tommy contacted John Ike, and told us he'd found a singer that he wanted us to come up to Austin to hear. Tommy was more or less the middleman. [Roky] was super intensity, you know what I mean? Everybody was really impressed with him right away, and immediately we decided we ought to get together.

JOHN IKE: Stacy said, "If we can get *that* kid, we're going somewhere."

ROKY (*RNR*): I went over to their house and listened to them pick and I just, I couldn't believe it, man. Benny says, "Well, we're going to outer space," and flipped on the echo chamber and [it sounded] like a flying saucer takin' off. You just wouldn't believe them.

JOHN IKE: Roky just sat there. Because we didn't know any of his songs, we may have played something like "You Really Got Me" and stuff like that. We played blues jams, and Tommy started blowin' on this jug. And we didn't know what to think of that.

ROKY (*1973*): Tommy said he had [the] idea of the amplified jug, and started. He could really do far-out [stuff]—good bird calls [*laughs*]!

MIKEL ERICKSON: They proceeded to lock themselves in this room, and all this music started coming out like I'd never heard before. They jammed and it was strange . . . and [there was] the titter-tattering of what you found out later on was this guy blowing into a jug. The police beat on the door to get them to turn it down and Tommy told them, "Everything's OK, OK? It's an experimental thing. Everything's groovy. Everything cool." So they said, "No it's not!"

Jim Langdon's Nightbeat

Deck Club Halloween Party To Be Real Blast

That big Halloween party at the Commodore Perry's Deck Club should turn out to be a real blast.

Constructing the haunted house for the Saturday night affair is KEN JOHNSON, new director of the Austin Civic Theater.

Included in the gala spook package will be dummies with knife-in-chest; hairy spiders feeding on blood; and a real, live fortune teller to tell fortunes of those who dare.

At 10:30 p.m., there will be a special dance show featuring all the popular dances from the Roaring Twenty-Flapper era, to the present day dance fads such as the twist and the frug.

Both band and dancers will be on hand to provide this entertainment.

All the waiters and bartenders will be decked out in costumes belonging to the Boston (Mass.) Opera Company, and manager GENE RAY and wife PAT will both be sporting spooky costumes for the big party.

Deck Club members are reportedly already preparing their Halloween costumes for the affair, and local actors plan to be on hand to help pull off the "new twist" masquerade.

●

Heard a new band Thursday night at the Swingers Club. The group, a five-piece rock 'n' roll combo called The Wigs, is fronted by 21-year-old drummer-vocalist RUSTY WEIR, oldest member of the band.

Other members are JESS YARYAN, bass; BENNY ROWE, guitar; JOHNNY RICHARDSON, (lead) guitar; and BILLY WILMOT on organ. Most of the boys also sing background on several of the numbers.

The bright young group has had little exposure on the Austin club scene, devoting most of their efforts to private engagements such as high school and fraternity parties.

On first hearing, the most impressive aspect of the band (aside from the strong vocals of the drummer) seemed to be their relaxed control of volume and the level of the band. On songs with three-voice passages, none of the lyrics were obscured by over-amplification, as is the case with so many young rock 'n' roll groups.

●

New owner-manager at the Cimmaron Club, 4900 South Congress.

His name is MIKE REARDON, and he takes over managerial duties for RAY DONLEY.

This weekend at the club he plans to bring in LITTLE LOU, while RONNIE CELLS will provide the musical entertainment Sunday through Tuesday of next week.

●

One of the few good turnouts at any Austin club Thursday night was at the Jade Room, where ROKY ERICKSON and the Spades enjoyed one of their best crowds at the club todate.

While there, I got to hear the other of two new tunes written by Erickson and soon to be recorded by the band—it's called "We Sell Soul."

Every time I catch the group, my feeling that Roky is one of the most exciting young singers to play this area is reaffirmed.

●

Friday and Saturday night at the Top Hat, the Crowns will be playing along with a couple of A Go Go Girls to add to the visual pleasure.

Manager AL SACHS has also scheduled the Cossacks of San Antonio for a Tuesday night engagement at the club.

Above: A clipping from Jim Langdon's "Nightbeat" column in *The Austin Statesman*, part of his coverage of the rise of Roky and the Spades, October 29, 1965.

Jim Langdon's Nightbeat

Le Lollypop Admits It's Licked

Well, it looks as though there was some truth to those rumors after all.

The word is now that tonight will be the last night for Austin's first discotheque club, Le Lollypop.

A tremendous business slump of late, coupled with a mountain of back debts seems to have initiated the club's downfall.

Some of the Go Go girls have already landed dancing jobs with other local clubs that turned discotheque after Le Lollypop appeared on the scene.

The beer lounge business is tough enough in this part of the country, but it seems the private club business is even tougher.

Dropping by the Iron Gate Restaurant Friday afternoon, a rather distinguished threesome —PRESIDENT LYNDON B. JOHNSON along with wife LADY BIRD and daughter LYNDA BIRD.

Tonight at Municipal Auditorium — DOUG CLARK and The Group.

The popular rock 'n' roll band has recorded a number of hit tunes in recent years.

Tickets for the show will be available at the door, with the combination show-dance scheduled from 8:30 till 11 p.m.

Coming Monday night at Municipal Auditorium — the big Country Spectacular.

The giant country and western show will feature top recording artists GEORGE JONES, MARTY ROBBINS, HANK SNOW and DON GIBSON, along with three separate bands.

The nation's number one country and western disc jockey MAX GARDNER of KOKE will emcee the show.

New Go Go Girls at the Jade Room:

Manager MARJ FUNK has hired two new Go Go dancers for her weekend entertainment to go along with the Rhythm Kings.

They are JACKI KELLENDORF and PATTY BADILLO, the latter formerly with Le Lollypop.

On Wednesdays and Thursdays, Marj says she doesn't need dancers to put on a show.

ROKY ERICKSON and the Spades, along with their growing following take care of that all by themselves. The band is sounding better and drawing bigger crowds each week.

By the way, the group will make it down to San Antonio this Sunday to make the master tapes for their new record—two tunes written by Erickson himself.

Speaking of San Antonio, JOHN BUSTIN and I had an opportunity to chat with GLENN TUCKER, amusements editor of the San Antonio Light this week, via split screen television on KLRN, Channel 9.

According to Tucker, Dixieland — and especially The Landing — is really booming in San Antonio now.

Tucker said the Alamo City now boasts two of the top-ten nationally ranked Dixieland bands in the country —The Happy Jazz Band (playing the landing) and the Alamo City Jazz Band, the only Dixie group featured last summer at the Corpus Christi Jazz Festival.

On the local Dixie scene, if you haven't made it yet, the Fire Plug Five will be plugging away again Sunday night, 8:30 till 11:30, at the New Orleans Club.

The Austin Statesman

Jim Langdon's Nightbeat

Johnny Tillotson Headlines UT Minstrels

Saturday night — 7:30 — Gregory Gym:

JOHNNY TILLOTSON headlines the 1965 UT Cowboy Minstrels.

Backing Tillotson will be the seven-piece "rock" band, The Fendermen, along with three swinging A Go Go Girls.

Featured Go Go Girl with the band is a booming blonde known as NATALIE, who will provide most of the bumps and grinds for the show.

The Cowboy Minstrels are held annually for the benefit of the Austin Council for Retarded Children. Last year, the Cowboys contributed $5,000 to the Council.

Also scheduled for the show will be the announcement of Texas Cowboy Sweetheart to be chosen out of a field of 14 beautiful misses.

•

Live scene at El Pepino club at 885 East 6th Street on Thursday nights.

Checked by the club last night and heard FREDDIE GOLDSMITH and the Derbies performing a rhythm and blues set. With them were to A Go Go Girls known as The Entertainers.

As of a few weeks ago, the club has taken on a new look. Owner SIMON GIL has moved the bar back to the back of the room, thus making more room for dancing.

•

Booked tonight and tomorrow night at the Carousel Lounge, 1110 East 52nd Street — The Crossfires, a young rock 'n' roll band out of Fredericksburg.

The four piece band, whose members are ages 12, 13, 14 and 15, has played a few other local night spots and received good response.

Club owners MR. and MRS. CECIL MEIER, report the young band finished seventh out of 50-some-odd contestants in the 'Battle of the Bands" in Dallas recently.

The attractive North Austin club features live entertainment only on weekends.

Good news from the Swingers A Go Go Club:

Management reports some 500 people turned out for Wednesday night's GEORGE JONES booking, and were well pleased by the top country and western artist's show.

Booked for the club tonight is a band out of San Antonio

The discotheque club will follow up Saturday night with another top country and western attraction, BOBBY BARE.

The same set of dancing girls provide the visual entertainment, be it rock 'n' roll, or A Go Go country and western style.

•

Swung by the Jade Room Thursday night.

ROCKY and The Spades are still packing them in and, in fact, are playing to an even more diversified audience than ever before.

On hand Thursday night were the usual crowd of young rock 'n' roll fans, as well as a few small children with parents, a few horned-rim glasses adult spectators, and members of the ultra-cool bearded set.

When a band can draw that diversified an audience, their music has to have some universal appeal to it.

By the way, Jade Room owner MARJ FUNK will be in San Angelo tonight where she will watch her band director son, RICHARD, put on one of his contest-material half-time shows.

Top: "Nightbeat" in *The Austin Statesman* from November 6, 1965.

Bottom: November 19, 1965.

Opposite top: November 30, 1965.

Opposite bottom: December 2, 1965.

By JIM LANGDON
Staff Writer

Nightbeat

The 11th Street To Open Under Id Management

What was perhaps the most consistent night spot and meeting place for Austin folk music and jazz enthusiasts is now defunct.

The Id coffee house, formerly at 407 West 24th Street, is no more, but taking its place will be something even better.

Opening soon under Id management will be The 11th Door at 11th Street and Red River — site of the old Jazz Room. The club will present folk music and after-hours jazz just as the old Id did, but now, customers whose musical tastes are curbed by coffee and soured by cider will be able to purchase beer within the legal selling hours.

The management will revert to coffee-only for its after-hours operations. More on this later.

•

On the black tie beat, more than 500 people are expected for the gala invitational champagne party at Cambridge Tower Wednesday evening.

The party, scheduled from 7 to 9:30 p.m. in the London Bridge Room, will celebrate the formal opening of three new businesses in the Tower.

Hosts for the evening are MADELEINE AUBRY of Madeleine Aubry Associates; MR. and MRS. E. R. SHARP of the Sharpes (fashion specialty shop); and WADE SIMPSON and GORDON MANN of HMS Gifts.

Top names on the 750-couple invitation list include such notables as PRESIDENT and MRS. LYNDON B. JOHNSON and GOVERNOR and MRS. JOHN CONNALLY.

The party is a prelude to the official open house all-day Thursday and Friday.

Providing music for the party will be the DAVE WILLIAMS cocktail trio through the PAULA CRAIG agency.

•

The Commodore Perry Deck Club, which has been operating on an abbreviated schedule for refurbishing, resumes on its regular time table Wednesday.

Looking to the fall, hotel manager ROD MORGAN reports that one of the entertainment features to be continued will be the special Dixieland Night once a month.

Already booked for a return date Sept. 23 is the popular Happy Jazz Band of the famed Landing in San Antonio.

Also still on the card is the HERB FIELDS Trio for Monday through Thursday, which expands to a quintet for the larger weekend crowds.

•

Checking in at the Jade Room at 1501 San Jacinto, I caught a young rock 'n' roll combo called The Spades which has been booked at the club for Wednesday and Thursday nights through October.

The youthful group, just returned to the Jade Room from a week-long engagement at Le Lollypop, is fronted by Beatle-haired singer and lead guitar player, ROKY ERICKSON. Other members of the band, ranging from 16 to 19 years of age, are ERNIE CULLY, JOHN SHROPSHIRE, JOHN KEARNEY and JOHNNY ELI.

Among the new-dance enthusiasts in the crowd last Thursday night were DOUG COOPWOOD of the Iron Gate Restaurant; BOBBY BALAGIA of LeLollypop; and Austin real estate man TOMMY PRICE.

Still going strong on weekends is the Jade Room's regular band for the most part since 1962—The Rhythm Kings.

The six-piece Negro combo is headed by trumpeter ALVIN PATTERSON, and includes brother ROY PATTERSON on piano and organ; JIMMY JORDEN, alto sax; LARUE BANKS, drums; NICK RYRES, bass; and LARUE MAYES on trombone.

Three of the group, who, incidentally, all chip in on vocals, have masters degrees in music.

With live entertainment now booked four nights a week at the Jade Room, owner-manager MARJORIE FUNK looks to a lively business this fall.

Jim Langdon's Nightbeat

New Club Seeks Charter Members

Applicantions for charter membership were mailed out this week by The Club Seville, located in Austin's new WILBUR CLARK Crest Hotel.

The Embassy Room of the club is due to open the early part of this month along with the hotel itself.

The plush new room was decorated and designed by Hotel Designs, Inc., of La Jolla, Calif.

•

Friday at the Coliseum—an all-star rock 'n' roll show headed by "Mr. Dynamite" himself, JAMES BROWN.

Filling out the bill will be other recording stars such as BOBBY BYRD, JAMES CRAWFORD, "BABY" LLOYD, VICKIE ANDERSON, T. V. MAMMA and the Flames.

Brown, whose big hit "Papa's Got A Brand New Bag" backed by a full 18-piece orchestra.

•

Dropped by the Jade Room this week to hear the new band there—a four-piece combo called The Squires.

The Spades, a local group that had built a strong weeknight following at the club is now in the process of rebuilding after losing lead singer and guitarist ROKY ERICKSON.

Erickson has reportedly joined another band from Arkansas coastal area.

While the Spades are regrouping, the Squires may end up with some of the band's previous bookings.

•

With the Holiday Season fast approaching, Austin's "Over 29" dance club is making preparations for two big events scheduled for late December.

First on the bill will be the club's Christmas dance, featuring the music of the JAY LEUTWYLER.

Following this will be the annual Mistletoe ball slated for Dec. 30.

LEE KOHLENBERG and his orchestra is booked for this year-end activity.

•

Though it's still in the distant future, the Texas Heritage Folk Festival steering committee has announced that folksinger PETE SEEGER has agreed to appear on next year's festival.

Also confirmed are the New Lost City Ramblers.

•

No word has yet been received on the personnel of the STAN GETZ Quartet, scheduled to play Municipal Auditorium Thursday, Dec. 9, on the CEC Concert bill.

Local jazz buffs are hoping that one of those members will be the talented young vibist GARY BURTON, who launched his professional career with the GEORGE SHEARING Quintet while still in his teens.

Getz, himself, has practically dominated the tenor sax jazz scene for the past 20 years, beginning with the JACK TEAGARDEN band at age 15.

DEC. 6 THRU 12, 1965

FUN 40 + 10

4 PM WEEKDAYS, 9 AM SATURDAYS WITH KELLEY

12 MIDNIGHT WITH DAVIS & JAY

			LW
1.	LOOK THROUGH ANY WINDOW	HOLLIES	4
2.	Cara-Lin	Strangeloves	1
3.	Turn! Turn! Turn!	Byrds	3
4.	I Hear A Symphony	Supremes	2
5.	Fever	McCoys	5
6.	Thunderball	Tom Jones	42
7.	Remember You/Just Out Of Reach	Zombies	7
8.	Here It Comes Again	Fortunes	6
9.	I See The Light	Five Americans	11
10.	Pity Me	Sonny Oceans	14
11.	Let's Get Together/Cast Your Fate	We 5	17
12.	Goodbye Babe	Castaways	21
13.	I'm A Man	Yardbirds	9
14.	1-2-3	Len Barry	8
15.	Take A Heart	Sorrows	16
16.	It's My Life	Animals	22
17.	I Can Never Go Home Anymore	Shangri-Las	25
18.	I Won't Love You Anymore (Sorry)	Leslie Gore	26
19.	A Well Respected Man	Kinks	28
20.	Go Away From My World	Marianne Faithful	44
21.	It's Good News Week	Hedgehoppers Anonyous	29
22.	Boys	Peter Best of the Beatles	48
23.	You Didn't Have To Be So Nice	Lovin' Spoonful	30
24.	Universal Coward	Jan Barry	27
25.	Who'll Be The One	Rob London/Rogues	23
26.	I'm Satisfied	Sam Remo Golden Strings	39
27.	The Little Girl I Once Knew	Beach Boys	40
28.	You're Gonna Miss Me	Roky/Spades	49
29.	Sunday And Me	Jay/Americans	32
30.	Get Off My Cloud	Rolling Stones	18
31.	Mystic Eyes	Them	10
32.	Roses and Rainbows	Danny Hutton	12
33.	Princess In Rags	Gene Pitney	38
34.	Tell Me	Strangers	33
35.	Won't You Please Crawl Out Your Window	Vacels	19
36.	Girl From The North Country	Plymouth Rockers	50
37.	Until It's Time For You To Go	Buffy Sainte-Marie	—
38.	Over and Over	Dave Clark Five	43
39.	You Better Be Careful	Golliwogs	PIK
40.	Hide Your Love Away	The Silkie	37

KAY-ZEE KLIMBERS

41.	Everyday	Moody Blues
42.	The Blues Peddlers	Dick Campbell
43.	Walk Hand In Hand	Gerry/Pacemakers
44.	Ebb Tide	Righteous Bros.
45.	Yesterday	Matt Monroe
46.	Just Like Me	Paul Revere/Raiders
47.	Please Don't Fight It	Dino/Desi/Billy
48.	She's Just My Style	Gary Lewis/Playboys
49.	An Invitation To Cry	The Magicians
50.	Gloria	Them (Return Disc)

JAZZ Spotlights

NIGHTLY 11 PM WITH JAY/WILSON

BEAUX J. POOBOO
by
LES McCANN LTD.

Here's a really groovey sound from KAY-ZEE's LIMELIGHT collection. Cuts include really fascinating things like "BATMAN" and "THIS COULD BE THE START OF SOMETHING BIG," that smash Steve Allen tune. Les wails a couple of numbers, too. Hear it spotlighted nightly on JAZZ PERSONIFIED only on KAZZ radio, Austin!

top Pop

8 AM WITH RUFFIN/HALLMAN

			LW
1.	MY NAME IS BARBRA, TWO	BARBRA STREISAND	1
2.	Whipped Cream & Other Delights	Tijuana Brass	2
3.	The In Crowd	Ramsey Lewis	3
4.	Going Places	Tijuana Brass	5
5.	The Sound Of Music	Soundtrack	4
6.	My Name Is Barbra	Barbra Streisand	8
7.	September Of My Years	Frank Sinatra	7
8.	I'm The One Who Loves You	Dean Martin	6
9.	Gentle Is My Love	Nancy Wilson	9
10.	Tony Bennett's Greatest Hits, Vol. III	Tony Bennett	11
11.	The Great Race	Henry Mancini	14
12.	Sinatra '65	Frank Sinatra	10
13.	My Fair Lady	Soundtrack	12
14.	Dear Heart	Andy Williams	13
15.	Only The Best	Ferrante/Teicher	15
16.	The Wonderful World of Antonio Jobim	Antonio Jobim	18
17.	Houston	Dean Martin	19
18.	Fiddler On The Roof	Original Cast	16
19.	Ramblin' Rose	Nat King Cole	17
20.	There's Love, & There's Love	Jack Jones	23
21.	The Sandpiper	Soundtrack	21
22.	Mary Poppins	Soundtrack	20
23.	Judy And Liza Live At The Paladium	Garland/Minnelli	25
24.	The Shadow Of Your Smile	Astrud Giliberto	24
25.	Summer Sounds	Robert Goulet	23

folk

8 PM NIGHTLY WITH JAY/WILSON

REQUEST LINE OPEN EVERY NIGHT

			LW
1.	THERE BUT FOR FORTUNE	JOAN BAEZ	6
2.	Cu Cu Rru Cu Paloma	Nancy Ames	1
3.	Red Velvet	Ian/Sylvia	2
4.	Nancy Whiskey	Allen Damron/Carol Hedin	5
5.	Kevin Barry	Pete Seeger	10
6.	In Hills Of Shiloh	New Christy Minstrels	14
7.	That's My Song	Carolyn Hester	7
8.	Brennan On The Moor	Clancy Bros./Makem	12
9.	Today	New Christy Minstrels	8
10.	One For The Money	Damron/Hedin	17
11.	Until Its Time For You To Go	Buffy Sainte-Marie	23
12.	Farewell	Judy Collins	13
13.	It's Plastic	Serendipity Singers	21
14.	The Last Thing On My Mind	Tom Paxton	15
15.	Farewell, Angelina	Joan Baez	25
16.	Dylan's Dream	Bob Dylan	16
17.	Early Morning Rain	Ian/Sylvia	—
18.	Tomorrow Is A Long Time	Judy Collins	19
19.	Young Men	Womenfolk	—
20.	Try For The Sun	Donovan	—
21.	Time	Pozo-Seco Singers	—
22.	Girl From The North Country	Bob Dylan	24
23.	Brandy Leave Me Alone	Gale Garnett	—
24.	Little Bit Of Rain	Harry Belefonte	PIK
25.	Yonder Comes The Blues	Fred Neil	—

SHOWTIME

3 PM WEEKDAYS WITH HALLMAN

MONDAY:	KISS ME KATE—Original Cast
TUESDAY:	FIORELLO—Original Cast
WEDNESDAY:	TAKE ME ALONG—Original Cast
THURSDAY:	ECCO/THE BIG VALLEY—Soundtracks
FRIDAY:	THE SKYSCRAPER—Original Cast
MONDAY (13th):	BLOOMER GIRL—Original Cast
TUESDAY (14th):	GENTLE RAIN/PINK PANTHER—Movie Scores

Above: KAZZ-FM radio survey from the week of December 6, 1965, with the Spades charting at #28.

REVERBERATION
(DOUBT)

Formation and Bust

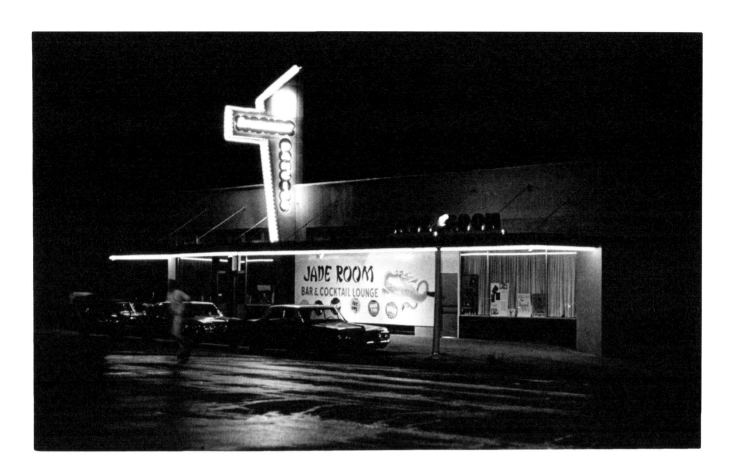

Top: The Jade Room: 1501 San Jacinto Boulevard, Austin.

Bottom: The 13th Floor Elevators' infamous business card, from December 1965, featuring the earliest-known graphic use of the word "psychedelic" in connection with popular music. The idea to depict the band's name emanating from an eye and pyramid was Tommy Hall's, but the card was designed and executed by UT art student John Cleveland, who also painted the band's drumhead and later designed the cover of their first LP.

Within days of their first meeting, Roky visited the Lingsmen at the Dunes. Since it was a foregone conclusion that they should work together, he sat in for one song only, "(I Can't Get No) Satisfaction." Just as the Lingsmen had been rushed into forming, so were the 13th Floor Elevators.

One night, John Ike was talking to a man at the bar who reminded him of Johnny Cash but in fact was Johnny Fisher, the head of the state narcotics commission.

> JOHN IKE: We had a couple of policemen that were the security guards, and they said, "D'you know who you're talkin' to there? That's the head of the state narcotics commission. You boys better get out of here. You're talking to the Man. He wants you guys." I said, "Thank you very much."

The Lingsmen left Port Aransas immediately.

▲ **WHEN EVERYONE** reconvened in Austin, all hell broke loose. There had been no time to establish whether Roky was the Lingsmen's new singer, or whether they were Roky's new backing band, and while Roky had the gig, John Ike owned the equipment and wanted to protect his family's investment. There hadn't even been enough time to discuss the new lineup: Benny wanted his electric fiddle included, and while the idea of Tommy playing bass was briefly entertained, there was an immediate split over whether he should be involved at all. While Stacy felt a huge debt for Tommy's help in finding them a new singer, John Ike only saw a threat to his control.

> JOHN IKE: See, we were on the run, really: we had no singer, we had no money, we had no food, we had no dope. Tommy had a house, he had food, he had dope—and he got us Roky, so he got us a gig. We had nothing. Roky had everything: he had a band, he had a gig, and he was writing songs. Tommy took all that away from him.

> POWELL ST. JOHN: They had rehearsals, and they all showed up and argued like hell. You wouldn't think enlightened people would argue like that, but they did. Mostly between Roky and the other members of the band. It was in the spirit of working things out, and having got into a band after that, I realized you get together and part of rehearsal is screaming at them.

The new band needed a name, and, as was already becoming typical, this became another battleground for control. While John Ike recalls that the idea came at the first meeting, Clementine is equally certain that it didn't.

ROKY (*1975*): There's not a thirteenth floor in a building, so we said "We're playing on it." It was like, if you want to get to the thirteenth floor, ride our elevator!

JOHN IKE: We sat down and said, "We've got to have a name for this band." I said, "How about the Elevators?" Clementine liked that name and said, "Oh, well we've already thought about that." But they hadn't, because we went directly from the band room to the table in the kitchen and I'd thought of it. And then she thought of "the 13th Floor," and we put the "13th Floor Elevators" together as a name—well, she did. The next day, Tommy comes over and he says, "How about 'the 13th Floor Elevators?'" At that point, Tommy claimed that he thought of the name. But Tommy was a liar and a thief.

CLEMENTINE: No, the band name came later than that first meeting. I remember very clearly the evening that the band was named. At the time I was writing a gothic novel, and I was lying in bed with Tommy and he said, "We're trying to come up with a name for the band; do you have any suggestions?" So I said, "Well, there are a lot of black bands that have names that kind of sound like this: Miracles, Temptations . . . Why don't you call yourself the Elevators? And he goes "Ah! That's good!" So he goes back into the living room and comes back about fifteen minutes later and he goes, "They liked the Elevators, but it's too short—it needs to have more tacked on to it." And my favorite number is thirteen—it's my lucky number, plus it stands for *m* in the alphabet, which is marijuana, plus most buildings do not have a thirteenth floor—so why not the "13th Floor Elevators"?

At the next meeting, Tommy suggested they all drop hallucinogens and see where it took them musically.

STACY: When you first turn on, everything is really clear and you're really organized. You know what you want to do and you do it. It looked so easy at first.

JOHN IKE: Tommy gives me a gelatin capsule full of it. He said, "Here, take this." I said, "No, thank you." Then Stacy comes in, "Hey, man, listen. You've got to take that acid or you're not going to be in a place with us." And Benny comes in and says the same thing. So I said, "OK, what the hell." I took that stuff. I was playing the drums here and the walls started to move. My brain was out of control. I was terrified of Tommy. I had the worst trip anybody could imagine. I didn't want to do anything but crawl around in the front yard of this house and look at the fields. It's weird. It might be fine for some people, but I'm not the same. I just didn't want to take anymore.

Opposite top: "Nightbeat" in *The Austin Statesman* from December 8, 1965.

Opposite bottom: "Nightbeat" in *The Austin Statesman* from December 11, 1965.

Jim Langdon's Nightbeat

Catch Lightning Hopkins for Traditional Blues

For the finest in traditional blues, catch LIGHTNING HOPKINS at the 11th Door this week.

Flanked by harmonica player BILLY BIZOR, with CLEVELAND CHENIER on rub board, the durable Houston blues guitarist has been putting on some of the best of his night club shows since he opened last weekend.

And the response has been equally good.

Manager BILL SIMONSON reported turning away more than 100 people Saturday night alone, and when I dropped by the club Tuesday evening, there was an exceptional week-night audience on hand to dig Lightning.

Hopkins will be playing the 11th Door through Saturday.

•

As previously mentioned, the big "Last Nail" party at Wilbur Clark's Crest Hotel was quite a blast.

Here are just a few of the guests who attended the affair. fair:

Col. JAMES T. GRIBBLE, commander, Bergstrom Air Force Base; White House press secretary BILL MOYERS and his assistant, JOSEPH LAITIN; COKE STEVENSON JR., Liquor Control Board administrator; and councilwoman EMMA LONG, along with husband STUART.

Also on hand were bank president HOWARD COX of Capital National, LEON STONE of Austin National; JOHN BURNS of City National; and ED WROE JR. of American National Bank; as well as JOE STJEPCEUICH of Texas State Bank.

Miss Austin Aqua Beauty, VICKI HUDSON, was escorted by Vice Commodore and MRS. STEVE PRICE; and Aqua Festival Duchesses DIANA BUTLER and BETH MARSH were escorted by MR. and MRS. ROD KENNEDY.

Sprinkled throughout the gathering were representatives from nearly all the local news media including JON FORD of the San Antonio Express.

•

Well, it's happened again.

Dino's is closed.

Former Dino's manager CHARLES WILLIAMS will now team up with DONALD FREY for a crack at the Cimmaron Club on South Congress.

Opening date for the Cimmaron was set for Wednesday, 4 p.m. to 12 midnight, with music by Dino's regulars, LITTLE LOU and JIMMY MOSES.

•

The new band that former Spade leader ROKY ERICKSON has joined is scheduled to play the Jade Room Wednesday and Thursday of this week.

Name of the new band is the "13th Floor Elevators" and consists of two guitars, bass, drums and amplified jug.

Locals in the group are Erickson and juggist TOMMY HALL, who have joined with three other muicians from the Port Aransas area.

At present, the Spades (without Erickson) are in the process of reorganizing.

•

Coming up Jan. 7—a big "Battle of the Bands" sponsored by Austin Civitans.

Most of the competition will consist of local teenage rock 'n' roll bands.

More details on this at a later date.

Langdon's Nightbeat

Blues Singer Closes Booming Stand

Closing out at the 11th Door tonight after a booming 10-day stand — Texas blues artist LIGHTNING HOPKINS.

The great blues singer and guitarist has been packing 'em in at the club, even on the week nights.

Coming up next weekend in the blues and folk vein will be three outstanding performers, including the first guest appearance of Port Arthur blues singer JANIS JOPLIN.

Miss Joplin, who returns to Austin after a few years on both East and West coasts, is playing a Houston coffee house this weekend.

On the after-hours scene tonight — a new blue-type quartet headed by guitarist RICHARD SILOM.

•

Roky Erickson's new band the 13th Floor Elevators opened the Jade Room Wednesday and Thursday nights.

The band drew good crowds both nights despite competition from one-night appearances of ROY HEAD (Wednesday at The Swingers) and STAN GETZ (Thursday at Municipal Auditorium.)

While Roky is still as exciting as ever, and the personnel of the new band sounds good individually, the group will need a little time to jell to match the continuity of the old Spades.

And those who might have been curious as to the contribution of the amplified jug in the new group were probably disappointed, for the jug, even amplified, was hardly audible over the amplified guitars and bass.

•

Word has it that Downtowner Club manager STEVE KAZMAR has been cut from the club as part of a sweeping cost-cutting move by higher-ups.

On the way, according to rumor, are additional cost-cuts that will affect entertainment as well as bar beverages.

With the new year close at hand, it may be that "quality" will become last year's word.

•

Dropping by the New Orleans Club this past week was CBS's HARRY REASONER.

Wonder if Austin's "Old World Night Club" will make one of the network's "REASONER REPORTS."

•

Reflecting on Thursday night's STAN GETZ Concert at Municipal Auditorium, few listeners there came away with any doubt as to who is the best ballad stylist in the jazz world today.

While turning in his usual top-notch performance on the up-tunes and bossa nova numbers, the genius of Stan Getz reached its forte in the ballad bag.

And his sidemen on the show —vibist GARY BURTON; bassman STEVE SWALLOW; and drummer ROY HAYNES — rank with the top musicians in the country on their respective instruments.

My only regret was that young Burton did not have the opportunity to display his rare skills on vibes to a greater degree.

While he was featured on a couple of tunes (one of which he composed himself) and took a couple of choruses on other charts, it was hardly the fair showing one would expect to be given a musician of his great talent. On tunes like "Summertime," which he has soloed on so nicely on record, and some of the straight blues numbers, Burton did not eve get a chorus.

But when he was allowed t play, he really wailed. As JOHN BUSTIN pointed out i his review of the concert, Bur ton's "Funny Valentine" alon was worth the price of admission.

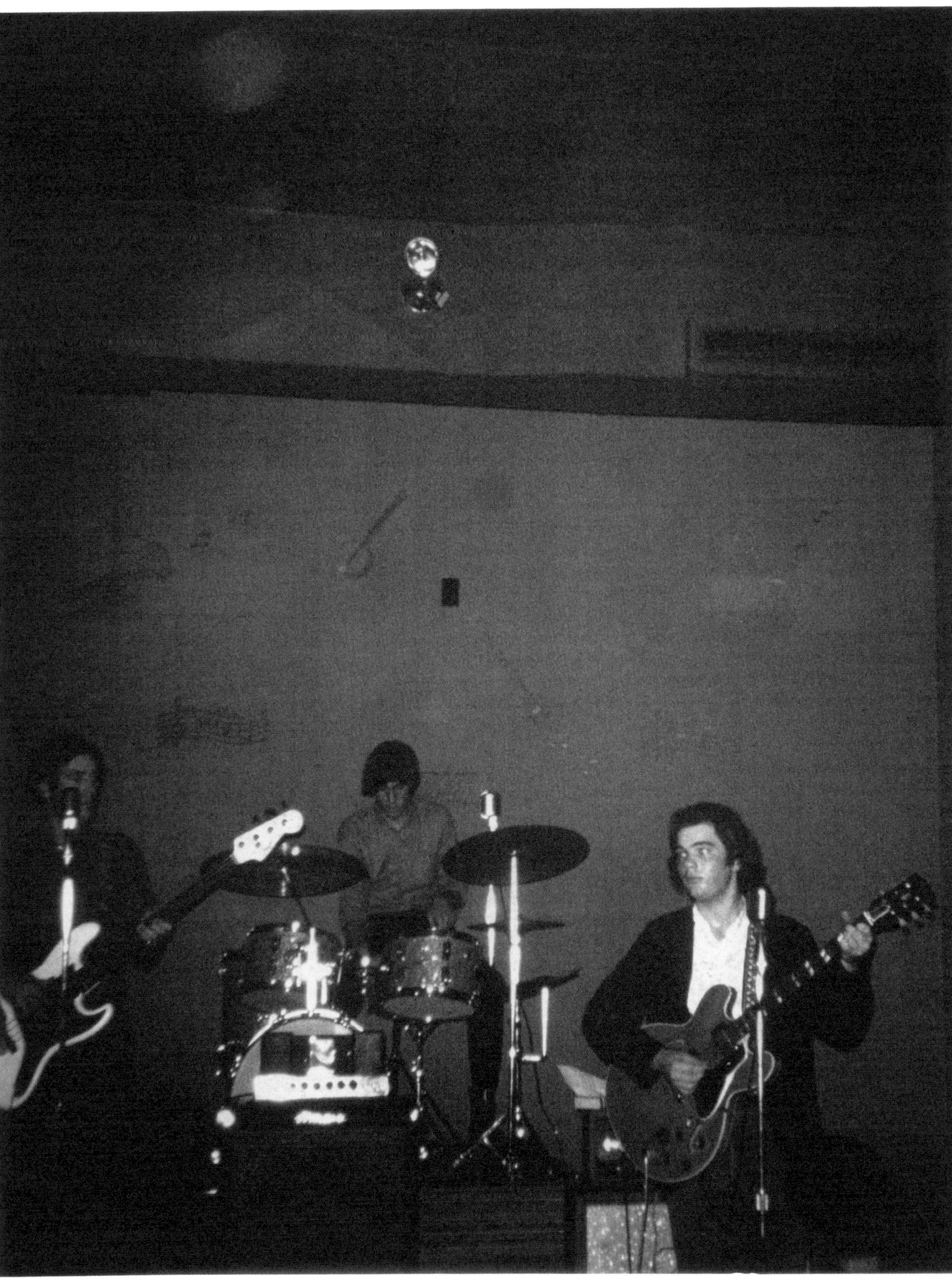

STACY (*K*): John Ike kept saying, "God, I can't believe this is happening." He kept looking really shook up, and I said, "What's wrong, man?" "We're going to heaven, man, that's Adam and Eve. And we're dying." I said, "Listen, John Ike, you're on a rib. That's Tommy and Clementine, and we're just out here on acid." Benny was in a pretty groovy place, but he was mocking a lot of Tommy's philosophy. Tommy told us we might have a bad experience where we thought we were dying—he explained about rebirth, and nobody really had any idea, of course. Once we'd had an experience, we all had this spiritual thing that happened together. I mean, it was really a religious thing. We just all came on together and we were in a wonderland. And ol' Tommy had put us, with his knowledge, into a clear state. And it was like you were totally free.

TOMMY: We were naive. It was my idea that we would "play the acid." We all took acid, but John Ike had a bad trip. So that was the first hole that we had in the group—because my idea was, we would all be on acid, and then we would reinforce one another as we played. We played some shows when we were on acid and we had people come up to us saying they were more stoned now, digging our group. It had done that to their heads.

STACY (*K*): We got tee'd into a trip together—just really some of the greatest experiences I've ever had in my life, musically, were on acid. I remember one time, we were playing and we were working on a song, and it would be good, but it would have some kind of force; I can't explain it [except] that it was like another dimension, like a wave, a wall . . . it only happened maybe six or seven times the whole time we were together, and we never got it on record, but it emotionally affected me, raised me up.

JOHN IKE: That's the first and only band I ever really could say that I formed. Of course, without Roky—there's no telling what would have happened if Tommy hadn't gotten Roky. That was a monumental task, and all it took was three hits of acid and Tommy had control of his brain. Tommy was twenty-two years old and Roky was eighteen years old. And Tommy had dope—Roky liked dope. Then Tommy and I locked horns right away, because I said to Tommy, "I'm handling the money in this band. This is my band." See, I got a bass player, lead guitar, and a drummer. I said, "I pay everybody." I wasn't taking any more for myself, but I wasn't going to trust Tommy Hall, the guy I'd just met, with my future. Because he ripped them off bad.

GEORGE KINNEY: [Roky] used to tell us, "Put bread crumbs on the trail when you go on psychedelic experience, so you

Opposite: The 13th Floor Elevators (left to right in photo: Benny, John Ike, Roky) at what was most likely their first performance: December 8, 1965, at the Jade Room. Photo by Roky's proud mom, Evelyn, seated in the front row of tables.

can find your way back," just like the old Hansel and Gretel nursery rhyme. Early on, Roky never did get too far-out—he had a way back, and it was very down-home. People who didn't know Roky never knew that side of him—very deeply-rooted in the physical.

TOMMY (*AC*): One day, Clementine and I went tripping with Roky. At some point, Roky wanted to go home. Clementine thought he should come down more off the acid before we dropped him off at his mom's, but Roky insisted it was cool. I agreed and we dropped him off. I regret that to this day . . . The next thing we knew, a day or so later, we found he was in Austin State Hospital! Tary and I knew someone who worked at the hospital, and he left a door unlocked for us. We went there and broke Roky out.

CLEMENTINE: I think it was the second time [Roky] got high with us. [Evelyn] was the one who decided he was out of his mind and needed to be hospitalized when he was high. He was high and she thought he was crazy. Tommy and I had said, "Please, don't make us take you home—we don't think you're gonna be safe there." "Oh, of course I'll be safe with Mom!" "No, please don't do that. What if she sees you like this?" "She'll be fine." And she had him committed! I do know that while he was high, he was subjected to shock treatment, and that was when the biggest damage was first done.

JOHN IKE: Tommy'd sit in the corner at rehearsals and blow away in the corner. That first gig, Sandy set up the stage and it was *not* discussed that Tommy would play. He sidled up there and started blowin'. We didn't like it because he was louder than everybody else—he had a microphone right up to his mouth.

SANDY LOCKETT: I engineered the first gig. They were using whatever could be gathered together, basically Fender equipment. It was so difficult with the jug and the open mics and the extreme—for that time—volume. I used a remarkable rig consisting of stacks of KLHs and lots of Dynaco Mark II amplifiers.

JOHNNY GATHINGS: The Jade Room, the first one. I was excited—they had it pretty much together. John Cleveland, the artist, was on the door greeting everyone as they came in; he looked really wild! Stacy was nervous—he had stage fright [*laughs*]. He was always worried about what he looked like, if his hair was OK. He was more worked up about the music though—he was the guts of the band, he had the heavy sound. First gig, they weren't really too confident they were good, [but] the music was excellent. Roky was fantastic—it just came natural to him.

Opposite: Roky with the Spades (left to right: Roky, Ernie Culley, John Eli) at the Jade Room, playing his final contracted shows in December 1965.

The
Spades

Opposite top: The band (left to right: Benny, Roky, Tommy, Stacy) in Waterloo Park, down the street from the Jade Room, late 1965. Supposedly the band's first (unused) publicity photo (without John Ike).

Opposite bottom: An early frat party performance (December 1965 or early 1966). Left to right: Tommy, Benny, Roky, John Ike, Stacy.

EVELYN ERICKSON: I thought it looked [like] good fun [*laughs*], sweet innocence. Roky came over and asked me, "How did we sound?" And I said, "Well, they don't sound like they're all together. Like, each one had their own drummer they were listening to."

CLEMENTINE: I got in touch with ["Nightbeat" columnist] Jim Langdon . . . I said, "Jim, you've said wonderful things about the Spades, and I don't want to influence you, but I want you to hear these people." Well, he was not terribly happy with the new group because it did not compare to the tightness of the Spades, but they hadn't been together long enough to get really tight, musically. We didn't mind that his review was less than wholehearted and less than enthusiastic; after that he produced much better reviews.

BOB SIMMONS: In a time when there was a devout seriousness to all we post-college would-be beatniks were up to, it was obvious the 13th Floor Elevators were decidedly serious about making a major impression on us and maybe the planet. The Jade Room gigs were where they started working out who they would become. The management complained about the volume. So did the neighbors. Tough. It was obvious the volume was part of their overwhelming charm. The lady who ran the Jade Room had to let the volume come with the band—either book them or not. She had the wisdom to survey the crowd they were attracting and say, "OK, play as loud as you like. Keep it on ten, Stacy." If I hadn't taken the pictures, I'd never remember anything.

ROKY: [The Elevators] would play with the feedback from the guitars. We would put our amps on each other and it would create what we called "the third voice"—trying to form the feedback into a separate tune.

POWELL ST. JOHN: The times that I saw them live, I believe that they were on acid. It sounded as though they were operating as a single being, a single unit. They were intuiting one another to an extent that I had never seen before. It didn't look like they had practiced the stuff; they were communicating almost telepathically.

Tommy commissioned John Cleveland, a UT art student, to design the band's business card, which depicted the words "psychedelic rock" emitting from a pyramid-and-eye motif. Although there had been earlier usages of the word "psychedelic" in relation to music, Cleveland's business card is the earliest, most overt piece of psychedelic artwork for a band that exists. He also painted the band's drumhead in a similar style, as well as one-off posters for the Jade Room window (none of which are known to have survived).

Top: Roky and Stacy locking into the "Third Sound" at the Jade Room.

Center: Unknown woman and "Nightbeat" columnist Jim Langdon dancing at the Jade Room—note the papier-mâché dragon in the background.

Bottom: Benny and John Ike at the Jade Room, December 1965 or early 1966.

While John Ike wanted Tommy out of the group immediately, Stacy felt a huge debt to him—not only for introducing them to Roky, but also for LSD, which he felt transformed him as a musician. Stacy reciprocated by asking Tommy to write lyrics to some of the riffs he'd been working up. He gave Tommy the structure of an anti-school song, originally titled "Who Am I?" Unimpressed, Tommy added "multidimensional textures," and transformed it into "Thru the Rhythm"—a manifesto to break ties "with books that rehash the same old lies" and seek new forms of knowledge.

One night before Christmas 1965, the band returned to their motel room to find FBI agents waiting for them. One of Stacy's friends had dodged the draft and been hiding out in their room. The motel owners, Ray and Helen Boles, played detective, keeping a record of the group's activities which they then passed to the Austin Vice Squad: "Roger 'Rocky' Erickson, George E. Kinney and J. Thomas Hall" were named—"members of a small, local jazz band, playing in the Austin area," believed "to be using and trafficking marijuana." In haste to get home for the holiday, Stacy left his bill unpaid and a coat hanging in the closet with marijuana in the pocket.

> STACY (*K*): This guy had come from Houston and smoked some joints up in our apartment, and dumped the seeds and ashes in this sack by the stove, and this other guy left a coat with weed in the pockets. So they got all those little bits together, and that's what they popped us for.

Regardless of whose coat it was, its pocket had a sports shop receipt with Stacy's name on it. The owners of the North Lamar Hotel called the police at 9:30 a.m. on Christmas morning and the vice squad arrived within fifteen minutes. The consequences of this oversight impacted the rest of Stacy's life. The ensuing court case curtailed not only his creative but also his physical freedom: he'd soon have to apply for a travel permit simply to attend a rehearsal.

> STACY (*K*): We found out later that they'd been tracking us more or less since we were in Port Aransas.

▲

> **GORDON BYNUM: IT WAS** breathtaking, the precision. It was like those ice skaters—how can they do it? And so I said, "Would you like to come to Houston?" and offered them a chance to record.

On January 2, 1966, the Elevators prepared for their first recording session. Bynum booked them with producer Walt Andrus at his studio in Houston and created a new label named Contact (as in "contact high") especially for the release. Benny was billeted with Roky for last-minute rehearsals of his bass parts to "You're Gonna Miss Me," the obvious choice for first single. Of course, this decision caused a backlash: the band was accused of poaching the Spades' singer to steal his potential hit song. Worse still, Roky was obliged to still perform with the Spades until his contracted bookings ran out.

> WALT ANDRUS: I didn't know a lot about them then—they just came in and did it. And it was a mono recording [with] everybody standing around with some microphones I'd put around the studio. Real simple. Roky was probably the most exciting singer I ever worked with—he had that charisma, and an intelligence that he could do anything he ever wanted [with].

The band's LSD use, meanwhile, carried significant risk.

Opposite: The infamous letter to Stacy from "Schofield," detailing the drug deal that would seal the band's fate. Despite the date at the top, the envelope postmark confirms this was mailed in January 1966.

> Q: Where was Tommy getting [the LSD]?
>
> STACY: From somebody in New York sending it to him in packages.
>
> Q: Did you feel like it was pure stuff?
>
> STACY: I felt like it was, yeah. It was capsules; I think it was Sandoz. Occasionally, we got some bad acid but not really—once in a while it might have strychnine or speed or some stimulant. Some of those were bummers, but generally we always tried to get the best acid. That was one thing we tried to do.
>
> Q: Did you ever play without dropping?
>
> STACY: Oh yeah, once in a while, but not that much.
>
> Q: Was it a lot different?
>
> STACY: Yeah, it was. It didn't feel [like] such a spiritual thing. I'd be more self-conscious and hung up about my personal thing and, like, when I was on acid, I could be free and in a very loose manner.
>
> Q: It helped your music, then?
>
> STACY: When I listen to the music now, I don't think it really did, but as far as my feeling for the music, it was much more—as far as playing it, it was a lot more intense. Like, I feel I was a lot more imaginative on acid.

In an effort to procure hallucinogens, Stacy made contact with someone named "Schofield" at Dartmouth College in New Hampshire. A written response was sent to "Stacy Sutherland, North Main Street, Kerrville," but was delivered to the family home of Johnny Gathings, Stacy's old friend. Johnny's sister, already suspicious about what Stacy was getting her brother into, intercepted the letter and tipped off the police before forwarding it to Stacy's new lodgings at the Bellaire Motel, 3412 S. Congress, in Austin. This, in turn, helped connect the vice squad in Port Aransas with the Travis County police force in Austin.

1/17/65

Stacy –

Will be able to make trade – can get hash & acid relatively easily. Acid will come in caps, so there will be no difficulty. Thought at first I could only get it in sugar cubes, but now there will be no problem.

Took my first acid trip Sat. nite – Sun Morning. Very interesting, very revealing. Smoked hash at same time – for a while, anyway – quite a combination – you can go strange places – nice places.

Write & tell me details – how much acid you want, if you can trade Gold, what ratio, etc –

Schofield

Address –

312 South Wigwam
Dartmouth College
Hanover, N. H.

JOHNNY GATHINGS: John Ike didn't want to take [LSD], so I said, "I'll take it."

JOHN IKE: See, Stacy said, "John Ike, give me the acid Tommy gives you, and I'll give it to Johnny—he needs it." So I said OK—he was my friend, we were getting along at the time. Stacy gave Johnny the acid and also a bottle of Romilar. Johnny flips out, and his sister calls the vice squad in Austin and says, "Their names are John Ike Walton and Stacy Sutherland, they own such and such a car, and they're at this hotel." Tommy [had] asked to borrow my car—he didn't tell me where he was going, or what he was doing. Tommy returned from Mexico with twenty-six pounds of Acapulco Gold.

On the evening of January 26, Harvey Gann and two of his vice squad sergeants, preparing for the bust, staked out Tommy's house until 2:00 a.m.

JOHN IKE: We saw the vice squad officers in the alleyway one day before the bust, and Tommy said, "Don't worry about getting busted—[surveillance officer] Gerding will give us a call and say, 'Get cool or we'll have to bust you.'"

Earlier that day, policemen Leonard Flores and E. L. Conner applied for a search warrant for room eighteen of the Bellaire Motel. Due to a "lack of activity," they didn't execute their search and waited until the following evening, when Gann decided to also raid Tommy and Clementine's at 8:20 p.m.

JOHN IKE: Well, Gerding didn't call, and just about an hour before the police came in to bust us, Stacy, Roky, and Tommy dropped some mescaline, so they were peaking while they were getting busted. I was at the back door—there was a .45 automatic sticking in my face as soon as I started down the steps, and they said, "Get back inside the house." I went back in there and he went to the front . . . [and] they had me sit down and take my boots off and looked for drugs—individually searched all of us.

STACY (*K*): Tommy's little step-kids kept saying, "Those aren't men, Mama, those are *policemen.*" Everybody was sitting around on mescaline, and we'd been smoking, there was pipes, and like, they just walked in on us—it was too much of a trip. Sure, that Tommy was hot; they used to call him "Tommy Turn-On." He was just flabbergasted. He just didn't think it was going to happen. It just blew his mind.

CLEMENTINE: We had grass in our garage. Now I had heard that Gann, if he got any of the Elevators alone, would make sure some of the younger members of the force would beat the hell out of them, because he felt that they were influencing the young people of Texas in a really bad way. I was lying in

Opposite: Austin Police Department surveillance photos of Tommy and Clementine's house at 403 E. 38th Street—showing John Ike's van parked in front of the garage, where most of what remained of the twenty-six-pound haul of marijuana was stashed under a couch—January 26, 1966.

400
E. 38TH ST.
AVENUE H

Above and opposite:
Austin vice squad evidence photos taken during the bust at Tommy and Clementine's house.

FRESH FOOD
GREEN
HEAD
Lettuce

Above: Austin Police Department photo of John Ike, Tommy, Roky, and Stacy sitting in the bay window in the front room of the house during the bust, January 27, 1966. John Ike: "Everybody was on mescaline: Tommy, Stacy, and Roky just turned on as the cops came in. Clementine rose up and said, 'I want to go too. He's my husband and I want to go with him.' They called her father and told him that they had busted all of them for heroin and her mother had a heart attack and died. All of our mothers came the next day. They knew we were in serious trouble."

bed when they busted in [and when] I realized that they really were gonna take Tommy, I called my father and said, "Come get the children, I've got to make myself get arrested." And so, I went up to them and I said, "You're gonna have to arrest me. If you don't, I'll do something that'll make you arrest me." They finally obliged me, and I'm glad, because I was put into the same car and Tommy made it safely to the police station without ever having been beaten up. They knew the dope was in the garage, but they just enjoyed throwing all the china on the floor, and [turning] all the drawers out. And the children were hysterical, they were screaming, and my father came and my father took command—he was an army officer. He took command and sorted it all out so that the police could do no more damage in the house.

The twenty-six pounds of grass stashed in the garage was presumably ready for the trade with Schofield. Although we don't know the split of LSD and hash proposed, twenty-six pounds of grass could translate into 10,000 hits of LSD—and given the shelf life of LSD, this was clearly for more than just personal use.

While the police now had evidence against Stacy (turned over to the police on Christmas by the owners of the North Lamar Hotel), Tommy, and, allegedly, John Ike—having supposedly found "a small amount of marijuana from the floorboards of [a] 1966 Chevrolet Greenbrier, Texas 1965 Registration License PGL 462," his vehicle—their real target was Roky, the visible spokesman for the new movement.

JOHN IKE: They put Roky and I in a squad car—and Roky had already moved out of that [house] and there was nothing in there—and one of these guys reaches in his pocket and says, "Look what I've found, Roky, look what I found in your house." They were asking Stacy, "What do you think of LSD? Tried any of that?" "Oh no, that stuff's too scary, I'd never try any of that stuff," and he was buzzing on mescaline anyway. I was just terrified. Back then, a marijuana bust was like heroin.

CPT. HARVEY GANN: In the beginning of the sixties, the [drug] problem became acute. The Beatles, Dylan, and Roky Erickson and all that group came along, and that was contradictory to what the police were trying to do: keep a lid on the drug problem . . . Like anything else, the squeaking wheel gets the grease, and the ones out in front making the most nuisance of themselves are going to get the most attention. If you're out there trying to get attention, you're going to get it. You'd have to be an idiot not to see this was going to get you in hot water.

LT. BURT GERDING: To me, as both a policeman and as a citizen, I felt it was an assault on my culture. So it made it almost a personal thing.

Opposite left: *Austin Statesman* account of the bust and its aftermath, January 29, 1966.

Opposite right: Post-bust mug shots of Tommy, John Ike, and Clementine (Roky's and Stacy's file photos were later replaced with mug shots from subsequent arrests).

STEPHANIE CHERNIKOWSKI: It was very, very frightening, because in youth there's a level of invulnerability that you ascend to. You assume you're protected because you're basically moral and good, so you really don't think they're going to get you. I think that's why a lot of people went home quickly and a lot of doors were locked and windows were pulled. I remember that as a night of drawn drapes, everybody sealing themselves in at home.

LYNN HOWELL: I was in the Jade Room the night word came that the Elevators had been busted, and all of a sudden half the room got up and ran straight to the bathroom, and I swear the toilets flushed for half an hour!

EVELYN ERICKSON: Jim Langdon called me and said, "I think you ought to know, Roky's in jail." I was home alone with four kids—Roger was in California on business—so they were all asleep. I got dressed and went down to the jail and asked if I could talk to Roky, and they brought him out. I had a couple of jokes, because I was scared, going down to the jail at two o'clock in the morning, alone. They treated me really nice, so I told him the jokes and he laughed and I told him we'd need a lawyer. I was just scared; they said he was caught with marijuana. We were paranoid after that.

DONNIE ERICKSON: I was in eighth grade when they got busted, and the teacher was like, "There's that guy whose brother got busted this morning." So, there was a lot of shame in that. They were magical, you know, till the time when we heard about the bust.

POWELL ST. JOHN: The whole situation in Austin was that drugs were coming into the community, and there were certain people that were always under the suspicion just because they looked like they might [use drugs]. I was one of those. And then coming out with a band that openly advocates taking psychedelic drugs blows your cover. After they began to perform publicly, I became more paranoid than I'd ever been. I would imagine they had a list of people who went to the gigs. It was really a very fascistic kind of setting. As it turned out, my paranoia was not baseless: we were under surveillance all the time. Why they didn't actually bust anybody but the Elevators, I don't know.

The effect of the bust was that the Elevators were trapped inside the state boundary for six months awaiting trial. As paranoia became rife, many of the band's contemporaries fled to California, where they would contribute to the growing San Francisco scene. Although Austin's underground had been among the earliest psychedelic subcultures in the United States, for the time being it was stunted.

Rock-Roll Outfit Out On Bond

Members of the 13th Floor Elevators, local rock 'n' roll musical group, left the sixth floor Travis County jail Friday after being held overnight on dope charges.

Released on $1,000 bond were Roger (Roky) Erickson, 18, leader of the group known as "Roky and His 13th Floor Elevators," John Walton, 19, Stacy Southerland, 20, James Thomas Hall, 23, and Hall's 26-year-old wife, Cleamentine Hall.

All were charged Thursday night with illegal possession of marijuana by Detective Sergeant Leonard Flores in the Justice Court of Frank McBee. Attorney Jack McCelland signed their bond.

The four musicians and Hall's wife were arrested Thursday night in Hall's apartment at 403 East 38th Street.

Vice squad Lieutenant Harvey E. Gann, and Sergeants Lee Conner, Flores and Robert Jones — armed with a search warrant —made the arrest.

Gann said about two pounds of marijuana were confiscated. He said marijuana was found in a car as well as in two other apartments — at 3412 South Congress where Walton and Southerland live, and at 404 East 18th where Erickson resides.

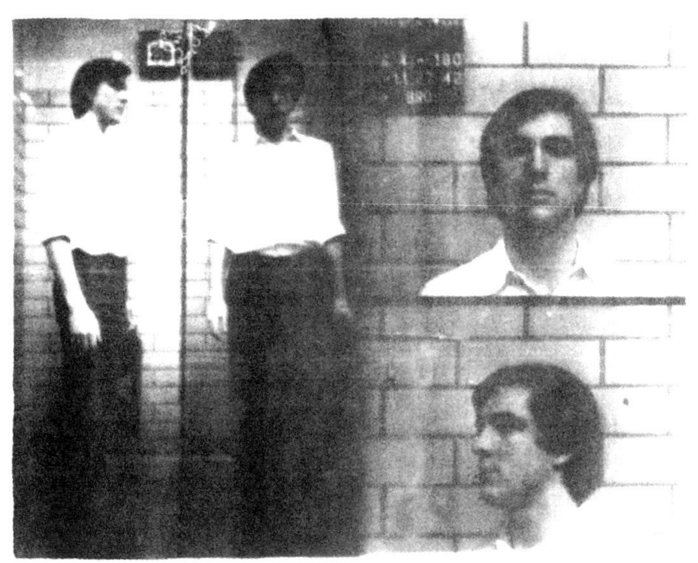

While the bust denied the band the opportunity to promote their music outside the state, they also became victim of a local radio ban: curiously, Austin's KNOW station banned their single the same day as the bust. The Elevators were also dismissed from the Jade Room—but subsequently welcomed at the New Orleans Club, which became their new base. Meanwhile KAZZ-FM championed the band with weekly live broadcasts from the New Orleans.

> GILBERT SHELTON: I remember seeing the Elevators at the New Orleans Club. I remember that most or all of them had very, very short hair because they had just been busted. They didn't seem too enthusiastic, but I thought they were pretty good. The electric jug seemed sort of out of place, although later I came to see that it was important to the identity of the group.

With their future hanging in the balance, the band returned to Andrus Studios in either February or March to record an album's worth of material for posterity. The record would consist of the band's live set: side one would be cover material and non-psychedelic original songs, while the manifesto to enlightenment would unfold on side two. Although the LP as it was originally recorded would go unreleased until 2009, its contents put the Elevators ahead of all their competitors (even the Beatles, who recorded their psychedelic masterpiece, "Tomorrow Never Knows," in April 1966).

But amid the band's newfound legal troubles, further interpersonal friction was emerging. Benny was the first to crack.

> JOHNNY GATHINGS: I liked Benny a lot. He whipped Tommy one time at the New Orleans Club. He got after him because he didn't like Tommy, not at all. Didn't need the jug in the band.

> BENNY: Tommy Hall. The old head. See, he couldn't play music, but he played jug. He had good rhythm and he had writing skills, so he was the main man. I didn't like him too much, but he was smart; he had direction in the form of a pure little thing that comes from your soul. Tommy was just too smart for me to even comprehend: if he got mad at me, you know, he'd metallize me around. I got real tender from that.

More troubling than any personnel issues, though, was Benny's difficulty adjusting to the band's new drug regimen.

> BENNY: Roky stung me on DMT and I said, "Fuck you, this shit is poison." We sat on a rocky ledge out there and smoked before we knew what was what, but I knew where it was going—straight to hell.

On February 22 at the New Orleans Club, Benny's precarious state became apparent.

SANDY LOCKETT: The New Orleans had no stage. The performers stood right on the floor, same level as the dancers. The fellows had indulged remarkably before the gig, and it was a very hot evening—the place was packed, so it got extremely hot and everybody was sweating. Benny finally got down to a T-shirt with holes in it and a falling-off pair of blue jeans. He was shaved to a buzz cut, and there was sweat running all over him. And as he continued to play bass he began to get a stranger and stranger expression on his face . . . After a while he began to pick up one foot and then the other, and look at his feet while he was playing. Finally, at the end of the set, he rushed off into the restroom, where he said, "I'm bleeding! I'm bleeding! I was standing out there and blood started coming out of the roots of my hair and it dripped down my shoulders and across my chest and down into my pants and I was stepping in it and everybody out there dancing was dancing in my blood!"

▲ **BY THE TIME** the Elevators reached Houston to play La Maison, the venue had moved to its third location in an old Weingarten's grocery store, on 1420 Richmond.

JOHN IKE: It was a gutted supermarket—they put a bandstand up there and that was it. It was a hole. No decoration or anything. They had go-go girls dancing on each side of the band, no light shows, [and we had to] bring our own PA.

GORDON BYNUM: At La Maison, I met this guy Jim Stalarow . . . I was a college kid who wanted to record groups. I'd never dropped acid; I was frightened to. Jim held up two thumbs and his index fingers and made a triangle, and he said, "You know, there is such a thing as the 'pyramid of ascending knowledge.' Most people are down here on the lower level—they don't understand that much, and as you move up the pyramid the width decreases, and so the knowledge becomes more condensed. When you reach the actual top of the pyramid, you can explain the essence of life with one word." As he said that, he looks at me with a straight face, as serious as he could be. "I know that word." But he refused to tell me what it was.

Amid the chaos of the time, Stalarow became the Elevators' manager.

CLEMENTINE: I have no idea how [Stalarow] managed to take over, but he had a fast line and he just sort of pushed things around, and we went, "Well, at least we're going somewhere." There had to be someone who would get these guys out onstage; there had to be someone with some kind of a connection.

Jim Langdon's Nightbeat

Ban on Record Here Somewhat Strange

In case you're wondering why you haven't heard The Thirteenth Floor Elevators' new record on Austin's leading rock station, it's because KNOW refuses to play it.

And that is somewhat strange considering that the record is selling quite well here. In fact, REED's Music Co., 805 Congress, reports that the new record is one of the hottest selling 45rpm singles they have ever handled.

Since last week, when the record was released, it has sold head-and-shoulders above any other single cut in their racks.

Therefore, the band, headed by ROKY ERICKSON —the same group that has been packing the Jade Room on week nights — was understandably curious as to why the record was not being played on the local station.

So a representative of the band made a trip to KNOW to seek an explanation and this is what he was told:

Number one, that too many people had called the station asking to hear the record; and (two) that the record was no good, anyway.

Now, on the first point, the station's thinking was apparently that the calls were all coming from a small group of people, namely the band or close friends of the band.

Judging from the record's local sales, as well as the capacity crowds that pack the Jade Room week nights when the band plays, the station's first point seem highly unlikely.

As to the quality of the record, this is, of course, a matter of individual taste. But I have heard the record, and at least two KNOW staffers have told me personally that they thought the record was pretty good and should be played.

The decision to pull the record, the two sides being "You're Gonna Miss Me," and "Tried To Hide," was made by KNOW DJ LOU HOUSE, who was reportedly "bugged by the numerous phone calls.

Had the decision been made by anyone else, it might have been understandable, since at least two of the KNOW DJs act as managers for rock 'n' roll outfits. But this does not enter into the picture in House's case.

As I said, many people obviously think the record is good. Both sides are original compositions written by members of the local group.

But the strangest thing about the entire affair is the station's refusal to support a local group, while raving on about mediocre efforts from Houston and Dallas.

And, of course, in such cities as Houston and Dallas, the local rock or "Top Forty" stations are always the first to champion their area's local efforts.

One station in town is playing the record, however, and that's KAZZ-FM. Unfortunately, not everyone owns an FM radio.

Perhaps, with luck, the record will go well elsewhere. Then the station would be forced to reconsider its decision.

But, it it did go well in other places, then the group would not need the kindness of House or KNOW.

Top: "Nightbeat" column, January 27.

Bottom: "Nightbeat" column, February 10. First known use of "psychedelic rock" in print. Langdon: "I think [the Elevators] regarded me as somebody who would say nice things about them in the paper, help further their career, but I know Roky viewed me as much older than I really was! I tried acid twice. There were some people who were [taking acid at gigs]—usually you knew who they were; probably a pretty small minority of people who would actually be out in a public place stoned on acid."

Jim Langdon's Nightbeat

Unique Elevators Shine With 'Psychedelic Rock'

WHERE THE ACTION WAS:

Two Austin night spots shared the mid-week spotlight for hard swinging action on the rock 'n' roll beat Wednesday night, and neither rain nor hail could dampen the burning excitement that raged in both clubs.

At the New Orleans Club it was ROKY and the 13th Floor Elevators blasting out "Psychedelic Rock" for more than 300 people who jammed the club, while over at Swingers A Go Go, veteran rock 'n' roll star JERRY LEE LEWIS put on a dazzling show for a full house of some 500 persons.

Considering the weather, plus the fact that about 3,000 opera fans were making the scene at Municipal Auditorium, where the New York Met was closing out its Austin stand with a production of "Susannah," it was a pretty active night on the local front, all the way round.

Lewis, who first hit the pay-dirt, nationwide with his recording of "Whole Lot of Shaking Going On," put on the usual exciting show expected of such a star in his field.

A product of the ELVIS PRESLEY era, Lewis has outlived many of the teenage idols of his age due to his unusual competence as a musician. Even when he is not singing, the Bogalusa, Louisiana, native can generate excitement with his knock-out piano and organ playing.

Pianist DON ADELMAN, who plays the New Orleans Club on Sundays, was out to catch his high school idol Wednesday. He recalled another time when Lewis played Austin when, after the show, Adelman asked him if he could play anything other than rock.

According to Don, Lewis proceeded to whip out the "best arrangement of Malaguena I've ever heard."

The band backing him this trip, mainly out of Memphis, did their share in putting on a good show too. At the end of one of the wilder numbers, the entire band, including the drummer, was standing and wailing atop amplifiers, piano benches and trap stools.

Meanwhile, at the New Orleans Club, "Psychedelic Rock" was showing its effect on the wildly enthusiastic audience. The place was so jammed one could hardly move, which prompted owner ANDY PORTER to book the band for every Wednesday and Thursday night at the club from here on.

I, for one, would be reluctant to try to define "Psychedelic Rock" or attempt to outline just what it is supposed to do. But this much is certain: the Elevators are a unique group. No one has ever heard anything quite like the sound they put out, anywhere, and their appeal is not confined to members of the younger generation. This was apparent when scanning the crowd and discovering a good many middle-agers swinging right along.

Radio station KAZZ-FM was on hand Wednesday and presented a 30-minute, live broadcast of the band from the club. KAZZ staffers BILL JOSEY and RIM KELLY are among the band's biggest supporters.

In all, it was a wailing evening, and from the size of the crowd on hand for the band's debut at the New Orleans, it looks as though the scene can do nothing but grow.

•

By the way, ANDY PORTER isn't standing still with the acquisition of the Elevators.

With the Austin Civic Theatre declaring that jazz did not enhance its image, Porter has picked up the BLUE CREW for Sunday nights at the club.

This means the entire ACT Sunday jazz scene, session included, will simply move over to the New Orleans Club as of this Sunday.

House band will be the same as it was at ACT, featuring tenor man FRED SMITH, pianist JAMES POLK, drummer GERRY STORM and bass man LUIZ NATALICIO. There is a good chance the BOB SARDO Trio may be on hand this Sunday as well. ERNIE MAE MILLER still plays downstairs on week nights.

So where's the action? For the moment, at least, it looks like it's all happening at the New Orleans.

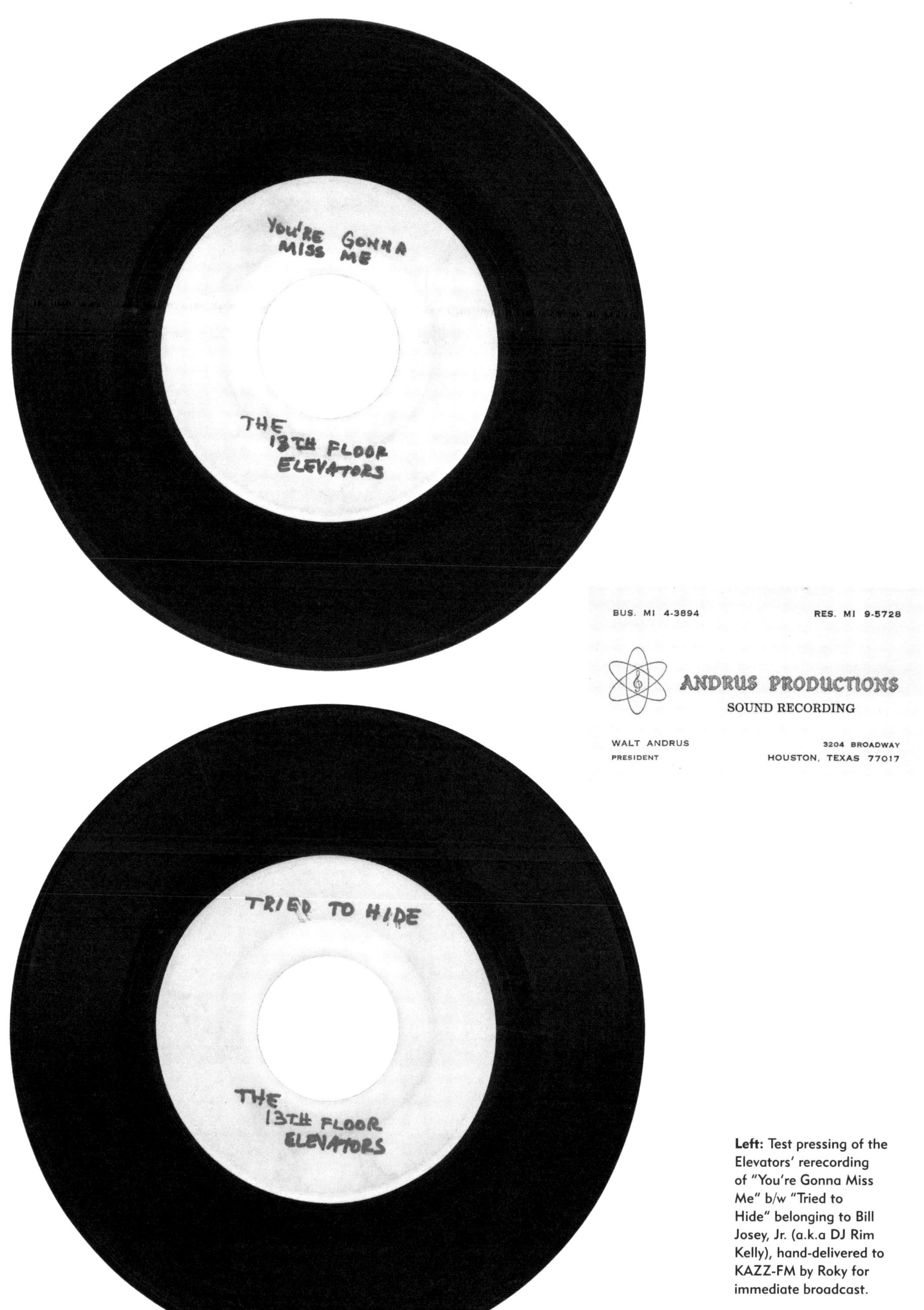

Left: Test pressing of the Elevators' rerecording of "You're Gonna Miss Me" b/w "Tried to Hide" belonging to Bill Josey, Jr. (a.k.a DJ Rim Kelly), hand-delivered to KAZZ-FM by Roky for immediate broadcast.

Right: Producer Walt Andrus's business card.

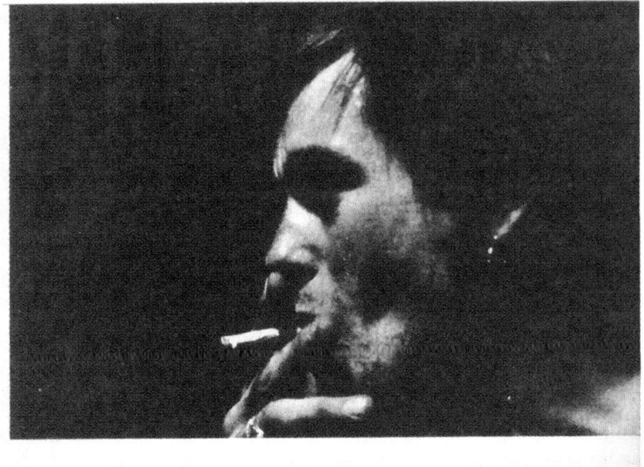

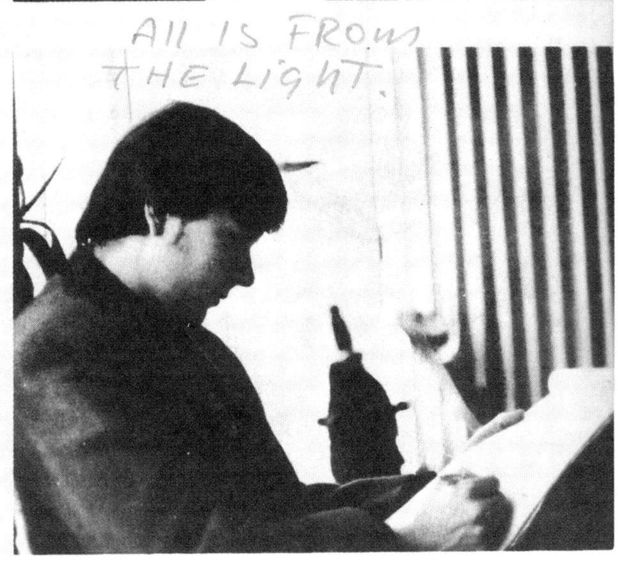

Above: A page from Stacy Sutherland's personal copy of Bob Simmons's one-off publication *Nightbeat* (unrelated to Jim Langdon's newspaper column), published December 1966 and containing many of his photos from the New Orleans Club, with Stacy's inscription reading "All is from the Light." Simmons's writeup: *"The Elevators moved to San Francisco to undergo the refining processes of the star producing machineries. Their first album on the IA label will be released by the time this issue sees print. And though their music, at least in Austin, remains a part of the underground currents of the hip generation, local attempts to hide the Elevators under the carpet become less successful as their nationwide recognition increases. The local top 40 station, relenting to public pressure, has lifted both its 'ban the Beatles' and 'ban the Elevators' policies, and Elevator performances are carried into Austin homes via national TV networks. The Elevators are expected to return to Austin in late December, and with luck, and the cooperation of some farsighted local concert promoter, Austin will again experience the mystique of last summer's Elevation."*

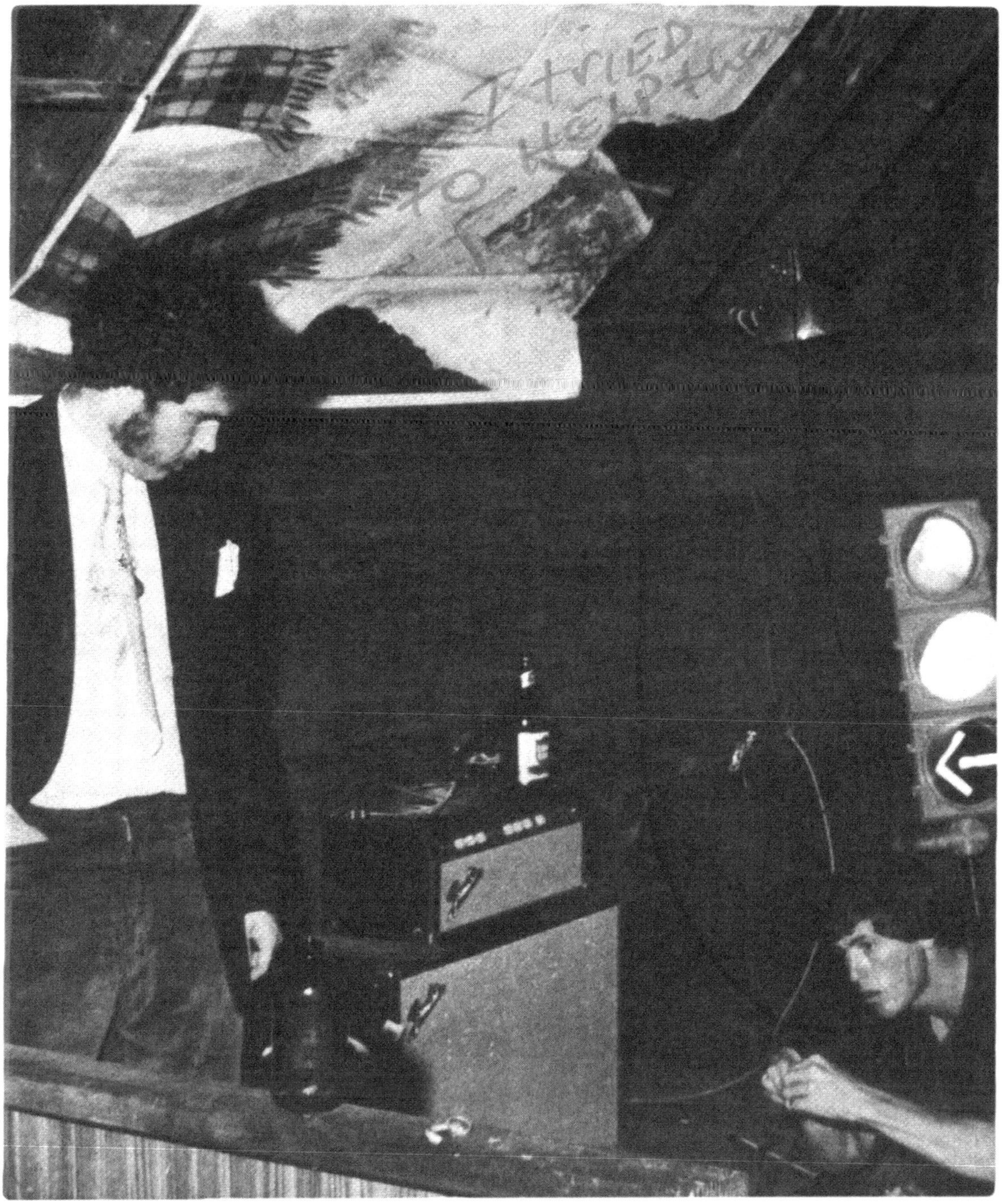

Top: Benny with "Fat Charlie" Prichard of Conqueroo, February 1966, at a costume party at the Caswell House in Austin (Conqueroo's HQ) circa February 1966. Benny had blown the bass amp by running his fiddle through it. Stacy's photo notation reads "I tried to help them." Bob Simmons: "I remember the 'costume party' at the Caswell. Bob Brown of Conqueroo wrapped a Japanese tatami mat around himself and came as a taco. I stole that traffic light myself."

Bottom: Front cover of Stacy's copy of *Nightbeat*.

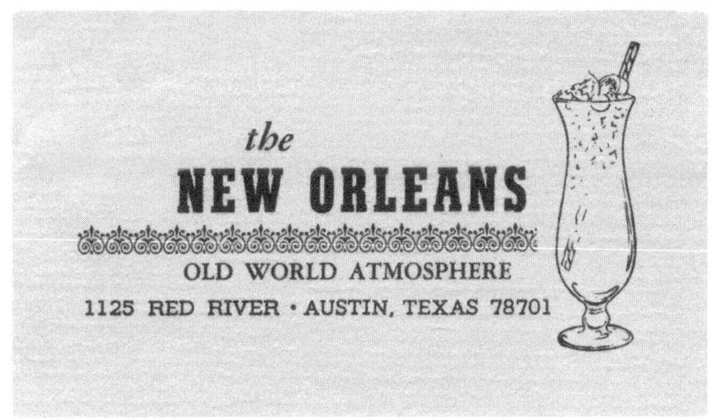
the
NEW ORLEANS
OLD WORLD ATMOSPHERE
1125 RED RIVER • AUSTIN, TEXAS 78701

Opposite top: The New Orleans Club, 1125 Red River Street, early 1960s.

Opposite bottom: Tommy and Roky photographed by Bob Simmons at the New Orleans Club, circa February 1966.

Top left: The band's manager Jim Stalarow at the New Orleans.

Top right: Benny performing at the New Orleans.

Bottom left: Stacy at the New Orleans.

Bottom right: Letterhead from the New Orleans.

Top right: Nailing down John Ike's kit at the Jade Room.

Center right: John Ike's painted bass drum head, featuring art by John Cleveland.

Center and bottom left: The Elevators, shot by Simmons at an afternoon sound check at the New Orleans Club, February 1966.

Opposite: Live at the New Orleans, early 1966, photographed in color. Diana Driver: "I was sixteen when I went with my brother Cliff and a group of his friends to the New Orleans Club to see the 13th Floor Elevators. It was the first time I'd ever been in a club, and I was thrilled to be included. Of course, I'd heard of Roky Erickson and the Elevators—after all, I was going to Travis High School, and everyone there knew about him and his band. I remember that the music was loud, the bar was filled with smoke, and the place was packed with people. Some were there to dance and others were just there for the music. At the time, I was more interested in folk music—Joan Baez, Bob Dylan, etc.—than I was in hard rock 'n' roll, so I wasn't very appreciative of the fact that I was witnessing rock 'n' roll history. Cliff had asked me to bring my camera, which I did, and he took pictures of the band and the crowd. Decades later, I found the pictures in an old envelope that also included additional family pictures. Because of high school gossip, I knew about the drugs and later learned of Roky's admittance to a mental hospital. But I didn't know much and wasn't too interested in any of the details. Looking back, I'm appalled at what the authorities put him through."

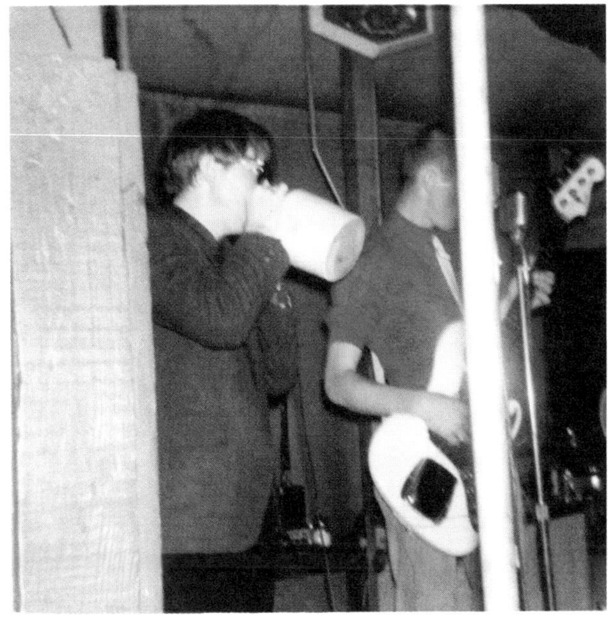

Above and opposite: At the New Orleans in mid-February, with haircuts fresh from the courtroom.

Opposite: The Elevators at the New Orleans, shot by photographer Ralph Y. Michaels. Michaels: "After basic training and schooling, I reported to my first and only duty station: VIII US Army Corps in Austin. Not a military base at all; I lived six blocks from work and about the same from the New Orleans Club. I've always been an 'aircheck' hobbyist, since the late fifties. At some point in late 1965, I visited the studios of KAZZ-FM. And I kept going, and I was always welcomed—and then the Elevators surfaced."

Top left: John Ike at the New Orleans.

Top right: Scratched Polaroid of the band lip-syncing live to "You're Gonna Miss Me" on KTRK Houston's *Larry Kane Show*, taken by Glenn Pitts (one of the show's resident dancers) one Saturday morning in late January–February 1966.

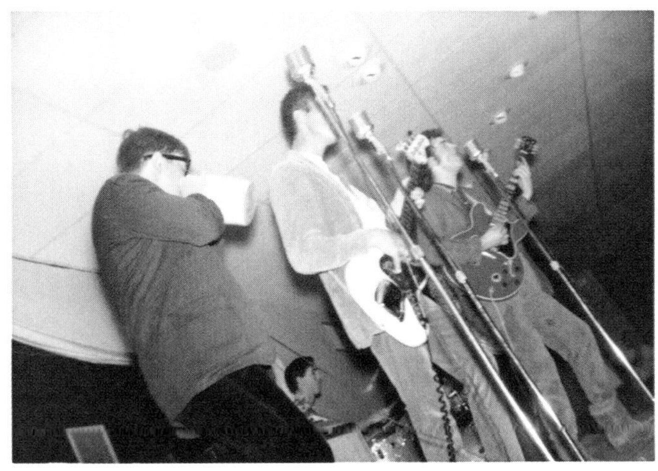

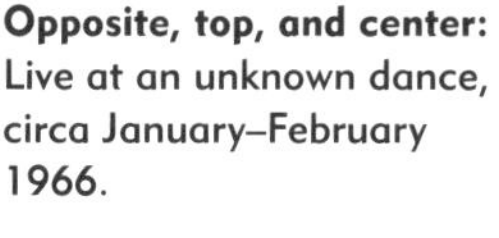

Opposite, top, and center: Live at an unknown dance, circa January–February 1966.

Bottom: The band's earliest known handbill, for a show in Palestine, Texas, on February 24th.

ANGELS Attic Presents...

13th Floor ELEVATORS FEB. 24th

& Latter Daye Saintz

ON the Courthouse SQUARE

PALESTINE

8 till 12 $2.00/Person

Below: Performing at La Maison Teen Club in Houston, circa February–March 1966.

▲ **ON MARCH 12**, the Elevators played a benefit concert for Texas bluesman Teodar Jackson at the Austin Methodist Center, during which they shared the bill with another rising star of the Austin scene.

BOB SIMMONS: I have a terrible memory of the Teodar Jackson benefit. Roky came on. Janis sang with Roky (if I remember correctly) and the Elevators. I took a whole roll of film—for me this was costly. After the show, as I was changing film cans ... I noticed that the camera had stripped out the little holes that advance the film, and the film had not gone through the camera: I missed the whole damned event, photographically speaking. I regret that moment to this day. I still think Janis watched Roky and something in her snapped to the kind of abandon and release that Roky did: "Wow! That's it!" Not to take anything away from Janis as a singer—it's just, she was learning how to be a "rock star," and Roky was the best she had seen.

At the Teodar Jackson show, Tommy watched Janis from the wings and made a comment that was immediately seized upon: "What if Roky and Janis sang together?" This, in turn, led to the enduring myth of Janis Joplin having, at some point, joined the Elevators.

ROKY (*1975*): Janis Joplin blew your mind just to meet her, as much offstage as she did onstage. She was so real of a person that it's no wonder she made it. We did some benefits together. We loved her. She needed to get her own name more than as just a member of the Elevators—she had to be known as Janis Joplin, and I had to be known as Roky Erickson.

TARY OWENS: It was one of her first major appearances in Austin. She was toying with the idea of a singing slot in the Elevators. Janis was very influenced by Roky. At that point she was doing acoustic blues. She didn't sing with them at that event.

CHET HELMS: [Janis] told me she'd been performing with the 13th Floor Elevators. She always belted, but her screaming, that came from Roky. What became clear to me was that there was a dramatic change in her stage presence.

JIM LANGDON: Janis was doing a single stand-up blues/folk-oriented [set]: acoustic guitar, or her autoharp, "Going Down to Brownsville," "Codeine"—very much in the blues-to-folk idiom. She never said anything to me about playing with the band. I know other people had this dream marriage in their heads: getting Roky and Janis together.

JOHN IKE: When we played the Methodist Center, that was the first gig we played with her. She had her guitar and she walked up to the microphone and she did her thing. And then we got up there and we did our thing and that was it. She never joined us singing. She didn't know our songs. I don't know where people get this "Janis Joplin was playing with the Elevators" [idea], because that never happened.

▲ **WITH HEAT FROM** the cops rising in Austin, the band did the sensible thing and relocated to Dallas, the closest thing Texas had to an entertainment capital. Sales of "You're Gonna Miss Me" had taken off regionally, and interest from the William Morris Agency was enough for the band to try their chances. Compared to Austin or Houston, Dallas had many garage and frat bands with a host of small- and medium-sized record labels to facilitate them.

Soon after their arrival, the Elevators appeared live on the TV show *Sumpin' Else* before headlining a show at the massive Market Hall the same day. The band knew they'd need to work hard to establish their profile and to reclaim "You're Gonna Miss Me"—which, in their absence, had been adopted as a popular cover tune by local bands. On more than one occasion they'd arrive at a club to hear the opening band performing their hit. As a result, the Elevators opened and closed their set with "You're Gonna Miss Me" just in case anyone missed it.

The Spades' version of the single had been available for less than a day before the Elevators poached both Roky and the song. Despite charting momentarily on the KAZZ-FM survey, it died a quick death sales-wise (and is now a major collectors item). Still, radio play of both versions continued to cloud ownership of the song.

At the time, it was common practice to release a record on a small local label, establish a regional hit, and then license to a larger label for national distribution with the long-term view of making a cash-in album. Gordon Bynum consulted pop impresario Huey Meaux—"the Crazy Cajun," responsible for the Sir Douglas Quintet's 1965 international hit, "She's About a Mover"—who introduced him to the Houston Records pressing plant, where he pressed 500 copies. Unbeknownst to Bynum, however, Meaux also ordered further batches of "You're Gonna Miss Me" and began hawking the record himself.

With Bynum out of sight, the band worked with a new producer in Dallas on a follow-up single. Dale Hawkins, whose "Susie Q" charted at #7 in 1957, was now operating as an A&R man for the local Abnak Records label and had successfully signed the Five Americans' "I See the Light" to Hanna-Barbera Records with an album deal attached.

DALE HAWKINS: I heard the [Elevators] and thought they were commercial, and took them to Sumet [Sound Studios]. I felt insecure in signing them to the label I was working for, because it was rather shaky at the time. I recommended that they continue to work with [engineer] Bob Sullivan, since the rapport there was compatible.

Opposite: The Elevators at La Maison.

Top right: Roky at the Teodar Jackson benefit concert, March 12, 1966.

Left and opposite: The Elevators onstage at the Teodar Jackson benefit concert at the Methodist Center in Austin. This was the only time they shared a bill with Janis Joplin in Texas.

ELEVATORS

ELEVATORS

BOB SULLIVAN: What I remember most was their demeanor. They were so stoned out that you could walk in and say, "Hey, the building's on fire," and they'd say, "Cool, man" [*laughs*]—they were just that laid back.

The band recorded Tommy's new psychedelic song "Reverberation" with the slower "Splash One," by Roky with Clementine as cowriter, as the B-side.

Meanwhile, another music biz hustler, Kendall Skinner, had designs on acquiring "You're Gonna Miss Me" for his label, the International Artists Recording Corporation. The label's origins constitute their own complex saga. Once International Artists' original founder, Fred Carroll, had signed his band the Coastliners to the Back Beat label, he decided to recoup his $35 startup costs by selling the name and label stampers to a conglomerate of Houston businessmen. The new IA consisted of: two lawyers, Bill Dillard and Noble Ginther, Jr., neither of whom had any music industry experience; Lester J. Martin, a recording studio owner; and music publisher Kendall (Ken) Skinner. Despite the name, they had neither international artists, national artists, nor even any local acts on their roster. Greedily hoping to discover the Texan Beatles, IA signed the 13th Floor Elevators instead. When they signed a licensing deal with IA to promote their single nationally, the band neglected to mention that they were already under contract with Bynum. Dillard argued that if IA was to invest in promotion, they should have the rights to a followup LP, but the band flatly refused, aiming to bypass IA and sign with a major label.

GEORGE BANKS: I was in the office when everyone was signing contracts. Benny was always very sharp—he read the contract, and he whips out his fiddle, and plays what he thought of the contract. Didn't even speak!

GORDON BYNUM: They had gone to Dallas and—this was really bizarre—I got a call from a guy and he asked me if I [owned] copyright of the name "13th Floor Elevators." John Ike went and registered the name and then he called me, and I told him I had an idea for a song for them to do, and he said, "Well, we're not going to record for you anymore and we're not interested in any of your ideas." That's what happened.

When Bynum discovered "You're Gonna Miss Me" had been released by IA, he contacted Dillard. Not only had the label repressed his record, but Skinner had removed Bynum's name from the label and credited himself as both producer and publisher. When Dillard discovered Bynum already had a full LP recorded, he immediately repressed the record, reinstating Bynum's credits and subsequently cutting a deal to license the band's unreleased LP.

This turn of events is the reason for the Elevators' later characterization that they were sold by Bynum to IA. The label's possession of the "Bynum tapes"—the first LP—would be held over the band's heads for years: IA would threaten to release the tapes right up until 1968, when they finally dubbed them with applause and put them out as a live album. The

The Austin Statesman Tuesday, March 15, 1966

Jim Langdon's Nightbeat

Benefit Blues Concert Big Success

Verdict on Sunday's TEODAR JACKSON benefit blues concert here — complete success, in both appeal and purpose.

The concert, staged at the Methodist Student Center before a standing-room-only crowd of more than 400, featured perhaps the finest package of blues talent ever assembled under any one roof in Austin.

It would be practically impossible to single out any one performer over any other — all were in such rare form.

blues man MANCE LIPSCOMB. Especially effective was his use of a pocket knife in playing blues guitar, a haunting sound that nearly brought the house down.

Lipscomb, along with the local rock band, The 13th Floor Elevators, are Austin favorites wherever they play. The Elevators wrapped up the afternoon's entertainment in typical blasting style, receiving their usual great response.

But the most exciting portion of the program may well have been created late in the second half of the show by Port Arthur blues singer JANIS JOPLIN — the only female performer on the bill — who literally electrified her audience with her powerful, soul-searching blues presentation.

After opening with the grim and gutty "Codine," Miss Joplin changed over to her "soft voice" and a delicate treatment of "I Ain't Got a Worry" which produced an almost spellbinding effect.

Then back with a raucous interpretation of "Going Down to Brownsville," and for her encore, one of her own compositions called "Turtle Blues," which she calls "simi-auto-

The Austin Statesman
Thursday, March 17, 1966
Page B10—Austin, Texas

NIGHT BEAT

By JIM LANGDON

The 13th Floor Elevators, Austin's hottest rock group, will be heading for Dallas next week where they hope for a shot at the big time.

The band will be featured two nights a week at a large Dallas club, and will use Big "D" as their headquarters for booking out on other jobs.

As a tribute to the band, more than 500 persons turned out at the New Orleans Club Wednesday night to catch the group in its last local club date.

Top: Langdon's "Nightbeat" review of the benefit concert for Texas bluesman Teodar Jackson, March 16, 1966.

Center right: Jim Langdon's column (here styled as "Night Beat") from March 17. The New Orleans Show referenced was broadcast by KAZZ-FM and survives.

Bottom: Having made their first television appearance on Dallas's *Sumpin' Else* show on March 25, 1966, at 4:00 p.m., the Elevators went on to headline this show at the massive Market Hall that evening.

Thursday, April 28, 1966

• • •

Two exciting scenes set for Thursday and Friday of this week:

At the 11th Door, it's blind blues singer-guitarist DOC WATSON, who will play Thursday through Saturday at the Club. He's being brought to town through the aid of folk collector TARY OWENS.

Next door at the New Orleans Club Thursday and Friday evenings, it's the rousing sounds of the 13th Floor Elevators, in town between Dallas engagements.

The rock group is the all-time crowd-drawer at the club.

• • •

Austin American-Statesman

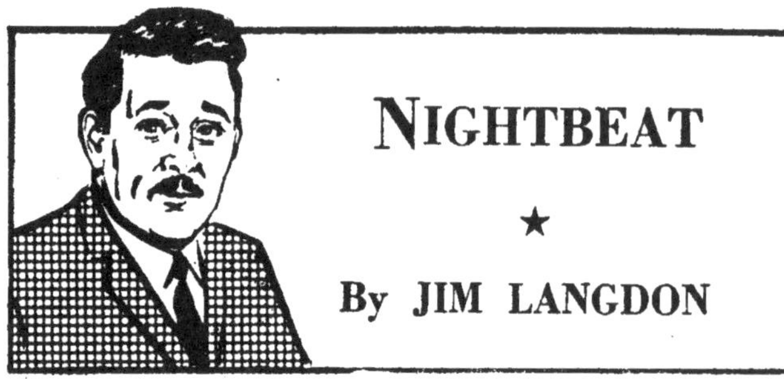

•

Still on guitars, it was like old home week at the New Orleans Club Thursday and Friday evening where ROCKY ERICKSON and the 13th Floor Elevators made dramatic return appearance at the club.

Dramatic, in that some 1,000 people showed up over the two night engagement, literally jamming every available corner of the club, both indoors and out.

It was really amazing, witnessing the walls of people, set in motion to the psychedelic sounds of the group which, if anything, has improved since its last dates in the Austin area.

And this was where the action was. From the latest in "POP" outfits and hair styles, to the more conservative customers . . . all reacted much the same to the band's exciting rhythms.

And that reaction was affirmative.

•

The Austin American

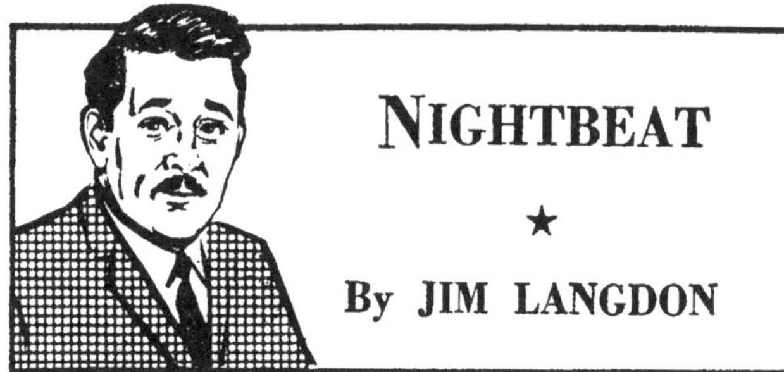

•

After going over big in the Dallas-Fort Worth area, where they appeared in concert with The BYRDS, the 13th Floor Elevators will return to the New Orleans Club for a two-night stand next week, Wednesday and Thursday.

Top left: "Nightbeat" from April 28, 1966, featuring an ad for an Elevators performance at the New Orleans.

Top right: "Nightbeat" column recounting the band's return to the New Orleans.

Bottom right: "Nightbeat" from May 20, 1966.

band didn't want the old recordings issued, as they'd since written new material and progressed musically, but they were also stalling for time; the recordings' being "no good" was a justification that they hoped would allow them the time they needed to sign with a major label.

Meanwhile the "You're Gonna Miss Me" fiasco rolled on. No sooner had the single started to chart on the lower regions of *Billboard* than IA discovered their new signing on, of all labels, Hanna-Barbera Records. They'd contacted Huey Meaux about picking up the option on "You're Gonna Miss Me," and a representative from the label had arrived to pay Meaux an advance and collect tapes.

Meanwhile, Dillard was out in California to meet a record promoter whom Skinner had contacted on IA's behalf.

> LELAN ROGERS: I was at an R&B label called Omen Records. We were trying to get some hits, and we weren't. About that time, a guy named Ken Skinner showed up, and he had about four or five records on International Artists Records. I heard one that I liked, and that was because of the jug, and that was "You're Gonna Miss Me." I thought, "I can work this record for you."
>
> BILL DILLARD (*AB*): Lelan noticed the guy who owned a pressing plant in the parking lot. Lelan said, "That's who I was taking you to see." So Lelan introduced me—Dalton was his name. Lelan said, "We have a hit: 'You're Gonna Miss Me' by the 13th Floor Elevators." Dalton literally turned white. Lelan said, "What's wrong?" Dalton said, "Hanna-Barbera said the record belonged to them. I've been pressing it for them." I said, "How many did you press?" He got real iffy. I said, "Well, how many have you shipped?" And he got real iffy. I said, "I think you need to get on the horn. I've got a bunch of people out there promoting this record, and they've got another job as of now: looking for this record. And if I find one copy—*one copy*—of this record on the Hanna-Barbera label, there's going to be a new name on that building." And we did find one—in Miami.

Dillard confiscated the record stampers and switched pressing plants—from Houston to "Rainbo [*sic*] Records" in Los Angeles. Amazingly, "You're Gonna Miss Me" continued to appear with a number of different IA label variations, including one that even listed the label name as "A.I." All told, the record appeared on thirteen different label variations over various repressings by the end of 1966.

▲ **DIVORCED FROM** their LSD supply and with marijuana being too dangerous to possess, the Elevators soon began resorting to drugstore highs to elevate their performances. Roky and Stacy joined Tommy in his favorite: Romilar, a codeine-based cough syrup whose effects were reportedly a sense of focus and well-being, but were in truth quite the opposite. Much to his annoyance, John Ike now had to drag the zoned-out Roky and Stacy off the sofa and into the van. While Tommy, by contrast, was always ready for gigs, his pinprick pupils and bluish-tinged lips—well-known side effects of Romilar—helped further the band's reputation as weirdos and alienate them from the straight elements within the music industry. Benny's libation of choice was Listerine, the alcohol-based mouthwash, though he also liked Valo and Vick's inhalers, which contained extractable amphetamine. Benny and Stacy also liked barbiturates and Quaaludes, and when things got seriously degenerate, they sniffed glue.

After Bynum's bookings ran out, the band suffered through a number of poorly planned shows set up by Jim Stalarow and decided to fire their ersatz manager. Stalarow's sacking allowed John Ike to take control of the band's management: he soon engaged a new booking agent named Jerry Ray and approached his mother to finance a "13th Floor Club" in another former grocery store on Dallas's North Collett Avenue.

> JOHN IKE: Things were looking pretty good: we did a TV show, we've got a hit record here in Dallas—let's open up a club. We looked into the building and—spent about $2,000 or $3,000 on it, my mother did. My mother was quite a business lady, and she was into helping her boy and the band. It looked like we had a future.

But before long, John Ike's bid plans were thwarted by a parking technicality, and the "13th Floor Club" never materialized.

In late April, the Elevators made their triumphant return to Austin's New Orleans Club, though they were actually back in town to attend their grand jury hearings. In preparation, Evelyn Erickson had mobilized her prayer group and the Waltons had hired Les Proctor—an ex-DA with political clout—in an attempt to persuade the grand jury to be lenient. Nevertheless, both attempts failed, and the police complaints were upheld.

On May 13, the band opened for the Byrds at the Will Rogers Auditorium in Fort Worth. The show was reported to have been a huge success by Jim Langdon, and while both Roky and Tommy remember it that way, John Ike remembers it being a disappointment, as they had had to play outside on a thrown-together stage in the parking lot instead of in the main auditorium.

In late May, the group left Dallas and hit the so-called "'A' Road Tour" (highways 6 and 1960 out of Houston toward Addicks, Alief, Arcola, and Alvin), making stops in Austin to attend various court hearings and to appear at the New Orleans. The Waltons' lawyer Jack McClellan made counterclaims against the police, arguing that the evidence from the bust had been gathered illegally, and issued subpoenas for the arresting officers, hoping that a pretrial hearing would reveal the cops' testimony prior to the actual trial.

While the endless courtroom drudgery dragged on, the band put Benny on a trial of their own, with Stacy also facing charges. Benny disapproved of Tommy's dealing activities, but Tommy—a drug purist, when it suited him—objected to Benny's increasingly severe addiction to speed.

LOUANNS

Tues., May 10 - 8 p.m. - 12

END of SCHOOL DANCE

CANNIBAL

and the

Headhunters

"Land of A Thousand Dancers"

THE

PREMIERS

'Farmer John'

The 13th FLOOR ELEVATORS

Dallas' Own Penthouse Five

An EXPLOSION From HOUSTON, TEXAS

A NATIONAL HIT!

"YOU'RE GONNA MISS ME"

THE 13th FLOOR ELEVATORS

IA 107

OWNED and DISTRIBUTED BY:

INTERNATIONAL ARTISTS RECORDS

1005 Americana Bldg. Houston, Texas, (713) CA-8-1244

TW	KIST LIST -- WEEKENDING AUGUST 13, 1966	LW
1.	Sweet Pea - Tommy Roe	2
2.	Sunny - Bobby Hebb	1
3.	Mothers Little Helper/Lady Jane -Rolling Stones	4
4.	Seven and Seven is --- Love	7
5.	Psychotic Reaction - Count Five	9
6.	Some Good Guys, Etc - Standells	11
7.	Over, Under, Sideways, Down - The Yardbirds	8
8.	'Lil Red Riding Hood - Sam the Sham	5
9.	Sunshine Superman - Donovan	12
10.	Summer In The City - Lovin Spoonful	6
11.	They're Coming To Take Me Away - Napolean XIV	3
12.	5-D (Fifth Dimension) - The Byrds	13
13.	See You In September - The Happenings	14
14.	You're Gonna Miss Me - 13th Floor Elevators	19
15.	Distant Shores - Chad & Jeremy	22
16.	Guantanmera - The Sandpipers	23
17.	Alfie - Cher/Cilla Black	28
18.	This Door Swings Both Ways - Herman's Hermits	24
19.	Stop! Get A Ticket - Clefs of Lavender Hill	31
20.	Trains and Boats and Planes - Dionne Warwick	26
21.	Almost Persuaded - David Houston	29
22.	Yellow Submarine - Beatles (Album)	-
23.	Tar and Cement - Verdelle Smith	27
24.	Blowin' In The Wind - Stevie Wonder	-
25.	Too Many People - The Leaves	35
26.	Born a Woman - Sandy Posey	-
27.	Summertime - Billy Stewart	30
28.	I Couldn't Live Without Your Love - Petula Clark	33
29.	A Million and One - Dean Martin/Vic Dana	34
30.	Misty - Groove Holmes	36
31.	Cast Your Fate to the Wind - Shelby Flint	-
32.	Working in a Coal Mine - Lee Dorsey	38
33.	Can I Trust You - The Bachelors	37
34.	We'll Be United - The Intruders	-
35.	Long Days Care - Thee Sixpence	39
36.	Go Ahead and Cry - The Righteous Brothers	-
37.	Respectable - The Outsiders	40
38.	God Only Knows - The Beach Boys	-
39.	The Joker Went Wild - Brian Hyland	-
40.	Let's call it a Day, Girl - The Razor's Edge	-

HIT BOUND SOUNDS:

ARE YOU READY -------------RANDY THOMAS

Out of This World ---------The Chiffons

Kissin' My Life Away ------The Hondells

I Don't Want To See You ---His Majesty's Coachmen

Summer Kisses -------------Floyd & Jerry

Top left: Poster for the May 10 "End of School Dance" at Dallas club Louann's.

Top right: International Artists ad for "You're Gonna Miss Me" from *Cashbox* magazine, July 30, 1966.

Bottom: August 13 radio survey from KIST-FM ("the Kist List") in Carpinteria, California, featuring "You're Gonna Miss Me" at #14.

Top: The band's initial September trial date is announced in *The Austin Statesman*'s July 28, 1966 edition. It would soon be moved to August 8, ensuring the band a more favorable outcome.

Bottom: Stacy's probation agreement, issued on August 8, 1966.

The Austin Statesman Thursday, July 28, 1966

Rock 'n Rollers' Trial Sept. 19

District Judge Mace Thurman Jr. has set a Sept. 19 jury trial date for members of a local rock'n roll band accused of illegal possession of marijuana.

The trial date was set at 147th District Court docket call Thursday for Roger (Roky) Erickson, 19-year-old leader of the group known as "Roky and his 13th Floor Elevators", John Ike Walton, 19, Stacy Keith Southerland, 20, James Thomas Hall, 24, and Hall's wife, Clementine.

The group and Hall's wife appeared in court for the regular docket call Thursday.

They were arrested at Hall's 403 E. 38th St. residence last January and charged by city detectives with illegal possession of marijuana. Police said they had been under surveilance for about a month before the arrests were made.

CONDITIONS OF PROBATION

THE STATE OF TEXAS : IN THE 147th JUDICIAL DISTRICT COURT OF TRAVIS COUNTY, TEXAS

VS. : 8th DAY OF August, 1966

Stacy Keith Southerland : CAUSE NO. 37,010

In accordance with the authority conferred by the Adult Probation and Parole Law of the State of Texas, you have been placed on probation this date, 8-8-66, for a period of 2 years TDC by the Honorable Mace B. Thurman, Jr., Judge 147th Judicial District Court of Travis County, Texas.

It is the order of the Court that you shall comply with the following conditions of probation:

(1) You must obey all orders of the Court and the Probation Officer;
(2) Commit no offense against the laws of this or any other state or the United States;
(3) Avoid injurious or vicious habits (including the use of narcotic or habit forming drugs and alcoholic beverages);
(4) Avoid persons or places of disreputable or harmful character (including not frequenting or going about places where intoxicating beverages are sold);
(5) Report to the Probation Officer as directed;
(6) Permit the probation Officer to visit you at your home or elsewhere;
(7) Work faithfully at suitable employment as far as possible, subject to the approval of the court and/or the Probation Officer;
(8) Do not change employment or place of residence without the permission of the Probation Officer;
(9) Remain within Travis County, Texas, unless permitted to depart by the Court and/or the Probation Officer.
(10) Support your dependents;
(11) Pay your fine, if one be assessed, and the costs of Court, in one or several sums, and make restitution or reparation in any sum that the Court shall determine, to wit:

Court Cost:$10.70

You are hereby advised that under the law of this State, the Court shall determine the terms and conditions of your probation, and may at any time during the period of probation alter or modify the conditions of your probation. The court also has the authority at any time during the period of your probation to revoke your probation for violation of any of the conditions set out above.

The Court has placed you on probation, believing that if you sincerely try to obey and live up to the conditions of your probation, your attitude and conduct will improve to the benefit of the public and of yourself.

Witness our signatures this 8th day of August, 1966.

Stacy Sutherland
Probationer

Presiding Judge

Roger L. Ranney
Probation Officer

Advertisement from the *Irving Daily News* of Irving, Texas, hyping the Byrds show (with the Elevators opening) on May 13 at the Plymouth Park Music Center.

TARY OWENS: Benny went really off the deep end. He was the first visible casualty of the band. It was as much speed as it was acid; mixing the two. Benny was too wired. You could just see it. He was too out there.

BENNY: I had shaved my head, and they were just devastated. That's when Tommy really pulled away from me. But I did what I did. Mainly I got out of the Elevators because it was a little bit too much for me. I wasn't a good enough bass player anyway.

STACY (*K*): [Benny's departure came about] in a negative way. Just taking speed all the time, staying up three or four days at a time. He wouldn't come to practice. I loved ol' Benny so much, man, and I was guilty of the same thing. I started out with him, shooting a little speed, going to gigs, half of them on acid and us on speed. I started to get real nervous, and you know what speed does: you get uptight and ready to snap at people. Ol' Benny was wanting John Ike to fight him and Tommy, cursing each other like dogs. They told him, "Look, you're in a bad place, you're on methedrine. Quit!" They told me the same thing.

JOHN IKE: Tommy and Roky came to Stacy and said, "Benny's shootin' speed. We gotta get him out of the band." See, if Benny was in the picture, I had the majority of the band. It was my band. Because I got Benny and Stacy. [But] Benny was not a very good bass man. He was a violinist and he didn't think *bass*. I couldn't play drums to his bass part comfortably.

With Benny out of the band, the Elevators turned back to their original choice for the role: Ronnie Leatherman.

RONNIE: First time I saw the Elevators was the first time I played with them. It was kind of hard. Felt pretty much out of place all night, especially since they had such a following and, of course, a lot of [their fans] really liked Benny. There was a lot of people glaring at me.

On July 28, *The Austin Statesman* reported that the band's trial had been set for September 19 before Judge Mace Thurman, the "hanging judge"—so named because in drug-related cases, he was never lenient nor gave probation.

Once again, Evelyn mobilized her prayer group. Luckily, the group included the District Attorney's wife, who successfully appealed to her husband to bring the trial date forward to August 8, when Mace Thurman would be on vacation and D. B. Woods, an elderly, non–criminal judge, would be presiding.

JACK McCLELLAN (*K*): They had the wrong address on Roky's search warrant—they had Tommy's number on Roky's street. In their sloppiness, the narcs blew it. They planted him anyway, with stuff they'd found at Tommy's house. That sprung Roky.

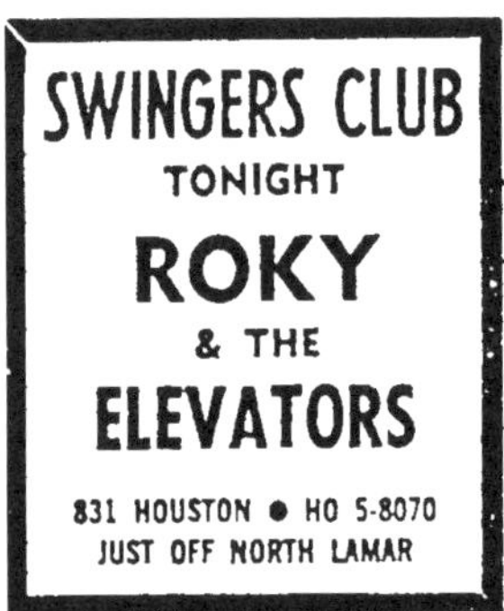

Austin Statesman advertisement for a June 20, 1966, performance at Austin's Swingers Club.

As for the rest of them, because they were the first group of white middle-class kids to get busted, the DA wasn't that interested in putting them in the penitentiary.

CLEMENTINE: We went in absolutely terrified, and we were absolutely bamboozled when it wasn't the horror we thought it would be. Everybody was telling us that we would never be heard of again. And the way the DA described our stash was, "We examined a small amount of marijuana." Now, it's true that he only examined a small amount, but there was a large amount. But the judge heard the words "small amount," and when the judge heard that, he says words to the effect of, "Well, don't ever do this again, boys." And we came out of there alive only because of the fact that a switch had been pulled on the judges and the DA set it up. And he could only have done that because of his wife, and his wife could only have done that because of Evelyn's prayer group.

Clementine and John Ike's cases were dismissed outright, Roky's case was dismissed on a technicality, and while Tommy and Stacy pleaded guilty, they were given only two years' probation.

Despite the seemingly favorable outcome of the trial, the implications of the bust would remain with the band members—particularly Stacy—for years to come. At the time, it was common practice for a court to remove offenders from the environment in which they had committed a crime in order to make it harder for them to re-offend, so, on August 8, as part of the judgment, Lelan Rogers (IA's newly appointed promotions man in Los Angeles) was named as the "responsible citizen" who would aid the probation services and vouch for Stacy and Tommy's every movement. Although this still allowed the band to perform, it now gave the record company total control over the band; neither Stacy nor Tommy could even enter a place licensed to sell alcohol, or travel to rehearsals, without having been granted signed permission.

On August 13, with probation cleared and filed for San Francisco, the band hit the road to join their friends—Janis, Chet, Jaxon, and the rest—in the former Beat utopia and new home of a burgeoning psychedelic culture.

III

I'VE GOT LEVITATION

BILL GRAHAM PRESENTS IN SAN FRANCISCO

13TH FLOOR ELEVATOR

GREAT SOCIETY

SOPWITH CAMEL

FRIDAY AUG. 26

SATURDAY AUG. 27

FILLMORE AUDITORIUM

WES WILSON '66

Photo by Herb Greene

TICKETS SAN FRANCISCO: City Lights Bookstore; The Psychedelic Shop; Bally Lo (Union Square); The Town Squire (1318 Polk); Mnasidika (1510 Haight) BERKELEY: Campus Records; Discount Records; Shakespeare & Co. MILL VALLEY: The Mod Hatter SAUSALITO: The Tides Bookstore; Rexall Pharmacy.

The band stopped to perform pickup shows in Redding, Fresno, and at Bill Quarry's "Teens 'n' Twenties" dance in Sacramento, where they were approached by a keen young promoter named Steve Tolin. While John Ike gave him the initial brush-off, Tolin persisted, recognizing an opportunity to promote a band on the brink of national success. He pitched an offer even John Ike couldn't refuse—if they'd divulge some of their future bookings, he'd arrange to have the band's fee doubled. John Ike agreed and wished him luck.

The Elevators finally arrived in San Francisco on August 25, amid further chaos: they were booked with Van Morrison and Them at the Longshoremen's Hall on Fisherman's Wharf (where Kesey's Trips Festival had been staged in January, along with the first Family Dog shows the year prior). The day the band arrived, the Yardbirds were playing at 3:00 p.m. at Bill Graham's Carousel Club—and since the Elevators were booked to play his main venue, the Fillmore Auditorium, the next day, they decided to report to Graham's office.

> CLEMENTINE: They were slated to play Longshoreman's Hall through one manager, and at the same time [fellow Austin-to-SF transplant] Travis Rivers decided he was our manager too, and set us up to play at the Fillmore. I vividly remember, Tommy and Roky and I were hauled into Bill Graham's office and absolutely cut into little pieces. He said, "You do not come into this town and sign up to be exclusively with me and be at the same time at Longshoreman's. You cannot do that." He says, "I'm an old street fighter, and you'll never work again." Bill Graham was not happy, but even Bill Graham could be charmed by Roky. Roky was irresistible.

After the dressing-down from Graham, the group loped off to see the Yardbirds. Jeff Beck was supposedly suffering from "exhaustion," and the previous day's show at the Monterey County Fairgrounds had been canceled. The Carousel show was the first time Jimmy Page took over lead guitar and Chris Dreja switched to bass (Beck would eventually leave the band in San Francisco). Unfortunately, the Elevators' bandboy Cecil Morris also decided to see the Yardbirds—without unloading the van.

Opposite: Wes Wilson's poster design for the band's only appearance at the Fillmore, on August 26–27, 1966. They performed only the first night, with locals Sopwith Camel as openers. The following night, the Elevators were replaced by Country Joe and the Fish and the Great Society. This poster started a trend amongst Californian promoters for billing the group as "Elevator" and not "Elevators," a tendency the band was unable to control, apart from at the Avalon. The rare first run of this popular poster and handbill were printed prior to the show on thin paper stock that reflected ultraviolet/blacklight. Subsequent second and third printings match the same stock as the postcard version of the handbill and do not reflect UV light.

RONNIE: The first day we were there, our bandboy went to see the Yardbirds at 3:00 in the afternoon and came back to the van and my bass amp had been stolen, my bass guitar, Stacy's Super Reverb [amp], and John Ike had a Gibson banjo and a Roberts reel-to-reel four-track recorder [stolen]. He'd brought it to record the shows. We had to go find stuff to play that night.

With bookings at the major ballrooms, a hit single, and record company support, the Elevators were able to re-equip at Sherman Clay's legendary music store, and they took full advantage—ordering new Standel amps and, for Stacy, a new Gibson 330 guitar and a Twin Reverb amp. Ronnie acquired a West German Klira—a violin bass similar to Paul McCartney's Höfner—but, until his new Standel arrived, he'd have to make do with the bass amp belonging to Jack Casady from the Jefferson Airplane. Although the theft further diminished John Ike's claim over the band, their new gear was far from free: the group was now encumbered by large monthly repayments to IA in addition to the existing debt owed to Mrs. Walton.

RONNIE: Longshoreman's Hall was the first night in San Francisco. We were supposed to be booked with Them [but] they got busted for pot, and I'd have loved to have met Van Morrison. We had seen some big crowds, but to see wilder crowds, people really into doing their new thing—that was our first night, and it was unreal. We played probably a little louder than most of them. We usually turned everything as far as it would go.

JAXON: That was the only show I remember Roky's mother being at—I think she realized this was a big move away from the protective little island that they had going in Texas; she was concerned, but she was basically the beaming, proud mother.

Despite having many Texan allies in town, the Elevators were soon brought up to speed with the politics of performing in San Francisco. There were two major players: Chet Helms and Bill Graham. Prior to the Elevators' arrival, both promoters had shared alternate bookings at the Fillmore Auditorium until a feud broke out and Chet relocated his Family Dog productions to the Avalon Ballroom. Despite their Texan connection with Chet, the Elevators were inadvertently booked at the Fillmore and arrived at hipster ground zero with short hair and a pop hit.

CLEMENTINE: We had a number-one hit—we're suspect. We had short hair—we're suspect. Two strikes against us. We had come from the trial, and we all looked like what later would have been described as "punk rockers." Somebody said we were the first punk rock band—we weren't; we were just forced to cut our hair.

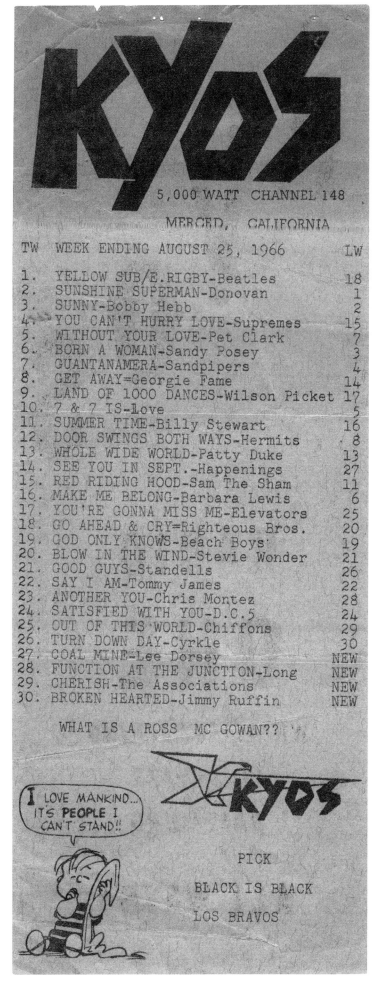

Top left: Ad from the *Royal's World Countdown* underground newspaper for the Elevators' first show in San Francisco on August 25, 1966, opening for Them.

KYOS

5,000 WATT CHANNEL 148

MERCED, CALIFORNIA

TW	WEEK ENDING AUGUST 25, 1966	LW
1.	YELLOW SUB/E.RIGBY-Beatles	18
2.	SUNSHINE SUPERMAN-Donovan	1
3.	SUNNY-Bobby Hebb	2
4.	YOU CAN'T HURRY LOVE-Supremes	15
5.	WITHOUT YOUR LOVE-Pet Clark	7
6.	BORN A WOMAN-Sandy Posey	3
7.	GUANTANAMERA-Sandpipers	4
8.	GET AWAY=Georgie Fame	14
9.	LAND OF 1000 DANCES-Wilson Picket	17
10.	7 & 7 IS-Love	5
11.	SUMMER TIME-Billy Stewart	16
12.	DOOR SWINGS BOTH WAYS-Hermits	8
13.	WHOLE WIDE WORLD-Patty Duke	13
14.	SEE YOU IN SEPT.-Happenings	27
15.	RED RIDING HOOD-Sam The Sham	11
16.	MAKE ME BELONG-Barbara Lewis	6
17.	YOU'RE GONNA MISS ME-Elevators	25
18.	GO AHEAD & CRY=Righteous Bros.	20
19.	GOD ONLY KNOWS-Beach Boys	19
20.	BLOW IN THE WIND-Stevie Wonder	21
21.	GOOD GUYS-Standells	26
22.	SAY I AM-Tommy James	22
23.	ANOTHER YOU-Chris Montez	28
24.	SATISFIED WITH YOU-D.C.5	24
25.	OUT OF THIS WORLD-Chiffons	29
26.	TURN DOWN DAY-Cyrkle	30
27.	COAL MINE-Lee Dorsey	NEW
28.	FUNCTION AT THE JUNCTION-Long	NEW
29.	CHERISH-The Associations	NEW
30.	BROKEN HEARTED-Jimmy Ruffin	NEW

WHAT IS A ROSS MC GOWAN??

KYOS

I LOVE MANKIND... IT'S PEOPLE I CAN'T STAND!!

PICK

BLACK IS BLACK

LOS BRAVOS

Right: A radio survey from KYOS in Merced, California, the week of August 25, 1966—showing "You're Gonna Miss Me" at #17.

CHET HELMS: [Bill] Graham never lets the truth get in the way of a good story. Actually, they never did [play for Graham]—the first show that they were booked to do there, they didn't do. It was booked by a guy named Curly Jim. They thought they were coming to play for me, and when they arrived here and learned they were not playing for me, they refused to play for Graham.

David Harris and Greg Shaw's fanzine, *Mojo Navigator Rock 'n' Roll News* (now regarded as possibly the first music fanzine and a later inspiration for *Rolling Stone*), had recently turned on Graham and his choice of bookings—the Turtles, Sam Sham and the Pharaohs, the Wailers, the Mindbenders—as "commercial, Top 40, schlock shit." It also reported, in issue #3: "The Thirteenth Floor Elevator [*sic*] is a local band, apparently having no connection with a group out of New York having the same name, which group has reportedly broken up."

It was not a great career start in their new city. Despite the Elevators' being the show's headliners, Grace Slick, then with the Great Society, was the center of Wes Wilson's poster design. In fact, the Elevators played only the first night, supported by Sopwith Camel; on the second night Country Joe and the Fish replaced them.

ROKY: Fillmore? Big show, real jam-packed, crowded with people.

TOMMY: We did our show on Friday, which was our opening show, a special thing I guess. And Bill Graham hated us. He thought we were really amateurish and stuff like that, and we were kind of schizoid from the whole trip. And we settled down. We started playing better shows.

The Beatles arrived in San Francisco to perform what became their final live show on August 29. Like the Elevators, the Beatles also had a poster designed by the Fillmore's legendary house artist, Wes Wilson. While the Beatles—unable to replicate psychedelic studio masterpieces such as "Tomorrow Never Knows" before a live audience—soon resolved to retire to the studio, the acid-fueled Elevators had arrived with an electric jug, determined "to put the acid into the music."

Further differences with the new "San Francisco Sound" soon became apparent. The Elevators were conceived from the outset as an uncompromising, loud electric psychedelic rock band. From their Texan point of view, the locals were still figuring which end to plug in their new electric guitars.

HOUSTON WHITE: Those motherfuckers [in San Francisco] couldn't play: the Grateful Dead were really awful, and Jefferson Airplane were grim; they just weren't happening. Big Brother and the Holding Company were awful—if it hadn't been for Janis they'd have never gotten across the street. And that was the thing: the Elevators were so obviously in command of their instruments, and they had it together.

Still, the local tastemakers were becoming receptive. The Dead's Jerry Garcia even attempted to namecheck the band in *Mojo Navigator*, calling them the "13th Story Elevator" and likening their style to the "San Francisco Sound," noting that they sounded a little like Big Brother. Meanwhile, the Elevators' old friend Janis Joplin had left town for Chicago days before their arrival.

JAXON: The Elevators knew they had a way into the West Coast through the fellow Texans on the music scene, and making it in the ballroom scene was going to be their big shot. Janis Joplin had done it from Texas. I saw them alongside Van Morrison doing "Gloria"—[he] used to throw back his head and let out the screams, but Roky had the scream that would knock your socks off. I thought they had the songs, the good looks, the talent—they could have made it big. And here I am, loving their music, sitting back in the Avalon and checking out the reaction, and the Californians didn't know what to make of it. The jug is very frenetic, and these people who were trying to be *so cool* and *so laid back*, it was a little too much for them. I could see right away it wasn't the same reception as you got with Quicksilver [Messenger Service], the house band. The Elevators weren't loaded down with beads and bangles—the hippies out there were vain, show-off people, and the Elevators weren't into that. They were wearing their scruffy clothes, old boots. They were not into the paraphernalia, so that intimidated [audiences].

STACY (*K*): I really and truly don't feel like anybody was in the place—out there, at that time—that we were in. I'm not saying we were necessarily wise in what we'd been doing, but we'd been taking acid constantly, I mean, for long periods of time. And Tommy was really a genius—he knew so much about religion and philosophy that he'd lecture to us. It was just constant. Those bands out there, they didn't really take acid till later. [They] didn't affect me spiritually, like most of my favorite musicians, but they were a bunch of kids too. They'd be passing round gallon jugs of acid through the audience, and you'd walk around, and there was just smiling faces. It was in the days of the actual innocence, the flowers and love . . . of course, it got rank.

Q: Did you take acid for the first Avalon performance?

RONNIE: Oh yeah, Tommy didn't let us go on without taking it. I always took a little; he always took a lot [*laughs*]. I usually took a half or a quarter—I wasn't quite ready for the whole thing yet. Those first few days, I was pretty new at it.

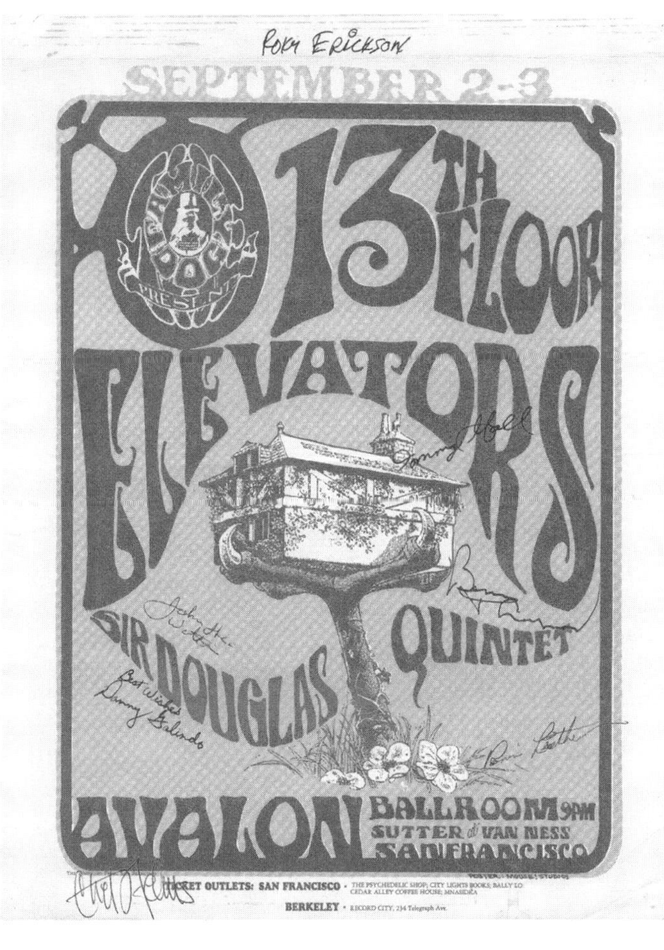

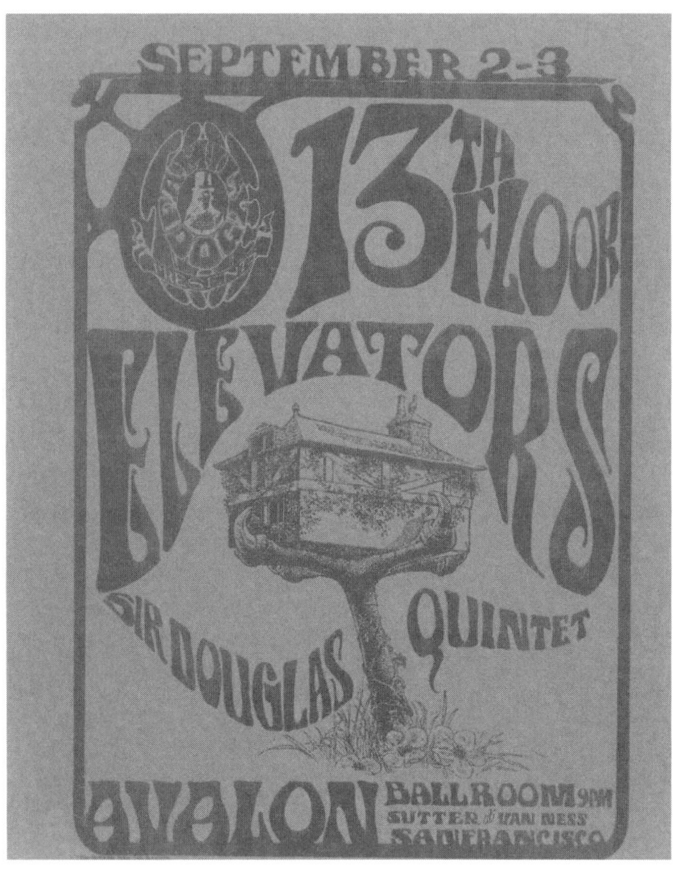

— ADMIT ONE $2.50 —

THE FAMILY DOG PRESENTS

DANCE-CONCERT

13th FLOOR ELEVATORS
with
SIR DOUGLAS QUINTET

SEPTEMBER 2 - 3 *9P.M.*

AVALON BALLROOM
SUTTER AT VAN NESS SAN FRANCISCO

The [Avalon] show I thought was great—I thought [it] went real well. I mean, it was a big place and it was full all the way to the back.

JOHN IKE: The Fillmore was a dump. The Avalon was a palace. We loved to play there. They gave away free acid at the door; it was a heaven for us.

Most of the members of the Grateful Dead attended the Elevators' first Avalon show, and John Ike recalls being approached as he left the stage with an invitation from one of the Deadheads to meet the band; not having a clue whom she was talking about, he passed. Tommy also recalls meeting the members of the Dead after the Avalon show and being invited out to Muir Woods—however a meeting wouldn't actually occur until Janis Joplin returned from Chicago. As Jaxon noted: "Janis had it made at that point, so she was in a position to be a benevolent angel."

CLEMENTINE: One of my favorite things that we did was we stayed with the Grateful Dead. Janis took us out [to Muir Woods]. There was also her band [Big Brother and the Holding Company], the Elevators, and the Grateful Dead. They had an old girls' camp with giant redwood trees. And up in the top of these redwood trees, they had built a deck to get high in. The safest I've ever felt in my whole life was up at the top of these redwood trees turning on with the Grateful Dead, because we knew there was no way police could bust us . . . And the thing that I liked so much—the musicians were very generous with each other, and hospitable, and not in the least bit competitive—it was a very loving time.

On the night of the successful Avalon show, Steve Tolin—the keen young promoter the Elevators had encountered in Sacramento—reappeared. He'd made good on his promise to double the fees for the shows John Ike had told him about. As a result, he was hired as the band's new booking agent.

STEVE TOLIN: I was simply getting them jobs. I watched the Elevators playing, and I saw the reaction in the crowd, and the Elevators tore up the evening. The kids loved them; they were a phenomenal group. They were getting a lot of airplay, and I was delighted to pick up a national group. I wasn't exposed as to whether they were on LSD, which was not my world.

Opposite top left: Handbill for the Elevators' first Avalon show, designed by Alton Kelley and Stanley Mouse, featuring an illustration by Robin Jacques lifted from the 1964 publication *Book of Dragons* by Ruth Manning-Sanders, September 2–3, 1966. Known as FD24 in the series of Family Dog productions, shown here is type "A," signed by Chet Helms and various band members. At least with Jaxon commissioning the posters at the Avalon, the band's name was spelled correctly.

Opposite top right: Avalon poster featuring the same design. There were two printings: one before the show, identified by the "Bindweed Press" printing credit, and one after, with FD24-2 notation.

Opposite bottom left: Type "D" handbill—the rarest of the four variations printed for the show.

Opposite bottom right: Ticket for the Avalon show.

"13 Floor Elevator"

DESIGNATION AND APPLICATION FOR MEMBERSHIP
IN THE

American Federation of Television and Radio Artists

LOS ANGELES LOCAL

1551 North La Brea Avenue — HOllywood 4-5123

AFFILIATED WITH THE AMERICAN FEDERATION OF LABOR

(1) I hereby apply for membership in the AMERICAN FEDERATION OF TELEVISION AND RADIO ARTISTS and in the Los Angeles Local thereof, and agree to be bound by each and every provision contained in the Constitution of the American Federation of Television and Radio Artists, in the Constitution of the said Local, by such amendments to said Constitutions as may hereafter be made, and by any and all by-laws, rules, regulations, orders and resolutions of the Federation and the Local, whether now in force or hereafter enacted. I agree that the said amendments, by-laws, rules, regulations, orders and resolutions are binding upon me as of the date of their lawfully taking effect, regardless of the rights, if any, vested in me prior to such date.

(2) I hereby designate the American Federation of Television and Radio Artists as my exclusive agent for collective bargaining purposes in any and all matters dealing with the radio industry, television, records, electrical transcriptions, any other means for mechanical reproduction, and any other matters or industries within the jurisdiction of the said Federation. I hereby further authorize the said Federation to delegate its right to be my collective bargaining agent to the said Local or to any other subdivision, agent or affiliate of said Federation.

(3) I hereby authorize the said Federation or the said Local, or other subdivision, agent or affiliate of the Federation, to enter into agreements with my employers or their representatives, requiring my membership in good standing in the said Federation as a condition of entering into and continuing my employment, and I hereby express my desire that such an agreement be consummated.

(4) I further authorize my employer to deduct from my compensation my dues, assessments and obligations to the Federation and the Local at such periods as the Federation may designate, and to pay the same directly to the Federation or the Local. It is understood that this authorization is irrevocable for a period of one year from the date endorsed hereon, and is thereafter revocable by me in writing only, delivered to the Federation and the Local.

(5) The above designations and authorizations are completely independent of my status as an applicant for membership under paragraph "(1)", and of my status as a member.

(6) Enclosed herewith is $________ covering the first payment of dues and initiation fees. (See reverse side.)

(7) I affirm that I have truthfully answered the questions on the reverse side hereof.

Dated 9-11, 1966 — 13th Floor Elevator

ROKY ERICKSON
(SIGN HERE) PROFESSIONAL NAME (PRINT HERE)

ROGER ERICKSON
(SIGN HERE) LEGAL NAME (PRINT HERE)

1169 McALLISTER S.F. CALIF.
(STREET) (CITY AND STATE) (ZIP CODE)

Telephone Numbers____ Soc. Sec. No.____

Agent's Name____ Phone No.____

Engagement & Date____

(FILL IN BOTH SIDES)

American Federation of Television and Radio Artists — OFFICE COPY

OCT 3 '66 105533 LA

13th Floor Elevator

singer — AFTRA-P

INITIATION	CURRENT DUES	PENALTY	TOTAL
100.00 a/c	(Where the Action Is 9/11/66) (American Bandstand 9/24/66)		

INITIATION / NATIONAL / LOCAL / TOTAL / BALANCE DUE

$ ____ IF PAID CURRENTLY WITH

PERIOD ENDING

Roger (Roky) Erickson 73443
1169 McAllister
San Francisco, Calif.
452-80-6827

Above: Roky's AFTRA contract and payment stub for the band's appearances on *Where the Action Is* and *American Bandstand*. The band got paid in advance, as filming didn't take place until the week of transmission: *Where the Action Is* was aired on September 26, and *American Bandstand* was broadcast on October 29 (the show's Halloween special).

Opposite top left: *Record World* advertisement for the "You're Gonna Miss Me" single, September 10.

Opposite top right: Poster for a show at the Solano County Fairgrounds in Vallejo, California, September 9.

Opposite bottom left: Handbill for a show at the Santa Rosa Veterans Memorial Building, September 10.

Opposite bottom right: Handbill for a show at Bill Quarry's "TNT" ("Teens 'n' Twenties") event featuring the Standells as well as—coming up on September 23—"13th Floor Elevator."

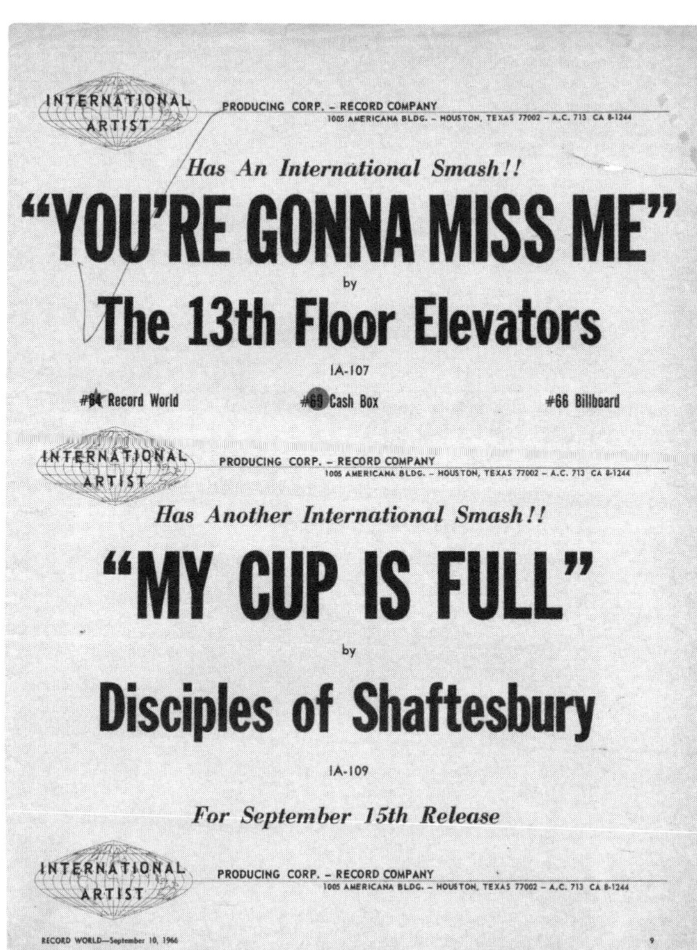

Golden Star Promotions
Presents

13TH FLOOR ELEVATOR

plus

The J.C. Battle of Bands runner-up

THE CHOSEN FOR

and

THE SOULS

FRI. NITE, SEPT. 9

SOLANO CO. FAIRGROUNDS

VALLEJO

8 p.m. to 12 Midnight

DRESS CASUAL

ONLY $2.00

GOLDEN STAR PROMOTIONS presents

13TH FLOOR ELEVATOR

and

The

NEW BREED

WITH THEIR HITS – "GREEN-EYED WOMAN" AND "I'VE BEEN WRONG BEFORE"

SAT. NITE, SEPT. 10

8 p.m. to 12 Midnight

Santa Rosa Vet's

Adm. only $2 MEMORIAL Don't Miss It!

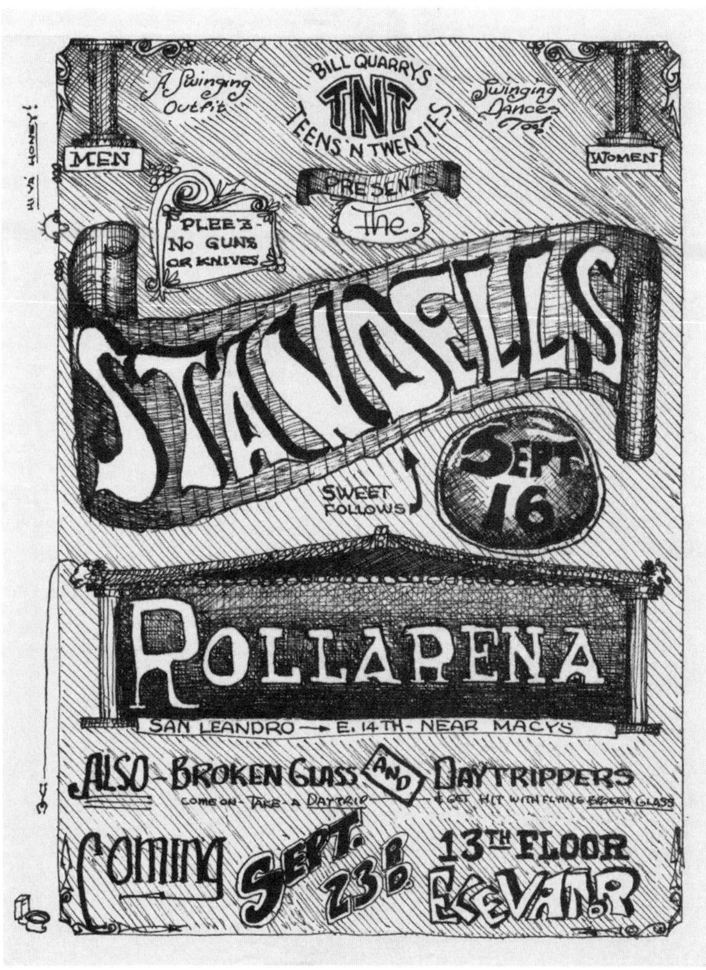

Monday September 26, 1966

Morning

6:30 5 KIDS AND COMPANY
12 LEAVE IT TO BEAVER—Comedy
6:35 10 FARM REPORT
6:40 6 FARM REPORT—Clark Bolt
6:45 42 GOD IS THE ANSWER
7:00 4 6 6 7 TODAY
COLOR Scheduled guests include playwright Edward Albee and sportscaster Joe Garagiola, who discusses the National League pennant race. (Two hours)
5 THREE STOOGES—Comedy
12 NEWS—Richard Roll
42 MARY MELODY—Children
7:05 10 NEWS
7:15 3 FARM NEWS, WEATHER
7:25 5 NEWS AND WEATHER
7:30 3 DOMINGO PENA—Discussion
5 10 COLOR NEWS—Wallace
10 CARTOONS—Children
7:55 5 10 NEWS AND WEATHER
8:00 3 B'WANA DON—Children

BOYS! *Earn extra spending money. Join TV Guide's Young Merchant program today. Fill out and mail this coupon.*

TV GUIDE, P. O. Box 66354
Houston 6, Tex. (S.T.) P65

Name______________Age____
Address____________________
City________State______Zip____

5 10 10 42 CAPT. KANGAROO
Mr. Green Jeans shows some ducks and flying squirrels. (60 min.)
12 MIKE DOUGLAS—Variety
Actor Chuck Connors is this week's co-host. (90 min.)
8:15 9 WHAT'S NEW—Children
8:30 3 JACK LA LANNE—Exercise
8:45 9 SPANISH LESSON
9:00 3 DIVORCE COURT—Drama
4 6 6 COLOR EYE GUESS
5 7 10 10 CANDID CAMERA
9 HISTORY AND GOVERNMENT
42 ROMPER ROOM—Children
9:25 4 6 6 COLOR NEWS-Vanocur
9 SCIENCE—Lesson
9:30 4 6 6 42 CONCENTRATION
5 7 10 10 BEVERLY HILLBILLIES—Comedy
"The Beverly Hillbillies" begin a series of daytime reruns as Jed strikes oil. Jed: Buddy Ebsen. Granny: Irene Ryan.
12 JACK LA LANNE—Exercise
9:45 9 LIBRARY AND LITERATURE
10:00 3 12 SUPERMARKET SWEEP
4 6 6 42 CHAIN LETTER
COLOR Actress Ruta Lee and TV host Dennis James are the celebrity guests.
5 7 10 10 ANDY GRIFFITH
9 HISTORY AND GOVERNMENT
10:25 9 SPANISH—Lesson
10:30 3 12 DATING GAME
4 6 6 42 COLOR SHOWDOWN—Game
5 7 10 10 DICK VAN DYKE
10:40 9 CHANGING EARTH—Science
11:00 3 12 DONNA REED—Comedy
4 6 6 42 COLOR JEOPARDY
5 7 10 10 LOVE OF LIFE
9 HISTORY AND GOVERNMENT
11:25 5 7 10 COLOR NEWS—Benti
9 SPANISH—Lesson
10 CONSULT DR. BROTHERS-Talk
11:30 3 12 FATHER KNOWS BEST
4 ED DUNN—Variety
5 7 10 SEARCH FOR TOMORROW—Serial
6 6 42 SWINGIN' COUNTRY
COLOR Guests: Tommy Leonetti ("Wayward Wind") and Gale Garnett.

A-22 TV GUIDE

6 Corpus Christi 10 Corpus Christi
6 Temple-Waco 10 Waco

10 BETTER LIVING—Russell
11:45 5 7 10 GUIDING LIGHT—Serial
9 SE HABLA—Spanish
11:55 6 6 42 NEWS—Newman

Afternoon

12:00 3 12 BEN CASEY—Drama
An expectant mother must undergo brain surgery that could result in the death of either the mother or the child. Barbara: Brett Somers. (60 min.)
5 NEWS—Jim Abbott
6 6 NEWS AND WEATHER
7 10 NEWS, FARM REPORT AND WEATHER
9 HISTORY AND GOVERNMENT
10 TEN ACRES—Johnny Watkins
42 CARROUSEL-Mamie St. George
12:10 7 WOMAN'S WORLD-Jean Boone
12:15 5 OUR TOWN—Discussion
6 CATHY'S CORNER—Women
10 KARTUNE KLUB—Children
12:25 9 LIBRARY AND LITERATURE
12:30 4 6 6 COLOR LET'S MAKE A DEAL—Game
5 7 10 10 AS THE WORLD TURNS—Serial
42 BEN CASEY—Drama
See 12 Noon, Ch. 3 for details.
12:45 9 SPANISH—Lesson
12:55 4 6 COLOR NEWS—Dickerson
1:00 3 12 NEWLYWED GAME
4 6 6 COLOR DAYS OF OUR LIVES—Serial
5 7 10 10 PASSWORD—Game
COLOR Danny Kaye and June Lockhart are this week's celebrity guests.
9 HISTORY AND GOVERNMENT
1:25 9 SPANISH—Lesson
1:30 3 12 A TIME FOR US—Serial
4 6 6 42 DOCTORS—Serial
5 7 10 10 HOUSE PARTY
COLOR Art Linkletter's guest is 12-year-old pianist Ginny Tiu.
1:40 9 CHANGING EARTH—Science
1:55 3 12 NEWS—Marlene Sanders
2:00 3 12 GENERAL HOSPITAL-Serial
4 6 6 42 COLOR ANOTHER WORLD—Serial

September 26 **Monday**
Morning-Afternoon

5 7 10 10 TELL THE TRUTH
9 HISTORY AND GOVERNMENT
2:25 5 7 7 10 COLOR NEWS—Douglas Edwards
9 SCIENCE—Lesson
2:30 3 12 42 NURSES—Serial
4 6 6 YOU DON'T SAY!-Game
COLOR Actors Hal March and Majorie Lord are the celebrity guests this week.
5 7 10 10 EDGE OF NIGHT
2:45 9 SPANISH—Lesson
3:00 3 12 42 DARK SHADOWS-Serial
4 6 6 MATCH GAME
COLOR Singer Anita Gillette and TV personality Les Crane are this week's celebrity panelists. Host: Gene Rayburn.
5 7 10 10 SECRET STORM
9 HISTORY AND GOVERNMENT
3:25 4 6 6 COLOR NEWS—Floyd Kalber
3:30 3 12 42 WHERE THE ACTION IS
Performers: Lee Dorsey and the Thirteenth Floor Elevators.
4 MERV GRIFFIN—Variety
5 POPEYE—Cartoons
6 COLOR COLONEL CHRISTOPHER—Children
6 LOVE THAT BOB!—Comedy
7 GENERAL HOSPITAL—Serial
10 LEAVE IT TO BEAVER-Comedy
10 SEARCH FOR TOMORROW
3:45 10 GUIDING LIGHT—Serial
3:55 41 NEWS—Andres R. Morin
4:00 3 MOVIE—Adventure
"Elephant Boy." (1937) Rudyard Kipling's classic about a native boy in India. Sabu, W. E. Holloway, Walter Hudd. (90 min.)
6 BOZO THE CLOWN
7 UNCLE JAY—Children
9 BOOK BEAT—Interview
10 LITTLE ORPHAN ANIMALS
10 BEN CASEY—Drama
See 12 Noon, Ch. 3 for details.
12 MOVIE—Melodrama
"The Fast and the Furious." (1954) A fugitive from the police hitches a ride with a girl. John Ireland, Dorothy Malone, Bruce Carlisle. (90 min.)
41 INFORMACION AGRICOLA
42 LEAVE IT TO BEAVER-Comedy
4:05 10 CARTOONS—Children

TV GUIDE A-23

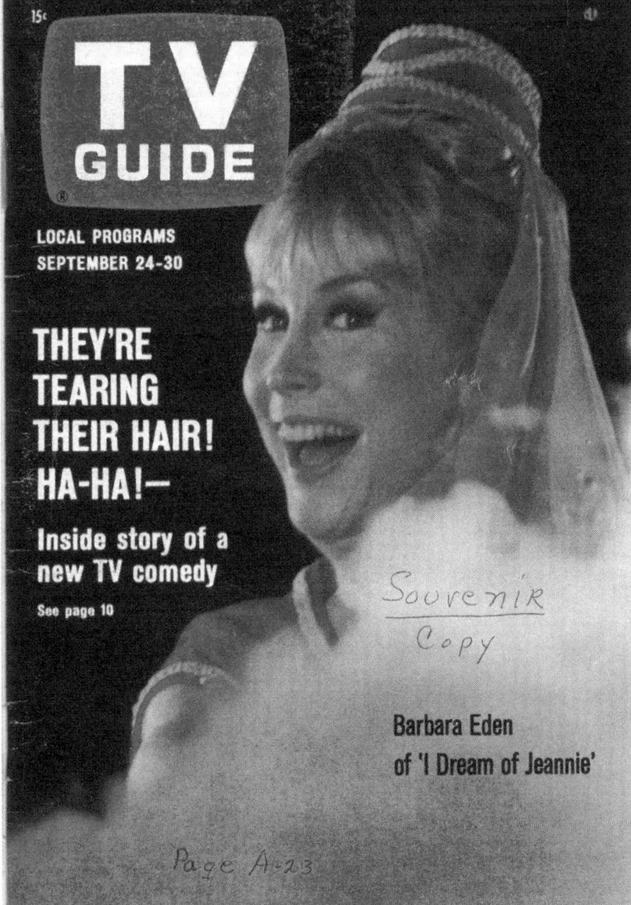

Above: Interior spread and cover from Ronnie's parents' *TV Guide*, the September 24–30 edition, featuring the band's first national television appearance: their September 26 performance on *Where the Action Is*.

Tolin concentrated on booking them as a pop act—ensuring they played every bandstand, fairground, armory, Rollarena, and veteran's hall in the Bay Area. He even got them to sign AFTRA contracts for a performance on Dick Clark's *Where the Action Is*—yes, the Elevators were set to appear on national TV.

Back in Houston, as "You're Gonna Miss Me" progressed up the weekly charts, IA reviewed the "Bynum tapes" for a follow-up single. They selected the cover of Buddy Holly's "I'm Gonna Love You Too" backed with "Splash 1"—believing that the songs would appeal to the wider market while showcasing the band's Texan heritage. This choice conflicted, however, with Tommy's wish to showcase his messianic, acid-informed manifesto songs, so the band returned to Texas to record a new version of "Reverberation," with Bob Sullivan and Bynum attending on IA's behalf. Despite coming directly from San Francisco, Tommy didn't have a supply of acid for the session, and as Ronnie recalls, the band smoked DMT instead. Powell's song "The Kingdom of Heaven" was recorded as the proposed B-side. After mixing on September 21, the band headed back to San Francisco the following day.

> JOHN IKE: Our manager [Steve Tolin], he told us, "I've been contacted by Capitol and Columbia Records, and they want you guys to sign with them." We said, "Oh no, we can't sign with them; we're happy with our record company." *Happy with our record company?* We were, at the time: they'd got us out of town, we had a number-one hit all over California, we had all the dope we could smoke, we had girls, and we had rock 'n' roll. [*Laughs*] What else is there? We had it all and we owed it to Lelan Rogers.

Considering they often performed three times a day, surprisingly little from the band's most active period has survived in terms of ephemera, photos, or advertisements. In fact, the only known photos of the Elevators in California are from a KFRC boat party. September 23 ("Marathon Day," as it became known) began when the band boarded a boat at 6:00 a.m and performed at 7:00 a.m., which Tommy particularly recalls because, evidently, he couldn't stop laughing when the faces of the DJs—realizing the Elevators were performing "drug songs"—turned white.

Next, the Elevators boarded a plane and flew to Encino to mime poolside at Dick Clark's house for *Where the Action Is*.

> STACY (*K*): [Dick Clark] was a pretty sharp character, I thought, in real life, but as soon as that camera came on, it was all young, healthy, vibrant, American . . . Stern businessman. That smile is all show; you can believe that. We did *Where the Action Is* [and] it was as nuts for him as us.

Regardless of what Clark thought of the band, he was impressed by Tolin, and offered him a PR job with his production company. But the Elevators weren't done: immediately after filming was finished, the band flew up to San Leandro

WHERE THE ACTION IS!

to perform at another of Bill Quarry's "Teens 'n' Twenties" Rollarena shows, after which they drove to yet another undocumented show in San Rafael. Ronnie remembers that the band seemed to develop a pattern of playing every four days—Tommy had deduced that LSD takes four days to clear the system before its full effects could be experienced again.

> CLEMENTINE: There was one marathon tour that they took of California where they played three different shows in one night—in very far apart, out-of-the-way places. They sweated while they were out there, and then [had to] travel through cold weather to the next show and get up there in damp clothes and perform outdoors, and do it again three nights in a row. And all of them held up. Roky had all the words right, and the musicianship was perfect. I don't know how they had the stamina to do all that and be high at the same time on LSD, but they did. At a country-type place, they tried to bust us, but Roky saved us. We got stopped by the police, and they seemed to know who we were—they were treating us like heavy drug people. I sat in the back seat with Roky and a policeman, and he turned to Roky and said, "I've been questioning you now for about twenty minutes—I bet you're ready for a shot!" And Roky was all innocence, looked at him and said, "No, thank you, I don't drink." And the guy left us. Roky could get away with murder, he was so genuine.

The intense month ended with a show in San Bruno followed by a return headline appearance at the Avalon, supported by house band Quicksilver Messenger Service.

> LIZ HENRY (fan): They had top bill over everybody we'd heard of. We were going, "They're getting top billing over Quicksilver Messenger Service!" And everybody, all the other bands, were going, "You're with *the 13th Floor Elevators*?" I mean, bands like Big Brother!

The consensus—or what the band termed "informed paranoia"—was that the authorities in Texas were catching up with them on the West Coast. The state of California banned LSD on October 6, 1966. The same week, "You're Gonna Miss Me" reached its peak of #55 on the Billboard chart after a long, solid climb, only to vanish entirely the next week. The band feared they had been victims of another shutdown.

The army also caught up with Roky.

> Q: The draft board were after in you SF?
>
> ROKY: *After?!* Ten times!
>
> JOHN KEARNEY: There's the draft board thing and the strangeness concerning it. I had the impression Tommy was in the driver's seat: he was going to guide [Roky] through beating the draft. I think Tommy's method was to beat Roky as well.

Opposite: Stills from the *Where the Action Is* performance.

Best Wishes, Danny Galindo

OH MOTHER

SHE'S A FINK

BILL QUARRY'S TEENS 'N TWENTIES

PRESENTS

TRUCKS USE LOW GEAR

OF SOUND

GENTLEMEN

MEN & WOMEN

WHATS GOING ON HERE?

ELVIS STARS

BARRY CARLOS IS A SWEET FELLOW

YOU'RE GONNA MISS ME

EVER SEE A PREGNANT ELEVATOR

SNOT

DRWG. DON RYDER

ALSO - STATON BROS.

AND THE WILD! ELEMENTS

13TH FLOOR ELEVATOR

SEPT. 23

plenty of free parking

ROKY ERICKSON

rollarena

SAN LEANDRO - E-14TH NEAR MACYS

Part of the strategy to thwart the draft board seems to have been for Roky to turn up at the hearings having smoked a ton of Asthmador cigarettes and taken acid, then to complain of back pain. By now, however, the draft board was onto Roky's ruse of turning up tripped out and sent him for a spinal tap.

After six intense weeks of touring, tripping, and, now, contending with the draft, it was Roky's turn to crack.

JOHN KEARNEY: Asthmador—it was over-the-counter belladonna. It's related to the datura root, which the Indians used in Mexico, for their visions. It has a nasty reputation. Roky was *not* crazy when he came back from Frisco. Roky started to play up the crazy routine. And me and the ol' boys still argue this one—when it started, it was an act, but now it's the only way he knows.

SANDY LOCKETT: [Roky] definitely made all the attempts to seem as fucked-up as he could for the draft board. It soon became clear that they had serious plans for that boy. He'd toked up on Asthmador cigarettes and showed up in a complete mess. [The cigarettes] imitated a lot of the symptoms of various respiratory afflictions, and they also put you into an opium haze—and that, together with the various things he'd take for gigs, just finally kicked him over.

JOHN IKE: In California [Roky] walked out on the stage on a bummer, forgot all of the words to all the songs, and says, "I can't play, man." He went and drew a blank on the stage. I said, "Don't worry about it, Roky. Stacy and Tommy and Ronnie and I'll play."

RONNIE: Well, he did that at more than one time. He just kind of spaced out and would just turn around and start playing [guitar].

TOMMY: Everything was perfectly normal, until all of a sudden, he couldn't do the words.

ROKY: Well, I had to go to do some tests. And then I had to have a spinal tap done so I could tell them I was sick, and didn't want to join.

Q: Was there actually anything wrong with you?

ROKY: No.

Q: You faked it.

ROKY: Yep, right . . . I told them I was having pains in my back so I couldn't work in the army.

Q: Pretty frightening?

ROKY: Yep.

Opposite: Handbill for the previously advertised September 23 "Teens 'n' Twenties" show, at the San Leandro Rollarena, signed by various band members.

JAXON: Don McGrew [and I] made a point of going over to where they were living. Tommy and Clementine were [saying], "Roky's not doing too well today; I don't think it would be good for you to see him." It was very frustrating, but I got the impression they had taken main control of the whole concept of the group. There wasn't that "hang out" kind of thing. And the one time we attempted to do it, we were basically run off by Clementine and Tommy. They were both getting into the voodoo wizard trip. Tommy got worse as time went on, with gowns and staffs with magical *da de du* . . . I've got to be honest, I blame Tommy for the whole troubles of the band out there. They were so intent on orchestrating the whole thing, instead of letting Roky see people that he knew, who could have [been] a reality link, instead of cloistering him away from the world.

ROKY: I was walking along the street, and the cops picked me up and wanted to see my identification. Apparently I didn't have the right ID—I was from Texas. If you weren't from San Francisco, you were a risk to them. So they took me to a mental hospital and checked me in. And luckily, it was a nice place, for the bigwigs.

SANDY LOCKETT: Well, Roky was really nuts by that time. He'd taken too many strange things, and that probably kicked him over the edge. We had to pry him out of San Francisco State Hospital. They were going to try both electro- and insulin-shock therapy, so we knew we had to get him out of there. Tommy and I had to sneak up there in the middle of the night and commando-raid him out the back stairs.

Another problem facing the band is that they'd lost track of one another. Roky, Tommy, and Clementine had taken an apartment at 1169 McAllister, in the Lower Haight. At the time, this was a predominately African-American neighborhood, and the locals didn't take kindly to the hippies' taking over the cheap rents. The final straw came when the group returned from touring to find the apartment entirely stripped. Everything—Tommy's record collection, photos, and clothes—was gone. Although they suspected the landlord was responsible, the house was also in a known heroin area. Ronnie recalls that the burglary came on the heels of a demonstration that spilled into a series of street disturbances, resulting in National Guardsmen patrolling the streets for several weeks.

JOHN IKE: Stacy lived in San Francisco—Ronnie, Cecil, and I lived in San Pablo, and the only time we had any contact with those people was at the gigs. We didn't know what they were up to. If I didn't go and get them in the car, they were always late. Tommy left California and went to Texas to visit and came back, and that goddamn Rambler broke down and I had to pay for the goddamn flight he took from Arizona to California—had

Opposite: Poster for the band's September 30 show at San Bruno's National Guard Armory.

SAN BRUNO
A-GO-GO
PRESENTS
THE
13TH FLOOR
ELEVATOR
THE
INMATES
THE
WESTMINSTER V
FREE DOOR
PRIZES
FRI.
SEPT.
30
8:30 PM
NAT.
GUARD
ARMORY
ADMISSION 2.00
3RD AVE. - SAN BRUNO
C. Thayer
Advance tickets can be purchased at the following locations:
SHERMAN CLAY
Hillsdale Shopping Mall, San Mateo
A.B.C. MUSIC
San Mateo Ave., San Bruno
BRONSTEIN MUSIC
Grand Ave., South San Francisco
OR CALL
588-5674

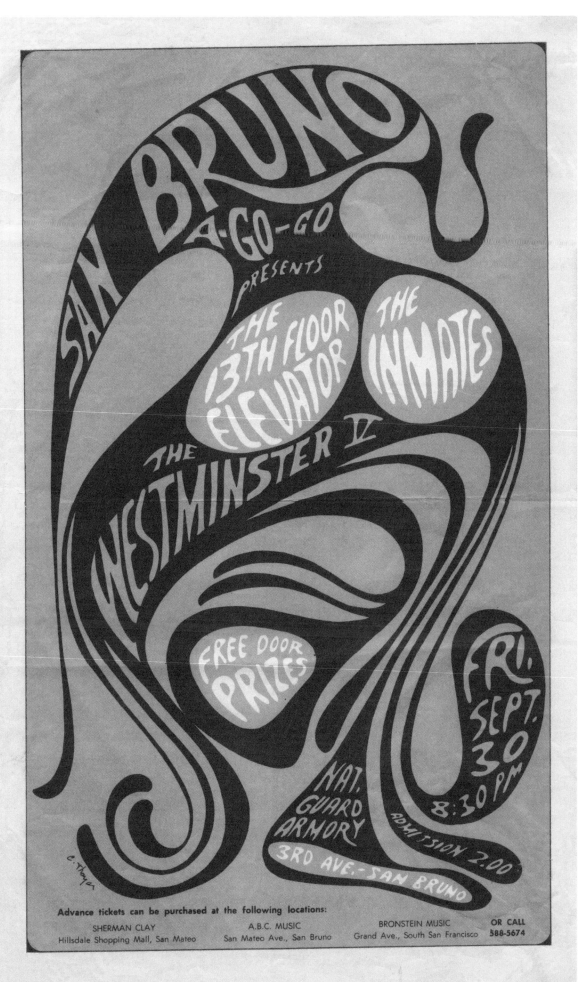

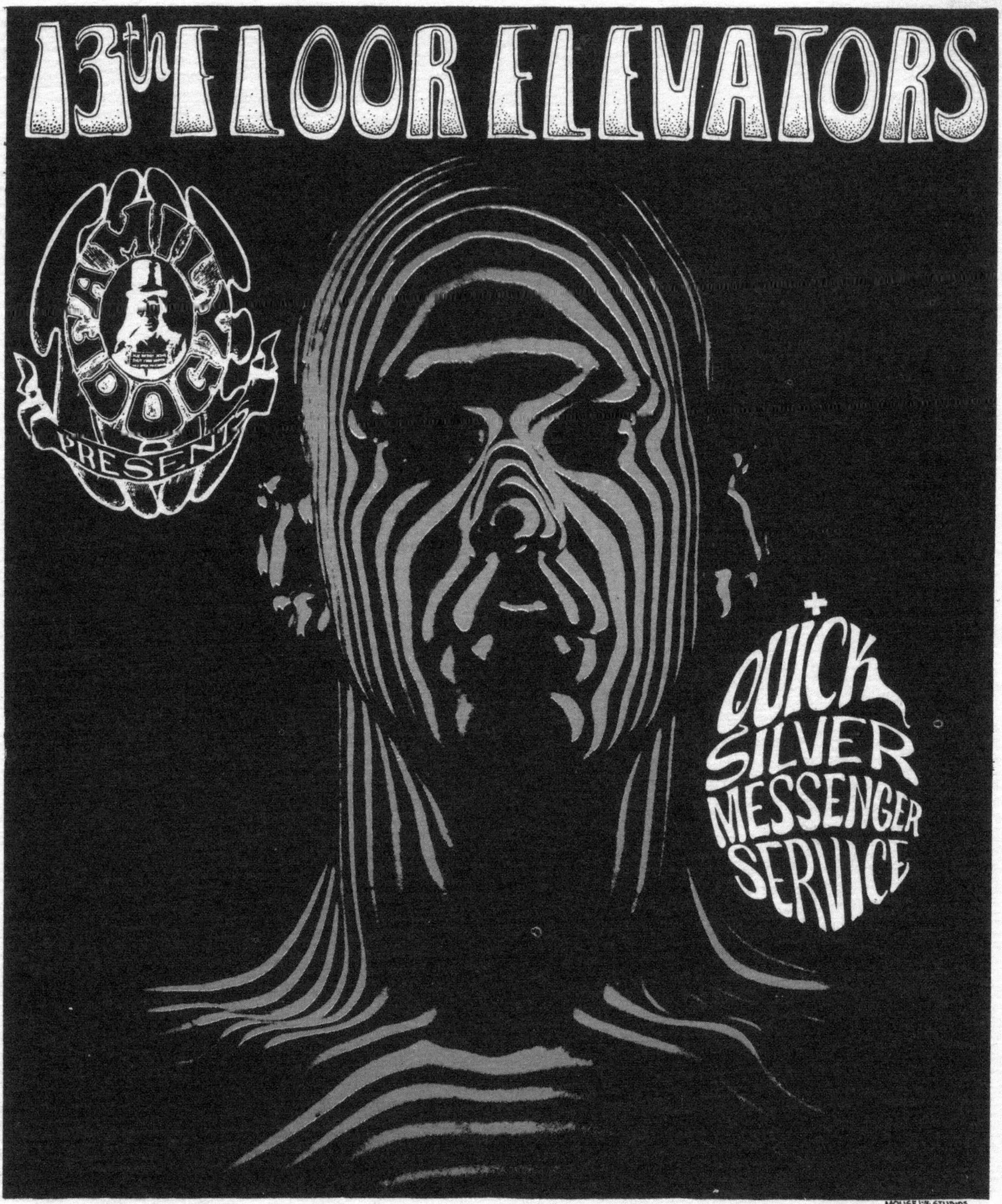

13th FLOOR ELEVATORS

FAMILY DOG PRESENTS

+ QUICK SILVER MESSENGER SERVICE

TICKET OUTLETS:	*SAN FRANCISCO*	THE PSYCHEDELIC SHOP; CITY LIGHTS BOOKS; BALLY LO; CEDAR ALLEY COFFEE HOUSE; MNASIDIKA; DISCOUNT RECORDS (North Beach); SANDAL MAKER (North Beach)
	SAUSALITO	TIDES BOOK SHOP; SANDAL MAKER
	BERKELEY	RECORD CITY, 234 Telegraph Avenue
	MENLO PARK	KEPLER'S BOOK STORE

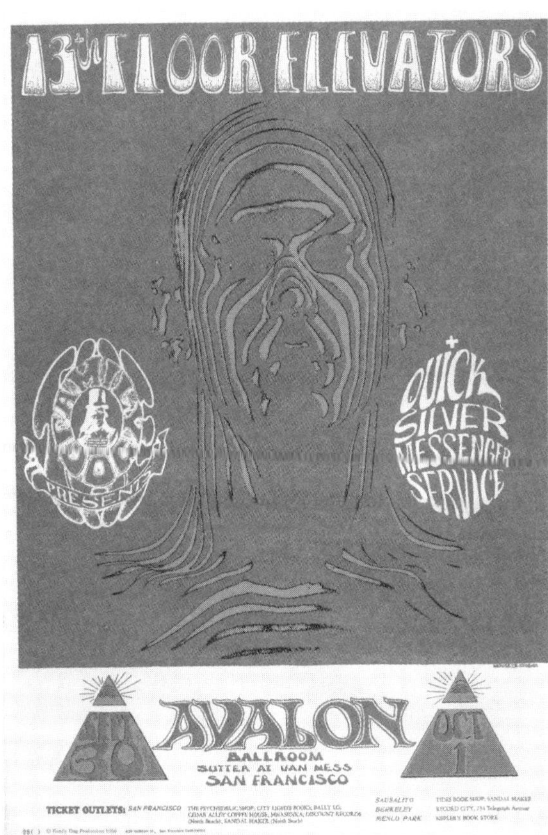

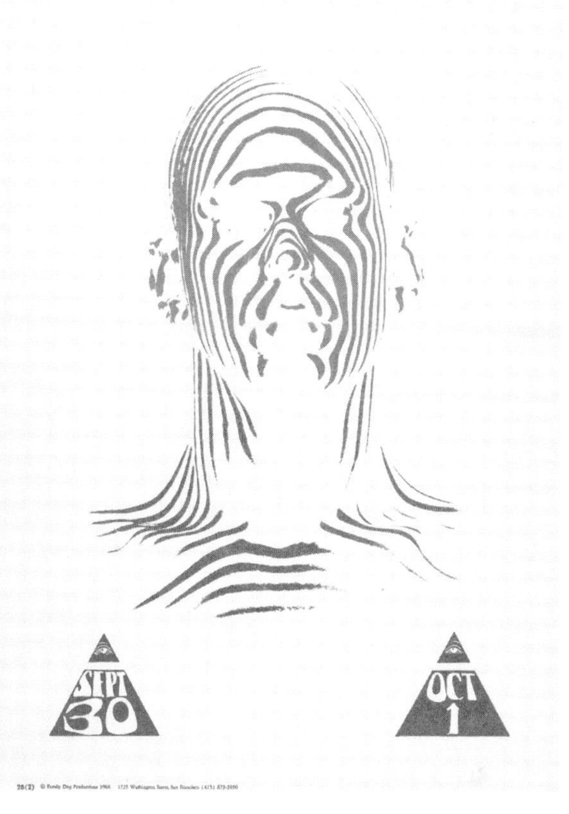

Opposite and above: Handbill and poster variations for the band's September 30–October 1 appearances at the Avalon, designed by Alton Kelley and Stanley Mouse using a December 1954 cover image from *Life*. Known as FD28, there are three known original printings of the poster. Shown is the handbill (**opposite**), the first poster printing with rare "split fountain" color gradation from top to bottom (**top left**), the second printing identified by the "28(2)" notation (**top right**), and two unfinished color separations from the original Bindweed Press printing (**bottom**).

to charter a flight to get to the gig. I was pissed, because he went back to Texas. Tommy, he was constantly going back and forth.

Q: Why?

JOHN IKE: Well, we can't talk about that.

Q: Dealing?

JOHN IKE: I suppose. I'm not sure; definitely maybe [*laughs*]. I mean, Stacy would ride a cab out to our house in San Pablo, and he'd be broke. And this happened every weekend. I'd say, "Stacy, why are you broke, man? I just gave you three hundred bucks." We played the Avalon Ballroom, we were playing all around the Bay Area, and making good money. Tommy really got a lot of money from Roky and Stacy and didn't provide them with anything but hamburgers and acid. They were broke, always. Coming to me for money. I was the manager. I handled the money—I wouldn't let Tommy do it.

ROKY (*KUT*): I didn't have much money, because Tommy Hall hogged all our money. I didn't enjoy that all that much, that Tommy Hall had all the money and I didn't . . . but I still had a good time.

STACY (*K*): John Ike and Ronnie were staying . . . seems like it was Larkspur, outside San Francisco. Already there was a bunch of clashes going on. We just got together for gigs—that's about all the group was really doing at that point. A lot of the first negative waves started in San Francisco. All kinds of delusions started to develop, like religious. Like, one time we felt like we were delivering a message; I can't explain it—it felt like we were obligated. That's what I was trying to explain about Roky, when he kept turning on after he started flipping out—it was an obligation that he felt, because of what he *believed* to be true. And we were starting to get heavy kickbacks.

JOHNNY GATHINGS: Stacy and I got high [and] we went down to Haight-Ashbury and found these caves, and there were a bunch of heroin addicts that were really sick and we went and preached to them, with our Bibles. We were getting kinda far-out and scary. We got too high. You don't mix religion with LSD.

JOHN IKE: The main thing that was hard was watching Roky; it was depressing what was happening to him. And then, somehow, Tommy got him back to a situation where he could go in and do the first album.

JERRY LIGHTFOOT: Stacy told me the idea was to play the ballrooms out there [in San Francisco] and get a deal. Well, Stacy told me [IA] threatened to come out there and take all his equipment, and said, "We want you to come back and make another record." They could have done anything at that point, they were wide open . . . it snapped it. The idea was to go back, straighten up, make this great record—and it just didn't work out. Sandy Lockett can probably tell you exactly. That's what Stacy told me.

SANDY LOCKETT: It was a very confusing period. And by that time, International Artists' plot had thickened. That was a strange bunch of people: Noble was just a rich guy who didn't quite know what to do, Lelan Rogers, who is a strange kettle of fish if there ever was one, and then there's this unusually crew-cut carrottop, Bill Dillard, who was kind of a strange, fringe lawyer type. And they were in the recording business for something besides the record business; I don't know what.

STACY (*K*): The first album we cut, it was really a bum deal. They'd been telling us we'd be going to Nashville for the first album. They called us from California to Texas and wanted us to do a few sides. And we came down here, and they got into a big hassle with us about money—the time of the year and all this. They said, "Y'all are either gonna cut the album this weekend or we're gonna release all these tapes we've got." And they meant it. And they were trash tapes, just studio jams and shit.

With four tracks already recorded and deemed useable, they drove nonstop from San Francisco to Dallas on October 9 to finish an album's worth of material with Bob Sullivan at Sumet Sounds, where they were also introduced to Lelan Rogers for the first time.

LELAN ROGERS: My first meeting with them was when they turned up at Sumet in Dallas. They drove back from San Francisco and [we] met, and we started recording there at two or three o'clock in the morning. It was fun.

JOHN IKE: Tommy was sitting on a stump in a vacant lot in Dallas, at three o'clock in the morning, with long hair, and he was meditating, and here come the cops. Stacy had stashed a little weed in the studio. They flushed it down the toilet but it didn't flush, it just floated to the top! [*Laughs*] And so Lelan was out there trying to talk them into leaving. And they wanted to know why this guy was meditating on a stump at three o'clock in the morning [*laughs*].

Bob Sullivan recalls Tommy going outside and "yodeling"—in fact, he'd gone out to practice the jug part to "Roller Coaster," the first song intended for recording, only to attract the attention of a passing police patrol.

TOMMY (MF): We first did "Roller Coaster," and I really busted that up and everybody hated me—you know, went off-key and stuff. But it wasn't my fault, 'cause I just wasn't ready for my part. But when I heard the recordings, I realized that it really worked. I looked at what I was doing primarily from a writer's standpoint, and was kinda just playing along with the band—and luckily that's how the band felt also.

JOHN IKE: The jug was so loud in that song, "Roller Coaster," that it drowned out a lot of the lyrics. That's what I hated about the jug. Roky was singing, doing real good and then here comes this jug. You know, Lelan piping in the jug, "Put the jug on ten!" You know? [*Laughs*] "They don't care about the lyrics—it's that jug that makes people like the Elevators!" That's the way Lelan felt about it.

Q: Did Lelan ever give you trouble about the performances?

ROKY: No, he never did, really. He'd say, "Could you boys speed it up a bit—we're paying for this time," or something like that, and I'd say, "Who is this weird man with the white hair?" He was weird-looking; his head was red as a beet.

LELAN ROGERS: They were usually a one-take band. And they had their ideas about what they wanted it to sound like. And I was more of a babysitter than I was a producer, I'm the first one to admit that. We just locked the doors and we would do one take, and then play it back, and if they liked it, we'd take it and go on to the next one.

BOB SULLIVAN: The 13th Floor Elevators came in and tuned up, and they were playing so loud. The vibrations on the building . . . I mean, the control room windows were rattling; I thought the putty was going to come loose. No one produced them, really. They just went in the studio and said, "We're going to do this; let's do it." None of this stuff had overdubs. We nailed some of those songs the first take. I mean, we'd play it back and they'd say, "That's great, let's go to the next one."

LELAN ROGERS: We went back to the hotel after the session, very tired, and we were going to get a bite to eat, go to bed. And they were having a gathering of socially prominent people at this hotel; they all had their tuxedos and evening gowns on, and I walked into the coffee shop with this group. Just keep in mind the era: we were socially unacceptable. But I had my two lawyers with me, so they couldn't kick us out. It was obvious we couldn't get waited on; people were trying to get rid of us. So I told the cashier, "I don't want to create a big scene, but this is a very famous recording group from England, and if the people in here find out who they are it'll create pandemonium because they'll all be wanting autographs. Just get us some scrambled eggs and then we'll go."

SUMET SOUND
STUDIOS

5652 Daniels Avenue
Dallas, Texas

Quantity	Item	Amount
	Oct 9 1966	
4h.	Studio @ 50.00	200.00
6h.	Edit and Mix @ 25.00	150.00
	Oct 10 1966	
3½	Studio @ 50.00	175.00
4h	Post mixing Edit @ 15.00	60.00
4	201 Tape @ 3.50	14.00
3	[illegible] Tapes @ 15.00	45.00
	2% Tax	[illegible]

Name International Artists

Address [illegible] Americana Bldg
Houston, Tex [illegible]

SERVICE OR MATERIAL ORDER NO. 2226

DATE 10/9-10/66

TERMS NET 11/10/66

No statement will be mailed. Please pay from this order.

The foregoing services and/or materials were performed or received and are accepted and, in consideration thereof, the undersigned customer agrees to pay Sumet Sound Studios, at Dallas, Texas, the amounts shown due above. If default is made in payment of amount due hereon, such amount will bear interest at rate of 7% per annum from date due until paid and if amount of this order is collected through court proceeding or by an attorney, the undersigned customer will pay an additional amount equal to 15% of amount due hereon or $25.00, whichever is the greater, as reasonable attorneys' fees.

Signature of Customer or Representative

Top: An invoice for recording time booked at Dallas's Sumet Sound Studio on October 9 and 10. Payment reminders continued to be sent for these sessions right up until 1968.

Bottom: Poster for the Elevators' concert on October 14 in Fresno.

Following pages: Interior of the program issued for the band's October 15 show at the College of San Mateo, featuring misattributed photos from the September 23 KFRC boat party show in San Francisco Bay. These are the only known photos of the band in California due to the number of robberies they experienced while there.

THE
13TH FLOOR
ELEVATOR
Sound
built on harmonic
of past traditio
that bends its listener
into another dimension
...a fourth illusio
of harmonic
...rising and palpitatin
through levels of structured ton
...five operators of a new machin
whisper into the voi
inviting its listeners to an initiatio
of their soul into a new understanding o
...what was ...what is ...what will b
Join the group and rise to a new heigh
while a passenge
on THE THIRTEENTH FLOOR ELEVATOR

RONNIE LEATHERMAN

ROCKY ERICKSON

STACY SOUTHERLAND

TOMMY HALL

TOMMY HALL

STACY SOUTHERLAND

RONNIE LEATHERMAN

JOHN WALTON

JOHN WALTON

ED DOYLE PRESENTS
FLOOR ELEVATOR
THE BAYTOVENS
THE HARBINGER COMPLEX
THE CANADIAN FUZZ
THE IMMEDIATE FAMILY
THE NIGHT CAPS
THE STANTON BROS
IN CONCERT
SAT. OCT. 15
COLLEGE OF SAN MATEO
8:30 P.M.
ADMISSION 3.00
ADVANCE TICKETS:
CSM STUDENT COUNCIL OFFICE . A B C MUSIC, San Bruno . SHERMAN CLAY, Hillsdale
or CALL 588-5674

ED DOYLE PRESENTS
FLOOR ELEVATOR
THE BAYTOVENS
THE HARBINGER COMPLEX
THE CANADIAN FUZZ
THE IMMEDIATE FAMILY
THE NIGHT CAPS
THE STATON BROS.
IN CONCERT
SAT. OCT. 15
COLLEGE OF SAN MATEO
8:30 P.M.
ADMISSION 3.00

THE BAYTOVENS
THE HARBINGER COMPLEX
THE CANADIAN FUZZ
THE IMMEDIATE FAMILY
THE NIGHT CAPS
THE STATON BROS.
IN CONCERT
SAT. OCT. 15
COLLEGE OF SAN MATEO
8:30 P.M.
ADMISSION 3.00

ED DOYLE PRESENTS
FLOOR ELEVATOR
THE BAYTOVENS
THE HARBINGER COMPLEX
THE CANADIAN FUZZ
THE IMMEDIATE FAMILY
THE NIGHT CAPS
THE STATON BROS.
IN CONCERT
SAT. OCT. 15
COLLEGE OF SAN MATEO
8:30 P.M.
ADMISSION 3.00

Opposite top: Handbill and postcard for the San Mateo show.

Opposite bottom: Front and back cover of the San Mateo program.

> So she said, "Who's in the group?" I said, "It's the Rolling Stones, that's Mick Jagger sitting there"—pointing at Roky—and she said, "Oh my God, my daughter's bought all their records; let me get an autograph." So she runs over and Roky is sitting, saying, "Wow, man, what's going on?" And I said, "Just sign." We finally got to eat.

The only real problem during the sessions was that Tommy was short of the penultimate song for his planned psychedelic concept album. The track would be a warning to the curious traveler not to fail in his quest, because the ultimate goal was next: the album's closer, "Kingdom of Heaven." Roky had taught "We Sell Soul," the B-side of the Spades single, to the rest of the band in the back of the van from San Francisco. Once Tommy contrived to fit his lyrics to the melody, the song became "Don't Fall Down."

> RONNIE: We spent hours on "Don't Fall Down" and then we gave it up because everyone was too tired . . . and then we went to Houston, to Jones Sound Studio. I don't know why we didn't finish in Dallas . . . And the worst part was they remixed [the album] after we mixed it and sent it off to California to have it pressed. But I always liked Lelan. He really wanted to work with us, but he had to deal with the lawyers that had no idea about the music business.

After having acetates cut for what they believed to be the final mix, the band hit the road back to San Francisco, performing shows in Albuquerque, Santa Fe, and Fresno en route. However, not only did IA remix the entire album, they also resequenced the running order to start with the "hit," thereby ruining Tommy's intended overarching concept (however true this actually was, since several of the songs were written by Roky, Stacy, and Powell without his involvement).

> STACY (*K*): Tommy was writing some of those explanations for the songs and, you know, they weren't really the explanations at all. Like, "You're Gonna Miss Me" Roky had made before we'd even started . . . Whatever, it freaked me out. But he kept telling us, "Man, this is going to cause a stir." He says, "These people have never seen anything like this," and he says, "This is going to cause a controversy." And, in a sense, it did.

They returned to headline a large show for KFRC on October 15, at the College of San Mateo. Organized by Steve Tolin, this was clearly a big event, with six other bands playing before the Elevators. The promoters had also gone over the top on the advertising—printing handbills, postcards, and even a program with photos of the band from the KFRC boat trip (but with incorrect names attributed throughout).

In addition, it was the Avalon Ballroom's first anniversary that night, which was marked by a series of shows all weekend, the details of which have blurred in people's memories. The Sunday event is remembered

Big Brother & the Holding Company
Family Dog
Presents
The Sir Douglas Quintet
THE DOG WILL BE ONE YEAR OLD THIS SUNDAY
A SURPRIZE VISIT ON SUNDAY BY ?
SAT OCT 15
SUN OCT 16
LIGHTS BY BEN VAN METER & ROGER HILLYARD
AVALON BALLROOM
9 PM · SUTTER AT VAN NESS SAN FRANCISCO · 9 PM
TICKET OUTLETS:
SAN FRANCISCO THE PSYCHEDELIC SHOP; CITY LIGHTS BOOKS; BALLY LO; CEDAR ALLEY COFFEE HOUSE; MNASIDIKA; (North Beach) SANDAL MAKER (North Beach)
SAUSALITO TIDES BOOK SHOP
BERKELEY RECORD CITY, 234 Telegraph Avenue
MENLO PARK KEPLER'S BOOK STORE
FAMILY DOG © 1966 MOUSE STUDIOS
THE BINDWEED PRESS, SAN FRANCISCO

as "All-Texan Night," featuring Janis Joplin with Big Brother, the Sir Douglas Quintet, and the Elevators—who, due to the uncertainty of their return, were billed as "a surprize visit." Jerry Garcia and Pigpen from the Dead also formed a one-off jam band called the New Peanut Butter Sandwich, which included David Getz (Big Brother) as well as David Freiberg and Gary Duncan (Quicksilver).

Opposite: Poster for the Avalon's first anniversary show, remembered by many as "All-Texan Night." The Elevators are the teased "surprize visit on Sunday."

LIZ HENRY: The Grateful Dead are going, "We're on the same bill as the 13th Floor Elevators!" The Grateful Dead could not believe that [the Elevators] played a gig on acid—they were astounded.

PAM BAILEY: The keyboard player, Pigpen, he was going, "They don't really play a gig on *acid?!*" Eight million years later I tell this story and people go, "Yeah, sure, the Grateful Dead, *ha ha . . .*"

MOJO NAVIGATOR, *ISSUE 9*:
[The New Peanut Butter Sandwich] did a very long and boring pseudo Butterfield Blues instrumental. The most interesting group musically was the 13th Floor Elevators. They are a really freaky group. They look strange, they sound strange, and they are all good musicians, doing all original material. The lead singer, whose voice is truly odd, also plays guitar pretty well. The drummer is excellent. They have one guy who does nothing but boop-boop-boop with a jug. The songs they do are new and different.

Meanwhile, back in Texas, the arrival of John Cleveland's eye-popping album artwork, followed by Tommy's mind-boggling sleeve notes (a breakdown of each song's meaning and its relation to his concept of the LP as a pathway to enlightenment), caused Dillard and Ginther at IA to hit the roof. Luckily, Lelan intervened: not only did he lift the eye and pyramid—complete with thirteen floors—from the back of the dollar bill and plant it in the center of the back cover alongside Tommy's explanatory notes, but he also—on the other side of the pyramid—provided a set of name-dropping music industry insider blurbs, in order to try to identify them with the album.

SANDY LOCKETT: The cover very nearly got rejected, which would have been a tragedy.

JOHN IKE: We were delighted to have Lelan. When he saw that cover, he loved it. I mean, here you are in a record store—how could you turn that down? Everything else has a photograph of somebody on it, you know? And you come across that—you'd buy it, just to see what's inside!

Tolin, now working for Dick Clark Productions, booked the band for a second national TV appearance, this time for the Halloween special of the prestigious *American Bandstand*. While the rest of the band flew down to Los Angeles the morning of the filming, Tommy was forced to drive. He'd left a beaker of acid out—enough for the entire band's next show—but unfortunately Clementine, thinking it was for her, drank the whole thing. She was out for three days.

> CLEMENTINE: Just when I was coming out of it, complete with trenchmouth and shot kidney, we went south to do *American Bandstand.*

Tommy dropped Clementine off in Santa Barbara to stay with Russell Wheelock, an old friend from Texas (who would later take photos for the *Easter Everywhere* sleeve in 1967). John Ike—hoping to avoid the hassle of transporting his drums on the plane and assuming the studio would supply a kit—took only took his painted drumhead. Upon arrival, the band was ushered into dressing rooms and told by an officious production assistant to don gorilla costumes. They refused, and when news reached Clark, he came backstage and told the production assistant to "Go tell Paul Revere and the Raiders to do it; they'll do anything!"

During the performance, Roky hammed it up with a Chuck Berry duckwalk while Stacy stood motionless, doing his best to menace the camera. John Ike, meanwhile, could be briefly glimpsed hidden behind the cut-out jungle set, miming on imaginary drums—there was, of course, no studio kit available.

> ROKY: We asked Dick, "Would you ask us who's the head of the band?" And so [after the performance] he comes up and says, "Well, who's the head of your band?" [And Tommy says] "Well, we're all heads." This was on nationwide TV!

The *American Bandstand* Halloween special aired on October 29, 1966, and marked the Elevators' last stand as potential nationwide pop stars. While the rest of the group flew back to the Bay Area, Roky and Tommy decided to check out the Los Angeles scene. Starting in 1965, droves of Rolling Stones/Byrds clones had swarmed the Sunset Strip area until, in late October, local business owners demanded that the city impose a curfew to curb the twenty-four-hour lifestyle. The police moved in, resulting in the "Sunset Strip Riots," later immortalized in Buffalo Springfield's song "For What It's Worth." These riots, just kicking off when Roky and Tommy arrived in town, cemented the Los Angeles trip as another missed opportunity; "You're Gonna Miss Me" didn't chart as well in LA as it did in other parts of California, and while the Strip had plenty of clubs—including Pandora's Box, the Whisky a Go Go, London Fog, and Gazzarri's—that helped showcase local bands such as the Byrds, Buffalo Springfield, Love, the Seeds, and the Doors, the Elevators failed to register there. In any case, the clock was ticking against the band at this point: their three months' probation period (August 25 to November 25) during which they were allowed to perform was running out.

TRANS-TEXAS AIRWAYS
Houston, Texas
AIR FREIGHT DOMESTIC AIRBILL
NON-NEGOTIABLE

RECEIVED BY CARRIER AT: [ ] SHIPPER'S DOOR [ ] CITY TERMINAL [X] AIRPORT TERMINAL

ROUTING: AIRLINE ROUTING APPLIES UNLESS SHIPPER INSERTS SPECIFIC ROUTING HERE

CHARGES: [ ] PREPAID [X] COLLECT

DELIVERY will be made to consignee at a point where delivery service is available unless instructions to deliver to city terminal or airport terminal is specified in, "Instructions to carrier" below.

LETTERS SIGNIFY AIRPORT OF DEPARTURE
33- AUS 294-551

IMPORTANT: Carrier will complete all items below bold line EXCEPT SHIPPER'S C.O.D. Weights and classifications are subject to correction.

FROM: SHIPPER: John Cleveland
STREET ADDRESS: 1106 W. 22
CITY: Austin ZONE STATE: Tex

TO: CONSIGNEE: International Artists
STREET ADDRESS: 1505 Americana Bldg
CITY: Houston ZONE STATE: Texas

BY: SHIPPER OR SHIPPER'S AGENT: X John Cleveland
SHIPPER'S NUMBER

DESTINATION AIRPORT CODE: HOU.
CONSIGNEE'S NUMBER

IT IS MUTUALLY AGREED THAT THE GOODS HEREIN DESCRIBED ARE ACCEPTED IN APPARENT GOOD ORDER (EXCEPT AS NOTED) FOR TRANSPORTATION AS SPECIFIED HEREIN, SUBJECT TO GOVERNING CLASSIFICATIONS AND TARIFFS IN EFFECT AS OF THE DATE HEREOF WHICH ARE FILED IN ACCORDANCE WITH LAW. SAID CLASSIFICATIONS AND TARIFFS, COPIES OF WHICH ARE AVAILABLE FOR INSPECTION BY THE PARTIES HERETO, ARE HEREBY INCORPORATED INTO AND MADE PART OF THIS CONTRACT.

CARRIAGE HEREUNDER IS SUBJECT TO THE RULES RELATING TO LIABILITY ESTABLISHED BY THE CONVENTION FOR THE UNIFICATION OF CERTAIN RULES RELATING TO INTERNATIONAL CARRIAGE BY AIR, SIGNED AT WARSAW, OCTOBER 12, 1929, UNLESS SUCH CARRIAGE IS NOT "INTERNATIONAL CARRIAGE" AS DEFINED BY THE CONVENTION (SEE CARRIER'S TARIFF FOR SUCH DEFINITION). AGREED STOPPING PLACES ARE THOSE PLACES (OTHER THAN THE PLACE OF DESTINATION) SHOWN UNDER ROUTING OR AIRLINE ROUTING AND/OR THOSE PLACES SHOWN IN CARRIERS' TIME TABLE AS SCHEDULED STOPPING PLACES FOR THE ROUTE.

NO. PCS/PKGS.	DESCRIPTION OF PIECES AND CONTENTS MARKS · PACKING · NUMBER	WEIGHT	COMM'TY GRP. NO.	ROUTING TO	ROUTING VIA	RATE
1		13			TT	Min. Chg.

INSTRUCTIONS TO CARRIER: Deliver

[ ] CASH [ ] CREDIT

	PREPAID CHARGES	COLLECT CHARGE
INSURANCE	$	$
WEIGHT-RATE		5.00
WEIGHT-RATE		
WEIGHT-RATE		
PICKUP		
DELIVERY		1.50
EXCESS VALUE TRANSPORTATION CHARGE		.70
ADVANCES		
SHIPPER'S C. O. D.		
C.O.D. FEE/OTHER		
TOTAL CHARGES	$	$ 6.20

DECLARED VALUE agreed and understood to be not more than the value stated in the governing tariffs for each pound on which charges are assessed unless a higher value is declared and applicable charges paid thereon.
DECLARED VALUE $ 250.00
AMT. COLL. $

PCS/PKGS. LENGTH X WIDTH X DEPTH = CU. IN. DIMENSIONAL WGT. LBS.

33- AUS 294-551
LETTERS SIGNIFY AIRPORT OF DEPARTURE

EXECUTED BY TRANS-TEXAS AIRWAYS (AGENT'S SIG.) Stewart
AT: Austin Tex
DATE 10/20/66
TIME A.M. P.M.

COLLECT

Paid R. 222
10-21-66

FORM ACT. AIR CARGO, INC. WASHINGTON, D. C.

PRINTED IN U.S.A.

6 ...NSIGNEE'S MEMO (NOT AN INVOICE)

The 13TH FLOOR ELEVATORS--Austin's gift to psychedelic rock--cut an album last week in Dallas to be released on International Artists Label. Powell St. John, local folklorist, singer, musician, songwriter, magician has penned three of the titles: "You Don't Know How Young You Are," "Kingdom of Heaven," and "Monkey Island." And the rest are all Elevators originals, hallucinated by Roky Erickson and the crew: "Roller Coaster," "Tried to Hide" (a new cut of the hit single), "You're Gonna Miss Me," "Splash I," "Reverberation," "Fire Engine," and "Don't Fall Down." The last two were also waxed on a single. Cover artist is John Cleveland, local doodler artiste superb. The single will be released in about a week; the album will be available in two to three weeks on the west coast, sometime thereafter in Austin. To speed things up--harass your local retailers!! Reed Music is your best bet.

THE WIGS--still at the Jade Room Wednesdays and Thursdays.
BABY CAKES--at Swingers on weekends.
CONQUEROO--in dance

Gentle Thursday is coming...

By Georges Courtelaine:

Top: Shipping document for John Cleveland's *Psychedelic Sounds* artwork, dated October 20.

Bottom: October 17 article from *The Rag* detailing the *Psychedelic Sounds* release.

Saturday 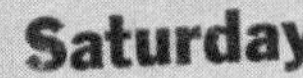 October 29, 1966

Morning-Afternoon

5 13 24 33 49 COLOR KING KONG—Cartoons
8 11 27 35 COLOR FRANKENSTEIN JR.—Cartoons
10:30 3 12 21 COLOR SPACE KIDETTES—Cartoons
5 13 24 33 49 COLOR BEATLES—Cartoons
8 11 27 35 COLOR SPACE GHOST—Cartoons
11:00 3 12 21 COLOR COOL McCOOL
5 13 24 33 49 COLOR CASPER—Cartoons
8 11 27 35 COLOR SUPERMAN—Cartoons
11:30 3 12 21 JETSONS—Cartoon
COLOR Rosey the maid falls in love.
5 13 24 33 49 COLOR MAGILLA GORILLA—Cartoons
0 11 27 05 [illegible] LONE RANGER—Cartoons

Afternoon

12:00 3 12 21 TOP CAT—Cartoon
COLOR Rookie Patrolman Prowler wants to reform the city.
5 24 33 49 COLOR BUGS BUNNY—Cartoons
8 11 27 35 COLOR ROAD RUNNER—Cartoons
13 COLOR CHAMPIONSHIP BOWLING
12:30 3 12 21 SMITHSONIAN
COLOR Can bones tell us about history? At the Smithsonian Institution, osteologist Al Myrick, who studies bones, discusses their form and function in prehistoric animals. Cameras show dinosaurs, flying reptiles, lizards and the bone structure of man. Host: Bill Ryan.
5 MOVIE—Musical
COLOR "The 'I Don't Care' Girl." (1953) A producer working on a screen treatment of Eva Tanguay's life finds several different people claiming to have "discovered" her. Mitzi Gaynor, David Wayne, Oscar Levant. (Two hours)
8 11 27 35 COLOR BEAGLES
24 33 49 COLOR MILTON THE MONSTER—Cartoons

1:00 3 12 21 ANIMAL SECRETS
COLOR "Travelers on the Wing." Anthropologist Loren C. Eiseley visits Hawk Mountain, Pa., to examine the migratory habits of birds. Using films and stills, he tells how bird watchers track flights; and how, why and where birds migrate.
8 MOVIE—Double Feature
1. "Trouble Makers." (Comedy; 1948) While operating a sidewalk telescope, two of the Bowery Boys sight a murder in a nearby hotel. Leo Gorcey, Huntz Hall, Gabriel Dell, Helen Parrish.
2. "World Without End." (Science Fiction; 1956) On a space flight, four scientists break the time barrier and land on earth in the year 2508. Hugh Marlowe, Nancy Gates, Nelson Leigh, Rod Taylor. (Three hours)
11 27 35 COLOR TOM AND JERRY—Cartoons
13 COLLEGE FOOTBALL—Ohio State vs. Minnesota
The Ohio State Buckeyes play the Gophers at Minneapolis. See 2 P.M. Ch. 5 for details. (Live)
24 33 49 COLOR HOPPITY HOOPER—Cartoons
1:30 3 PANORAMA—Jay Lawrence
COLOR Host Jay Lawrence discusses bond issues 13 and 14 with Dr. Paul Briggs, Cleveland schools superintendent.
11 YOUR COLLEGE GUIDE
12 COFFEE AND QUESTIONS—Genevieve Blatt
21 LITTLEST HOBO—Drama
24 33 AMERICAN BANDSTAND
Guests: Billy Stewart and the 13th Floor Elevators. Host: Dick Clark. (60 min.)
27 MOVIE—Double Feature
1. "The Flying Missile." (Drama; 1950) A submarine commander fights to prove his theory that V-2 rockets can be launched successfully from underseas craft. Glenn Ford, Viveca Lindfors, Henry O'Neill, Carl Benton Reid.
2. "Frontier Gal." (Western; 1945) Escaping from a posse, a young man runs into a female saloon owner—and is married to her at the point of a gun. Yvonne DeCarlo, Rod Cameron, Andy Devine, Fuzzy Knight. (Three hours)
35 TO BE ANNOUNCED
49 CLUB RANDY

A-8 TV GUIDE

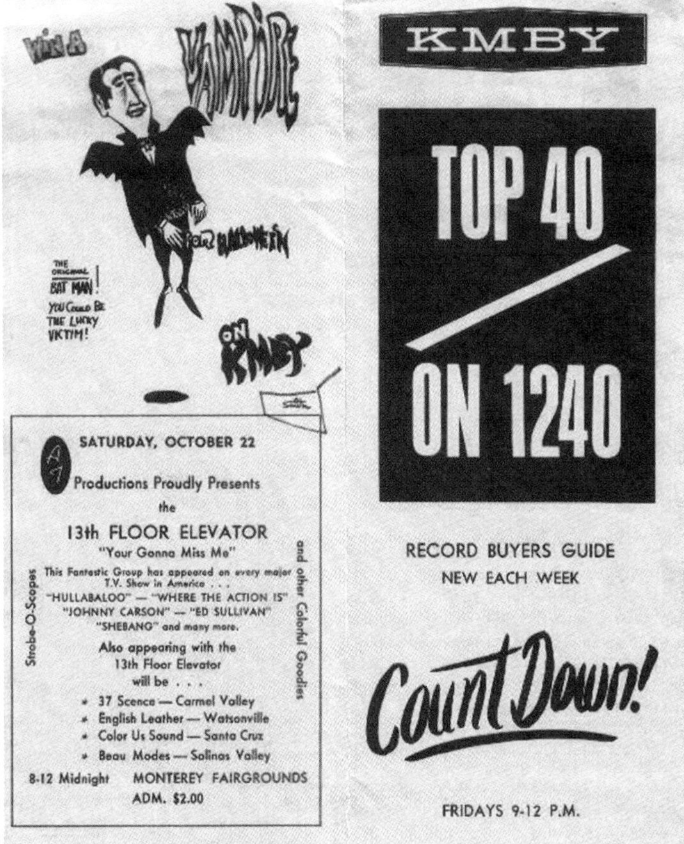

Top left and right: Ronnie's parents' *TV Guide*, listing the Elevators' October 29 appearance on *American Bandstand*.

Bottom: October 22 KMBY radio survey advertising the band's appearance at the Monterey Fairgrounds, erroneously declaring "This Fantastic Group has appeared on every major T.V. show in America."

Opposite top: Still from the *American Bandstand* performance, featuring the bizarre jungle set chosen for the episode.

Opposite bottom: Tommy to Dick Clark: "We're all heads."

k·z's HOT 30

1.	YOU KEEP ME HANGING ON	SUPREMES
2.	Good Vibrations	Beach Boys
3.	Devil With The Blue Dress On	Mitch Ryder
4.	Rain On The Roof	Lovin' Spoonful
5.	Stop! Stop! Stop!	Hollies
6.	Winchester Cathedral	New Vaudeville Band
7.	Louie, Louie	Sandpipers
8.	A Hazy Shade Of Winter	Simon/Garfunkle
9.	Reverberation	13th Floor Elevators
10.	All Strung Out	April Stevens/Nino Tempo
11.	Mellow Yellow	Donovan
12.	I Got The Feelin'	Neil Diamond
13.	If I Were A Carpenter	Bobby Darin
14.	Walk Away, Rene	Lefte Banke
15.	Let Love Come Between Us	Rubber Band
16.	Why Pick On Me	Standells
17.	Good Thing	Paul Revere/Raiders
18.	Nineteen Days	Dave Clark Five
19.	Great Airplane Strike	Paul Revere/Raiders
20.	Come On Up	Young Rascals
21.	Here Today	Robb Storme Group
22.	Happenings Ten Years Time Ago	Yardbirds
23.	The Bears	Fastest Group Alive
24.	Lady Godiva	Peter/Gordon
25.	Pandora's Golden Heebie Jeebies	Association
26.	Hippy Elevator Operator	W. C. Fields Memorial Electric String Band
27.	Help Me Girl	Animals
28.	Bringing Me Down	Jefferson Airplane
29.	Talk Talk	Music Machine
30.	East West	Herman's Hermits

RIM'S PICKS:

PEACE OF MIND—Cout Five	(Double-Shot)
I'M A BELIEVER—Monkees	(Colgems)
TELL IT TO THE RAIN—4 Seasons	(Phillips)

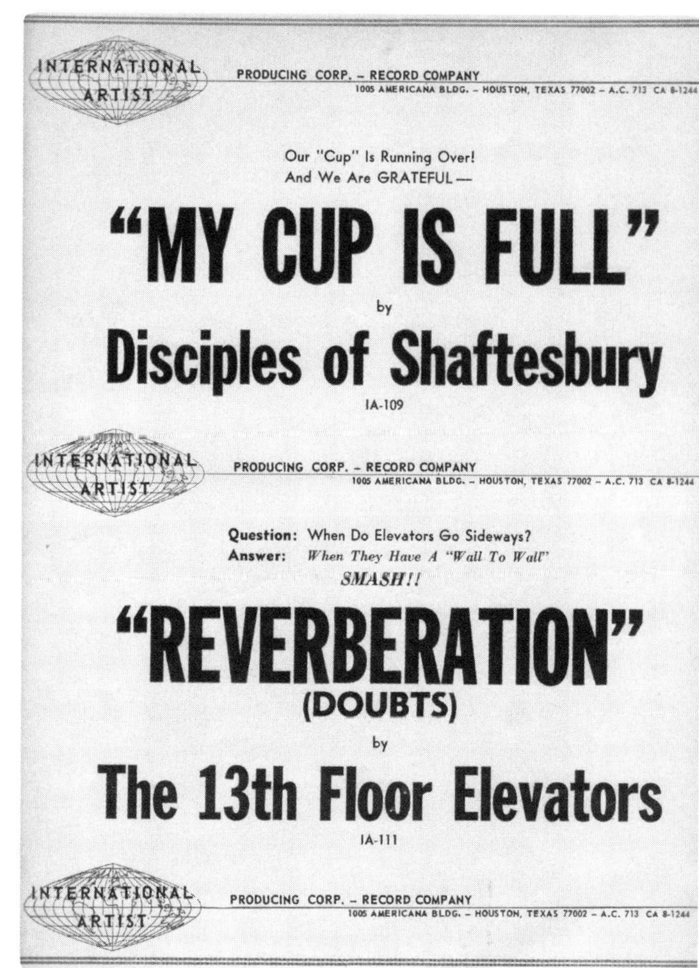

Ralph & Al Pepe Presents .... 9:00 to 1:00 a.m.

Thurs. Nite Nov. 10th

13th FLOOR ELEVATOR

SHOW TIME !! 9:00 and 11:00

The ★ Nite Riders

FREAK OUT! LIGHT SHOWS By: CONRAD

Santa Venetia ARMORY

ADMISSION $2.50

Veteran's Day Dance and Show !!

PHONE: 454-6165

Top left: "Reverberation" at #9 on the KAZZ-FM radio survey for the week of December 1.

Top right: Advertisement in *Record World* for the "Reverberation" single, November 5.

Bottom: Poster for the band's show at the Santa Venetia Armory, November 10.

▲ **WHILE RED DAY-GLO** hype stickers, printed for the jackets of the Elevators' new album, announced that the record "presents the hit singles 'You're Gonna Miss Me' plus 'Reverberation,'" the new single proved to be a flop. Released a couple of weeks prior to the full-length, it was reviewed by *Billboard* in their "National Breakout" selection on November 19, and the following week it entered the charts at #129 before promptly disappearing without a trace. Regionally, sales weren't much better—even back home, it only graced the KAZZ-FM survey at #22.

> STACY (*K*): I think if we'd stayed on a level like "You're Gonna Miss Me" a little longer, it would have been wiser too—instead of moving right up immediately into what we wanted to do. We went too fast.

> TOMMY (*MF*): We knew that it takes groups several albums to make it, but our problem was that we never could come up with a second single. We were a purely intellectual, album-oriented band, and still, at that time, everything was singles-oriented. Well, we tried a whole bunch of them. Roky wrote "You're Gonna Miss Me," and I should have made him write something like that.

Stacy, John Ike, and Ronnie moved their digs to Sausalito's Fireside Motel. Stacy liked the afterhours musicians' scene in Marin County: things came alive after the clubs in San Francisco shut down around 1:00 a.m. and often continued until dawn. One of the main venues across the Bay was the Ark, an old paddle steamer converted into a club; the trio of Elevators, along with many other leading musicians of the day, could often be found there, hanging out in jam sessions or just picking.

> JOHNNY GATHINGS: I remember the Fireside Motel. Moby Grape lived next door. Stacy liked Skip Spence; he didn't like all of them.

Moby Grape was a band formed around former Jefferson Airplane drummer Skip Spence. While Skip was much loved, rhythm guitarist Peter Lewis, the son of actress Loretta Young, was no friend of Stacy's. As it turned out, this was for good reason.

"The Grape" used the Ark as a rehearsal space, and shortly after their live debut, on November 4 at the California Hall in San Francisco (before an audience, according to Lewis, of five people and several hundred empty chairs), they performed a showcase there.

> CLEMENTINE: We went to hear the Grape at the Ark, and Stacy stood there worshipping these guys. Then one of the band members [presumably Lewis] got on the mic and said, "We've heard that the 13th Floor Elevators are in the audience, and we're not going to play anymore because we don't want them to steal any of our material." Stacy was in tears.

Only a week after their evidently disastrous debut, Moby Grape was booked as the Elevators' support act at the Avalon on November 11, for what would turn out to be the headlining band's final appearance at the venue. Fearing his band would be blown off stage by the Elevators, Lewis allegedly did everything he could to upstage them—even going so far as to sabotage their sound.

> CLEMENTINE: At the Avalon, playing with the Grape, when I was backstage, one of their guys [Lewis] said to the soundman to turn the voice up high and then low down—up and down. And then I realized they were doing it while the Elevators were on, to sabotage the show. Roky's voice would be so loud it would hurt your ears, and then you couldn't hear it. I made a beeline for Chet, and he raised hell with the guys.

The night after the Moby Grape debacle, Roky didn't bother showing up until fifteen minutes before the end of the set. During his absence Johnny Gathings had filled in on rhythm guitar while their bandboy Cecil attempted some vocals. The run of Avalon shows, meant to serve as the launch for the "Reverberation" single, had landed with a thud.

▲ **ON NOVEMBER 18,** the first order for *The Psychedelic Sounds of the 13th Floor Elevators* was received from Independent Music Sales in San Francisco. Although no firm release date appears to exist, promotional copies are known to have begun shipping on November 26 to all major US cities, while mono stock copies began shipping December 5 to the states where "You're Gonna Miss Me" had charted the highest: California, Texas, Michigan, and Florida.

Meanwhile, unbeknownst to the band, IA's Dillard and Rogers hired Houston DJ Chuck Dunaway from KILT-FM to supervise a stereo remix at Sumet on November 21 and 22, then mastered it, cut it to lacquers, and shipped it to San Antonio for pressing at the Texas 'N' Tanner plant. Though Bob Sullivan's personal safety master of the recordings proved he knew how to mic a studio for a solid stereo mix, the remix done by Dillard, Rogers, and Dunaway was anything but.

The Elevators had heretofore been blissfully unaware that the recordings they approved for mastering at Columbia Records in Hollywood had been swapped out for a remixed, resequenced, utterly compromised version, but when an advance copy reached them in San Francisco, the difference was immediately evident; whereas "You're Gonna Miss Me" had screeched off the original 45-rpm cut, the LP mastered version was dead. Angry and disappointed, they held a small listening party on a floating LSD lab in Marin County. Benny, who'd just arrived in town, was invited, but freaked out after absorbing a massive hit of LSD from laying on freshly-dosed sheets of blotter acid.

> ROKY: Yes [I saw Benny]. He said he was a changed man. He wasn't doing speed, wasn't using the needle. [But] people said,

whether he was changed or not, they didn't want him around because of what he had done.

TARY OWENS: Haight Street at the donut shop, it was probably two in the morning—I was tripping on acid; I'd gone down there to get some munchies. Benny comes into the place with his fiddle and a Bible. First, he starts playing the fiddle, and gets everybody's attention. Then he starts preaching. And it was really sad.

BENNY: I went through the meth analog, LSD, and cannabis . . . We had Benzedrine, Benzedrine, and Benzedrine daily: put it in the coffee. When you're considering "before you accuse me, you better take a look at yourself," you'll find out that that is you. That's the main theory I want to get through to you: the reason [for] the way I am to you is your fault.

The band had to headline one final Bay Area show on November 25—at Maple Hall, on 1522 Polk Street in San Francisco—after which their probation period was up and it was time to return to Texas and spend a late Thanksgiving with their families. The internal dynamic of the band had been spread too thinly in California, with Roky and the Halls in Oakland and the Hill Country boys in Sausalito across the Bay. Stacy was no longer buying the hippie rap, and he refused to accept Tommy's every word. If the band was to succeed commercially, they'd need to regroup in Texas. More than just needing to consider their options, they'd have to do some negotiating with IA, not to mention the probation department. While they hoped to be able to tour nationally to promote their album, there was also an alleged offer to tour Britain.

CLEMENTINE: They were horrifically homesick, and Stacy was the most—and he was so in love with his girlfriend [Laurie Jones]. Also, Stacy didn't like the California scene. He's not a surfer-type person. He liked the solid-rock Texas scene. The down-home was very important to him, and there was nothing down-home about San Francisco, with the hippie free love and dancing around and a lot of irresponsibility. It did not appeal to Stacy in the least, and he wanted home; his trips became longer and longer to Texas, and it became harder and harder to pull him out of Texas.

TOMMY: See, there was evils here [in San Francisco]. Stacy was trying to stay away from people doing smack. So it was the best thing; we were able to get back.

GEORGE BANKS: When the Elevators first got back to Austin from California, they were in some kind of recovery. I was never around them shooting heroin, but I know that was a problem out there.

Above and opposite: Packaging of *The Psychedelic Sounds of the 13th Floor Elevators*, with front-cover art by John Cleveland and Tommy and Lelan Rogers's dual writeups on the back.

THE PSYCHEDELIC SOUNDS OF:

The 13th Floor Elevators

Since Aristotle, man has organized his knowledge vertically in separate and unrelated groups---Science, Religion, Sex, Relaxation, Work, etc. The main emphasis in his language, his system of storing knowledge, has been on the identification of objects rather than on the relationships between objects. He is now forced to use his tools of reasoning separately and for one situation at a time. Had man been able to see past this hypnotic way of thinking, to distrust it (as did Einstein), and to resystematize his knowledge so that it would all be related horizontally, he would now enjoy the perfect sanity which comes from being able to deal with his life in its entirety.

Recently, it has become possible for man to chemically alter his mental state and thus alter his point of view (that is, his own basic relation with the outside world which determines how he stores his information). He then can restructure his thinking and change his language so that his thoughts bear more relation to his life and his problems, therefore approaching them more sanely.

It is this quest for pure sanity that forms the basis of the songs on this album.

YOU DON'T KNOW HOW YOUNG YOU ARE explains the difference between persons using the old and the new reasoning. The old reasoning, which involves a preoccupation with objects, appears to someone using the new reasoning, as childishly unsane. The old system keeps man blind to his animal-like emotional reactions.

THROUGH THE RHYTHM shows the results of applying the old system and its ramifications. The new system involves a major evolutionary step for man. The new man views the old man in much the same way as the old man views the ape.

MONKEY ISLAND expresses the position of a person who has just discovered that he no longer belongs to the old order.

ROLLER COASTER describes the discovery of the new direction and purpose to man's life, the movement in that direction, and the results. The pleasures of the quest are made concrete in FIRE ENGINE.

REVERBERATION is the root of all inability to cope with environment. Doubt causes negative emotions which reverberate and hamper all constructive thought. If a person learns and organizes his knowledge in the right way---with perfect cross-reference---he need not experience doubt or hesitation.

TRIED TO HIDE was written about those people who for the sake of appearances take on the superficial aspects of the quest. The dismissal of such a person is expressed in YOUR GONNA MISS ME

I'VE SEEN YOUR FACE BEFORE – (Splash 1) describes a meeting with a person who radiates the essence of the quest. There is an outpour of warmth and understanding at the instant of meeting between two such persons, just as if they have been friends for life.

DON'T FALL DOWN refers to the care that must be taken to retain and reinforce this state.

THE KINGDOM OF HEAVEN IS WITHIN YOU The Bible states in "Proverbs" that man's only escape from the end foretold in "Revelations" lies in his reinterpreting and redefining God.

"ELEVATORS"

This space is reserved for a word of thanks to all those people who have made the success of the Thirteenth Floor Elevators record "You're Gonna Miss Me" possible.

DENNY ZEITLER and the staff at Independent Music Sales in San Francisco. DENNY being one of the greatest promotion men to ever pick up a phonograph record.

GORDON BYNUM, a young, up-and-coming record producer who has a byword which is "right, right". When told the record by the Elevators was a smash, he simply stated "right, right".

CHUCK DUNAWAY of Radio KILT, Houston, a D. J. and Music Director with enough forethought to realize when the group was on Contact Records, a local company, that they had that certain something to put them in the class of HIT artists.

GARY STITES and JOE STANZIONE of Campus Record Distributors, Miami, Florida, who almost ended up with a nervous breakdown trying to break this record and keep it.

CAROL DALING at Concord Distributors, Cleveland, Ohio, whose persistence with her own radio stations finally paid off: and ARMEN BOLADIAN and his crew of Record Distributors, Detroit, who despite the tight play list, found a way: and JERRY LOVE of Alpha Distributors, of New York City, who tried - God knows he tried: and DON ANTI, Radio Station KFWB, Los Angeles, who tried twice and CHIC SILVERS in Washington who did everything in his power, even top ten and to JAY-KAY Distributors in Dallas who continually yelled "It's a smash everywhere" except in Dallas and kept right on trans-shipping and to ERNIE LEANER and his son BILL who knew I was over-due and tried and to CAROL at Tempo in San Francisco who was the very first to believe DENNY ZEITLER and gave us the Wizard Pick and last but not least to BILL GAVIN of the Gavin Reporter who believed in the record and stuck with us to the very end and to the many D. J.'s whom we have never met personally but who kept asking "What is that funny little noise in that record?"

Lelan Rogers

INTERNATIONAL ARTIST PRODUCING CORP.
Houston, Texas

MONO L. P. - 1 A - No.1

YOU'RE GONNA MISS ME
(Rocky Ericson)
ROLLER COASTER
(T. Hall - R. Ericson)
SPLASH 1
(C. Hall - R. Ericson)
REVERBERATION (Doubt)
(T. Hall-S. Sutherland-R. Ericson)
DON'T FALL DOWN
(T. Hall - R. Ericson)

CREDITS:
YOU'RE GONNA MISS ME
Produced by: GORDON BYNUM
All other tunes Produced by:
LELAN ROGERS

Engineer: BOB SULLIVAN at Summit Sound Studio, Dallas, Texas
Cover Design: JOHN CLEVELAND, Austin, Texas
All tunes in this L.P. Published by: TAPIER MUSIC CORP. B.M.I. Houston, Texas

FIRE ENGINE
(T. Hall-S. Sutherland-R. Ericson)
THRU THE RHYTHM
(T. Hall-S. Sutherland)
YOU DON'T KNOW
(John St. Powell)
KINGDOM OF HEAVEN
(John St. Powell)
MONKEY ISLAND
(John St. Powell)
TRIED TO HIDE
(T. Hall - S. Sutherland)

PRINTING BY TANNER 'N' TEXAS, INC. - 1422 WEST POPLAR STREET - SAN ANTONIO, TEXAS 78207

13th FLOOR ELEVATORS
MOBY GRAPE
FAMILY DOG PRESENTS
NOV. 11-12
AVALON BALLROOM
SUTTER at VAN NESS
9PM
SAN FRANCISCO
REVERB ERATION
Lights Benvan Meter & Roger Hilyard
Dance Concert

SAN FRANCISCO THE PSYCHEDELIC SHOP; CITY LIGHTS BOOKS; BALLY LO; CEDAR ALLEY COFFEE HOUSE; MNASIDKA; SANDAL MAKER (North Beach); HUT T-1 STATE COLLEGE
TICKET OUTLETS:
SAUSALITO TIDES BOOK SHOP
BERKELEY MOE'S BOOKS; DISCOUNT RECORDS
MENLO PARK KEPLER'S BOOK STORE
THE BINDWEED PRESS, SAN FRANCISCO

ROKY ERICKSON
13th FLOOR ELEVATORS
MOBY GRAPE
NOV. 11-12
AVALON BALLROOM
SUTTER at VAN NESS
9PM
SAN FRANCISCO
REVERB ERATION
TICKET OUTLETS:

13th FLOOR ELEVATORS
MOBY GRAPE
NOV. 11-12
AVALON BALLROOM
SUTTER at VAN NESS
9PM
SAN FRANCISCO
REVERB ERATION
TICKET OUTLETS:

13th FLOOR ELEVATORS
MOBY GRAPE
NOV. 11-12
AVALON BALLROOM
SUTTER at VAN NESS
SAN FRANCISCO
REVERB ERATION
TICKET OUTLETS:

RAG RAG
THORNE DREYER

ROCK

CONQUEROO - will be playing at that dirty brown building at 2513 San Antonio Fri and Sat nites. At the I.L. Club Wed and after hours Sat (1:30-4:30 am)
WIGS - Wed nite at the Jade Room.
REVISED EDITION - Thurs at the Jade Room.
LORD AUGUST AND THE VISIONS - Swingers, Fri and Sat.
13TH FLOOR ELEVATORS--- will be in San Antonio Friday the 16th.No more details.

GALLERIES

ART FACULTY-annual faculty show at Univ Art Museum. Runs gamut from paintings and sculpture to jewelry and tapestries.
MAVERICK STUDIOS---new gallery on S. Congress
LAGUNA GLORIA -- Annual sales and rental exhibit; Luiz Guzman exhibit of terra cotta sculpture, oils; Ferdinand Roten, original prints.

THE Theatah

Melodrama - Red Lion will start casting a new melodrama Mon nite at 7.

"Ionesco A' Troix," being presented by the Bijuberti Players, is well worth seeing. Gary Chason has directed three of Ionesco's one-acts, MAID TO MARRY, THE LEADER, & THE LESSON, in the basement of the Laos House, 19th and Rio Grande. The stage area is fascinating if miniscule. An intimate stage is placed in the center of a very narrow and very theatrical worship room of sorts with the audience seated on both sides. In staging THE LESSON, Chason has placed skrims between the audience and the stage. When the lights are put on the players, the front skrim is translucent while the one in back becomes a wall, blocking view of the audience over there. Makes the violence necessarily less intimate. THE LESSON failed to reach the crescendo of which it is capable. Sean Adams, good at the beginning, bungled his lines and failed to fulfill the demands of the climactic build. Pearl Coffey was fine. THE LEADER was my favorite, Harry Kinney and Linalice Carey doing admirably in that frantic diatribe on leader fetishism. Player piano music and use of a strobe light were fun, though I thought more could have been done with them. "Ionesco A' Troix" is worth seeing. It runs Friday and Saturday nites.

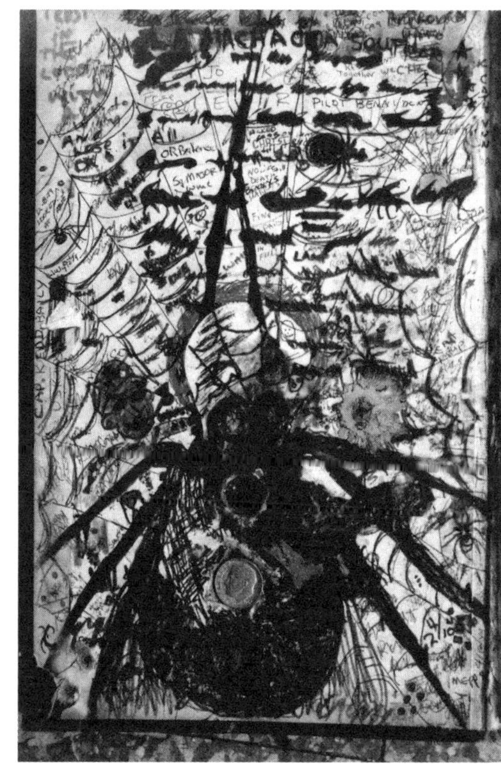

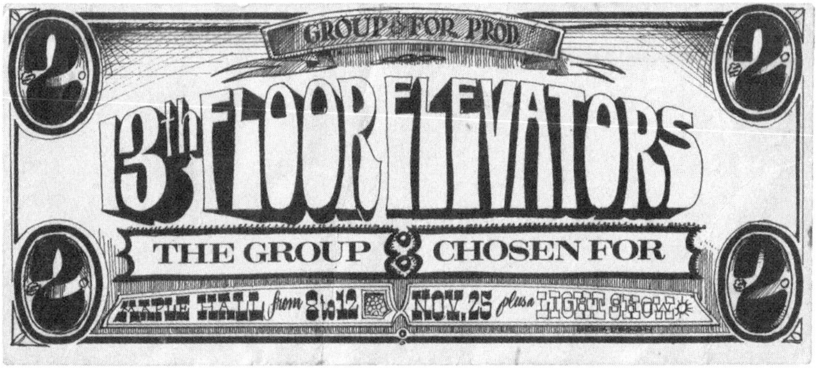

Opposite top left: Poster for the Elevators' final Avalon shows on November 11–12, to promote the release of the "Reverberation" single, supported by Moby Grape. Artwork by Steve Renick. Known as FD34, this poster underwent three printings: the first, prior to the show, with the Bindweed Press printing credit; the second with "split fountain" color gradation in the green fill; and the third with the notation "34-3."

Opposite top right: Handbill type "B" with orange ink—this copy signed by members of the band and Chet Helms.

Opposite bottom left: Handbill type "A" with purple ink.

Opposite bottom right: Handbill type "C," which came stapled into some copies of *Mojo Navigator* #10; once they ran out, they were replaced by a handbill for Country Joe and the Fish.

Top left: *Rag* writeup mentioning the Elevators' December 16 appearance in San Antonio.

Bottom left: Handbill of the band's final known California performance, November 25 at Maple Hall.

Top and bottom right: Benny's embellished Bible.

Opposite top left: An Erickson family portrait: Mikel; Ben; Evelyn's mother, "Mom K."; Donnie; Roky (home at Arthur Lane for Thanksgiving weekend); and Sumner.

Opposite top right: Left to right: Donnie, Evelyn, Ben, Roger, Sumner, Roky, Mikel at Christmas. The mural in the background was painted by Evelyn, representing the profile of each of her five sons.

Opposite bottom: Roky with Evelyn, November 27.

Following pages: Simmons's notorious negative *Psychedelic Sounds* review in *The Rag*.

LETTER TO STACY FROM LAURIE JONES [STACY'S GIRLFRIEND], NOVEMBER 1966:

I went back to Kerrville and rumors were circulating that you were in serious trouble again. Ronnie Leatherman was in town, where were you? I came back to Austin and more rumors were spreading. A few mornings ago I was walking to my 9:00 class and guess who do I see? Benny Thurman. I have never been so shocked in my life. It was exactly 8:45 in the morning and he was just standing against the wall. It scared me. I asked him what he was doing and he replied "Playing." Then he turned and ran down the hall saying, "I get the picture."

SANDY LOCKETT: Things were exceedingly rocky for Roky—oh, absolutely running scared all the time. Everybody tries to forget [the draft], but it was terrific with him. During the Christmas season, the draft guys got so hot on the trail, [and] I had to take him to a private psychiatrist in Houston. He was heavy-duty on the board of everything, and knew all the draft guys. I'd gone to him years before and had come to quite a good understanding with him, so I said, "Hey Ronald, this guy is completely nuts, and they're trying to get him in the army. I think you'll have no problem saying this in such terms that even the draft board can understand." He said, "Well, bring him over." After he'd done his magic, the draft distress eased off, but that still left the dope and the nuttiness distress.

The first review of the Elevators' album appeared December 12, 1966, in *The Rag*, a local Austin underground paper. Written by ex-*Ranger* staff writer Bob Simmons, it was decidedly less than complimentary. Nevertheless, it confirmed in print what everyone already knew: IA had failed the band.

BOB SIMMONS: I caught hell for my negative review. I wrote it in a fit of disappointment that the record did not really capture the sound and excitement of the band. It was a real quick and dirty effort by Lelan Rogers. I wanted them to sound like the Stones records, or the Yardbirds, and it just sounded tinny and strictly lo-fi. Everyone wanted [my review] to be a booster, but I couldn't in good conscience "boost" something that sounded so second-rate—in an audio sense. Truly, they were an amazing band.

The Elevators appeased their Texan audiences with return shows in San Antonio and Houston before heading their separate ways for Christmas. Most of the band headed for the Hill Country—including Tommy and Clementine, who went to her father's ranch outside Kerrville. While Clementine tried to persuade her daughter Laura to join her in San Francisco, Laura ultimately opted to stay with her horses on the ranch. While Tommy remained with the band in Texas (on probation), Clementine opted for San Francisco with her son Roland in tow. Although her relationship with Tommy and the rest of the band had begun to drift, she'd return when they needed her.

The Psychedelic Sounds of:
THE 13th FLOOR ELEVATORS
(International Artist LP)

Kirkwilson discusses

granted that anyone lived in a pretty how town so on ad infinum. our fathers moved through dooms of symbolic logic and their systems have been visited upon us: static words with static meanings: static thought processes: static and particular values in their rungs ladder-wise. here we go round the prickly pear (in our unawares). is there balm in gilead? will porter's healing oil help? where is surcease and what is her phone number?

solutions in a record album? nope. but help perhaps for the receptive and any record album whose liner notes begin "since Aristotle" might be expected to blow a few minds and does and mindblowing is the quickest first step toward mindrestructuring (remaining aware of the always inherent danger: that the blown stage becomes permanent). this particular album is wordlessly grand. Listening to it was the greatest charge i've had since the girl i danced with at the senior prom ate my carnation.

but with or sans metabolic explosions the elevators are among the finest psychedelic bands and it is forever wonderful to relate that they began right here in milk-white-on-the-colorado.

BOB SIMMONS

Well, well, what have we here? Why from the looks of it I would think "A special Christmas Album from the Thirteenth Floor Elevators." But no, it's just a cover designed by Austin artist John Cleveland. The colors (red and green) are quite timely though. If I didn't know better I would say what a clever marketing ploy. It would, unfortunately, however, be the only clever thing done on the whole effort. The album itself is such a vast agglomeration of mistakes, carelessness, pretentiousness, and just plain poor judgement that I am ashamed to admit that I shelled out the $3.87 that it costs at J.R. Reed.

The first thing that I would like to make a snide remark about is of course, The Album Notes. My thanks go out to the Elevators for taking the time and effort to explain their songs. The complex imagery and symbolism would be well nigh impossible to figure out without these difinitive aids. Then again maybe it's just the engineering of the record that makes them hard to understand. In any case it really overjoys me to find out that if I turn on I will be able to restructure my thought processes and I will be able to slip the bonds of Aristotelian thinking (as did Einstein). The wonders of Dope!

The whole product just makes me a little bit sad. It could have been nice. It isn't. The quality of the recording is such that the vocals are almost unintelligible. It's my understanding that there is a reason for this. The producers were afraid that if the words could be understood that they would be banned from air play. Considering most of the pop music that is receiving wide recognition currently they could have been a bit more courageous. If they are so afraid of Elevator material why did they sign them in the first place?

While I am asking questions, allow me to ask a few more.

Who is John St. Powell? Do they mean Powell St. John or is this some new face in the song writing crowd?

Why do they spell the song Reverberation/Revarberation two ways?

Why does Lelan Rogers have to thank everyone he ever knew on the album? Wouldn't letters be less expensive than typesetting?

Why... Oh never mind. Why don't they just shoot Lelan Rogers?

Luckily for the Elevators the album does say "The Psychedelic Sound." This will certainly assure them of a large market of aspiring hippy types who wouldn't dare miss the latest in mystique fetish objects Watch out psycheburbia! Here they come..."EEEEEEEYOW! Things go better with Coca Cola...

*o*o*o*

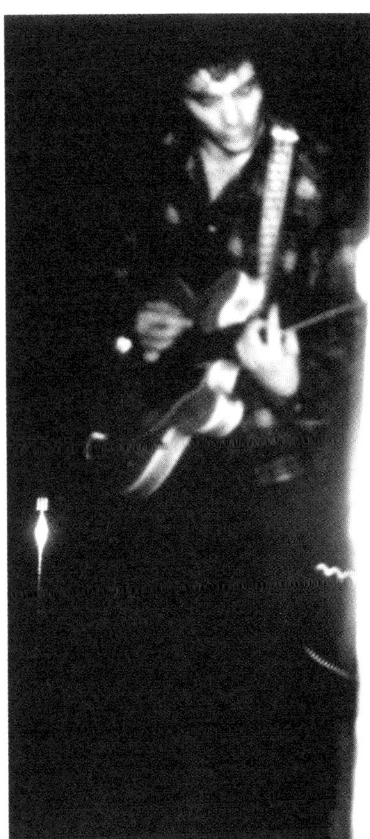

Above: The band at the Catacombs in Houston, December 1966, photographed by George L. Craig. Craig: "I knew Stacy, Benny, and John Ike from another band [the Lingsmen] that played at an outdoor pavilion on the beach at Port Aransas. After they met Roky and Tommy Hall they changed dramatically . . .they played at a place called Of Our Own, the Catacombs, and a few other small clubs in Houston. Tommy Hall lived in the same old house—converted to apartments—as a few friends, and we all started hanging out."

IV

SHE LIVES (IN A TIME OF HER OWN)

The Return

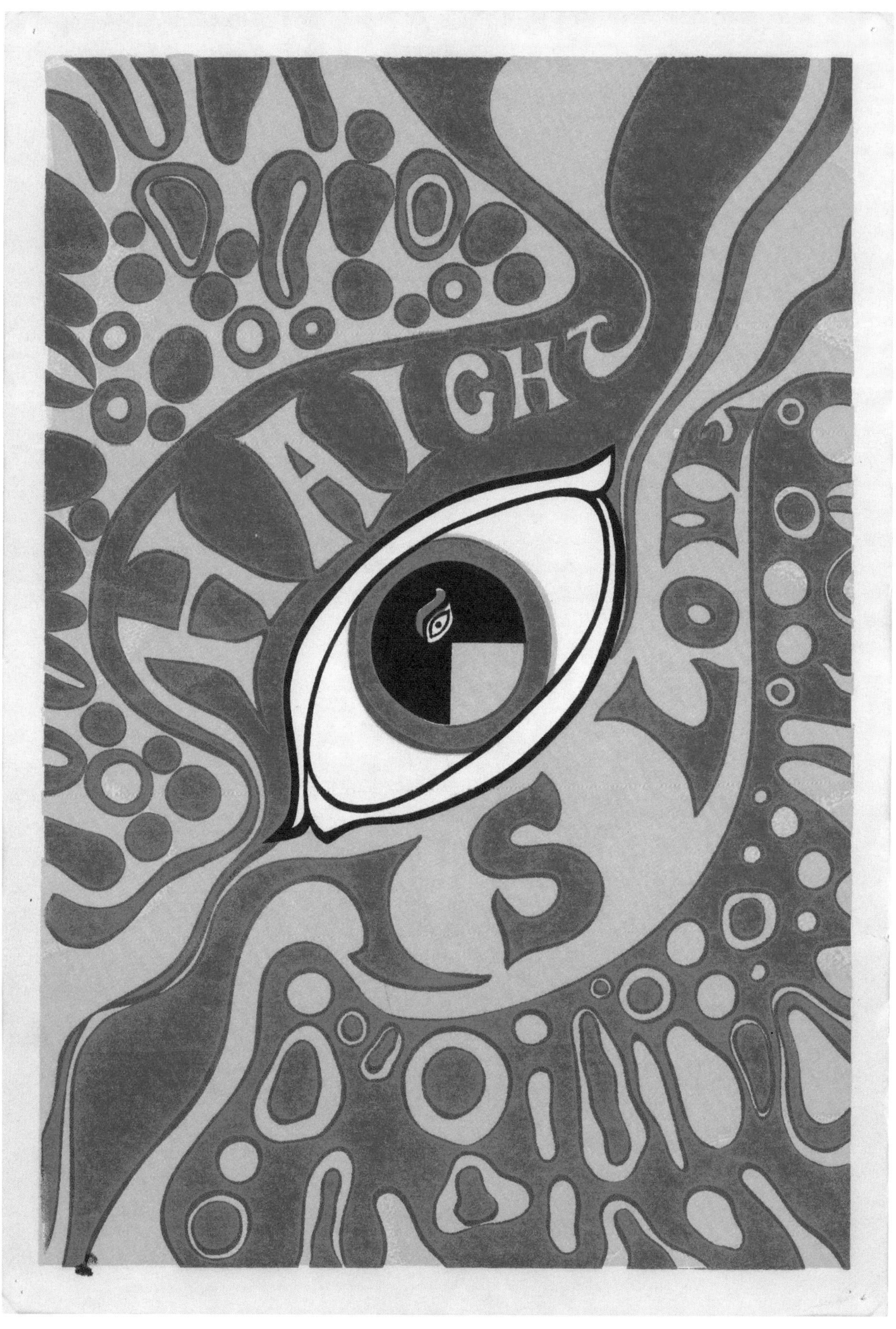

Above: "Haight Is Love" headshop poster design based on John Cleveland's artwork for *Psychedelic Sounds*. The art from this poster would be seen on the door of Peter Sellers's psychedelic car in the 1968 film *I Love You, Alice B. Toklas*.

The first printed acknowledgments of *The Psychedelic Sounds of the 13th Floor Elevators* came in the trade papers *Record World* and *Billboard* on January 7, 1967, followed by a "New Action Album" listing in *Billboard* on January 11. This was the same month the Doors' first LP was issued (recorded August–September), and two months prior to *The Velvet Underground and Nico* (recorded April–November). Finally, America had moved beyond its infatuation with the so-called "British Invasion" and started producing unapologetically American rock music, with the Elevators at the absolute forefront of a pioneering new musical genre: psychedelic rock.

The year started with a favorable and well-informed article in *The Austin Statesman*, also on January 7, under the headline "Local Rock 'n' Roll Band Back from Successful Tour," which avoided referencing their courtroom troubles (or, indeed, their difficulties on the West Coast). In reality, the band returned to a dire situation.

> SANDY LOCKETT: It was a dreadful period, and they were stuck in Houston. IA would not give them money but would pay their food, provided they got it from a particular restaurant—trying to keep a leash on them.

Indeed, the band's end-of-year statement showed that despite the sales of 60,000 records and income from four months spent touring the West Coast (for which every official show contract had had to be signed by IA), the band still owed $1,337.02 in recoupable debt to the label.

In spite of all this, the band, now back in Texas, expected IA to have details of an East Coast promotional tour nearly finalized. There was a big meeting of all concerned at the label. Realizing that IA was stalling (though it was too soon to figure out why), and informed by their experience in California, the band stopped wasting time and booked the Doris Miller Auditorium in Austin for January 7. The show was put on by the specially created "Electric Grandmother," a booking outfit set up by soundman Sandy Lockett with light show owners Houston White and Gary Scanlon. A feature of all the Electric Grandmother shows was a jam session between the Elevators and their support band, Conqueroo, held after the Elevators' main set.

> ROKY (*1975*): When we jammed with Conqueroo, they would do as much for us—I'm trying to explain—what I hope we did for other bands. We could just jam with them and feel like we had complete freedom to really blow some people's minds with our talent.

To capitalize on their new celebrity, Tommy decided to style the band's look. According to Ronnie, everything they wore supposedly conveyed a hidden meaning (now, of course, long forgotten): Tommy wore an ex-navy peacoat; Ronnie, a red velvet jacket, round John Lennon specs, and John Ike's father's pop-up wedding top hat; John Ike styled himself in his Frisco gear—frilly shirt, striped pants, and fringed "Indian" boots; Roky wore a tailored jacket with vintage dress shirt; and Stacy wore a red-and-black-checked hoodie that looked twenty years ahead of Seattle grunge.

The show was an outright success, so the Electric Grandmother next booked a show for February 10 at Austin's City Coliseum, a repurposed World War II aircraft hangar from the old Bergstrom Air Force Base. This was where Elvis had appeared in 1956 as part of Hank Snow's Grand Ole Opry tour, and where large revue acts—such as James Brown, and Ike and Tina Turner performed when in town. For the Elevators, it was a massive leap from the New Orleans Club, and by far the most ambitious show the band had played to date in Texas. But with more than 2,000 tickets sold at the previous month's Doris Miller show, they easily packed the venue. The only problem was that the venue was so vast, it stretched the capabilities of Sandy Lockett's sound crew.

> HOUSTON WHITE: We did one show at the Coliseum, which was not very good; we didn't have the sound equipment and it was not a good room.

Given the scale of their success, it is bizarre that the following day the band supported the Roy Head Trio in a small club in New Braunfels, seventy-five miles southeast of Kerrville, the middle of nowhere. Roy Head was one of Huey Meaux's white soul acts, whose "Treat Her Right" had been kept out of the national number-one spot in 1965 by the Beatles' "Yesterday." Head was a showman: his set featured, among other flourishes, the whole James Brown dropping-to-the-knees routine. According to Ronnie, Stacy found the act amusing, particularly since it came on the heels of the Elevators' delivering a "transcendent" performance—to fifty lucky attendees.

▲ **WHILE THE BAND** continued to push for an East Coast promotional tour, IA countered them by demanding new recordings. As the link between the valuable marketing buzzword "psychedelic rock" and the increasingly illegal mind-altering drugs to which it referred became clearer, IA elected—rather than risk another dangerous tour—to keep the band in Houston, only issuing records in hopes of another radio hit. Once again fearing "the Bynum tapes" would be revisited, the band agreed to record at Andrus Studio from January 17 to 20. However, they hadn't written or worked up enough new material for a whole LP, so only three tracks were recorded.

IA also wanted to capitalize on the success of the recent shows and insisted on promoting the next, in February at the Houston Music Theatre, "in association with the Electric Grandmother." Not only did they intend to record the show, they wanted to use it to launch a new single, "I've Got Levitation" b/w "Before You Accuse Me," culled from the recent studio sessions. Despite the fact that the stereo version of the new LP had only just

THE PSYCHEDELIC SOUNDS OF THE 13TH FLOOR ELEVATORS

International Artists 1.

The group states on the liner notes that all the tunes on the package are descriptive of the more meaningful life a body achieves through the use of psychedelic drugs. Perhaps. "Reverberation," "You're Gonna Miss Me."

Austin American-Statesman Saturday, Jan. 7, 1967

Local Rock 'n' Roll Band Back From Successful Tour

When Austin's 13th Floor Elevators left the Capital City for California at summer's end, the band was little known outside the State of Texas. Their following, though enthusiastic, remained a local one.

Such is not the case today, just a little more than four months later, as the group returns home for its first local engagement after completing a well received series of night-club and concert engagements throughout California.

Today, the Elevators are attracting fans from coast to coast, by virtue of a pair of single recordings and a new album on International Artist label; a pair of nationwide television appearances; and mention in various national magazines, the most recent of which was an issue of Newsweek a couple of weeks back.

The home-grown group of rock 'n' roll musicians will perform Saturday evening, 8 p.m. till 1 a.m., at Doris Miller Auditorium. The band will be featured at the combination dance-concert along with another local rock band — the Conqueroo.

Adding to the music will be the Jomo Disaster Light Show, a new concept in audio-visual entertainment first developed in the San Francisco area.

For the Elevators, the show will mark their first local appearance since drawing record-breaking crowds at several of the local nightspots last summer.

Four members of the original quintet remain: Singer Roky Ericson, lead guitarist Stacy Sutherland, jug player Tommy Hall and drummer John Ike.

Although the band relies largely on original material written by its members, it also includes in its repertoire new material from other promising young song writers. One such contributor is Austin harmonica player Powell St. John, who wrote three songs for the Elevators' new LP. St. John is currently in San Francisco.

Tickets for the Saturday night show are now on sale at radio station KAZZ-FM; Hemphill's No. 2; Travis Book Store and the Record Shop. Advance price is $1.75. Admission at the door will be $2.

The show is being presented by a local production company called The Electric Grandmother, an organization patterned after the famed Family Dog of San Francisco.

Master of ceremonies will be KAZZ disc jockey Rim Kelly.

Psychedelic Sounds Set For Austin

It all started in San Francisco, a product of the POP Generation, and now it seems destined to sweep the nation.

It's the "new" entertainment, and Austin is due to receive the first tremors from the quake Saturday night at Doris Miller Auditorium when the 13th Floor Elevators — an Austin-sired "psychedelic rock 'n' roll" band — returns home to headline a combination danco and concert.

The Elevators, recently returned from a highly successful concert and club tour of the West Coast, will be joined on the program by another "new thing" local group — the Conqueroo — along with the Jomo Disaster Light Show.

The "audio-visual happening" is being presented by the Electric Grandmother, an Austin-based production company which plans to present shows featuring local talent along with nationally recognized artists of the "hip" gender.

The show is scheduled from 8 p.m. to 1 a.m.

For those never having witnessed a light show presentation in conjunction with a dance-concert, the program will constitute a totally new entertainment experience. Visual effect devices include:

—Stroboscopic lighting, semilar to the flash effects of old-time motion pictures;

—Flashing patterns projected across the dancers and performers themselves, as well as walls and ceilings;

—Liquid light machines designed to create the illusion that walls are alive with movement and color, with both movement and color changes seemingly in correlation with the tempos and dynamics of the music.

The Austin show will be the first such large auditorium presentation in Texas. It will be conducted in the tradition that has made such San Francisco locations as the Avalon Ballroom and Fillmore Auditorium prime focal points of the new action.

Of course, to most Austin rock 'n' roll fans, the Elevators are no strangers. The young group had already attracted perhaps the largest following of any local musical aggregation before their departure for California and the West Coast. They return now with a new International Artist record album to their credit as well as having appeared on national television on both the "American Bandstand" show and "Where the Action Is."

Foremost in helping create the unique "psychedelic" sound of the band are lead singer Roky Ericson and amplified jug player Tommy Hall.

Emcee for the Saturday night show will be disc jockey Rim Kelly of radio station KAZZ-FM.

Advance tickets priced at $1.75 are available at KAZZ; Hemphill's No. 2; The Record Shop and Travis Book Store.

Tickets will also be available at the door (Doris Miller Auditorium, 2300 Rosewood) at $2 per person.

Top left: Review blurb from *Record World*, January 7, 1967.

Center left: *Austin Statesman* article, January 7.

Right: *Austin Statesman* article, January 8.

Top left: Drawn advertisement with map for the Doris Miller Auditorium show on the east side of town. From *The Rag*, January 2.

Top right: The Doris Miller Auditorium show poster, regarded as the first ever Texan psychedelic poster.

Bottom left: Handbill for the Doris Miller Auditorium concert using Mark Weakley's poster art.

shipped to stores in mid-January, the label, in lieu of a promotional tour, now wanted to issue a live version of *Psychedelic Sounds* and a new single.

FRIDAY,
FEB. 10th
8 P.M.
ELECTRIC
GRANDMOTHER
PRESENTS
13th FLOOR
ELEVATORS
CONQUEROO
JOMO DISASTER
LIGHT SHOW
CITY
COLISEUM
TICKETS:
PRE-SALE, $1.75 AT
KAZZ-FM, HEMPHILL'S #2,
THE RECORD SHOP, AND
TRAVIS BOOK STORE
$2.00 AT THE DOOR

Austin Statesman ad for the second Electric Grandmother show at the City Coliseum, February 10.

HOUSTON WHITE: [The third Electric Grandmother show] was done in conjunction with International Artists, and that's where we figured out what kind of assholes they were.

JOHN IKE: Oh, yeah, [IA] wanted as much as they could get. Because a new cover with "the 13th Floor Elevators" was going to sell at that point.

RONNIE: We came back [from San Francisco] mainly to record. We had just finished *Psychedelic Sounds* and [IA] were going, "Well, we need to start working on the next one," and canceled our East Coast tour. We had jobs booked on the East Coast, from Florida up to Maryland, you know—spreading our albums in that direction. I really think if we would have been able to do the East Coast, we could have gotten a lot bigger. And I think it would've held everybody together a little more. That's when [IA] had us there in Houston and we were going nowhere—we played the same club, the Living Eye, probably fifteen weeks in a row. It just went on and on and on. And that's when John Ike and I decided, "This isn't gonna go anywhere." Because we were playing there for $750, and we could have been playing in Florida for $2,400 a night.

▲ **THE HOUSTON MUSIC THEATRE** show would become a turning point in the band's career, albeit for all the wrong reasons.

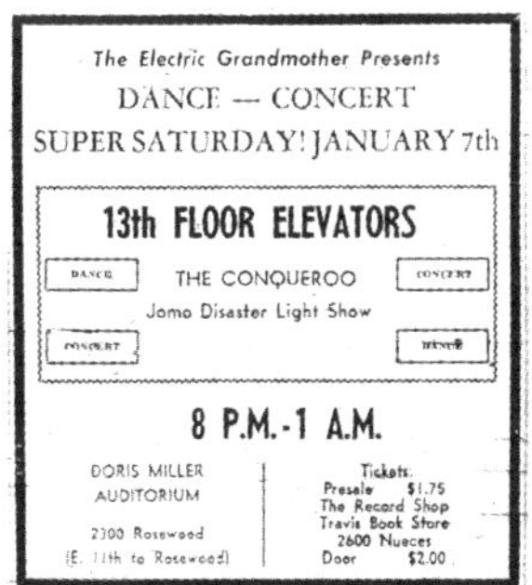

The Electric Grandmother Presents
DANCE — CONCERT
SUPER SATURDAY! JANUARY 7th
13th FLOOR ELEVATORS
DANCE
THE CONQUEROO
CONCERT
Jomo Disaster Light Show
CONCERT
8 P.M.-1 A.M.
DORIS MILLER
AUDITORIUM
2300 Rosewood
(E. 11th to Rosewood)
Tickets:
Presale $1.75
The Record Shop
Travis Book Store
2600 Nueces
Door $2.00

Advertisement for the Doris Miller show in the *Daily Texan*, January 5.

WALT ANDRUS: I always felt [IA] exploited the band's drug situation. I wasn't that close to it, but I had a very negative feeling about it. They used to carry the band around in a van that was locked from the outside, that kind of stuff. I tried to do one live album at the dome building [the Houston Music Theatre]. Frank [Davis, engineer] made some microphones that rotated on hydraulic booms—but Roky, he couldn't finish a tune. He'd come on and forget what he was doing.

LELAN ROGERS: The paranoia was terrible . . . knowing how bad the police wanted to bust them. Policemen used to get two dollars an hour when they worked off-duty, so I hired four or five rooms in the Holiday Inn and arranged to hire three or four people out of the vice squad to protect this superstar rock group that I was bringing to town. I got the detectives rooms on the same floor, and then brought the Elevators down from Austin to play, and so they were escorted and protected by the police for two days and nights. I had protection for a group they were trying to bust and they never knew it until afterwards.

Above: The Elevators perform at the Phi Gamma Delta frat-house, 300 West 27th Street, Austin, January 1967.

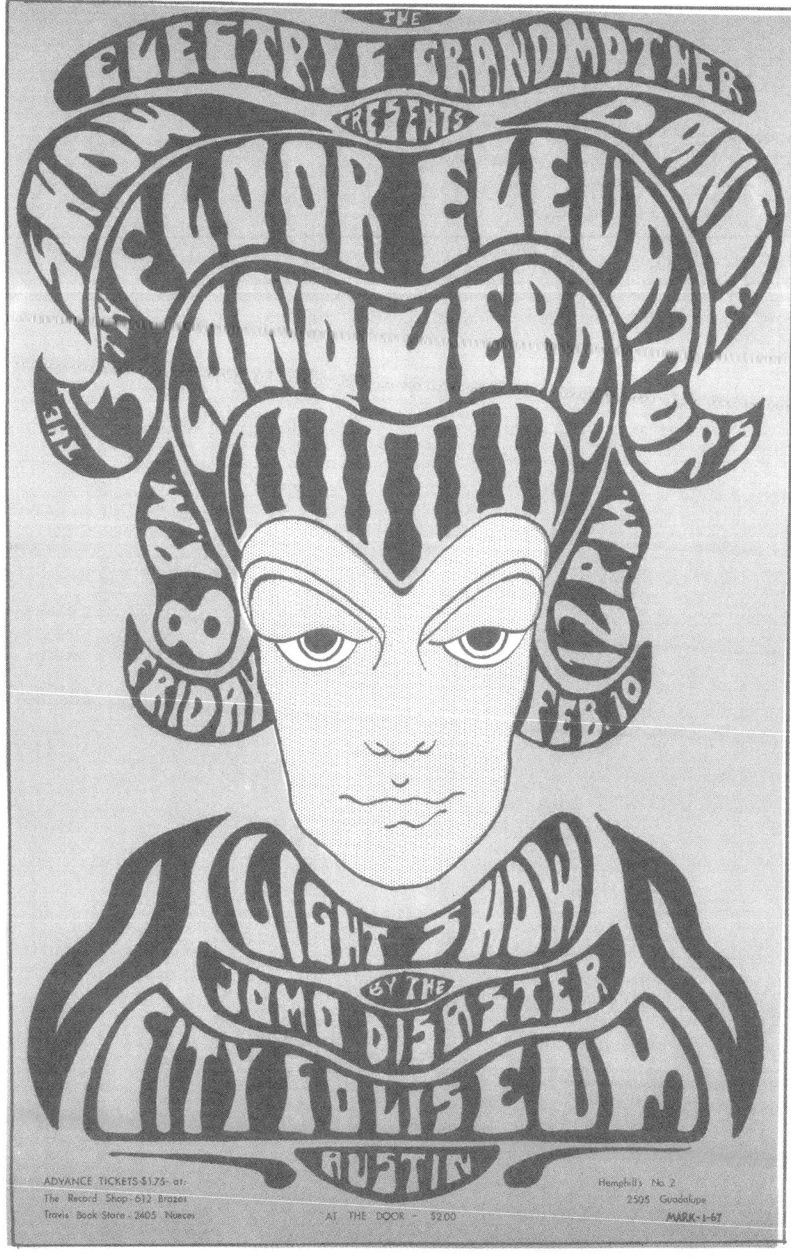

Above: Mark Weakley's poster and handbill for the City Coliseum concert. Following the success of the previous Electric Grandmother booking, Weakley was granted a larger print run and expanded palette, and the posters were sold at the show.

In his drawings of classical architectural monuments of

'New Rock' Show Set at Coliseum

The Electric Grandmother, a local production outfit, swings into action again at 8 p.m. Friday night at City Coliseum—for the second in a dance—light show series featuring top rock 'n' roll bands in the area as well as sidebar attractions of the "new thing" entertainment.

One of Austin's newest contributions to the new rock — the Thirteenth Floor Elevator — will headline the show along with The Conqueroo, another local group.

At least two other local bands are scheduled to perform in the Friday concert as well.

One of the features of the January show which will be continued is the last hour "jam session." This is where musicians from the various groups have a chance to get together and play whatever comes into their heads thereby producing sounds which have been tagged "psychedelic."

Tickets for the show are priced at $2 at the door or $1.75 advance. Presale locations include Travis Book Store, The Record Shop, and KAZZ-FM studios.

FRIDAY—FEB. 10

SWINGING CONQUEROO TAKES OVER FRIDAY AT COLISEUM
Ed Guinn, Bob Brown—to rock at psychedelic music, light show.

Here Tonight

'New Thing' Show Going to Houston

Austinites attending the "new thing" dance and light show Friday night at 8 p.m. in the City Coliseum will also be seeing a preview of what will be a major first for the City of Houston the following weekend.

The entire company will present the same show Feb. 18 at the Houston Music Theater.

It will mark the first time that the theater-in-the-round has opened its doors to any sort of rock 'n' roll show.

The "musical happening," featuring the 13th Floor Elevators, the Conqueroo and the spectacular Jomo Disaster Light Show, is being presented both in Austin and Houston by the Electric Grandmother, an Austin-based production company.

Musicians, light technicians and the entire management are Austinites.

And, the organization from which the Electric Grandmother received its inspiration — the Family Dog of San Francisco — also happens to be headed by former Austin residents.

The Jan. 7 debut for the production company attracted nearly 2,000 people at Doris Miller Auditorium.

Prices are $2 at the door and $1.75 in advance from Hemphill's No. 2, the Travis Book Store, the Record Shop and KAZZ-FM.

Both the Elevators and the Conqueroo are advocates of the psychedelic school of rock 'n' roll — a new wave of popular music which is fast dominating the rock 'n' roll scene.

The Jomo Disaster Light Show will feature new techniques picked up directly from New York by staff members.

Rim Kelly, KAZZ-FM disc jockey, will act as master of ceremonies.

Left: Article from *The Daily Texan* previewing the City Coliseum show, February 8.

Right: *Austin Statesman* article previewing the third Electric Grandmother production with the Elevators and Conqueroo at the Houston Music Theatre, February 10.

Opposite top: *Austin Statesman* article on the City Coliseum show, February 8.

Opposite bottom: Front page of the *Southwestern Texan*, reporting the band's booking at the Bellaire City Gymnasium in the southwestern suburb of Houston, February 1.

Following page: The Elevators live, probably at the Aztec Theater in San Antonio, January–February 1967. Photographed by Ronnie Leatherman's then-girlfriend, Dianne Honea.

Wednesday, Feb. 8, 1967

Happening

Fun Show Set at Coliseum Friday

The Electric Grandmother [illegible] into action again Friday, presenting the 13th Floor Elevators, the Conqueroo and other assorted bands, light shows and "musical happenings."

The [illegible]ond in this series of dance and light shows, the fun is set to begin at 8 p.m. in the City Coliseum.

Approxim[illegible] 2,000 Austinites turned out for the January show in Doris Miller Auditorium. One of the most successful features of the first show was the last hour "jam session," which will be continued Friday.

Master of ceremonies will again be Rim Kelly of KAZZ-FM radio.

Members of the production company's staff have visited New York since the last show and have returned with new equipment and new ideas for the February shindig.

Tickets sell for $1.75 in advance, $2 at the door and are currently on sale at Hemphill's No. 2, 2501 Guadalupe; Travis Book Store, 109 E. [illegible]th; the Record Shop, 81[illegible] Brazos; and at KAZZ-FM studios in Perry-Brooks Building.

"Art Nouveau" posters by Mark Weakley advertising the show are also available at the Travis Book Store.

Acto[illegible]

How

By [illegible]

AP [illegible]

HOLLYWOO[illegible]

did he ge[illegible]

That's what [illegible] has been wond[illegible] Robert Evans w[illegible] head of produc[illegible] ount Studios [illegible] stemmed from [illegible] Evans had been [illegible] admittedly "a [illegible] — and he had [illegible] movie in his li[illegible]

Yet he was [illegible] of running the [illegible] deals with st[illegible] directors and w[illegible] ally overseein[illegible] product, whic[illegible] scores of milli[illegible] year.

Evans has a[illegible]

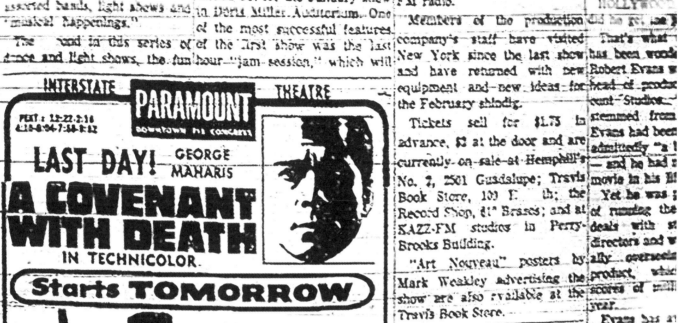

WILLOW AREA POOL PLANS UNDER CONSIDERATION

Willow Pool, a non-profit corporation, is now proceeding with plans to build the swimming pool and bath house on property located at 10500 Cliffwood. The cost of the pool and bath house is approximately $40,000. These facilities will be used by subscribing members in the Willow Meadows, Willowbrook and Post Oak Manor area.

The plans include a swimming pool, a wading pool, life guards, concession stands. Off street parking will be provided. This 2.9 acre tract is on Cliffwood, between Mcdermed and Tonawanda, near the Willow Park.

Memberships are open to residents in the above areas and additional information may be secured by calling any of the elected officers; Pres. Dr. Joe Kaufhold, 4302 Silverwood; Dr. Jack Westmoreland, 4110 Waycross; Vice-Pres.; Mrs. Kitten Carter, Treas.; 10303 Greenwillow; Max Millner, Secy. 4429 Waycross.

"Elevators" To Play at Bellaire Dance, Feb. 4

Nationally popular recording artists, the "13th Floor Elevators" will be on stage at this week's Bellaire teen dance at the Bellaire City Gym. Saturday, Feb. 4th at 8 p.m. Admission is only $1 per person for this performance.

One of the hottest groups on the nation's record scene, these boys from Austin, have had two singles and an album in the national charts within the past year. Teenagers from the Bellaire and Southwest area are invited to attend.

DOUG PETTIGREW

Doug Pettigrew, 15, is a 10th grade Bellaire High student. He attended the Nat'l. Scout Jamboree at Valley Forge in 1964 and is a member of Troop 298, sponsored by the Bellaire Christian Church.

Previous page: Dianne Honea's photos of the Elevators at the Holiday Inn Club in New Braunfels, Texas's Landa Park; February 11, 1967.

Above and opposite: The Elevators at the Holiday Inn Club in New Braunfels, shot by Bob Snider's girlfriend, Linda. Snider: "It was rather rare to be able to see the Elevators, so the distance—about eighty miles from Georgetown—did not seem prohibitive. I recall that the crowd was small, fifty people at most; this allowed Linda, my girlfriend (future wife) and I to roam about freely. She carried her Kodak Brownie camera. I would stoop down and lift her up above the crowd. As I recall, it was a very acoustically 'live' room with cement floors, I think cinderblock walls, and drop-in acoustic tile ceiling. The room acted as a well-tuned speaker cabinet. The jug filled the room in just the right way. The vocals were clear. I probably saw the Elevators a half dozen times: two 'bad' shows, two 'fair' shows, two where they were 'on their game.' One of those two transcendent shows was at the Jade Room; the other was this night in New Braunfels."

RZ ADN 10 PD FEB 6 1107A C ST- (BOOK 8 COPIES)

DLR--DONT PHONE

1. JERRY LOVE,/ALPHA DISTRIBUTORS, 20 WEST END AVE, NYK

DLR DONT PHONE

2. DAVE FOX AND AL CHAPMAN,/CHAPMAN RECORD DISTRIBUTORS, 2645 WEST PICO,LOSA

DLR DONT PHONE

3. RON ADAMS AND JOE STANZIONE,/CAMPUS RECORD DISTRIBUTORS, 6751 NORTHWEST 37TH COURT, MIAMI FLO

DLR DONT PHONE

4. JERRY MORRIS,/FIDELITY RECORD DISTRIBUTORS, 5301 SHILSHOLE AVE NORTHWEST SEATTLE WASH

DLR DONT PHONE

5. ARMAND BALADIUM,/DETROIT RECORD DISTRIBUTORS, 14344 FENKELL, DET

DLR DONT PHONE

6. DENNY ZEITLER,/INDEPENDENT MUSIC SALES, 800 MARIPOSA SFRAN

DLR DONT PHONE

7. DON AND JOE BANASHEK,/7-B PRODUCTIONS, 715 CAMP,NRLNS

DLR DONT PHONE

8. BILL LEANER,/UNITED RECORD DISTRIBUTORS, 1827 SOUTH MICHIGAN CHGO

=LEVITATION IS A VIRUS. HELP SPREAD IT WITH AIR PLAY.=

LELAN ROGERS

1967 FEB 6 AM 11 35

CFM FURN

INTERNATIONAL ARTISTS
1005 AMERICAN BLDG
HOU 77002

CA 8-1244/INTERNATIONAL ARTISTS, 1005 AMERICANA

SENT BY MRS CHUMLEY

DLR DONT PHONE

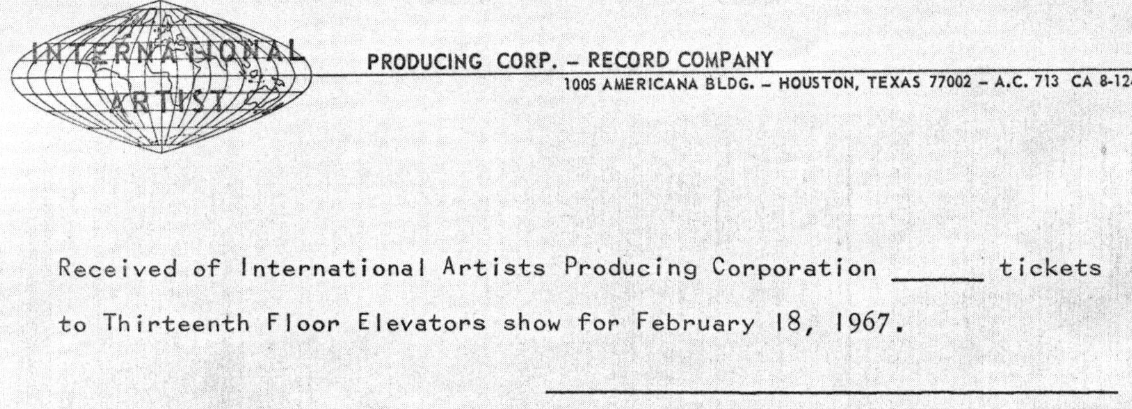

INTERNATIONAL ARTIST

PRODUCING CORP. - RECORD COMPANY

1005 AMERICANA BLDG. - HOUSTON, TEXAS 77002 - A.C. 713 CA 8-1244

Received of International Artists Producing Corporation ______ tickets to Thirteenth Floor Elevators show for February 18, 1967.

____

BY: ______________________________

DATE: ______________________________

JOHN IKE: Just before we went on, Stacy comes up to me and says, "John, I'm scared. I feel like a two-year-old child." I went and turned this over to Jack McClellan, my lawyer. I said, "Jack, Stacy dropped a bunch of acid, he feels like a two-year-old child. And he's gotta go on in thirty minutes." So Jack takes him outside and sticks a joint in his mouth. He gets him even higher than he was! [*Laughs*] Needless to say, it didn't work.

JACK McCLELLAN: This friend of mine was saying, "What's wrong with Stacy? You gotta take the sharp end of the acid off with some grass." Stacy was lying on the goddamn floor, groaning. This [off-duty cop] was about seven feet tall and 300 pounds, straight-looking, and he freaked Stacy out. He just looked like a big cop, standing there in that hotel room. Finally, this dude gave him a couple of joints and cooled him right out, but we practically had to carry him onstage. The kids loved it. No wonder the narcs considered it their sacred duty to eradicate these cats.

CHARLIE PRICHARD: It was hard to take the stage. There was no backstage—you used to have to go through the audience. I don't know how it was perceived, but it sure was weird being on that stage while it turns around, even though it does it really slowly—one spin every half hour. When you play, it's not unusual to focus on someone in the audience, and not necessarily to play at them, [but] it's nice to have something to relate to that's not disappearing to your right.

▲ **AFTER A SHOW IN** Houston, Peter Yarrow—of Peter, Paul and Mary—hung out with George Banks and returned to New York with copies of *Psychedelic Sounds*. He convinced Murray the K, the legendary DJ and promoter, to back an Elevators East Coast tour.

GEORGE BANKS: Peter Yarrow used to call me literally every week and say, "When are these guys going to get up here?" I dealt with Tommy, because he positioned himself as head of the group, even though it was Mrs. Walton's money.

TOMMY (*M*): We had a lot of trouble—like [John Ike] totally messed things up for us as far as the East Coast because he was always quibbling about who should manage us. We tried to book gigs in New York, but he called the people up and told them that [the right people] hadn't booked us and they canceled everything.

JACK McCLELLAN: IA wanted to send them all to New York. Lelan Rogers told me he'd just spoken to Murray the K, that they were all set up to do *The Ed Sullivan Show*. My theory was that they were going to get to New York City and be on the skids there, just like they always were, and would have lost track of each other, like San Francisco.

Opposite top: February 6 promo telegram for the "Levitation" single from International Artists: *"LEVITATION IS A VIRUS. HELP SPREAD IT WITH AIRPLAY."*

Opposite bottom: Ticket manifest from IA for the February 18 show at the Houston Music Theatre.

In addition to the possibility of gigs on the East Coast, international interest in the band was slowly building.

> LELAN ROGERS: Right after they released the first album, I took it to New York to a friend of mine who owned *Record World* [magazine], Bob Austin, and I met Michael Jefferies, who managed Jimi Hendrix. He'd just found Jimi and wanted to take the Elevators back to England with him, and he said he would make them as big as the Stones. And I called—and the guys didn't want to go.

> JOHN IKE: I remember Lelan saying Jimi Hendrix's manager wanted to take us to Europe, but that was bullshit. We didn't have the chance. You bet we'd [have gone]. We were starving here.

In spite of this denial, the last line of a letter from Laurie Jones to Stacy would seem to confirm the band's resistance to touring in Britain: *"Stacy, why don't you want to go to England this summer?"*

Barry Miles—co-owner of London's Indica Bookshop and Gallery, where John Lennon met Yoko Ono; editor of the underground newspaper *I.T.*; and general key player in the British underground—visited New York and returned to Swinging London with *Psychedelic Sounds*. Word was circulating throughout the city's cultural elite, but while the record found favor at the legendary King's Road boutique Granny Takes a Trip, with underground DJ Jeff Dexter, and even with Keith Richards (whose favorite song was "Don't Fall Down"), the LP apparently failed to reach the ears of Jimi Hendrix.

> KATHY ETCHINGHAM (Hendrix's girlfriend): We had a copy of the Red Crayola [*The Parable of Arable Land*, IA's second release, which Roky also played on]—I remember Jimi liked the artwork [by George Banks, who designed the Elevators' *Easter Everywhere* sleeve]. We did not have an Elevators record, and I don't remember them or any discussion with Mike Jefferies.

Sadly, the record didn't appear to have filtered into the Beatles' circle, although Sean Lennon would later confirm that a copy of "the eyeball album" was in his mom and dad's collection. Meanwhile, the Beatles' manager, Brian Epstein, was showcasing Hendrix at his Saville Theatre in London; by the time Hendrix reached Texas, in 1968, the Elevators were in tatters.

The LP did, however, reach Andrew Lauder, A&R at Liberty Records, who tried to license it for release in the UK. Unfortunately, IA demanded an absurd figure, so the only foreign releases were those that came in January: an extremely rare four track EP in France and a "You're Gonna Miss Me" single in Germany.

In February, the LP was name-checked in the February 11 issue of *Melody Maker* (the band's first mention in the foreign press), as part of an article breaking down the burgeoning American psychedelic scene furnished throughout with proselytizing quotes from Chet Helms, who had been on a visit to London.

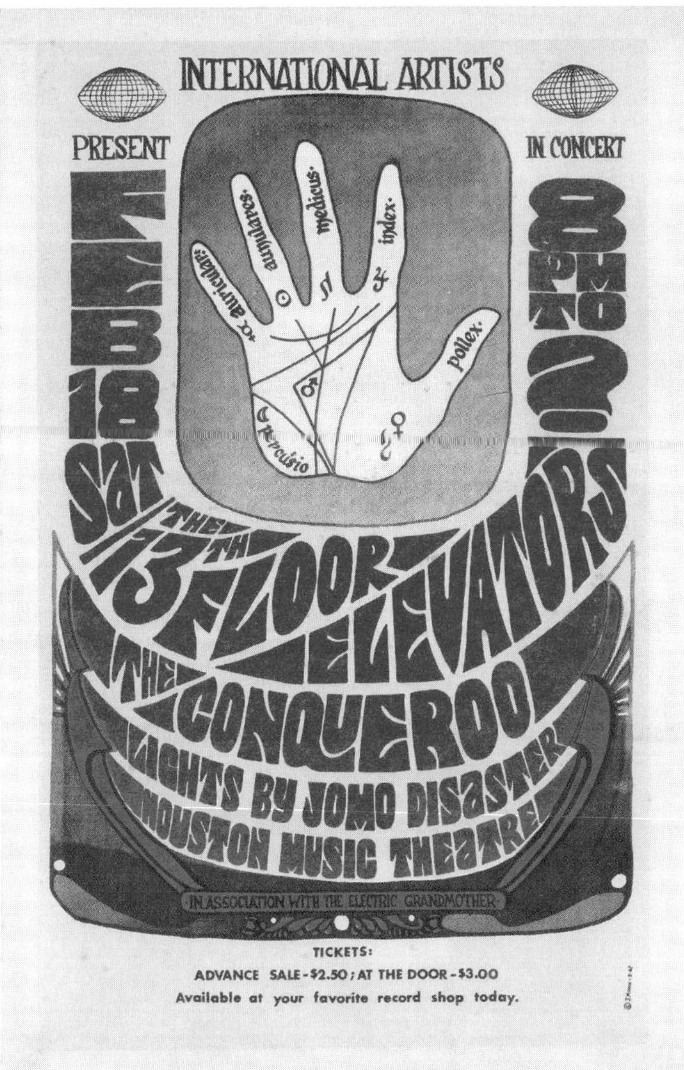

26

HOUSTON MUSIC THEATRE
SOUTHWEST FREEWAY AT FONDREN

FEB.
18
1967

INTERNATIONAL ARTISTS
RECORD CORP. Presents
13th FLOOR ELEVATORS
WITH
JAMO LIGHT DISASTER
IN CONCERT
SAT. EVE. 8:00 P.M.
Adm. $3.00

GLOBE TICKET COMPANY, DALLAS

SAT. EVE.
FEBRUARY
18
1967

HOUSTON MUSIC
THEATRE

26

Above: Poster, handbill, and ticket for the show at the Houston Music Theatre.

Opposite and below: The band being interviewed for college radio, backstage at the Houston Music Theatre, February 18, 1967. Stacy's bad trip took hold when the show's emcee—KILT-FM's DJ Russ Knight, a.k.a "Weird Beard"—changed into his costume. Stacy: "I went inside and the devil was there, and he had this tall pointed hat on, and he was the emcee for the show, 'Weird Beard,' the number-one disc jockey in Houston. And he looked at me and he had a goatee and a sorcerer's costume on . . . and I was bad and he knew it. And this narcotics agent that we hired to travel with us to guard us was standing beside me, and I didn't want him to know I was freaking out."

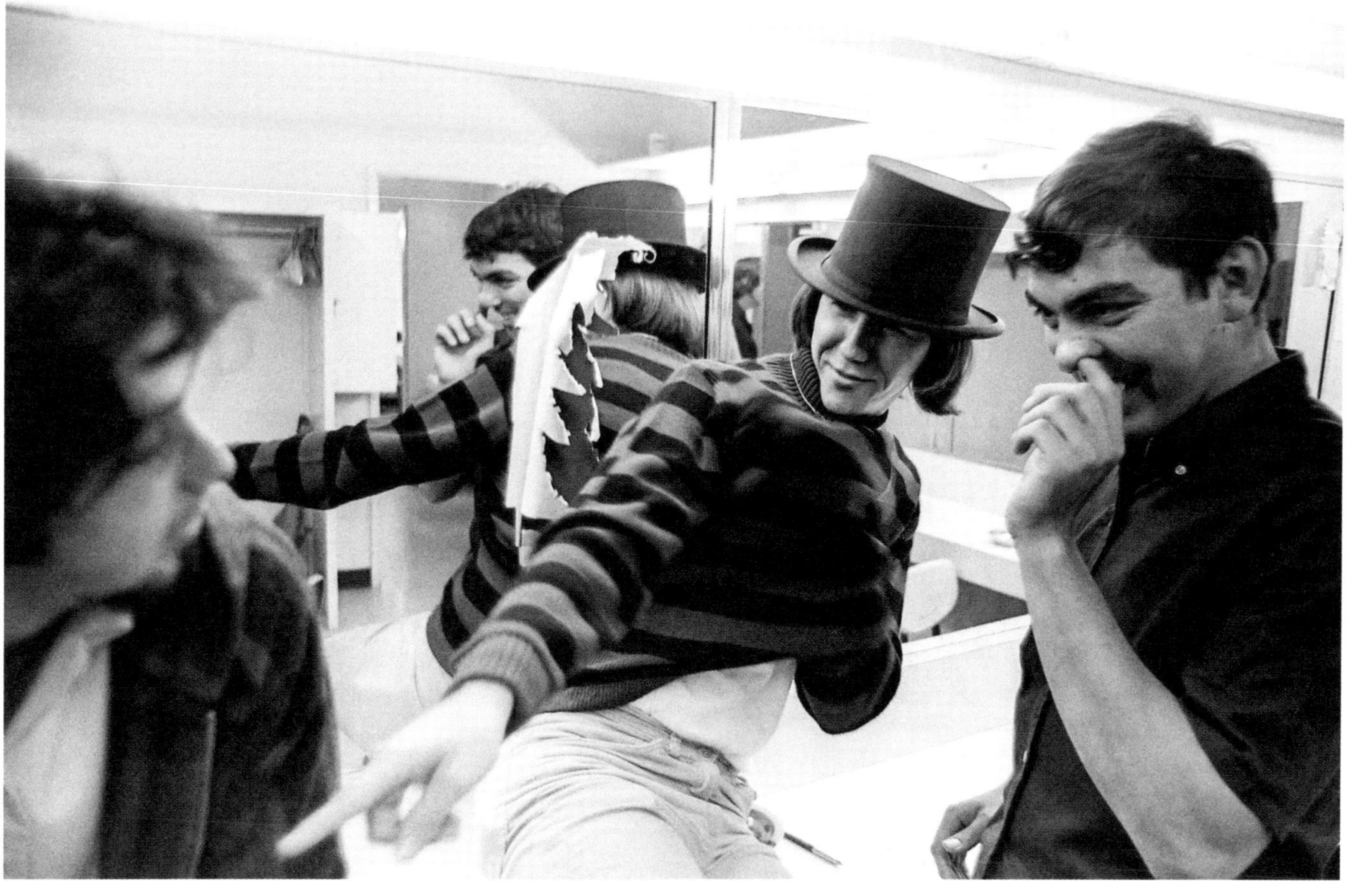

Above and opposite: Backstage at the Houston Music Theatre. Stacy: "And the devil walked up to me and started asking me how his pointed hat looked, and every time he twisted his pointed hat his nostrils would flare . . . I ran outside and looked up at the sky, and there were clouds of blood floating in the sky . . . and I called John Ike and Ronnie up and said, 'I've got to go to a hospital, 'cause I lost it.' And the show was starting, and as soon as I took off down the ramp, man, I looked down there and I saw the light show and the revolving stage—and it represented Hades, and Satan with his cape was leading us down into the arena."

Above: Dressing room portrait at the Houston Music Theatre. Budding high school photographer William Warner wrote to IA and was issued free tickets and a trip backstage, during which he documented Stacy's evolving bad trip and the show itself. Warner: "I knew nothing about the Elevators, but 'Reverberation' was on the radio all the time and they were a popular group, so I just cold-called Lelan Rogers [at] age fifteen. I'd got the reputation as the kid who photographed bands. He said, 'I'll leave two tickets for you at the box office—just go to the dressing room and ask.' So, I just showed up in the dressing room and did my thing, which at that point was pretty practiced routine, like going to work . . . [the] *Life* magazine–type idea of doing really composed pictures. Also interacting really directly with people."

Right and bottom: Onstage at the Houston Music Theatre. William Warner: "I was very taken with Roky's demeanor. He was very nice while I was photographing him. They seemed like a really nice bunch of guys. I knew nothing about drugs. I was very naive. The mood was somewhat spacey, you'd say now. The one thing I do remember is that Stacy seemed kinda out of it and John Ike was acting like he needed to lure Stacy out of the dressing room: 'This way, come on, come on.' To me that was just a curious detail—I didn't get what was really going on. I followed them down the ramp and was basically sat on the side of the stage. And the stage would revolve—go round and round. Whatever complaints people might have about the sound [on the recording of the show], that's astoundingly better than it sounded in person: it was a huge noise being played in a big echoey dome as the stage rotated, and sound would go away from you and came back to you as the stage went around. Impossible to tell what was going on, so I actually left at that point . . . when the jam with Conqueroo was going on, just as I was leaving, I got to the last row and had one frame of film left and made that one single shot of them all onstage. I have to point out I was fifteen; my father had to drive me down to this thing and pick me up."

▲ **BEYOND CHARTING** toward the lower end of the top thirty on both Austin's KNOW-FM and Houston's KILT radio surveys in mid-March, "I've Got Levitation" failed to catch on nationally. Broke and agentless, the band began picking up whatever live work they could muster, resulting in a schedule that consisted of frat parties, teen dances in school gymnasiums, and support slots.

> JERRY LIGHTFOOT: Last time I saw [the Elevators] do a meaningful gig was at the Living Eye in '67. I remember watching Stacy playing, and he set up a riff—"Levitation"—he sent this riff off, and with the echo it got to where the echo was chasing itself, and he set this whole thing up where it was chasing this lick around the room, literally. And John Ike and Ronnie were so on it, perfect . . . truly psychedelic. And then Roky just stepped up and blew your head off . . . it was fantastic! Fantastic!

> JACK McCLELLAN (*1973*): The way most bands tried to get that psychedelic hypnotic effect was just by turning up the volume. The Elevators had extrapolated on that and used a lot of feedback. Oh, it was chaos . . . It was such a homogeneous din, and yet there was something there. The teenyboppers loved Roky—he had lots of soul. Stacy was simply one of the best blues guitarists I'd ever heard, especially for a white boy. I tried to get them to listen to African music, get them into multiple rhythms and out of 4/4, so they could get the same hypnotic effect without all the god-awful noise and feedback. I figured once the newness of Tommy's gimmick wore off, they'd have some solid music to fall back on. Just before they split up, Tommy had begun to discernibly contribute to their overall sound. He never actually played the jug anyway, just the microphone. Once in a while they really swung; when Stacy was together and when they played the blues, I stopped whatever I was doing, grabbed a gal, and took her out on the dance floor and started to slide.

In April, Jack McClellan set up 13th Floor, Inc., installing himself as the legal department, Juanita Holman (the wife of his legal partner) as the secretary, and Emma Walton, John Ike's mother, as the backer. The idea was to set up a management company to counter IA's control of the band, force

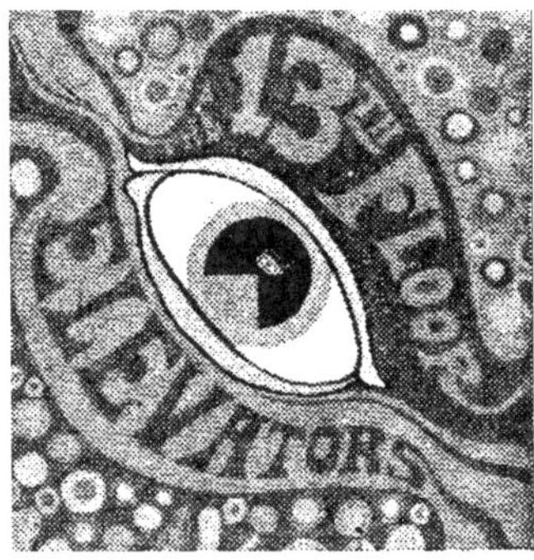

THE 13th FLOOR ELEVATORS

A true psychedelic sound is hard to capture, but it's been done here.

There is a spiritual feel to all the numbers in the albums, but especially "Reverberation".

The LP is selling like hotcakes in Greenwich Village, and it won't be long before it repeats the performance all over.

Review of *Psychedelic Sounds* in Go magazine #53, March 31, 1967.

KILT ☆ FORTY STAR SURVEY

HOUSTON'S MOST POPULAR SONGS

WEEK OF
MARCH 15 - 22

Song	Artist	Label
*1...HAPPY TOGETHER	THE TURTLES	WHITE WHALE
*2...STRAWBERRY FIELDS/PENNY LANE	THE BEATLES	CAPITOL
*3...DEDICATED TO THE ONE I LOVE	THE MAMAS & PAPAS	DUNHILL
*4...FOR WHAT ITS WORTH	THE BUFFALO SPRINGFIELD	ATCO
*5...HEY MISTER	THE FEVER TREE	MAINSTREAM
*6...WESTERN UNION	THE FIVE AMERICANS	ABNAK
*7...GEORGY GIRL	THE SEEKERS	CAPITOL
*8...THE 59th STREET BRIDGE SONG	HARPERS BIZARRE	WARNER BROS.
*9...BABY I NEED YOUR LOVIN'	JOHNNY RIVERS	IMPERIAL
*10..THIS IS MY SONG	PETULA CLARK	WARNER BROS.
*11..SOCK IT TO ME BABY	MITCH RYDER	NEW VOICE
12..MY CUP RUNNETH OVER	ED AMES	R C A
*13..I NEVER LOVED A MAN	ARETHA FRANKLIN	ATLANTIC
*14..IF YOU EVER FIND THE TIME	THE JONES BOYS	ATCO
*15..A LITTLE BIT ME/FLIP	THE MONKEES	COLGEMS
*16..SOMETHING STUPID	FRANK & NANCY SINATRA	REPRISE
*17..UPS AND DOWNS	PAUL REVERE & RAIDERS	COLUMBIA
*18..WONDERFUL WINO	GEORGE CARLIN	R C A
*19..RETURN OF THE RED BARON	THE ROYAL GUARDSMEN	LAURIE
*20..MORNINGTOWN RIDE	THE SEEKERS	CAPITOL
*21..DANNY BOY	RAY PRICE	COLUMBIA
*22..SIT DOWN I THINK I LOVE YOU	THE MOJO MEN	REPRISE
*23..KIND OF A HUSH	HERMAN'S HERMITS	M G M
*24..WHAT A WOMAN IN LOVE WON'T DO	SANDY POSEY	M G M
*25..RUBY TUESDAY	THE ROLLING STONES	LONDON
*26..COME BACK HOME	CHARLIE ROMANS	HICKORY
27..LEVITATION	13th FLOOR ELEVATORS	I A
*28..THE LOSER	GARY LEWIS & PLAYBOYS	LIBERTY
*29..KIND OF A DRAG	THE BUCKINGHAMS	U S A
*30..SHOW ME	JOE TEX	DIAL
*31..LIVE	THE MERRY-GO-ROUND	A & M
*32..BEGGIN'	THE FOUR SEASONS	PHILIPS
*33..EXCUSE ME DEAR MARTHA	THE POZO SECO SINGERS	COLUMBIA
*34..BERNADETTE	THE FOUR TOPS	MOTOWN
*35..DETROIT CITY	TOM JONES	PARROT
*36..CALIFORNIA NIGHTS	LESLIE GORE	MERCURY
*37..WALKIN' IN THE SUNSHINE	ROGER MILLER	SMASH
*38..THAT ACAPULCO GOLD	THE RAINY DAZE	U N I
*39..WITH THIS RING	THE PLATTERS	MUSICOR
*40..FRIDAY ON MY MIND	THE EASYBEATS	U A

* FIRST OFFERED ON KILT

KILT DISC 'COVERY OF THE WEEK

LOVE EYES — NANCY SINATRA — REPRISE

★★★★
GREATEST LOVE (Marsaint, BMI)
OH! DARLING (Modern, BMI)
Z. Z. HILL—Kent 460.

The r/b mood is slow and full of woo. There's no way to stop this well-done cut.

★★★★
FOR HE'S A JOLLY GOOD FELLOW (Ahab, BMI)
SWEET MARIA (Roosevelt, BMI)
BOBBY VINTON—Epic 5-10136.

Story of a wedding and a triangle. Bobby will pull tears with his sensitive reading.

★★★★
LEVITATION (Tapier, BMI)
BEFORE YOU ACCUSE ME (Arc, BMI)
THE THIRTEENTH FLOOR ELEVATORS —IA 113.

Thick folk rock with psychedelic dressing up. The kids will like the aura.

★★★★
PRECIOUS MEMORIES (Naro, ASCAP)
JUICY LUCY (Naro, ASCAP)
THE ROMEOS—Mark II 1.

Already breaking in certain areas, this haunting, funky, special instrumental will be large.

Top: KILT-FM Houston's radio survey for the week of March 15–22, showing "Levitation" at #27.

Bottom: Review of the "Levitation" single in the February 25 edition of *Record World*. "The kids will like the aura."

transparency, and secure the band a livable wage while they addressed their debts to Mrs. Walton.

> JACK McCLELLAN (*1973*): My attitude towards IA was: thumbs-down on the motherfuckers. Not only were they horrendous rip-offs as a record company, they couldn't even sell any fucking records! Mechanically, they put out an inferior product. The Elevators were about all they had, so they really wanted to hang on. As their manager, I engaged a booking agent and started getting them gigs. They were unbelievably popular; everybody wanted the Elevators. Why were they such paupers? They gave up everything to this company, all rights. They were like fucking slaves! In return, the company agreed to "do the best it can"—no standards spelled out to judge the record company's performance, no standards set out for accounting, nothing!

But McClellan's legal wrangling could go only so far in addressing the band's internal issues.

> JACK McCLELLAN (*1973*): Right away, it began to be apparent that the band was composed of two factions: Emma Walton being the actual forces behind one, with John Ike and Ronnie, the other being Tommy and Roky. Stacy was the swingman. Stacy was the band. He knew what gave the band its sound. By far and away he was the best musician . . . Stacy always appeared to me as being very confused about who he was . . . Sometimes he'd say, "Tommy's ruining my life." I tried my damnedest to get Stacy on my side and he'd vacillate back and forth. I don't know what Tommy was telling him—I can only judge by what Tommy did, which was give everybody acid all the time.

> JOHN IKE: Stacy would come to me literally in tears, whimpering because he was so terrified, so incredibly freaked. And Tommy would have a long talk with him and give him some more acid.

> STACY (*K*): It's not that I felt that I had to keep taking the drug. I didn't believe the drug was bad. I believed that it was good, if you can understand that. I thought of myself as being bad, but the drug was showing me that I was bad. All the time I believed it was here through God. I believed that it was really a means by which we could tap the source.

Jack got the Elevators a new agency, Talent of Texas, which booked them in Austin for a series of shows. While the band returned to both the Doris Miller Auditorium and the City Coliseum, the multimedia shows—despite promo materials promising "Laurel and Hardy movies, psychedelic slides, oil lights and strobes"—couldn't repeat the magic of the Electric Grandmother shows' gathering of the tribes.

Above: Performing at the Living Eye Teen Club, Houston, circa late February–May 1967.

On April 30, just three days after the official launch of 13th Floor, Inc., the *Houston Post*'s Scott Holtzman reported the next stage of the band's dissolution: "Rocky [*sic*] and Tommy have exited the 13th Floor Elevators, leaving them with no lead singer."

STACY (*K*): We wanted to blow off [Tommy and Roky]—at the time it was almost sane, considering the condition everything was in. I considered it, sure, because we weren't working and the group was breaking up. I was trying to find the best path to follow. At the time, Roky was spaced out—like, I had talks with his old lady. That's when John decided that we ought to get another singer. I don't know, it went from bad to worse.

▲ **WHILE THE BATTLE FOR** legal control of the band continued, Roky and Tommy moved back to Austin. While there, they formed a writing pact to produce the grand "Work." Tommy's interest in G. I. Gurdjieff and mathematics had evolved into a wider exploration of Eastern science, philosophy, and religious mysticism, all of which he was attempting to parallel with allegorical readings of Christian texts. This would distill into what has become the band's most critically-celebrated song, "Slip Inside This House."

CLEMENTINE: Tommy and I were driving around and I said, "My favorite thing to do when I find a beautiful neighborhood like this is just to slip inside the house mentally and picture myself walking up and down the stairs, and going into the living room and having something to eat or read." I loved to slip inside people's houses. And that's where he said, "Tell me that again!" But, that being said, Tommy required very little help.

ROKY (*1973*): I was beginning to write this thing; I thought it was like Beethoven, and somehow that vision gave me the energy to write. Tommy heard what I was doing and said, "That's out of sight—can I put these words to it?" I finished the music for the piece and he did the words. I didn't understand any of what he was talking about at the time.

TOMMY: I tried to communicate, but it is true that we never—I never—sat down and, you know, explained the lyrics to him.

JOHN KEARNEY: Suddenly Roky and Tommy were living upstairs in one of those cool, old apartments on West Fifth Street. We went round to visit, and Tommy had taken a lot of acid and he was working on "Slip Inside This House," reading a book called *Secret of the Golden Flower*. And he would come out and talk to me about what he was doing and mostly you just listened—he likes to do the talking—and it all made sense at the time, but he started to project his personality to such a degree of intensity that it was very hard for Roky to be Roky. Stacy, too, was very strong—Stacy had problems with Tommy's lyrics, said they were all "negative." Like all central, rural Texas people, [Stacy's] humor was rather caustic, but he was always distant—not in a way that he wouldn't talk, he wasn't shy; it was like a black cloud enveloped Stacy.

Meanwhile, a relationship was developing between Roky and his childhood friend George Kinney's girlfriend, Dana. There had always been a strong magnetism between the two, and Roky and George had a rivalry that often led to them dating the same girls. Though it had looked like that pattern was going to perpetuate here, Dana ended up marrying George on June 17.

Dana Morris, as she appeared in the 1966 announcement of her engagement to George Kinney.

DANA MORRIS: We married when I was four months pregnant. I loved Roky, and I didn't want to be touched or moved by Roky . . . I couldn't listen to Roky's music. It hurt me. So three days after Lenicia was born—George had gone to work—it was pouring rain and she'd been crying all night. And I hear a knock and Roky's standing there smiling. I said, "The baby's crying," so he said, "Give me the baby," and Lenicia stopped crying. I was spiritually—but not physically—able to get together with Roky.

JOHN KEARNEY: I remember the boys coming back [to Austin] for a brief bit—but it didn't turn into a brief bit. Therefore [it was] the classic mistake of "the hero returns and nothing happens." Roky was with a woman called Judith; Judith was a ball of fire. Roky stayed with me—we lived with George Kinney and his wife, Dana, and things [were] decidedly unhealthy. As it turned out, Roky and Dana were trysting as George worked hard to pay the rent. I remember an aura of degeneracy.

DANA MORRIS: I didn't want to be with George, and I missed Roky, but he'd met this girl named Judith and she was his first girlfriend he could write about . . . And I didn't want to be around him . . . or see Roky happy with another woman. She should have never made the mistake of telling me she was cheating on Roky. So I went to Roky, and Tommy was in the room, and I said, "Roky, you need to know she's going behind your back and cheating on you. It's just breaking my heart that she's doing this to you."

TOMMY (*1973*): We were living in Austin and I was pumping Roky full of Sri Yukteswar Giri's *The Holy Science* book, but this chick was really being shitty to him. She was running around with someone else. It was fucking up his head—especially if you're supposed to be this really super-cool singer. It just got to him, because he's not very egotistical. He just had a groovy way of doing things; he'd go on adventures. This chick couldn't understand that. I tried to say things to her, but she was the opposite pole to Roky.

Throughout May, the band struggled on, still performing their endless residency at the Living Eye in Houston. One story perfectly illustrates their plight. Tommy and Roky were at the Ericksons' family home, with a gig booked in Houston in half an hour. It was at least a ninety-minute drive, but they had no transport, so they borrowed Evelyn's car on the pretense of going to the store to buy her some groceries. After the show, they didn't have enough gas to get back to Austin, and had no money. The only answer was to pay Lelan a visit at 2.00 a.m., palms extended. Lelan was awoken and, after some persuasion, handed out five-dollar bills before being allowed to go back to bed.

BEAU SUTHERLAND. I can't tell you how many times Stacy would tell me that they'd get a contract to appear somewhere and they'd show up, holding their breath, hoping everybody [in the band] would get there. Sometimes it would be right down to the end.

Opposite top and bottom left: Roky onstage and in the dressing room of the Living Eye Teen Club, shot by William Warner.

Opposite bottom right and following page: Performance at the Living Eye, early 1967, photographed by Russell Wheelock. Wheelock: "There really were a lot of things about them that were really excellent in concert. I wasn't there to observe them in that way, only what would make a good picture. Roky could play but he [would] not stop. I remember him standing on top of a speaker playing, and everyone was saying, 'Stop, Roky! We've been playing this tune for thirty minutes.' They could never get him to stop, and there was an audience, but he just kept on going. I knew them enough to see they were trying to stop him, but hell—he was up on top of a speaker just playing away; he didn't see why he should stop. [But] it was good music. It was great."

JACK McCLELLAN (*K*): God knows what they lived on. See, Tommy was able to go in there to IA and get these piddling little handouts—maybe fifty bucks, to last him a couple of weeks. But all seemingly cool with Tommy, since he got to buy as much acid as he wanted. What did he care about eating or paying back his debts, or that Mama Walton was out thousands? He seemed to be sold on [IA boss Noble] Ginther personally, because he'd once dropped some acid with him. By the time I latched on the band's bankroll, the pattern was already established: any time they got a couple of hundred dollars together, Tommy would fly up to San Francisco, buy a bunch of acid, and fly back. I finally indulged John Ike to the extent of letting him buy a motorcycle, just because I felt Tommy had appropriated so much of their bread. He wasn't hoarding it for himself, oh no—he was spending it on all of them. But you can see why John Ike insisted on managing the band: so he could protect his share. I was supposed to clean up all that, and what I actually did was just accelerate the process of their disintegration. All this was irrelevant to Tommy. He was willing to sell his soul for stardom; he was willing to let himself be screwed by these straight guys. John Ike wasn't, [and] Roky didn't know.

Talent of Texas, the new booking agents, found it increasingly hard to book the band, because promoters were unwilling to take the risk. They came up with a cunning solution: the agency had a cover band, Bryan's Blokes, on their roster, and they began booking them as the Elevators' support band. This effectively meant the Elevators now had understudies: if the band was late or didn't show, Bryan's Blokes performed an Elevators cover set, with

the house lights darkened and the light show redirected to blind the audience so no one could see exactly who was onstage.

> RONNIE: [At the Living Eye] there was a band—they did all Elevators stuff. This one other band just copied everything. It was kinda nice, but they'd do it and then we'd play . . . that was kinda weird.

Ultimately, this scheme may have been a little too successful: Bryan's Blokes eventually began taking outside bookings as an Elevators cover band, and the situation became so confusing that some advertisements had to expressly reference "the original 13th Floor Elevators."

▲ **THE ELEVATORS'** confinement in Texas did not mean that their legal troubles were behind them, and on May 19, the cops decided to execute an arrest warrant for Stacy just as the Elevators were striking up the second song of their set.

> JOHN IKE: At the Living Eye [IA] hired an ex-narcotics cop to stay with us to keep the other ones away. The cop we had was in the dressing room while we were onstage, so the Houston vice squad comes in and arrests Stacy off [the] stage for possession of marijuana!

> STACY (*1977*): I had [police] jump up onstage and grab me when I was playing, right in the middle of "Fire Engine." I handed one of them my guitar; it was turned up full blast, it started screaming—he didn't know what to do with it. And they took me through the crowd, and [the crowd] started throwing Coke cups and stuff at them and started rushing at them, and they freaked out and pulled their guns and backed out to the car. And it really upset this one cop—man, he freaked out, because he thought they were going to mob him. And I was on acid and my head's spinning 'round. He got me in the car and he said, "I'm going to take you outside of the town, and I'm going to kill you. And I'm going to tell them downtown that you tried to take my gun away from me, punk." And he'd [lunge] at me, you know, and I'd jump and see stars . . . I didn't think they were really going to do it, but I was so freaked out on acid, man. When we turned out on the freeway heading out of Houston, I freaked out. I started saying, "Now wait a minute man, can we calm it down?" [*Laughs*] I freaked . . . They took me out of town and turned around. They just wanted to shake me up, and they knew I was on acid.

> Q: Bet you were really glad to get to a police station.

> STACY (*1977*): Oh yeah.

LELAN ROGERS: I know that Stacy got busted and Noble Ginther made some arrangements to get him set free, and it cost a lot of money. The big drain on IA was constantly trying to fight the law enforcement because the Elevators—they were not cooperating. They did what they wanted to do regardless, and it was always costing a lot of money. If there was any records of it, they would probably owe the record company forty or fifty thousand dollars, because [IA was] paying them a salary and paying their rent, they were feeding them, they were paying the studio time, they were leasing equipment.

Ginther tried and failed to get Stacy out on bond—set this time at $5,000—in time for the band's scheduled appearance on *The Larry Kane Show* the following morning, Saturday, May 20. As word had spread of Stacy's arrest, everyone tuned in to see if he'd been released. The band attempted to perform "Don't Fall Down," but Stacy's absence meant that Roky fluffed miming Stacy's guitar intro. "Never quite sure," as Kane put it after the performance. "Never quite sure that this is it."

Advertisement for the Doris Miller show in the April 13 *Daily Texan*.

Advertisement for the City Coliseum "All Night Round-Up Party," April 14.

EMMA WALTON (*K*): Roky is eternally fresh-faced and young. Neither he nor his mother will ever grow up. He is certainly artistic and poetic, but at the same time he has no mentality at all—as far as the logistics of becoming a successful performer goes. He goes into a strange state of high exhilaration, but he can go down into a state of severe depression just as abruptly. As for the boys, they each had a touch of fame out there in California, and I think it had great impact on each of them—perhaps, in John's case, to his detriment. I think if John hadn't had to hassle with IA so much about money, then he'd have been more inclined to go along with Tommy, but the constant conflict just made him a nervous wreck.

STACY (*K*): John Ike really felt bad because he didn't take acid. He was secretly ashamed—he wanted to take it but he was deathly afraid of it, and I could understand why.

JOHN IKE (*1973*): I couldn't believe the other guys weren't in the same condition I was when I took that stuff. I knew one thing—my mind was wasted and my body was wracked, and I had died and gone to heaven, the very first time. It was Tommy's trip that nobody could be a whole meaningful person unless he took psychedelic drugs . . . that was his hold on the band. Roky was going crazy, Stacy was going crazy, and I said, "Fuck you, man," but all Tommy could say was, "This band isn't just a way to make a living, it's a way of life."

RONNIE: [The biggest problem] was Tommy's idea that everybody ought to take acid all the time, especially when we played or practiced. We had been working out at Stacy's ranch, at the

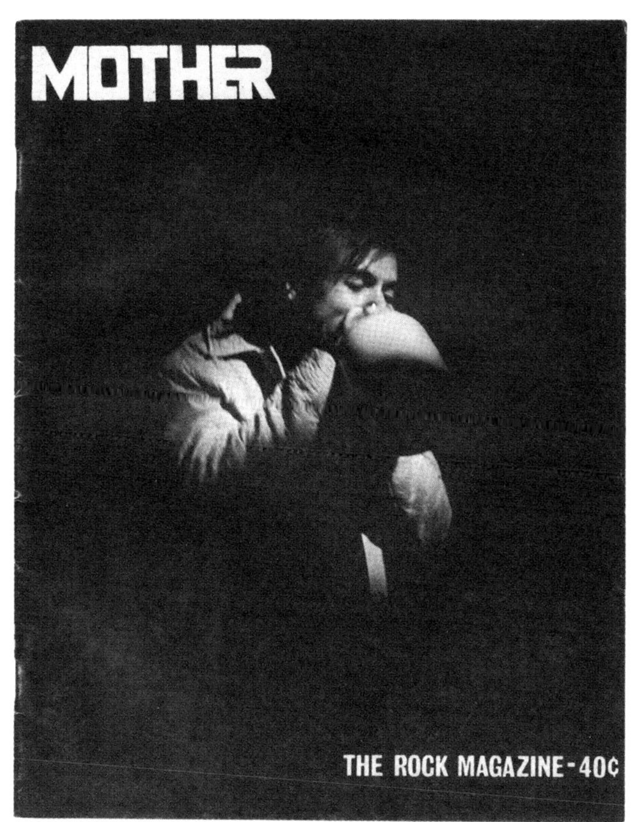

THE SMOLDERING BANANA PEEL

PRESENTS

THE 13th FLOOR ELVATORS

THE WIG

AND

THE GENTLE DEBACLE
PSYCHEDELIC LIGHT SHOW

AT DORIS MILLER
AUDITORIUM

THURSDAY NIGHT
APRIL 13
8:00 P. M.

Top left: William Warner's photo of Tommy gracing the cover of *Mother* #3, the final issue of Larry Sepulvado's Houston music fanzine.

Top right: Handbill for the Smoldering Banana Peel show at Doris Miller Auditorium, April 13.

hunting cabin, on "Slip Inside This House," and on all the other songs, but we never got to record them. We were trying to get Stacy and everybody to split with us, 'cause if we would have just held out . . . you know, a lot of ifs. There was a deal where Elektra Records wanted to buy us and offered, I think, $100,000, and IA didn't want [to] sell. But then [IA] promised that they'd get [the band] out on the road soon and bought them all new equipment: Standel amps, newer models than we had. And then three months later they took it all back. I just didn't trust them.

JACK McCLELLAN (*1973*): I have no evidence that they had serious discussion with any big record companies. I do recall having talked with one gentleman who indicated, "Yeah, if you can get them loose from International Artists, we'd be very interested."

In lieu of an East Coast tour and to break the impasse of the Living Eye residency, the band had been tentatively booking shows back on the West Coast. Chet Helms, clearly uncertain about the Elevators' ability to fulfill a headline booking, gave them a support slot with the Charlatans in late June. However, the real opportunity lost was the chance to perform at the massive Magic Mountain Festival in Marin County, where the band had been booked for June 10. Staged a week before the Monterey Pop Festival, this ambitious event drew an attendance of 30–40,000. Now regarded as the first full-scale rock festival, it featured the Doors, the Byrds, Jefferson Airplane, Captain Beefheart, the Seeds, and the Chocolate Watchband—among the best bands of the era.

While John Ike and Ronnie had previously hoped to get Stacy to split with them and reform the band in San Francisco, his recent arrest had violated his parole. This was the final straw for them, and, on July 6, the Elevators' classic lineup unceremoniously performed its last show together, back where it had all started, at the Jade Room.

In a familiar pattern, while the so-called Summer of Love took off in San Francisco, "the pioneers of psychedelic rock" (or what was left of them) retreated, spending the summer on a remote hilltop in Kerrville rehearsing a new rhythm section, before returning to Houston—this time, to record Tommy's masterwork.

Opposite top: Tommy and Ronnie onstage during the Elevators' penultimate show at the Living Eye Teen Club, May 19, 1967.

Bottom: The band plays along to "Don't Fall Down" on *The Larry Kane Show* minus Stacy, who had been arrested onstage at the Living Eye the previous night. March 20, 1967, 11:30 a.m. Betty Shumate: "We all enjoyed the Larry Kane TV show; we were grooving and dancing so often. The camera was part of the whole experience."

Top: The band with Ronnie's VW bug in the Living Eye parking lot, May 19, 1967. William Warner: "[This] was taken about an hour before Stacy was hauled off the stage by the Houston cops and busted. This happened on a Friday, as I recall. Although they completed the weekend gig, I think that was the last time they played that club."

Opposite top: Stacy onstage at the Living Eye. William Warner: "Stacy with freshly shorn hair . . . taken the day after the bust when the band was back at the Living Eye to play that night: May 20, 1967."

Opposite center and bottom: Performing at the Living Eye, shot by William Warner. Warner: "When I ran into the Elevators, it coincided with when I decided to quit going to school. I started living at the Living Eye . . . I think I saw every show [there]. The band at the Living Eye was still a really tight kick-ass band; they very much had it together. I think Roky and Stacy had a few problems, but Ronnie and John Ike were always on it and managed to start and end the songs properly. There was never any gross screwing up, which you saw later."

Above and opposite: Possibly the last photos of the classic lineup, shot by Betty Shumate at the Bellaire Gymnasium, May 27, 1967. Shumate: "I took the photos because they were my favorite band. I followed them wherever they went. The photos were tucked in with my photos of other bands I enjoyed as a teenager. I didn't take many, but I cherished those I did take. I'm especially excited about getting Roky in mid-scream! They were icons to all of us who were teenagers at the time. They were probably the most popular band in the state of Texas."

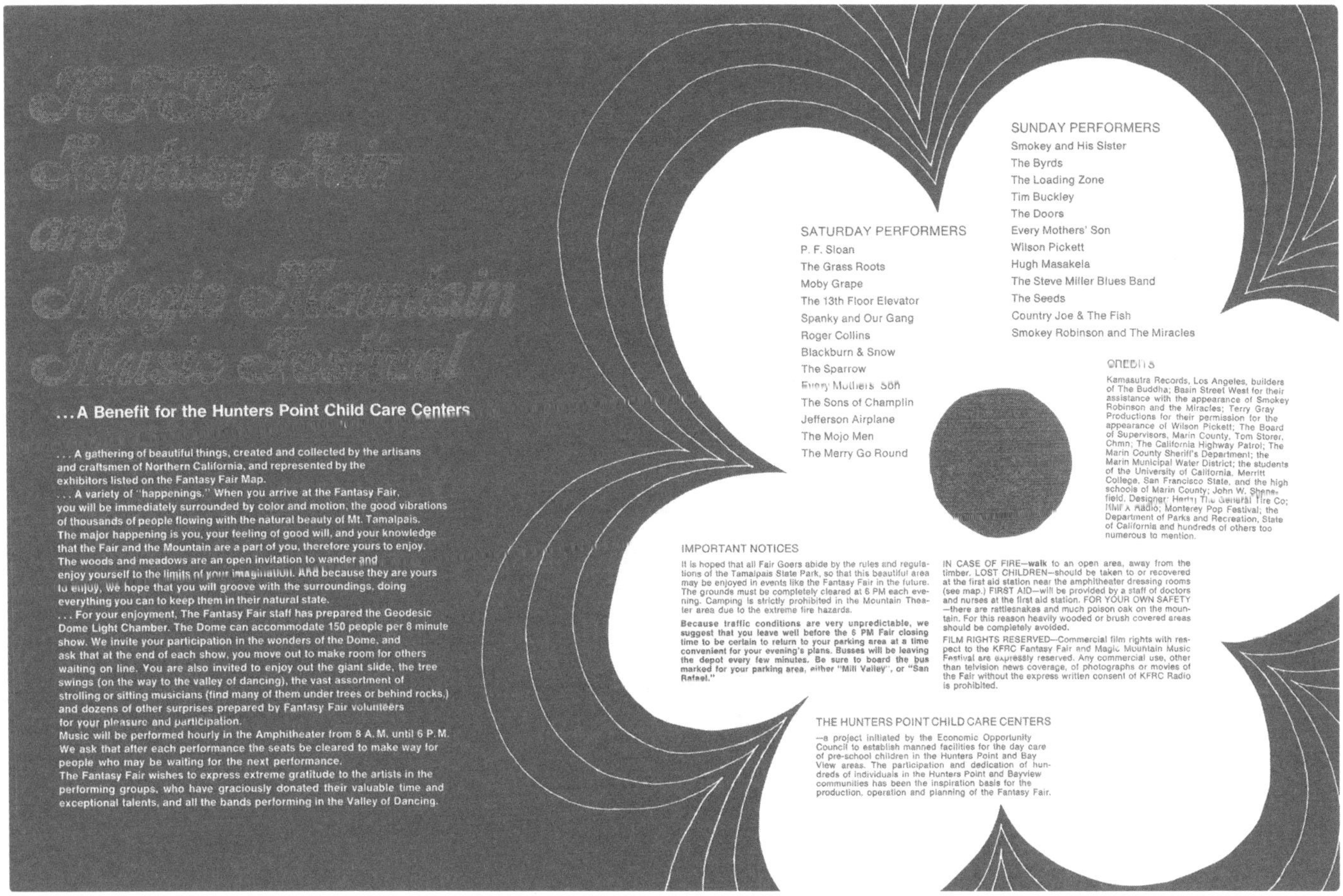

KFRC Fantasy Fair and Magic Mountain Music Festival

...A Benefit for the Hunters Point Child Care Centers

... A gathering of beautiful things, created and collected by the artisans and craftsmen of Northern California, and represented by the exhibitors listed on the Fantasy Fair Map.

... A variety of "happenings." When you arrive at the Fantasy Fair, you will be immediately surrounded by color and motion, the good vibrations of thousands of people flowing with the natural beauty of Mt. Tamalpais. The major happening is you, your feeling of good will, and your knowledge that the Fair and the Mountain are a part of you, therefore yours to enjoy. The woods and meadows are an open invitation to wander and enjoy yourself to the limits of your imagination. And because they are yours to enjoy, we hope that you will groove with the surroundings, doing everything you can to keep them in their natural state.

... For your enjoyment, The Fantasy Fair staff has prepared the Geodesic Dome Light Chamber. The Dome can accommodate 150 people per 8 minute show. We invite your participation in the wonders of the Dome, and ask that at the end of each show, you move out to make room for others waiting on line. You are also invited to enjoy out the giant slide, the tree swings (on the way to the valley of dancing), the vast assortment of strolling or sitting musicians (find many of them under trees or behind rocks,) and dozens of other surprises prepared by Fantasy Fair volunteers for your pleasure and participation.

Music will be performed hourly in the Amphitheater from 8 A.M. until 6 P.M. We ask that after each performance the seats be cleared to make way for people who may be waiting for the next performance.

The Fantasy Fair wishes to express extreme gratitude to the artists in the performing groups, who have graciously donated their valuable time and exceptional talents, and all the bands performing in the Valley of Dancing.

SATURDAY PERFORMERS

P. F. Sloan
The Grass Roots
Moby Grape
The 13th Floor Elevator
Spanky and Our Gang
Roger Collins
Blackburn & Snow
The Sparrow
Every Mothers' Son
The Sons of Champlin
Jefferson Airplane
The Mojo Men
The Merry Go Round

SUNDAY PERFORMERS

Smokey and His Sister
The Byrds
The Loading Zone
Tim Buckley
The Doors
Every Mothers' Son
Wilson Pickett
Hugh Masakela
The Steve Miller Blues Band
The Seeds
Country Joe & The Fish
Smokey Robinson and The Miracles

CREDITS

Kamasutra Records, Los Angeles, builders of The Buddha; Basin Street West for their assistance with the appearance of Smokey Robinson and the Miracles; Terry Gray Productions for their permission for the appearance of Wilson Pickett; The Board of Supervisors, Marin County, Tom Storer, Chmn; The California Highway Patrol; The Marin County Sheriff's Department; the Marin Municipal Water District; the students of the University of California, Merritt College, San Francisco State, and the high schools of Marin County; John W. Shenefield, Designer; Herty; The General Tire Co; KMPX Radio; Monterey Pop Festival; the Department of Parks and Recreation, State of California and hundreds of others too numerous to mention.

IMPORTANT NOTICES

It is hoped that all Fair Goers abide by the rules and regulations of the Tamalpais State Park, so that this beautiful area may be enjoyed in events like the Fantasy Fair in the future. The grounds must be completely cleared at 6 PM each evening. Camping is strictly prohibited in the Mountain Theater area due to the extreme fire hazards.

Because traffic conditions are very unpredictable, we suggest that you leave well before the 6 PM Fair closing time to be certain to return to your parking area at a time convenient for your evening's plans. Busses will be leaving the depot every few minutes. Be sure to board the bus marked for your parking area, either "Mill Valley", or "San Rafael."

IN CASE OF FIRE—**walk** to an open area, away from the timber. LOST CHILDREN—should be taken to or recovered at the first aid station near the amphitheater dressing rooms (see map.) FIRST AID—will be provided by a staff of doctors and nurses at the first aid station. FOR YOUR OWN SAFETY —there are rattlesnakes and much poison oak on the mountain. For this reason heavily wooded or brush covered areas should be completely avoided.

FILM RIGHTS RESERVED—Commercial film rights with respect to the KFRC Fantasy Fair and Magic Mountain Music Festival are expressly reserved. Any commercial use, other than telvision news coverage, of photographs or movies of the Fair without the express written consent of KFRC Radio is prohibited.

THE HUNTERS POINT CHILD CARE CENTERS

—a project initiated by the Economic Opportunity Council to establish manned facilities for the day care of pre-school children in the Hunters Point and Bay View areas. The participation and dedication of hundreds of individuals in the Hunters Point and Bayview communities has been the inspiration basis for the production, operation and planning of the Fantasy Fair.

Top: An opportunity missed: the band was booking its return to the West Coast at the height of the Summer of Love, as attested to by this poster/flier for KRFC Radio's ambitious Magic Mountain Music Festival, June 10–11, 1967.

Bottom: Poster for another return booking at the Avalon Ballroom—although Tommy later maintained that he would never have played alongside a band called "the Charlatans"—slated for June 1967. Mayo Thompson (of the Red Crayola): "We cooled our heels on Chet Helms's couch outside his office one afternoon, [and] couldn't help overhearing him talking to someone about the Elevators and their travel problems. As Mr. Helms's conversation seemed to go on . . . we left."

V

SLIP INSIDE THIS HOUSE

The Work

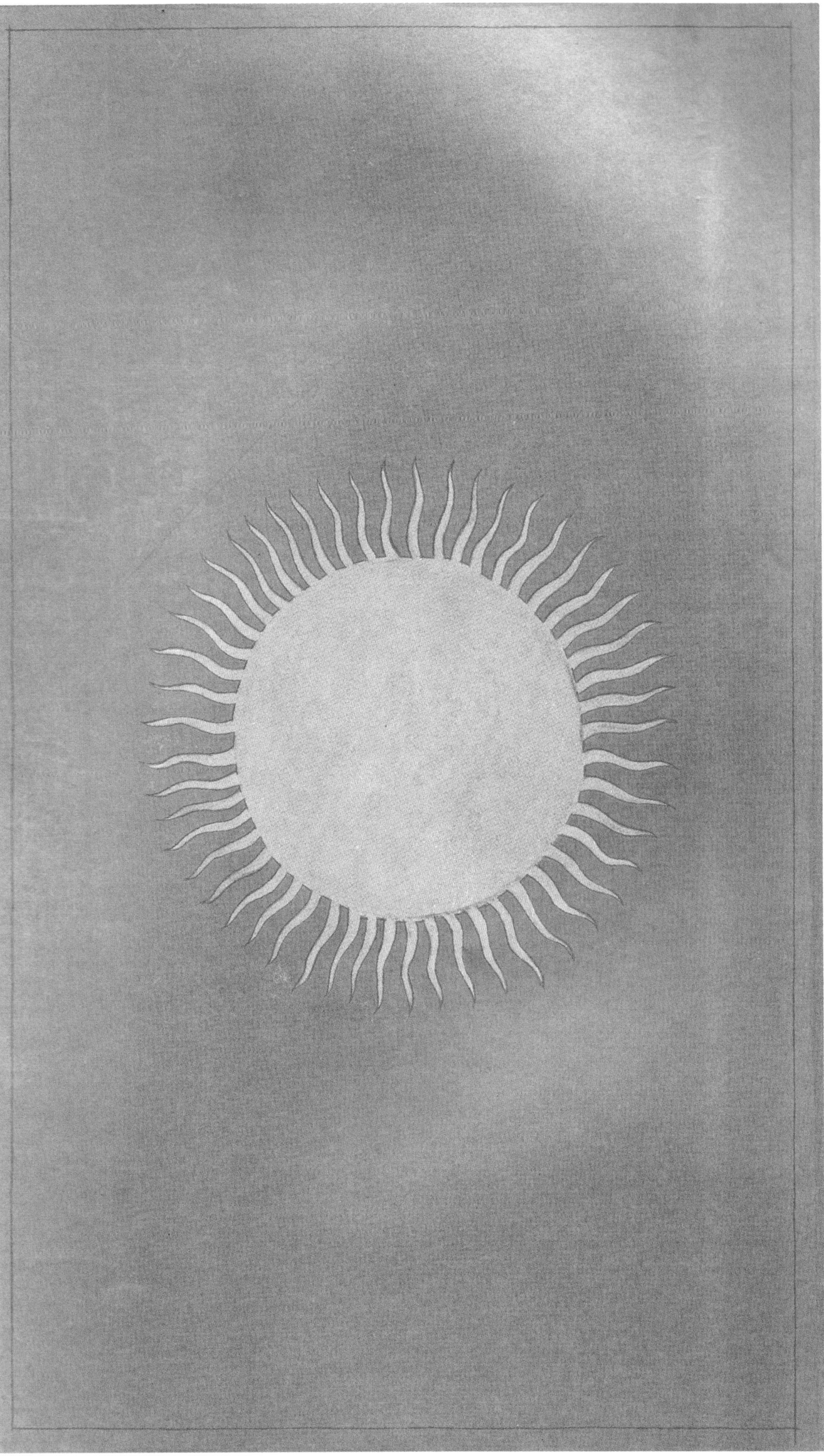

In mid-April 1967, Danny Galindo agreed to split the gas money with his friend Danny Thomas to drive from San Antonio to hear the Elevators play at the Doris Miller in Austin.

> DANNY GALINDO: I was a really big fan. Most of the time I was standing there with my chin on my collar, going, "Wow!" It was not just a band playing; the whole thing was an experience. It was all happening between the people in the crowd, and that's where the cultist thing came from: to make contact with human beings based on a totally nonverbal communication. That was an experience.

> DANNY THOMAS: My roommate invited me to go to Austin to hear the Elevators play at Doris Miller. That was the first and only time I ever heard the original band. I had never met any of them before.

En route, Galindo stopped off at a little hillside rail house on Riverside to score something for the concert. There, the "two Dannys" (as they soon became known) got involved in a jam session: Galindo on bass, Thomas on drums, and a mystery guitarist who'd thundered up on a motorbike, also looking to score before the concert.

> DANNY GALINDO: Stacy walked in the door and we didn't know who he was . . . So he pulled out his guitar and we kept on jamming. As I remember it, it was magic. I was totally blown away—that's probably one of the times I really impressed myself. Later that night, we went to the Elevators concert and the whole time I was digging them, but thinking, "Goddamn, man, there's no way in the world this band sounds as good as Stacy and Danny and me a few hours ago." I had had the foresight to give Stacy my name and Danny Thomas's phone number. A month later, I'm at school at Southwest Texas [State College], and Stacy calls. "Hey guys, would you guys be interested in playing with us? Can you be down here next week?" I said, "I'll tell you what, I can be down there this evening!"

At nineteen, Danny Galindo already considered himself a veteran of the Texas music scene. Born in San Antonio on June 29, 1949, he'd moved to

Opposite: Plate 36 from page 61 of *Tantra Art: Its Philosophy and Physics* by Ajit Mookerjee. The image, selected by Tommy while staying at the Western Skies motel during the *Easter Everywhere* sessions, was later redrawn by George Banks, aka "Flash Graphics," for that album's cover art. "Jyoti or light. Tempera painting in gold. Deccani school. C.18th century A.D. Light is the radiant manifestation of energy. The visible universe is the panorama of reflected forms created and produced by light. Private collection."

Austin to pursue a nursing degree with extra courses in dentistry, biology, and music. Inspired by the black music emitting from the radio circa 1962–63, he'd bought himself a Takamine electric bass and rented an amp.

Danny Thomas was born January 15, 1948, in Charlotte, North Carolina. Despite a formal musical training in the rudiments of composition, he, like Galindo, was mainly influenced by soul music, and had toured the Carolinas between 1960 and 1964 drumming with the Caravelles and spent two years in the Midwest with the Soul Brothers, opening for acts like Curtis Mayfield and the Impressions. After commencing his studies at Trinity College, San Antonio, in 1966, Thomas met and began performing with Galindo in impromptu jazz combos at pickup gigs outside cafes.

> DANNY THOMAS: I was caught between the military draft and life on campus; neither appealed to me. The call [came] from International Artists in Houston, to come to interview for the job as the Elevators' new drummer. I was in the car headed for Houston within an hour. I met the band the same day, at Noble Ginther's law office in downtown Houston. I arrived dressed in a coat and tie with shiny shoes and the guys in the band were in jeans and leather with Indian beads and cowboy boots. I had only smoked pot a few times, and had never taken drugs. I never auditioned; Roky and Tommy took Stacy's recommendation without question. We just drove to Kerrville [to Stacy's family ranch] and went to work. It was a magic summer.

For Stacy, making a proper album meant recording in a studio in Nashville, but he was persuaded by Tommy to stay in Houston to lay down the band's second record: Tommy's projected masterpiece, *Easter Everywhere*. Tommy had struck a deal with IA to fund a full month at Andrus Studios, which had been upgraded since their last session there to an eight-track recording desk. Being given time and the technical means to experiment in the studio appealed to Stacy—it was the next best thing to Nashville.

The Beatles released *Sgt. Pepper's Lonely Hearts Club Band* on May 26, 1967, marking the start of what would be known as the Summer of Love and of psychedelia as an international phenomenon. While the Beatles collected kudos, however, the 13th Floor Elevators, pioneers of the genre, retired to Stacy's family ranch in Texas Hill Country to rehearse, prep for the upcoming recording sessions, and play cat-and-mouse with local law enforcement.

> DANNY GALINDO: I thought Tommy Hall was very eccentric, and really my relationship with Tommy and Roky was very distant. I think they felt we were filling in. It was a real loss to them to lose John and Ronnie. First of all, they were an incredible part of their sound; second of all, they had played with them a long time. So Danny Thomas and I had huge shoes to fill. We did the best we could; but in the process, the sound of our music changed.

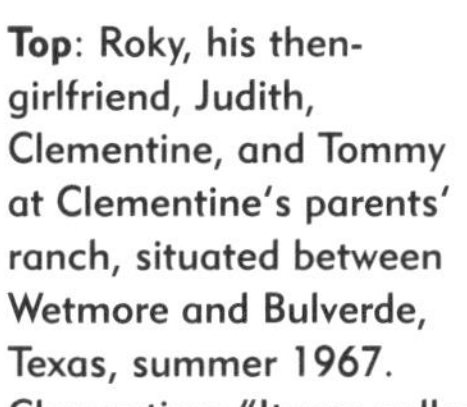

Top: Roky, his then-girlfriend, Judith, Clementine, and Tommy at Clementine's parents' ranch, situated between Wetmore and Bulverde, Texas, summer 1967. Clementine: "It was called 'Still Waters Ranch,' named by my parents after the creek that ran through it, as in 'He leadeth me beside the still waters.'"

Bottom: Danny Galindo, circa 1965.

DANNY THOMAS: The first night at Stacy's ranch, Roky played his guitar from dusk till dawn, on ten! I had never been in a band like this before. I was trying to lay down on my bunk and get some sleep. After going through that on my first night, anything after that was, "Well, this is the trip!"

STACY (*K*): We had a bunch of material, but if strange musicians get together, it takes months before they can really communicate. We didn't have time to get into each other's groove. It was much more mechanical, from that point on, than the original group. I think they saw it entirely as, "We have a record going." I don't think either of them were really interested in the trip at all.

DANNY GALINDO: By the time I got started, Roky was in the state where he couldn't tell me the chords to his tunes. Man, it was so hard for me. See, all the drummer had to worry about was tempo; I had to be there on every beat, you know, like [every] note. I had an incredibly tough time. Instead of telling me the chords, Roky would show me the position he was in, and I'd go, "Well, good?" It was never the same, but I became pretty good at reading him, so I could figure out when to get there by watching the guy's hand. Sometimes he could not remember the words, and he could not remember where he was at in the song. So it was very difficult to learn the material.

DANNY THOMAS: Roky's guitar playing adds something from another realm, something I can't describe. I'm a theoretically trained musician, and I know arranging; I'm not just a drummer who keeps the beat. Roky was self-taught to the point where he played what sounded good, even if he didn't know what the name of the chord was—but he would remember it. And it was absolutely avant-garde and way ahead of its time and unique in itself. In his rhythm playing, he's sort of like an invisible guitar player, but that gave it an "Elevator" feel—when you heard the first few seconds, you knew it was the Elevators. The reason why it should be credited to Roky [was] because it was a "wall of sound" approach, which was very difficult for me to get used to at first. John Ike used to drop by to check on our progress, and he and I became great friends. They were just used to the drummer taking the lead and keeping up, and whenever it started to lag, he would push them further and they would step up again. That was where they got their energy from. I got my energy from premeditated arrangements with planned hook lines and changes—what I call "stops, pops, and turnarounds"—so they had to adapt to my style, as well as me having to adapt to their style. I was a theoretically trained drummer who came from funksville, with a lot of syncopation—not just hellbent thrashing at the drums like John Ike. These musicians had never played with a drummer like me before, so they didn't know what was going on. "Slip Inside This House" gave me the opportunity to prove myself, and I kept it rock-steady through the whole song, but kept it edgy.

JOHN IKE: [Ronnie and I] took a lead guitar player with us [to San Francisco]: Johnny Richardson [from Austin band the Wig] and tried to get something going with different bands, but none of them panned out. He'd just got married, and he left his wife to go out there to hang out with a rock 'n' roll band. And she called him and said, you know, "Either get home or stay out there." [*Laughs*] He went back home.

RONNIE: I had an offer to play with [folk rock band] the Grass Roots . . . they were looking for a bass player, but I was still sticking with John Ike and trying to do something with him. I probably should have gone with them, because the next month they had a big hit.

DANA MORRIS: After I left George, Roky and I headed for Kerrville. George came to find us, and we're living in this hotel, taking acid, having the best time—teaching me the lotus position and how to leave my body. It was beautiful. We started getting a lot of flak because I'd left my baby with her father; the world was coming down on us, all our friends—a big scandal. People started coming 'round, friends from my old school, and they were going to beat Roky up—about eight of them. This is a small town, and they wanted to make sure I'm okay. Roky's in there washing dishes, so I say, "Everything's great—I'm with the man I love."

Meanwhile, the scene at the Sutherland ranch saw Stacy's family intersecting with the decidedly less sociable Tommy.

SIBYL SUTHERLAND: That was the weirdest boy I ever knew in my life. He was rude. I would try and talk to him, because I wanted to know something about him—after all, I was treating him. I would come and say something to him, and he would be reading some weighty tome, and he'd get up, close his book, and walk out. Just ignore me, like I wasn't worth answering, until I was just seething at him. Tommy picked up a roach and ate it—"It's just protein." If he hadn't got in there, [John Ike and the band] might have made it. Nobody knew anything about LSD at the time. They thought they'd discovered some great thing, where you could learn in minutes what it took a lifetime to learn; that it went through the cortex of your brain, and you would gain all this instant information . . . While they were out at the ranch, I was buying food and taking it out, but

WU 4178 (R 9-54) THE WESTERN UNION TELEGRAPH COMPANY

RECEIPT 1967 AUG 22 PM 3 07

OFFICE DATE 19

RECEIVED FROM International Artist

ADDRESS 1005 Americana Bldg CA81244

Fifty and no/100 Dollars $ 50.00

☐ Account for the month of 19

☒ Telegraphic Money Order

☐ Telegram or Cable

☐ Deposit on Collect Telegram Returnable after 24 hours

☐ Account No. FOR REMITTANCE

TO Tommy Hall

Address 413 Waterstreet

Place Kerrville Tx

MONEY ORDER CHARGES PAID	
Chgs	$ 80
Tolls	$ 149
Tax	$
TOTAL	$ 229

CR596

THE WESTERN UNION TELEGRAPH COMPANY

BY L Gehins

LUXURIOUS RI 7-2300

WESTERN SKIES MOTEL

Ike Fyfe

MANAGER

2806 OLD SPANISH TRAIL
HOUSTON, TEXAS

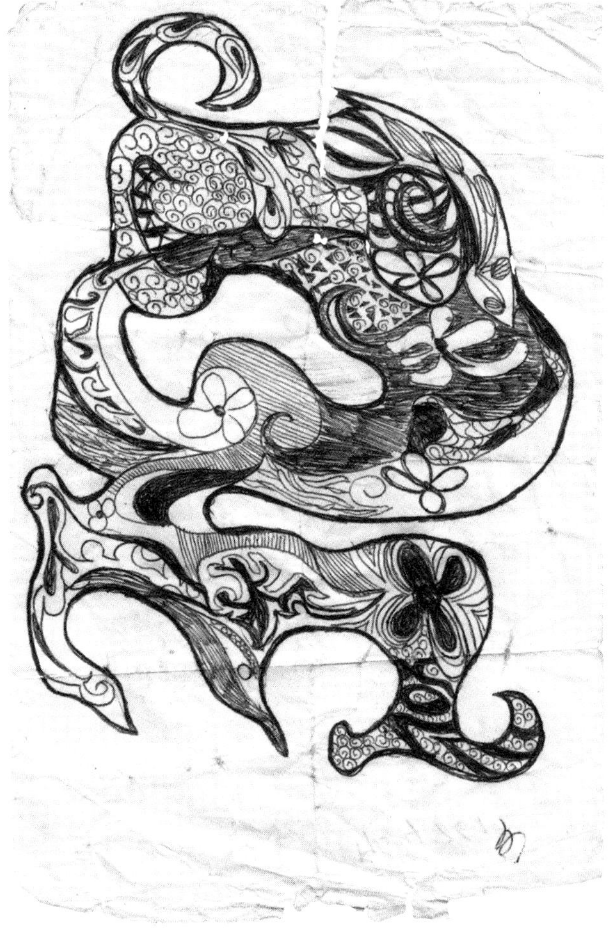

Top: International Artists' $50 album advance, wired to Tommy at Stacy's parents' address on August 22—basically, fuel money to get the band to Houston for the *Easter Everywhere* sessions.

Bottom left: Stacy's business card for the "luxurious" Western Skies Motel, where the band stayed for the *Easter Everywhere* sessions. Bobby Rector: "To show how bad this motel was—we checked under the bed to make sure we hadn't left anything and there was something under there so we pulled it out, it was a potato that had been growing in the mud and dust and had taken root in the carpet!"

Bottom right: Stacy Sutherland doodle with address for Houston's Western Skies Motel on reverse.

they would leave all the lids off the jelly jars and they would drink tea all day, which was alright by me, except they spilt it: sugar and tea all over the floor, and you stuck when you walked. I'd go out there and mop and mop, I'd find cups and things under trees . . . irresponsible. Finally, my husband told them to leave, and they left some appliance plugged in, and it burned and melted and it could have burned the whole house up.

▲ **THE PROCESS** of making the *Psychedelic Sounds* album had been one of simply documenting material that had been honed for six months on the live circuit. If it was any one member's album, it was Roky's; while supposedly a psychedelic album, his performances were way ahead of the time, making it more of a raw, almost punk recording. Although the new album was to be a showcase for Tommy's pathway to enlightenment (which had been denied him on the previous LP), Stacy would be the architect of the band's sound—his reward for staying. It would be recorded his way, with each instrument tracked separately, so that the final arrangements could be determined during mixing.

RUSSELL WHEELOCK: It was a heavy drug time. [They were] just stoned all the time when they were doing that album. Especially Roky, he was freaked; the bass player and the drummer weren't near as bad. The Elevators could play quite well stoned, but when you're in the studio, it requires more than just playing: making decisions and going back over things, and of course, they never played the same thing the same way twice. Stacy, as well as the drummer, were particularly exasperated because they couldn't get everybody to go—they'd get going and then somebody else was having some other kind of a problem.

WALT ANDRUS: I'm not someone who glorifies the drug culture; I never did do acid. I remember Tommy'd come through, and Roky would be sittin' on the couch, and he'd open his mouth, and Tommy would just throw stuff in. But they were burning it just so bright that everybody thought it was wonderful. They pretty well were organic in the way that they did things, and experimented with the sounds in the studio. Tommy tried to act like the czar of everything, but it pretty well gelled.

DANNY GALINDO: I think Frank [Davis, engineer] was frantic—we were impossible to work with and he had to work with us. He was in a very compromised situation; he recognized what was happening but he didn't act on it or speak on it. His body language told me that recording this album was driving him nuts, because he could hear a lot of things none of us wanted to hear. He had a more realistic perspective, and what sounded good to us sounded like shit to him. So, by the time you put all these tracks together, they sounded like a cacophony. There was always some sort of unrest, constant negative vibes; it was there all the time. Roky's guitar was so loud in there that you can't hear it. Roky wouldn't talk to me in a rational manner. He'd do things that made me mad, like hiding behind the amps. In the studio he seemed kind of lost; he'd gone beyond the point of being together, and a lot of what we were doing didn't make sense to him a lot of the time.

FRANK DAVIS: Stacy wrote the guitar parts, and he had a real definite flavor that was unlike everyone else's. Stacy was kind of down to earth, I guess—more than anyone else, but he could certainly get whacked out. In some ways he was the most traditional. Although the bass player and the drummer were great, they didn't have to do too much work. Stacy, Tommy, and Roky were really the nugget of it.

The band was under-rehearsed, and the new material still not fully developed; the resulting recordings lacked dynamic spontaneity. The solution was to perform the album live, then to meticulously overdub each instrument. Lelan, ostensibly still the producer, did little more than babysit them in the studio and make sure company time and money wasn't wasted.

STACY (*K*): Lelan was an ol' cat—he was the Silver Fox, he had those white shoes on, you know? He'd smoke weed with us. He didn't want [Dillard and Ginther] to know; he'd say, "Don't tell on me." I liked Lelan. He'd stand in on all our sessions. He really knew we were getting a bum deal, and really hated it, but he was providing for his kids.

Q: Did he ever do psychedelics?

STACY (*K*): No, he never did turn on acid.

LELAN ROGERS: Tommy, I remember, put a little acid in my cup of coffee while we was recording, and Stacy told me about it, said, "Don't mess with it, because that'll really put you in a different place." And I didn't, and I really got after Tommy after that. So what? We all got along good. They were just kids of the sixties.

However amicable Lelan found the band's approach, the usual agitation between members soon resurfaced.

DANNY GALINDO: It was tense between Roky and Tommy. Tommy wanted to be in control and wanted Roky to accept everything he suggested. Roky, having a mind of his own, didn't always agree with whatever Tommy was trying to get across.

Above: Lelan Rogers, Tommy, Roky, Danny Thomas, Stacy, and Danny Galindo during the *Easter Everywhere* sessions, held at Houston's Andrus Studios from August 25 to September 25, 1967.

Opposite, above, and bottom right: Tommy, Stacy, and Danny Galindo during the *Easter Everywhere* sessions.

Left and bottom: The two Dannys during the recording of *Easter Everywhere* in August and September. Photographer Russell Wheelock: "I knew Tommy while I was at university. While I was teaching in Houston, that's when the Elevators were doing their record in Houston and I went and photographed them . . . Guy [Clark, the other photographer present] might remember more, but we were there a substantial amount of time. I was focused on doing the pictures and I loved to go hear them because I really do think they were way ahead of their time."

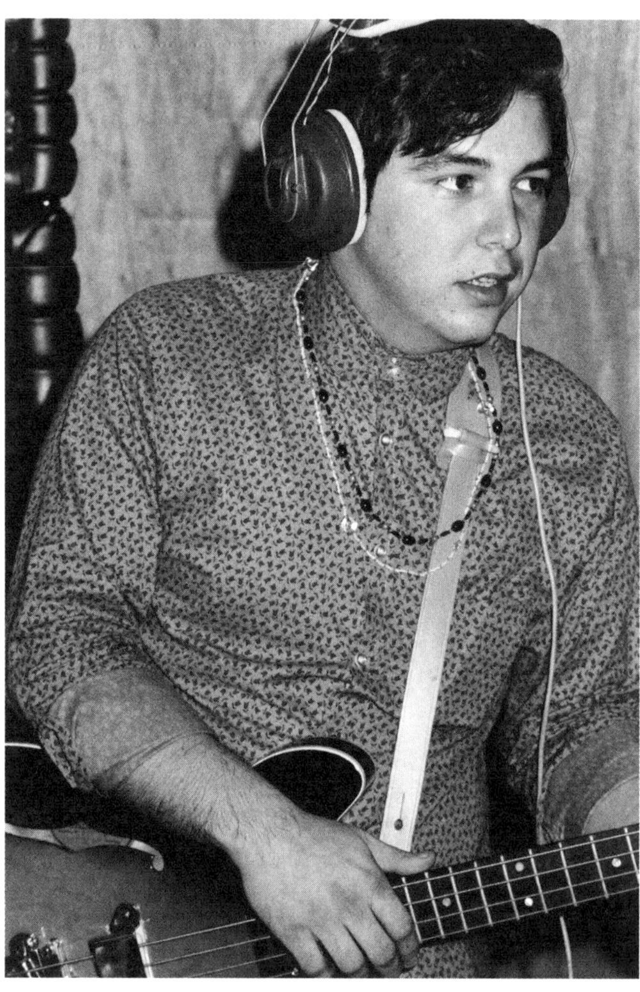

I felt Tommy's suggestions weren't always appropriate. [For instance] Roky couldn't learn the new lyrics, [and then] he'd learn them and Tommy would hand him a note and go, "No, do it this way." [*Laughs*] I could sense ol' Roky thinking, "You dumbass, I just got these old ones learnt and now you say, 'No, no, no, do these.'" I remember Stacy'd jump all over Tommy Hall when he'd do that: "Goddamn it Tommy! It's good enough! Can't you just leave it alone?"

ROKY (*1975*): When I first started [in the band], we were playing all this screaming feedback and everything, and now all we're doing is just "Slip Inside This House." There isn't enough feedback, and there isn't enough excitement in it. But the idea is captured. The Who came out with "Can't Explain," and they have lots of feedback and fantastic drumming, and they quit doing that and start doing stuff like "Tommy," and you're let down from it.

FRANK DAVIS: Tommy Hall never confronted me; I guess he thought everything, in this department, was taken care of. [But] on Roky's vocals, he would be right in his ear while he was doing it. The funny thing about it was, he was mostly right. I kind of hate that. He was the least musical, but he could hear the tone of voice, and not the interpretation, but the projected image from the timbre of the voice. He was great at it. The way I understand it, everything was symbolic; if you had come in off the street, you wouldn't have any idea what they were talking about. It would be just dope talk. Boy, I tell you, when they would be discussing the problems of the delivery of certain voice lines, it was like listening to Chinese verbiage. It was incredible, and if you ever caught a thread of where they were going, I swear, your feet would get off the ground. It was the most amazing experience, because they totally talked in these amazing analogies that were just extraordinary. Tommy had the words, [but] Roky could have read the dictionary and just given you chills.

STACY (*K*): It cramped [Roky], though. 'Cuz he's soulful, and Roky's used to rock 'n' roll all his life; he used his voice like an instrument, but when he's having to pronounce certain words and so forth, it's like he's having to read from an encyclopedia, you know? It's hard to find his vocal.

Tommy had become obsessed with every detail of Roky's vocal delivery: not just the pitch, tone, or timbre of his voice, but the very pronunciation of each word, any deviation in which could have potentially altered the semiotic or allegorical understanding of his precious lyrics, which had become heavily condensed esoteric aphorisms. The pressure was untenable; the situation eventually got so intense for Roky that he physically attacked Tommy and walked out of a session.

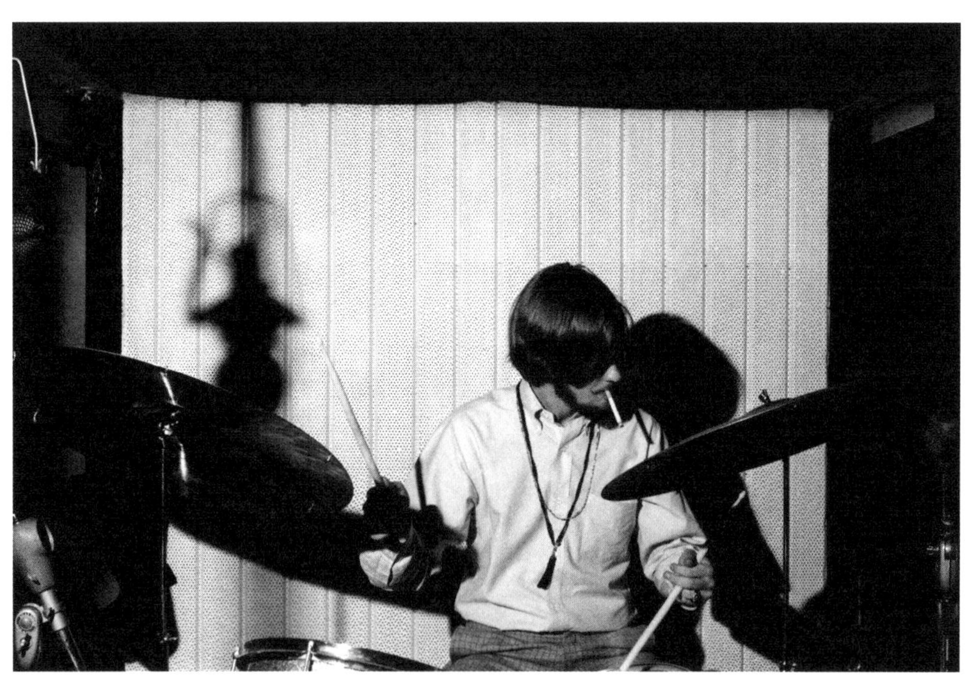

Top and left: Recording *Easter Everywhere*. Wheelock: "I saw them trying to put together that album and I knew it was going to be questionable because . . . the Elevators could play quite well stoned, but they didn't do anything else well stoned [*laughs*]. And that was the problem . . . Tommy was always conversational, even when he was really stoned. I felt he had his act together, whereas Roky didn't have his act together."

> FRANK DAVIS: Tommy was the lecturer and Roky was the one that was full of spirit. [The fight] was just, like, far-out. The fight wasn't anything compared to the irony; it was like the pope and some goddamn saint just knocking it out over which path to glory they should take . . . To see these people I'd come to consider saints coming to blows over something so tedious . . .

With the sessions hanging in the balance, Tommy sought out Clementine's calming influence.

> CLEMENTINE: [Our relationship] was a whole lot looser. I loved Tommy very much, but I didn't really want to possess him. [But] they started making *Easter Everywhere* and Tommy said, "You've got to get back here—we need you here when we're making *Easter Everywhere*."

Roky rallied upon Clementine's arrival, and she gently persuaded him back to the studio while the others were on a break. Alone with him in the booth, Clementine broke her silence and agreed to sing harmonies, and she and Roky taped a few songs together: an acoustic version of their cowritten "Splash 1," and one of Powell's, "Right Track Now." Roky had previously given Clementine a cassette of one of his quiet songs that had found little favor with Tommy, "I Had to Tell You." As with "Splash 1," Clementine penned some lyrics for the song. Roky had written a peculiar solo arrangement, which supposedly resembled ringing bells. Danny Galindo, the first to return after the break, panicked when he heard a song being worked up without him, and did his best to listen in, soon devising a guitar part derived from Clementine's vocal harmony. Much to his surprise, when Roky heard him playing the new melody, he ditched the original arrangement in its favor.

As the month drew to a close, there was no more time to luxuriate in limitless experimentation: final decisions had to be made. Tommy soon cracked under the pressure of delivering his masterpiece, briefly quitting the band—though Clementine convinced him to return, having burst into tears to demonstrate what the project meant to her. In the meantime, Stacy took the opportunity to swiftly record his contribution, "Nobody to Love." Despite Tommy's opinion that Roky should sing all the lead vocals, Stacy insisted that this song was far too personal, and he sang lead vocal for the first time.

Frank Davis and Walt Andrus were left the monumental task of editing and mixing the *Easter Everywhere* project together. They began on September 26, immediately after the sessions concluded. Various band members helped with the mixes and were allocated faders to operate—"playing the desk"—during the album's final mixes, which were finished on October 6.

> FRANK DAVIS: The mixes were the most extraordinary thing—like when you plan the movements of a ballet, the choreography was just extraordinary. It took three people on the board.

Following pages: Wheelock's portraits of the band taken during recording sessions.

Opposite: Roky, photographed by Russell Wheelock during recording sessions. Wheelock: "I was just trying to get good portraits, whereas Guy [Clark] was into getting something more exotic . . . my whole thing was good quality photographs, which is hard to do in the studio—not the best backgrounds and lighting and everything else."

TOMMY: During the mixes, there were all kinds of different speaker systems that we used, trying to get it right . . . I wish I could explain to you what an experience it was, doing that album. That was just something.

WALT ANDRUS: *Easter Everywhere* is something that no one will ever know how good that really was—because the mix! The clarity of the original recording was immaculate . . . I brought in some little itty-bitty speakers to see what it'd sound like on a car radio, and so the initial mix was real bottom-heavy, compensating for the small speakers. I offered to mix it for free, but there was too much wrangling going on over at IA. The original eight-track masters to it don't exist anymore, so you can never go and fix that. That thing was just beautiful, and all the pressings I've heard were . . .

The original artwork for *Easter Everywhere*—selected by Tommy from a book of tantric art—depicted a meditating yogi with seven chakras mapped along his body. The image was relegated to the back cover when Stacy objected on the grounds that the band had agreed not to reference one religion too heavily. In response, Tommy selected a less easily decoded allegorical representation of his ideas, resulting in the album's final cover image: a primeval yellow sun (containing forty-seven rays, an allusion to the forty-seventh problem of Euclid and its Masonic overtones) on a background of gold (itself a biblical symbol of divinity).

Although IA did afford the band a full month in the studio, the fact that the LP was mastered from the wrong mix highlights how amateurish the entire operation still was. In spite of the band's desire to present the album lavishly—using expensive gold ink on the front cover, full color band photos on the back, and a printed lyric inner sleeve—the package, like its predecessor, had a disconcerting crudeness that set it apart from mainstream product. In fact, it looked like a homemade record produced by a cult, which wasn't far from the reality of the situation. Still, the cover, like that of *Psychedelic Sounds*, has gone on to become an iconic symbol of the era—as, indeed, has the whole record: notwithstanding the chaos surrounding its creation and its commercial failure at the time, *Easter Everywhere*'s importance as *the* psychedelic album of the period has now been fully recognized.

▲ **IN MID-SEPTEMBER**, the band took a break from recording to debut their new lineup at Rice University in Houston. The show, according to William Warner, was an under-rehearsed mess.

WILLIAM WARNER: The absolute worst Elevators performance was at Rice University commons. The band couldn't start a song together, end a song together, decide what part of the song they were playing . . . Roky stood with his back to the

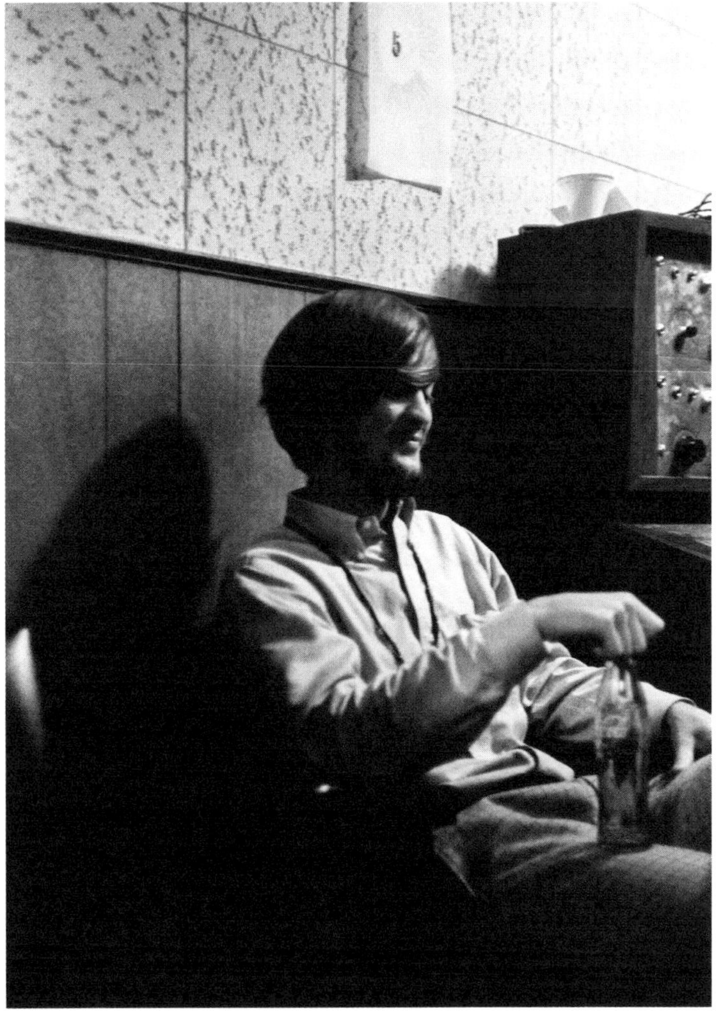

Opposite top: Tommy and Clementine, *Easter Everywhere* sessions.

Opposite bottom left: Danny Galindo plays the huge steel sheet percussion during the recording of "Earthquake."

Opposite bottom right: Clementine consoles a distraught Tommy.

Top left: Producer Walt Andrus in the studio.

Top right: Engineer Frank Davis and Lelan Rogers during recording.

Bottom right: Danny Thomas in the studio. Note the sun image—a motif from Mookerjee's book which would soon grace the album cover—on the paper above his head. The numeral 5 in the center of the sun carried significance as well: five band members, five songs per side, etc.

Top: Danny Thomas, Roky, and Stacy at the Dungeon Club in Spring, Texas, late October or November 1967. Warner: "[The Dungeon] was a club in North Harris County, North Houston [in Spring], opened very briefly, a true hole in the wall, a pit. I recall not wanting to drive all the way to Spring on a cold night. I drove out there to check it out, and the club wasn't even open. I ran into Roky, Stacy, and Danny Thomas; they were wandering around exploring. I took those photos, but I didn't hang around for the show."

Bottom: Handbill for the October 14 "Texas–OU Blast!" show at Dallas's Market Hall.

audience. If he did turn around, he'd mumble lyrics—often not the correct ones.

The band's next show, at a short-lived venue called the Dungeon in Spring, north of Houston, was just as poorly received. As the review in *Mother*—the Houston fanzine created by Larry Sepulvado and Cal Stanley—reported:

> *All thoughts of an Elevator reformation seemed to be cherished nostalgically. The new group left me doubting that it could be little more than an exploitation of their earlier reputation. Having sat through a performance of the Lost and Found and a fight that involved about fifty people, the 100 or so people drifted toward the main stage where the Elevators were to appear. Stacy and Tommy were first on stage, followed by a new drummer, Danny Thomas, and a new bass-man, Dan Galindo. Then Roky. Bluntly, Roky had looked better. They plugged in, sort of tuned up and broke into one of the worst performances I have ever witnessed by any group. They had no PA and the jug was inaudible. The new members understandably loosely faked their way through the seven or eight songs they played. What I had admired as the tightest most powerful rock band six months ago was now no better than the 100 or so bands I had seen try to imitate them. Roky's voice had lost that certain edge he used to maintain and what used to be an urgent plea was now more of a sympathetic plea. His screams that were once worth the price of admission were now nothing more than ragged shrieks.*

> DANNY GALINDO: See, Tommy tried to ritualize [the pre-show taking of LSD]. We'd all drop acid at the same time, maybe two or three hours before we were scheduled to play, and that way we would all be at the same level. I'd naturally defy it; it's not that I objected, but it was, "Well, Tommy, you know I was planning on taking some speed tonight, but I'll take some acid along with it." [*Laughs*]. I remember the [Dungeon] gig. By this time I was using a lot of speed. I hadn't quite crossed the line to addiction. When you're using a lot of speed there's magic, too; that's the problem, the drug-induced magic, and I was experiencing that.

With October came the annual "O.U. football weekend," when the rival University of Oklahoma Sooners played the University of Texas Longhorns in Dallas. The evening after the game was a traditional slot for huge local gigs, and the Elevators, advertised as "L.A.'s Hippest Psychedelic Group"—although "L.A." may have been a misprint of "I.A."—were booked for an event at the massive Market Hall convention center.

> DANNY GALINDO: It was terrifying. Mitch Ryder and the Detroit Wheels were the headliner; we were third up. It was, "Dear God," you know—we got up onstage, and I looked, and kept my head down and thought, "Keep going, keep going, keep

Opposite: Roky, shot by William Warner in Spring, Texas.

going"—man, I looked at the horizon. Awful. Terrible. In the first place, the people at that particular party weren't our audience; they were basically straight, middle-class, drunk types. They had no interest in what we were doing at all. I was so glad when it was over.

GEORGE BANKS: The O.U. weekend [was] a very big deal in Dallas. We all got very wasted, and I guess I must have been on a bit of a bad trip, and Roky asked me to sing with him onstage. And I really didn't want to go onstage. The entire environment that weekend—just a big drunk bash. And they played the convention center, which is huge; even though they were on the stage, which was eight feet high, the ceiling was almost endless. I got bummed out and Mikel [Erickson] had to walk me out of it. And I remember Roky singing "Walking the Dog," and I remember saying, "That's me!"

Meanwhile, back in Austin, the remnants of the Electric Grandmother team joined up with a twenty-year-old promoter named Don Hyde to mount a new venture: instead of hiring a different venue for each event, they decided to open Austin's first dedicated rock music venue, and Texas's first psychedelic ballroom, to be called the Vulcan Gas Company. Sandy Lockett would be the soundman, Gary Scanlon and Houston White's Jomo Disaster the house light show, and Houston and Hyde would book the bands. The idea was to create a home for the 13th Floor Elevators, who would finally have their own club.

DON HYDE: I got the lease for the Vulcan from Joe Dacey, who had a shoe store on Congress. I bought all my shoes from him growing up, and he knew me. This warehouse was for rent—316 Congress—so I went and looked at it with Joe, and he said, "$350 a month." There was no lease; it was strictly a handshake deal. But Joe had terrible pressure from everyone in town—city council, the mayor, the police, the newspaper, probably the governor—to kick us out. He came down there a couple of times unannounced on a Saturday night. He walked and looked around, and just shook his head and said, "I don't understand what everyone's getting so upset about—it just seems like a bunch of young people having a good time on a Saturday night." He said, "You keep on paying the rent and you can stay as long as you want." That was the deal.

The Vulcan was put together on a shoestring budget: wood piles around town were raided to build the stage, and old Salvation Army stands were converted into bathroom stalls.

LYNN HOWELL: It was a great big old room; no creature comforts whatsoever. Benches to sit on was about it—nothing as much as a table or chair.

Above and opposite: *Easter Everywhere* artwork, with the sun image on the front cover redrawn by George Banks (credited as "Flash Graphics"). Banks: "I had moved away from Houston, at the advice of my probation officer. I drove into town a few times and Tommy chose the photos from the *Tantra Art* book . . . [he] discussed the cover and got approval."

The packaging comprised a complex set of symbols and references, among them the idea that the square album cover (the shape symbolizing the material world) contained a circular record (the shape representing the spiritual realm), which in turn had a spiral etched into it (for the listener to follow and gain the information necessary for enlightenment). If listeners held the cover against their foreheads, the band's name would appear as a pair of flaming eyebrows, representing the sixth chakra, corresponding to the pituitary gland/third eye, above which would be the primordial sun representing the seventh/crown chakra, and above that, nirvana: "Easter Everywhere."

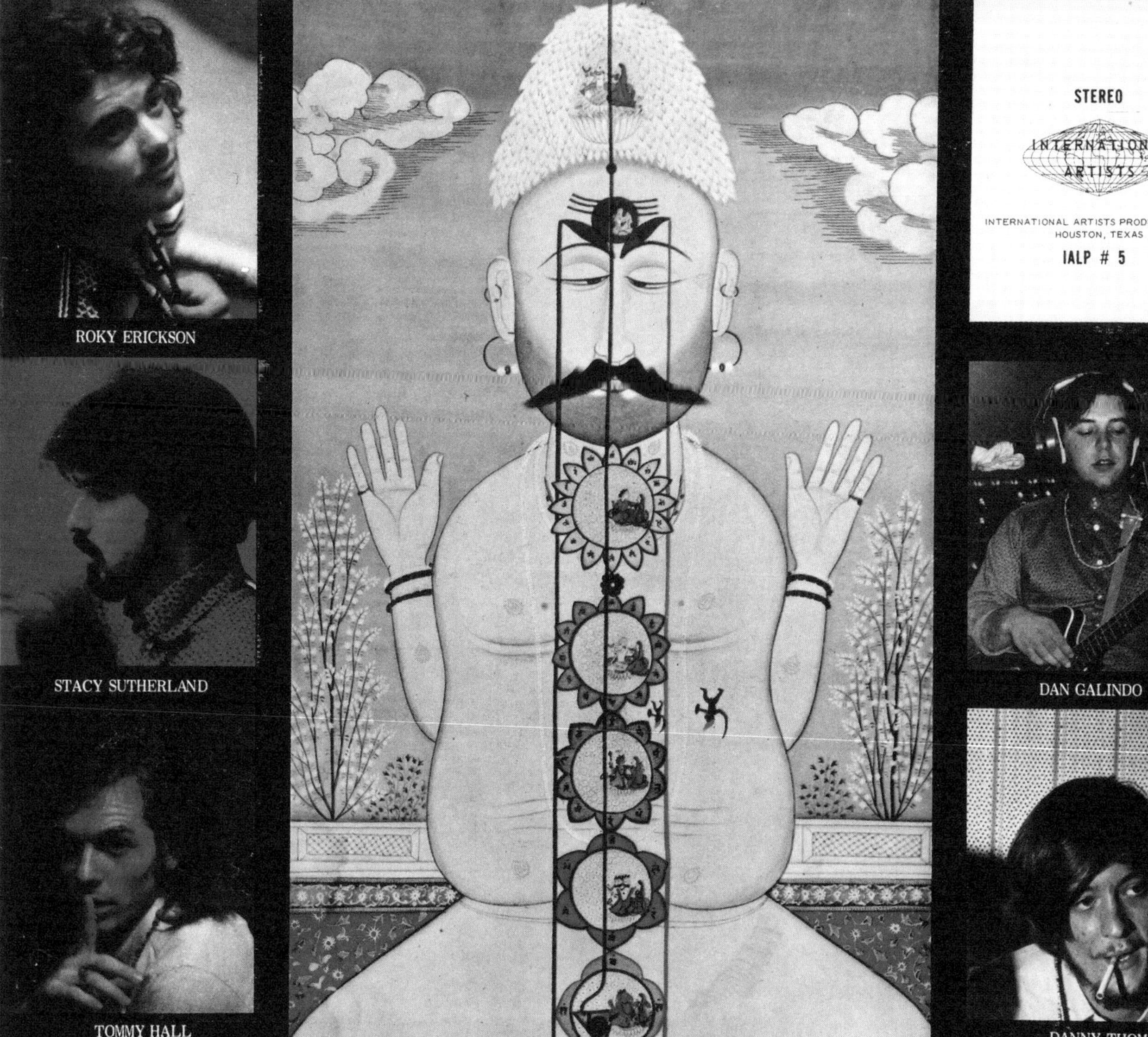

Side I

SLIP INSIDE THIS HOUSE
(Hall - Erickson) Tapier Music - B. M. I.

SLIDE MACHINE
(Powell St. John) Tapier Music - B. M. I.

SHE LIVES (In A Time Of Her Own)
(Hall - Erickson) Tapier Music - B. M. I.

NOBODY TO LOVE
(Sutherland) Tapier Music - B. M. I.

BABY BLUE
(Bob Dylan) M. Witmark & Sons - A. S. C. A. P.

Produced by: LELAN ROGERS
Recording Engineer: FRANK DAVIS
Cover Design: FLASH GRAPICS
Photos - GUY CLARK - RUSSELL WHEELOCK

Side II

EARTHQUAKE
(Hall - Erickson) Tapier Music - B. M. I.

DUST
(Hall - Erickson) Tapier Music - B. M. I.

LEVITATION
(Hall - Sutherland) Tapier Music - B. M. I.

I HAD TO TELL YOU
(Clementine Hall - Roky Erickson) Tapier Music - B. M. I.

POSTURES (Leave Your Body Behind)
(Hall - Erickson) Tapier Music - B. M. I.

Printing & Mfg. by TANNER 'N' TEXAS, Inc., 1422 West Poplar St., San Antonio 78207

The sparse interior, however, could be instantly transformed from the projection booth into a living mass of light and color.

DON HYDE: Gary Scanlon did the light show for the first six months. He was very influenced by Glen McKay's Jefferson Airplane light show ["Headlights"]. A lot of the expense of the club was buying the light show. I bought at least three oil slide projectors, and six or eight slide carousels and a sixteen-millimeter film projector: that was the basics of the light show. And Gary liked to take an image and repeat it six or eight times around the room. Lockett was supposed to be the Elevators' soundman. There were no [stage] monitors; our PA consisted of one horn and that was for the vocal, [and] everyone just played through their amps. There was a [mixing] board, and it had a little dial on it—it had one and ten and that was it; that was the Vulcan sound system. And Sandy would sit there with his beer at the beginning of the evening, and he'd take it from one to ten, and that was it.

GILBERT SHELTON: I just wanted to be involved in what was clearly such a fun project. I knew all the people involved already, with the exception of Don Hyde. I was just the first voluntary art director. The Vulcan Gas Company set aside a hundred dollars or so per week to print their posters. I was in charge of producing them. Someone found a printer who was willing to try the difficult technique of "split fountain" inking, where more than one color is used in a single printing—the colors being mixed and blended in the ink trough of the printing press itself. This, in effect, means that one achieves the effect of multicolor printing with just one or two runs of the press. Our printer was named Johnny Mercer, and he had his shop just off Sixth Street. We only did a hundred copies of each poster, and Johnny Mercer probably didn't make any profit—considering the amount of extra work he had to do. But he did win a prize as the best poster printer in Texas. I was mucho impressed by the posters for the San Francisco companies [like Jaxon's] the Family Dog . . . I copied the styles of the California artists: Wes Wilson, Rick Griffin, Stanley Mouse, Alton Kelley, Victor Moscoso, Bob Fried, and others. The Vulcan Gas Company posters had at least one superiority over the California ones, though: they were *bigger*.

DON HYDE: I knew John Mercer from when I was a kid; it was a big treat to go to his printing office with my father. He printed Western magazines—I loved the covers and the smell of fresh ink. He'd pat me on the head, [and say] "Here's a nickel, go buy a candy bar" . . . I couldn't understand why all the rockabilly and rock 'n' roll posters were so small,

Top and bottom right: Poster and both handbill variations for the shows at the Vulcan Gas Company in Austin on November 3–4, 1967, by Gilbert Shelton and Lieuen Adkins. Shelton: "The 'Pooh' poster was Lieuen Adkins's idea, and I just copied the drawings from the children's book *Winnie the Pooh*."

Bottom left: Cover of Mookerjee's *Tantra Art*.

Austin Statesman ad listing for the Vulcan show, November 1.

so I did an experiment that was 22 ½" by 28", and it came out beautifully.

SANDY LOCKETT: The morning of the opening, Houston and I were nailing together the stage when the police knocked on the door to carry away Houston. They dragged him off by the ear and did plenty of jeering—"I guess you guys won't be opening this evening." Well, they were awfully stressed when he was back by three o'clock and we went back to nailing the stage. It turned out to be a terrible mistake on their part, because what they were arresting Houston for was selling some LSD to a narcotics agent. Houston's lawyer pointed out they couldn't arrest him for selling LSD, because it wasn't illegal.

DON HYDE: We were all disappointed—the grand opening was supposed to be the Elevators, Conqueroo, and the Shiva's Headband, [but] for some reason the Elevators canceled, so we went ahead and figured it would be a warm-up; they played the second weekend. The club was built with the idea that the Elevators were supposed to be the house band; it was meant to be their home base. We thought that the Elevators would play once a month, if not twice a month. That didn't happen, and we had to scramble because there wasn't anybody in Austin to replace them. Johnny Winter was certainly talented, but a hundred people—that's all he could do.

When the Elevators finally took the stage at the Vulcan for a pair of weekend shows, things quickly went awry.

Ad for December shows at the Vulcan—the first of which was set to commemorate the anniversary of the band's first show at the Jade Room two years prior—from *The Austin Statesman*, December 8.

DON HYDE: On the first night, Friday [November 3], I was a little bit in awe of [the Elevators], so I stayed away from them. I'd known Roky since I was a kid, but I hadn't been in touch—we used to play together when we were five or six. But I [made] friends with Danny Galindo on Friday night; he was very friendly and outgoing. They did a very poor set on the Friday night. They just weren't on the same stage. It didn't even sound like they were playing the same songs. Just awful.

Q: This was the launch of the *Easter Everywhere* album?

DON HYDE: Yep, and it didn't work . . . And Danny was so mad about how bad it sounded that he threatened to quit, and not even play on Saturday. And so, I asked Danny, "Would it help pull things together if you guys took some acid?" And Danny said, "Yeah, that's what we'll do." So I gave him five hits, and they all took it at the same time, and they played great—maybe the best set I ever heard them play.

HOUSTON WHITE: A lot of folks seemed to have a remarkably good time.

Following pages: The band returns to *The Larry Kane Show* to perform "Slide Machine," November 11, 1967.

SANDY LOCKETT: Not without help.

DANNY GALINDO: We had an extraordinary gig down here at the Vulcan Gas Company. Oh God, was it incredible. Here's a whole segment of people that are coming under the wing of the cult, so to speak, and all of a sudden here is this beautiful place for us to go, that had all of the overheads and the pulsating blobs, you know, and the oils, and everything felt very secure because everybody in the joint was going, "Wow." You know? Everybody was making this contact that was really, felt really personal and warm—it was somebody you'd never seen in your life before, but that kind of magic was going around. I think that during that period of time it was the most liberated I'd ever seen Austin.

Even Stacy was happy: Sandy had found an organic way to create extra reverb using the building itself.

JOHNDAVID BARTLETT: In those days, you only had certain ways to get reverberation, [but] behind the stage there was a huge room, and back in the corner, there was a metal plate with a cistern that had been dug into the bedrock, into a big teardrop which was six feet deep. What they did was, they put a speaker down there, and dropped a microphone in there, and that was the reverb for the PA system for the Vulcan Gas Company. And that's when the arguments started: "That's too much reverb! That is way too much!" "No it's not—is there any way we can get more?"

▲ **WITH *EASTER EVERYWHERE*'S AUSTIN** launch complete, the Elevators headed to Houston, playing shows at Love Street Light Circus, signing records at a couple of in-store events, and making another appearance on *The Larry Kane Show*.

On November 20, Larry Sepulvado and Cal Stanley interviewed the band at the IA offices for *Mother*—the first and only interview published while the band was still together. Stacy didn't show up and Roky was "contemplating his existence," which left the talking to Tommy, with the two Dannys chipping in when allowed. Still, the interview provides a unique snapshot of where the band thought they were at the time. Despite Danny Galindo's enthusing over all the advertisements IA was going to place in the trade papers, none materialized. The band was most positive about the album's chances because other artists, such as the Doors and Hendrix, had helped establish a wider market for psychedelic rock. Although Tommy complained that many of the other groups who supposedly played psychedelic music were just imitating the sound, he also reaffirmed his belief in the power of the record album, its having another dimension, capable of reinforcing the written word.

Top left: Exterior of Houston's Love Street Light Circus.

Top middle and top right: Danny Thomas and Danny Galindo at Love Street. William Warner: "You had to go up a three-flight metal exterior staircase to get to the where the club was, the top floor of an old warehouse. The ceiling was two stories high, which is why the office was above the entrance. They had enough height to put a double deck for the lights. It was laid out in an odd way, in that up the middle, all the way to the stage, was pillow seating, and people would crash out, and around the edges were tables with seating."

Bottom: Roky, Diana Williams (the venue's resident dancer), and Stacy at Love Street. Warner: "By the time they were at Love Street, it was the *Easter Everywhere* [era]: they played all the stuff off the album: 'Slip Inside This House,' etc. Actually, they got a lot worse at playing the old songs. I'd say they were adequate at *EE* at that point, and progressively worse at playing 'Fire Engine' and 'You're Gonna Miss Me.' Then it reached a tipping point where they couldn't give a good performance."

Opposite top and bottom: The band in performance, framed by the Love Street light show. Warner: "Love Street was presented as a clean teen club, where your kids could go and be safe. But it was hard to buy that when the strobes were flashing and the girls were dancing and the band was playing. Most of the staff was ripped."

100 FT. LIGHT SHOW

13th FLOOR ELEVATORS

CONQUEROO FRIDAY ONLY

SHIVAS HEAD BAND SAT ONLY

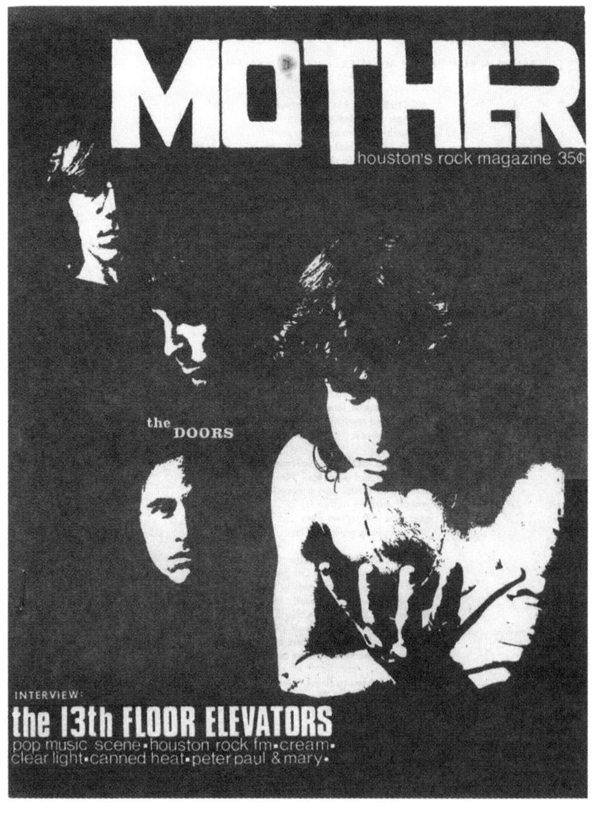

Top: Drawn advertisement in *The Rag* for the Elevators' Vulcan Gas Company shows.

Bottom: Cover of the first issue of *Mother* magazine, featuring the only contemporary Elevators print interview, circa December 1967.

Opposite and following pages: The *Mother* interview, reproduced in its entirety for the first time since its initial publication.

"ive seen your face before ive known you all my life
and though it's new your image cuts me like a knife"

A moment's thought, a couplet of verse; lyrics from a pop song--correct yet somehow inadequate descriptions of these lines taken from the recently successful recording, "Splash I".

As performed by the Clique, the song is a glossy, commercialized version of the original track penned by another Houston-based group, The 13th Floor Elevators. By comparison, the more recent version falls short of the original, yet it reached the top of the local charts: a reflection of the status of the pop scene locally, or perhaps a commentary on the sheer strength of the lyrics, apart from any musical encumbrance.

The music of the 13th Floor Elevators is not the proliferate volume of mediocrity that dominates Top 40 radio; nor is it at all akin to the less than elementary material produced on the local level, which seldom, if ever, makes the national charts.

Their sound is, and has been for several years, of the calibre of the music which spawned the West Coast Renaissance. In fact, it was the Elevators who first called their sound "Psychedelic", a term since used indiscriminately and erroneously by too many groups.

Their formula refined to its basic components is substantial lyrics carried on a driving, penetrating sound. The sound is the vehicle, which is the catalyst transforming effective thoughts into something more--the total experience that is the Elevators witnessed in person.

Live, they are a narcotic administered to the very fiber of your being. The sound is the medium, the volume is incredibly high, shooting straight through you. At times it is a depressant hitting the listener with a dull thud that falls upon numbed senses. Then it may suddenly become a stimulant, lifting you above the stabilized fixtures that surround you. At all times it is a continuous flowing medium of lyrics and electronic reverberations--a flowing resulting from the happy marriage of the lyrics and the music. The lyrics, devoid of their musical framework, stand on their own, but assume an even more dynamic property when fused with an electronic foundation.

The blaring quality of guitars at maximum volume underlaid with the haunting wailing of the jug and words whose meaning becomes a musical tool in themselves all serve to send the message home. This is the experience of the 13th Floor Elevators.

Are You Experienced?

The above theme on the 13th Floor Elevators was written well in advance of our securing an interview with them. It fittingly describes the reaction to an Elevators performance. What follows is an interview that was held at International Artists record company at 10 a.m. in the morning. Due to the early hour, Stacy Sutherland was unable to be there; and Roky Erikson, who was there, was still contemplating his existence at this hour. We hope this edited version of the interview will help reveal some of the questions concerning the cloak of mystery surrounding the Elevators.

Larry Sepulvado

AN INTERVIEW WITH THE 13TH FLOOR ELEVATORS

CAL STANLEY: Who picked the title for your new album, Easter Everywhere?
TOMMY HALL: Well, I did.
CAL: Any particular reason for it?
TOMMY: Well, it comes from the idea of Christ consciousness. And realizing that you can be born again; that you can constantly change and be reformed into a better and better person. It's like a progressive perfection and Easter Everywhere is sort of the combination or culmination of this idea as echoed in the public. It's like everyone is snapping to this; that there is a middle ground between the Eastern trip and the Western trip and that is by learning to use your emotion and realizing what emotion is and why it is there and how to control it from a pleasure point of view, so that you don't get hung up in a down place. It's just the idea of rising from the dead all over, everywhere.
CAL: How long have you been working on this album?
TOMMY: We just got together and started work on it. So we've been together what, about two months?
DAN GALINDO: Since the beginning of July.
CAL: So, it was put together in two months then?
TOMMY: All but two songs, "She Lives" and "Levitation", which were already recorded.
CAL: How did you develop your particular sound, the jug particularly?
TOMMY: We just wanted to make a music that could show a groovy place to people. So, we just tried to get together at as groovy a place as we could that had as many exposures, views, or photos of the different sides of the groovy place. A place that was evolving which you could come up from, all the time. Each of us tried to put his concept of that place and the total sum of it into our music.

Tommy Hall

Stacy Sutherland

DANNY THOMAS: It's like the lyrics have the main emphasis and the music is used as an accent and vehicle for the lyrics. In other words, the music is a bed for the lyrics to lie in, a bed of flowers.
TOMMY: It's half and half because the words are states of minds and the music is the emotion you feel with that state of mind.
DAN G.: I would like to interject this. Since this is the first go around for the present group, I feel our music will improve considerably. As the words get higher and carry more meaning our music will improve and take on new forms, new shapes, new ideas.
CAL: How do you go about putting one of your songs together? Who writes the music, who writes the lyrics or is it a group thing?
TOMMY: Sometimes Roky writes the music and sometimes Stacy. We'll get ideas from places or each other and I'll write a song about it. Then we all get together and arrange.
LARRY SEPULVADO: Who have been the previous members?
TOMMY: We've gotten a new drummer and bassman. The previous drummer's name was John Ike and the bassman was Ronnie Leatherman. We also had a previous bassman before that, Bennie.
LARRY: What band experience has the group had prior to the Elevators?
TOMMY: I've had none. Roky has been with another group.
DAN G.: I've had relatively little to speak of. I've been in it now over two years and most of that was spent looking for bands to play with...(laughter)...I just happened to be in the right spot at the right time.
DANNY T.: I was mostly playing on the East Coast; Virginia, North and South Carolina, and Georgia.
LARRY: Several months ago on the cover of Life Magazine, a poster advertising your appearance at the Avalon ballroom was featured with many other posters. What exactly took the Elevators out to the West Coast the early part of this year?
TOMMY: Because we were a band that presented states of mind.
LARRY: As far as psychedelic music, whatever that connotates, the Elevators were at the beginning of this movement as much as anybody.
TOMMY: Like we were the first group to advertise as psychedelic. Like we advertised as psychedelic and two weeks later the Grateful Dead played their first gig and they advertised as psychedelic.
LARRY: What was your impression when you originally arrived there?
TOMMY: It was a gas...(laughter)...It was just beautiful.
LARRY: Right now it seems most of the people that are there have turned into vegetables or...

TOMMY: No, not necessarily. It's like all the groovy people have left and are just doing their thing. When it first started out everyone said, "Hey, there are groovy people out there". So, everybody comes and they couldn't help what happened. Like they were all in different stages of evolution and the groovy people stayed together, so they could continue their thing.
LARRY: I've heard that The Dead have moved to New Mexico which is a sign that things are scattering out. There's not anything in San Francisco that you could consider a whole now, is there?
TOMMY: In any scene, you have to make your own scene. If you want to evolve you have to do it yourself. A certain amount is done for you but if you want to evolve faster you have to work. You have to go out and meet the people and sift through everybody and get finer and finer until you have got a nice scene and it's hard because there are so many people out there doing the same thing.
LARRY: How long were you out on the coast?
TOMMY: About two months.
ROKY ERIKSON: Was it that long?
CAL: With this thing going on in Frisco, why did you choose Houston as your base of operation?
TOMMY: Because the record company's here.
LARRY: From the bay area where did you go? People I know in New York have heard of the Elevators there. Have you played the East Coast?
TOMMY: No, we had a lot of trouble. That's why we have a new drummer. Like he totally messed things up for us as far as the East Coast because he was always quibbling about who should manage us. We tried to book gigs in New York but he called the people up and told them that the people hadn't booked us and they canceled everything. This made our record company mad and he sued our record company. So, we've had a lot of trouble as far as personnel and all of us working together.
LARRY: "You're Gonna Miss Me", your first record, received a lot of exposure, didn't it? Like your name has appeared in most of the periodicals when they list psychedelic groups.
TOMMY: Yes, we've been fortunate.
CAL: How do you feel your music stands in relation to the current musical scene?
TOMMY: We're just doing a different thing. Right now as our playing live gets better and better; well, like we're approaching it from a different view. We're approaching it from an emotional viewpoint rather than a musical one. As our music develops, we, as a group, develop emotion together.
CAL: It takes awhile to develop this group thinking, doesn't it?

Danny Thomas

TOMMY: That's true. It would be hard to compare us with anybody else because we're concentrating our thing on designing geometric states of mind. I think Dylan is doing the same thing. We're developing our music along the same lines...no, not the same lines but in the same way.
LARRY: One thing that I haven't understood is why the Elevators have not caught on nationwide. Through the somewhat collage of quality groups appearing now, this group has a distinctive sound which sets it apart from the others. Your lyric content, especially in your latest album, is as competent as anything available.
TOMMY: Well, one thing is that our record company has sort of been scared to do anything for us because of hassles with the past members of the group. Right now, they are behind us because we're together solid now.
CAL: Has that been the reason for the lack of publicity?
DAN G.: There will be publicity on this album. There'll be ads in Record World, Cashboard, Billbox. I mean Billboard...(laughter)...There will be publicity on this one.
LARRY: Talking about Billboard, they did feature the first album in their national album reviews, but it didn't move on the national charts.
DAN G.: That's because it didn't move enough.
TOMMY: We didn't push.

Dan Galindo

LARRY: Exactly where was it distributed and where did it sell?
TOMMY: Well, it's like we're putting out psychedelic music and we like to feel that it really is psychedelic. We have had a hard time selling in places where they don't understand psychedelic music. They don't know what to listen for. The psychedelic scene is spreading very fast but then we were sort of caught because people just weren't there when we were. The Doors and Jimi Hendrix are beginning to sell now and I think the market is changing in a good way as far as psychedelic music.
LARRY: That's why I have faith in the Elevators eventually making it nationally because you are sincere about what you are doing and did not jump on the bandwagon to capitalize on a trend.
TOMMY: What the other groups did was to just play the musical side of it. But things are different. This is not just music anymore. These people were playing it from this standpoint; they were just imitating the music.

CAL: Speaking of that, what was your reaction to the Clique's version of "Splash I".
TOMMY: It was groovy.
LARRY: Off the album, it was just another good cut but the vocal on the Clique's version did not convey this lyrical emotion. I didn't get the feeling that the words meant the same.
DAN G.: That arrangement seems like it was tailored for a particular market and in my opinion, was well done for the market it was intended to appeal to.
DANNY T.: It was arranged and produced very well.
LARRY: Clementine Hall is your wife, isn't she?
TOMMY: Yes, she's the one who thought of our name--The 13th Floor Elevators.
LARRY: That is her singing on "I Had to Tell You".
TOMMY: Yes. She wrote it and "Splash I".
CAL: What kind of plans do you have for the future?
TOMMY: We're going to tour the East and West Coasts and we have a new single that we have got to record.
LARRY: Your next single will not be from the album?
TOMMY: Well, "She Lives" will be released from the album.
DAN G.: We're going to be working on the single after that. It will be on our third album which International Artists would like us to have ready by February.
CAL: Or else?
TOMMY: We're in a groovy place right now with the record company. We just don't have any more problems.
LARRY: Whose idea was it to bring in Frank Davis as the recording engineer for the latest album?
TOMMY: It was all of ours. We wanted an eight-track studio.
LARRY: I saw you at the Frank Davis concert at the Jewish Community Center. That was really wild. That tape he played at the end of the set demonstrated he was really into something.
TOMMY: He really has some good stuff.
DANNY T.: That tape is going to be released as an album.
TOMMY: His mixing is very good. As far as mixing, he is a genius.
LARRY: Speaking of Davis, why was Guy Clark brought in to take photos for the album? He's been out of the public eye for quite some time.
DAN G.: He takes good pictures.
TOMMY: Guy is a very beautiful person.
LARRY: Is he working with the group in any way?
TOMMY: No, just the photos. I met Guy through Russell Wheelock, who also helped take the photos for the album. I've known Russell for a long time. I think it was Lelan's (Rogers, their producer) idea to use Guy.
CAL: Throughout your music, do you feel that you have one message or theme that you are trying to convey?
TOMMY: It's like we're all humans who have reached the point where if we all just give each other ideas, everyone will be able to come up. We're trying to work out the grooviest ideas we can. It's looking at phonograph records as a new book and a new kind of feedback man is giving himself. It's like man is talking to himself. Somebody can listen to a phonograph and go to a groovy place.
LARRY: That's what's good about your albums. If you let them, they can explore your mind. It can be an experience like reading a book.
DANNY T.: But it is more of an experience than that.
LARRY: It's an idea developed elsewhere in this magazine. This business of music being the literature of our times.
CAL: Like classical music, it's an emotional experience and from this standpoint your music is along the same lines. Like when some people hear this music, all they hear is noise or abstractions and that's all they hear.

Roky Erickson

TOMMY: Man has the power to identify with anything. If you want to turn yourself into a Coke bottle you can, and it's much easier on psychedelics. So, man in the future is going to be sitting in front of one of these albums, not necessarily ours, and the album will do a thing to him that would be like music and would not normally be expected. It would make him totally disassociate his actual ever-continuing self from his perishable egg shell earth presence and he would go to a completely different world. And the more he does that, the more he can learn about that world of immortality which is just a feeling. That's what we're trying to play in our music, the immortal theme, because it's like Christ said, "We're already immortal from in front". It's just knowing that feeling or mood that is what everyone is trying to put down on record for man to remember.
CAL: You are playing at Love Street this week and next?
DAN G.: Yes, we have a schedule around here somewhere.
TOMMY: Yes, this week and Thanksgiving. Then December 1, we play Austin, and then Bryan, and then we are off to Detroit. It's going to be real hard for us to play Detroit because we have to drive to San Francisco the following week. We will be in the Avalon the third week of December.
LARRY: Since you are going to Detroit, I assume there will be advance publicity? Has the album been out long enough for you to tell exactly how it has been received?
DANNY T.: 7,700 sold.
TOMMY: If it continues to sell like it is, it should be on the national charts in about three weeks.
CAL: Are you satisfied with your recorded sound? Is this the sound you're trying to get across?
TOMMY: It's like Scott Holtzman said, "There's a closeness that's just not there".
LARRY: Right. Because this is not the same thing when you see this live.
DAN G.: I would like to say one thing. Danny Thomas and myself, this is our first album. We had never played a job together. We had to do it the hard way, as hard as anyone could have done it. All this album is really , is an indication of the potential we have in this group. Our following albums will be much, much better and as the group tightens and the quality improves, so will our recordings.
LARRY: Earlier, I had mentioned to Tommy that the Elevators I saw at the Living Eye, earlier this year had a real tight sound. It was great.
DAN G.: Yes, but that group had been together for two years.
LARRY: I guess, everyone sort of feels the other out not only from within the group but establishing communication with the audience?
DAN G.: It's group communication and that's something we're developing right now. Danny Thomas and myself work together as much as possible. As we work, things will come more natural and soon we won't have to think about the beat. It will just be there. Danny will know what to do, I'll know what to do and along with Roky and Stacy we'll produce a picture, a musical picture with each part different but all fitting together perfectly. Right now there are a few spots and cracks but they are rapidly filling.
CAL: How can someone contact you for public appearances?
DAN G.: Artists Management Company, 1005 Americana Building, Houston.
CAL: That concludes our interview.
DANNY T.: As a final word, you might mention that the magazine you are getting ready to publish is working along the same direction as we are; that you are trying to do something better than the usual.
CAL: Thanks.
TOMMY: Larry, may I wish you luck on your magazine.
LARRY: Tommy, I thank you and the rest of the group for permitting this interview. We appreciate you giving us some of your time.

Although Danny certainly seemed optimistic in the interview about the band's future as a live act, this hopefulness was soon to sour. The band were booked to play five nights in a row between November 22 and 25: twice at Love Street Light Circus in Houston; then at Columbus Hall in Bryan, Texas; then at the Safari Club in Baytown; and, finally, back at Love Street for Thanksgiving on the thirtieth. The quality of the shows appeared to vary as much as the nightly lineup of the band.

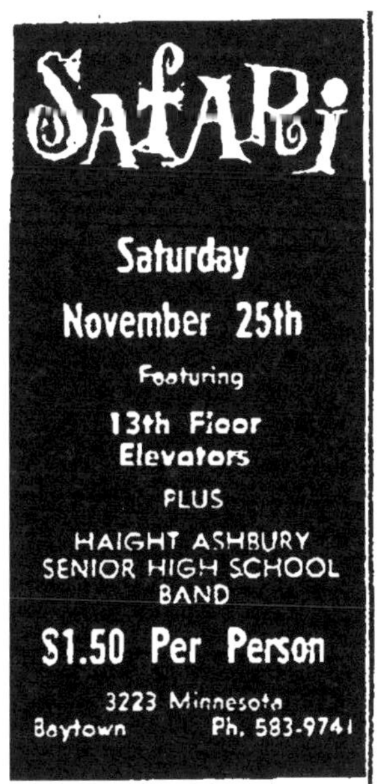

Advertisement for a performance at the Safari Club in Baytown, Texas, November 25.

DANNY GALINDO: One or the other [Roky or Stacy] wouldn't show up. So that resulted in the remainder of us having an incredible set, believe it or not. Because, for some reason, Roky wasn't usually very coherent in terms of his guitar playing—most of the time. But then a couple of nights at Love Street, Stacy didn't show up; all of the sudden, Roky found skill and played far beyond what I thought he was capable of—incredible playing. There was a night or two when Roky wasn't there, and we were able to reach the same place with Stacy. We switched into jam mode. Stacy would vocalize, do some of his tunes, and Tommy sang backup. Stacy used to hate that, [but] he just had to put up with it, and I could tell how much it got under his skin to hear that . . . We [also] had a big problem with Roky's volume. It was a way of tuning us out, so he could perform it the way he wanted to perform it. So, all the time, his amp was on maximum—wide open. Totally goofy. He'd come between all of us so we had to play to him, which broke the continuity. It got to where we felt we could play the songs better if Roky wasn't on guitar, and at a much later point that's what happened: we got Roky the smallest amp we possibly could and then we quit playing to Roky. We knew how to get through the material, so the three of us stayed together and went and it'd be up to him to keep up and we'd sound good. It was killer—he couldn't drown us out. I was never sure why he was doing what he did. He was unable to express his thoughts and feelings, so I think it was some of his frustration coming out.

Finally, in early December, the band was back at the Vulcan for what would turn out to be their last shows with the full lineup at the venue.

DANNY GALINDO: I think my last gig was at Love Street Light Circus in San Antonio [the sister club to the Houston location], and I believe Roky was about an hour late in coming down from the dressing room. He was in sheer terror; he got up onstage, and he looked around a few times, and he went back around his amp and hid. Luckily for me, I had a friend there that was a keyboard player; he came up and Stacy and I and him and Tommy just shook it, you know? But that was, for me, that was the point—the last straw. After the gig was over, I said, "I'm not going to be available anymore," and I left.

Opposite: An unknown show in Houston, late 1967.

Top: Handbill for the *Easter Everywhere* launch in Houston at Love Street, November 22–23.

Bottom: Illustrated ad for the Elevators at the Vulcan Gas Company from *The Rag*, December 8–10, 1967.

Opposite left: Listing for the shows in the December 4 edition of *The Rag*.

Opposite right: *Easter Everywhere* review in the underground *Chicago Seed* newspaper, volume 2, #6, April 1968.

THE ASSOCIATION---CEC at Municipal Aud, tomorrow at 8pm, if you can get in. VULCAN GAS CO.--13th Floor Elevators, Fri-Sun; Swiss Movement, Fri; South Canadian Overflow, Sat; Shiva's Head Band, Sun. JADE ROOM---Destruction's Children on Mon, on Wed is

continued on page 15

MANGELSDORFF'S REVIEW

13th FLOOR ELEVATORS: EASTER EVERYWHERE. International Artists IALP #5.

This side has been out a while without attracting much attention and perhaps there are reasons.

Here's a group with originality, mystic poetry for lyrics and an in-person act respected in San Francisco, which is dissipating its own efforts on record.

This band's potential is strong. Their guitars have a fine sound and they are smart in their use of electronic effects and when they get two leads going ("Baby Blue", "Earthquake"), you can see what a good wall they could have, a tougher Byrds, perhaps.

The trouble is that the lyrics and the music seem mutually distracting, The Elevator's use of dynamics is deficient, and they need to develop facets to their act, which might give them the projection they require.

Rocky Erickson's voice is distinctive and cuts through well, in fact he's almost always (recorded) way on top of the instruments. But there's an odd tone-deafness in his delivery (you thought Dylan was flat, hear Erickson do "Baby Blue"), he lacks nuances yet his insistent shout does not come off as chant or incantation either. Erickson's "country" roots show in "I Had to Tell You", and perhaps he should relax back into that bag to gain character.

The lyrics, well look at some. From "Slip Inside This House":

All your lightening waits inside you
Travel it along your spine
Seven stars receive your visit
Seven seals remain divine
Seven churches filled with spirit
Treasure from the angel's mine
Slip inside this house as you pass by

which is more typical than exceptional, or from "She Lives (In A Time of Her Own)":

Her love whips hard like wind and stars
in eager pain
She wins your thoughts and drives your
inner planes
She clears and shares a love the never
drains
She lives in a time of her own

or from "Postures (Leave Your Body Behind)":

In your wandering search for this
Only highest existence, consciousness
and bliss
By feeling more love for the sense
world your seeing
You raise your sense income and your
level of being
By finer and finer and finer agreeing
You leave... leave, leave
Leave your body behind

Their first lp was similar; originals which are mystical-acid paeans.

Erickson sometimes has to scuffle to phrase the lyrics into the tunes, but then so do most others. Dylan is an example of one who can scuffle without letting it detract from his act. But its often true here that the most ambitious poetry is yoked with the thinnest musical offerings. There is need for more sensitive arrangements, and better use of space. It's a shame when people ignore tunes like these, but they will until this act gets spruced up.

If you listen to "Tried to Hide" on their first lp you get an idea of what a sound this group could have. Like addition of a harp, as is used there (they use it here on "I Had to Tell You," but it sounds atypical) and their use of the cowbell (yes!) as a driving rhythmic device is excellent use of this forgotten implement. More and better developed blues would help The Elevators' sound and either their recorded cuts should be made shorter or their lyrics more brief and less involved; even Jimi Hendrix can't have his cake and eat it in respect to this.

"Levitation" is a hard-driving bitch, the only turn here I'd leave just as is. Good guitar slants and cymbal-bell work. "Slip Inside this House" is best combination of poetry and sound. "Earthquake" is fine in this respect, but my record has a recording goof which muffles the first minute or so of the cut. Maybe that widespread?

Since the group could stand better recording, a&r and supervision. Damn, I'd like the job myself, this group has what it takes, YES, they deserve to be more than an underground wraith.

"That sound" (a human voice, no shit) is again detectable all throughout this lp.

--Rich Mangelsdorff

STILL MORE

ROACHES

Fred Brooks, 21, former director of Nashville, Tennessee's controversial Li eration School, was sentenced today to four years in prison for draft refusal.

Brooks, a SNCC worker, pleaded not guilty on the grounds of his opposition to the war in Vietnam and his conscientious objection. His sentence was handed down by Judge William E. Miller.

Brooks' school was the subject of intense attack by the Congress last year, as various government officials charged that it "taught children to hate whites." --LNS

#%

URGENT: MISSISSIPPI FREEDOM INFORMATION SERVICE HAS STOPPED PUBLISHING. FIS is practically the last truthful source of information out of the state of Mississippi, but it is broke. It constantly has to deal with economic deprivation, lack of interest in the North and West, even bomb threats. Since its budget is very small, even $5 from each of the LNS members will revive it overnight. Send what you can, today: FIS, Box 120, Tougaloo, Miss. Request a sub., too. --LNS

Top and bottom: Poster, handbill, and ticket for the band's December stand at the Vulcan Gas Company, featuring Gilbert Shelton's art. Shelton: "That's clearly the ugliest poster that anyone ever did for the Vulcan Gas Company, and perhaps in the entire history of rock 'n' roll posters. Maybe it was because I was in a bad mood that week? It's liked mainly for the fact that it has the word 'pot' sort of halfway concealed in the middle of the drawing."

Opposite: Poster and handbill for an Elevators show that never happened: opening up for a Van Morrison–less Them, December 1967.

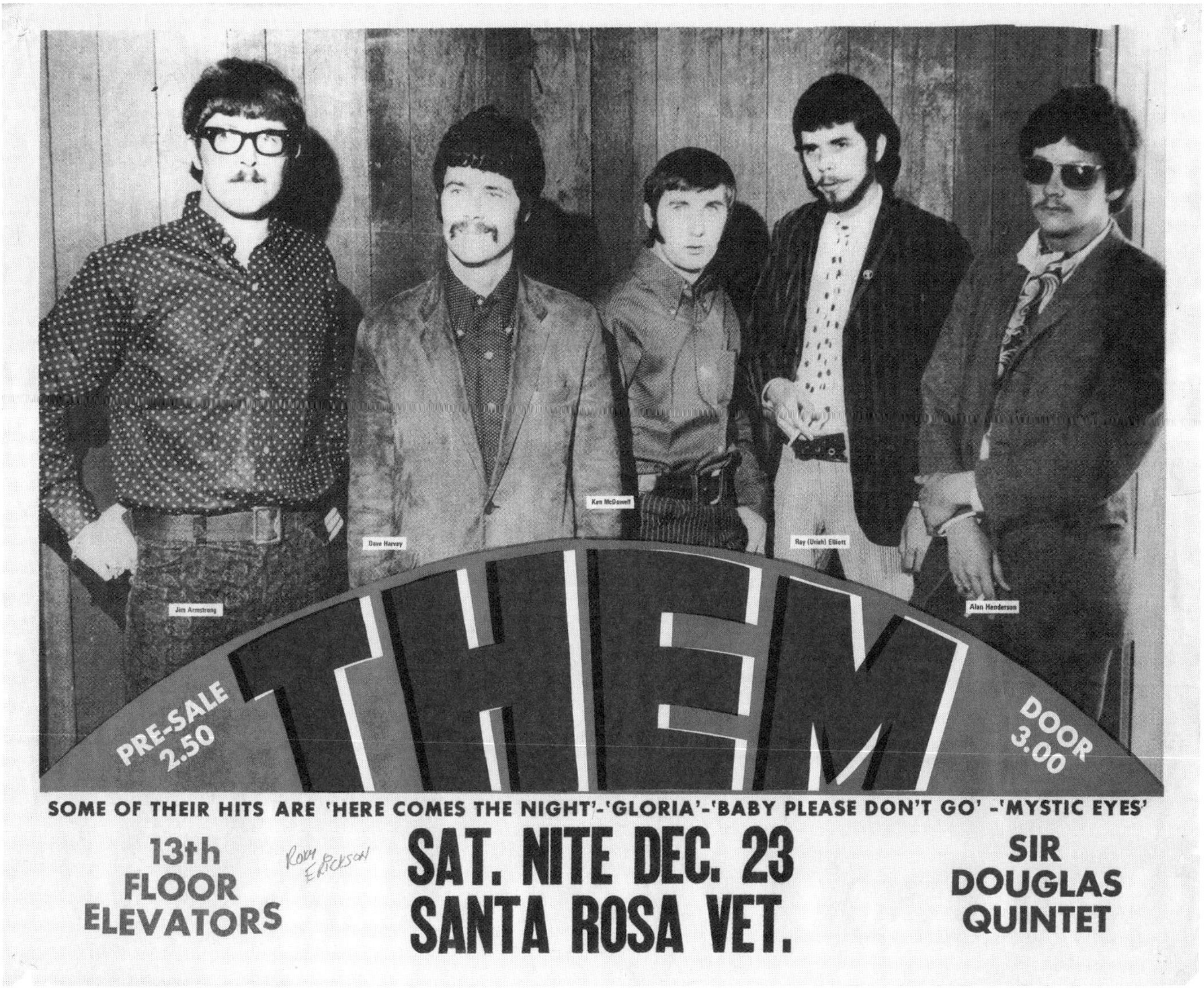

Jim Armstrong
Dave Harvey
Ken McDowell
Ray (Uriah) Elliott
Alan Henderson
THEM
PRE-SALE 2.50
DOOR 3.00
SOME OF THEIR HITS ARE 'HERE COMES THE NIGHT'-'GLORIA'-'BABY PLEASE DON'T GO' -'MYSTIC EYES'
13th FLOOR ELEVATORS
ROKY ERICKSON
SAT. NITE DEC. 23
SANTA ROSA VET.
SIR DOUGLAS QUINTET

THEM
PRE-SALE 2.50
DOOR 3.00
SOME OF THEIR HITS ARE 'HERE COMES THE NIGHT'-'GLORIA'-'BABY PLEASE DON'T GO' -'MYSTIC EYES'
13th FLOOR ELEVATORS
SAT. NITE DEC. 23
SANTA ROSA VET.
SIR DOUGLAS QUINTET

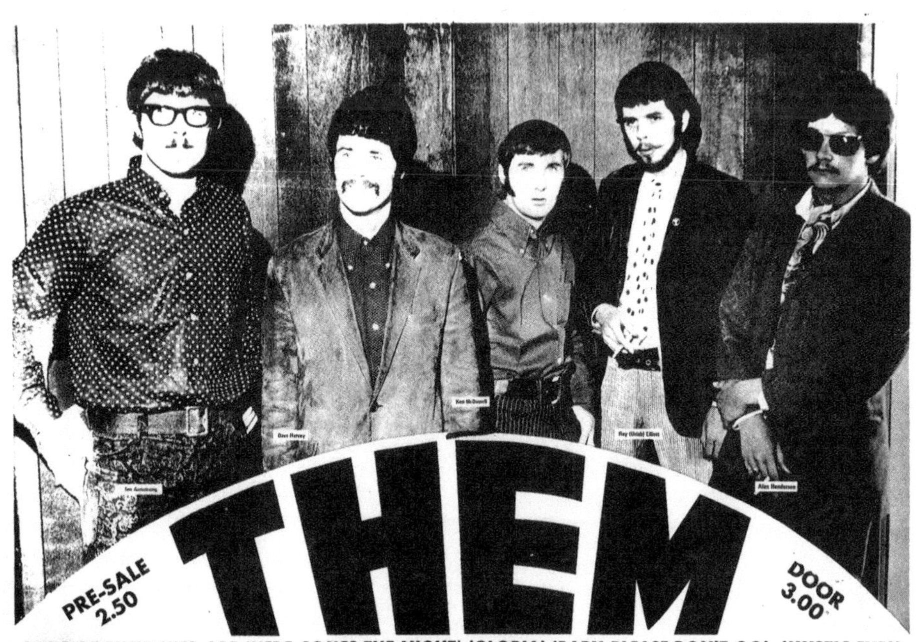

CITY OF KERRVILLE, TEXAS

SUMMONS FOR TRAFFIC VIOLATION

№ 29037

12 - 25 - 67
MONTH DAY YEAR

Stacy Sutherland
NAME

Box 864 Kerrville
ADDRESS

5161888 | 1A8012 Chev pickup
Operator's Lic. No. Car Lic. No. Make

8:30 AM PM

600 Blk Main st
LOCATION TIME

VIOLATION: Failed to yield right of way

Date of Birth: 5-28-46

CHARGES AGGRAVATED BY:

Drinking ☐ · Heavy Traffic ☐ · Near Collision: Pedestrian ☐ Automobile ☐ · SPEED: Slow ☐ High ☐

Dangerous Passing ☐ · No Observation ☐ · Slick Road ☐ · Weaving ☐ · Collision ☐ · Straddling Lane ☐ · Wrong Side St. ☐

Visibility Obscured: Buildings ☐ Cars ☐ Shrubs ☐ · Weather Conditions: Rain ☐ Snow ☐ Clear ☑

DIST.: Business ☑ Residential ☐ School ☐ Rural ☐

Cigarettes
ARRESTING OFFICER

I, Stacy Sutherland,
agree to appear at Corporation Court, City Hall, within ten days to enter a plea to the above charges.
Fines may be paid at the Police Department anytime before 10 days from date.

SEE REVERSE SIDE

Top: The court summons issued after Stacy's Christmas Day arrest. Sibyl Sutherland: "Well, he was taking a boy home that was drunk; of course, he wasn't supposed to be around drinking or anything [due to his probation]. And they arrested him."

Bottom: Tommy's girlfriend Gay Jones, at her parents' house over Christmas 1967.

VI

MAY THE CIRCLE REMAIN UNBROKEN

The Third Project

With *Easter Everywhere* having been released in November 1967, IA immediately wanted the band back in the studio. This time it was Stacy's turn: while Tommy was toying with a vague concept for an intended fourth LP called *The Beauty and the Beast*, Stacy had a backlog of unrecorded material. The band returned to Houston, where IA provided them with only a restaurant tab at Ogger's Diner so they could eat—believing any salary would just be spent on drugs, the label provided no cash. Still, Tommy treated this as a lifeline, and transferred the tab to Dobe's, a waffle shop on Louisiana Street where he ate practically every day for three months. For Stacy, too, it was the only guarantee of a meal.

> FRED HYDE: Tommy had the greatest apartment you've ever seen and he'd just hold court down there. He'd play albums and everybody would be loaded—you know, smoking DMT or hash or weed—and he'd just be running his rap all the time, and we'd all just be totally infatuated by everything that Tommy said. I think it was such an unsure time and he really appeared to have it together better than anybody.

> STACY (*K*): [Tommy would] have big crowds of people coming over to the house, and sitting around while he lectured. He started telling me, "I want to lecture for an hour [before] every performance." I started arguing with him about that—I knew that was bullshit. 'Cuz he'd get up there and start raving, "God is LSD," and these cops would come up and say, "You better collect that guy."

Despite a return booking at the Avalon Ballroom, the Elevators' weekly Love Street residency continued, with the band once more holed up at the rundown Western Skies motel. IA was in the process of acquiring the legendary Gold Star Studios in Houston, and in the meantime, Stacy worked up some of his new material at Andrus Studios with a curious Danny G. on bass. Danny thought it "smoked," and gave the engineer a tape—the demo of his new band, the Eccentrics—to record over. What was captured on that rehearsal tape displays an as-yet-unheard fluidity, drive, and authority for the band, especially compared to the *Easter Everywhere* sessions. Live in the studio, the group was superb, and Stacy realized that he didn't want or need the chaos of having Roky or Tommy there while he laid down the basic backing tracks.

> ROKY: When we first started the Elevators, the whole thing was to make sure everyone agreed on something before we did it. See, *Bull of the Woods* [the eventual name for the follow-up to *Easter Everywhere*] was the idea of not having the whole band agree to everything that was being done, so I don't really remember those songs—Stacy probably wouldn't even show

Opposite: Roky at Love Street, Houston, late 1967.

them to me. He would be paranoid, if he said anything to anybody about it, that his ideas would be rejected in the end.

In the wake of Danny Galindo's final departure, Duke Davis—from Houston's Starvation Army Band and the Grits (also signed to IA)—was drafted as the Elevators' new bassist. The band played about a dozen scattered shows over the next four months while they also attempted to start on the new album. As before, the quality of their performances varied due to the uncertainty of who would show up and what condition they would be in.

Ad for a January show at Baytown's Safari Club, previewing a return to the West Coast that was not to be.

DUKE DAVIS: It was kinda funny [being hired as the Elevators' new bassist] because of having met everybody in the summer of '65, and then a couple of years after that, I was working at IA records with Lelan Rogers. So I said, "Why not?" I was close to Danny Thomas; he was trying to bring me up to date with what had happened, how it had evolved. And I was close to Stacy; he was so far off into all the dark energies by then. There was a lot of tension between Stacy and Tommy. They pretty much stayed away from each other. Tommy—I wasn't around him that much. I knew Roky pretty well, but that could change from day to day. One time we drove up together from Victoria [a city south of San Antonio], and [Roky] got into this thing about Lenny Bruce for two days—he wouldn't let it go, he thought he was Lenny. He'd get off on tangents, and you couldn't keep up with him. I remember, we had a gig in Houston and he missed the gig because he was in the bathtub talking on the phone and he chewed on the phone cord and got shocked. All kind of weird things were happening with him. Tommy had the pep talk thing he'd do before we'd play: a lot of it was so far-out—he was almost talking like Roky. It was about what the purpose of the music was, in terms of the metaphysical realm. A lot of it didn't make a lot of sense to me. I was the new kid; I was trying to remember what key things were in. I felt, as far as the live thing, you just never knew what was going to happen—from the audience to the band. It was a pretty unique thing, and of course that was the connection with the audience, because probably seventy-five percent of the audience was on LSD as well; it always amazed me to watch the audience. We could sound great and we could sound terrible, and the audience was still right with us. They'd sing every word Roky sang, but there were times when Roky would be singing one song and playing another, and the band would be playing a third song. It was that crazy—but the audience would be right with it, and knew exactly what was going on. Weird.

SANDY LOCKETT: [Stacy] actually got one of the famous police department swimming lessons. Oh yes, it used to be a

TRAVEL PERMIT

Intra-State

TRAVIS COUNTY ADULT PROBATION OFFICE

Date 1-10-68

Name Stacy Keith Southerland Cause No. 32,010

Travel to: Houston Harris

Address - Street City County

Leaving 1-11-68 Returning 2-5-68

Purpose of Travel practice for record cutting

Manner of Travel If by Auto, Impala 1965 White

Make Model License

Companions if any members of 13th Floor Elevators

Instructions or comments:

Probationer Stacy Sutherland Officer Roger L. Rainey

Top: Travis County Probation Office travel permit for Stacy to attend practice sessions with the Elevators in Houston, signed by his 1966 court-appointed officer, Roger Rainey.

Bottom left: The Elevators' new bassist Duke Davis playing jug during a 1967 performance with the Starvation Army Band.

Bottom right: Clementine, as photographed by Mikel Erickson, back on the West Coast in San Francisco's Panhandle Park, late 1967.

Advertisement for a show at the Stardust Rollercade in the *Corpus Christi Caller-Times*, March 9.

common thing: a couple of rogue cops would take someone that had annoyed them to the bridge over Buffalo Bayou—about a thirty-five-foot drop—which was quite shallow, and they would simply throw you in. It was an open sewer, and difficult to climb out of. And his fears—physical and metaphysical—just overcame him, and I can remember him sitting on the end of the bed, just with the blue horrors—and you could mistake it for the DTs, or overdose, or something, but it was sheer human terror.

STACY (*K*): I felt emotionally upset about what we were doing. I felt we really had a lot of negative, satanic force. I didn't feel like we were doing the people a bit of good. It hadn't benefited us. I felt the message in the band was not what I wanted.

JERRY LIGHTFOOT: Stacy wanted to be invisible. He didn't want anybody knowing his business, and so he tried to separate himself. Everybody has this idea of bands being this communal thing: five guys who agree on everything. Ninety percent of the time it's one guy full of himself enough to get the thing done. It's not a democracy.

Stacy's misgivings about the band were compounded by his ever-worsening addiction.

JERRY LIGHTFOOT: Stacy was taking bennies [amphetamine]—he got to a point where he felt like he'd taken enough LSD. Tommy thought that was bullshit: "You're using Hitler's drugs now."

Q: Why did he switch to heroin?

JERRY LIGHTFOOT: It's a very isolated, cocoon type of thing. He was looking for some peace. Good God, everyone in the world knows what heroin does to you, but look at how many junkies there are.

STACY (*K*): I got into smack in Houston. I was depressed, but I had also been doing a lot of speed and I was really tired of it. I had a roommate who dated this chick, and she was supposed to bring over a gram of speed but she scored heroin instead. We were both leery of doing it, but we tried it and oh, it hit the spot. I wasn't planning on getting strung out; I was just gonna chip with it, and cut it off when it started fucking with me. And I didn't catch it. I just freaked out.

Opposite top: Victor Moscoso's poster for the projected February shows back at the Avalon in San Francisco.

Opposite bottom: January 3, 1968, *World Countdown* magazine listing for the Avalon show.

DUKE DAVIS: I remember the title *The Beauty and the Beast* being flown around, but by then [the third LP] had pretty much become Stacy's project. Roky was out of the loop, Tommy was totally removed; Stacy would go in the studio and record by

*Appearing in S.F. at the Avalon February 2-4 (Friday and Sunday) ELECTIC FLAG, 13th FLOOR ELEVATORS, MAD RIVER lights by: Diogenes Lanturn Works-February 3 (Saturday) FUGS. 13th FLOOR ELEVATORS, MAD RIVER lights by: Diogenes Lanturn Works-February 9-10-11 SIEGEL-SCHWALL, BUDDY GUY, HOUR GLASS, MANCE LIPSCOMB lights by: Jerry Abrams Headlights.

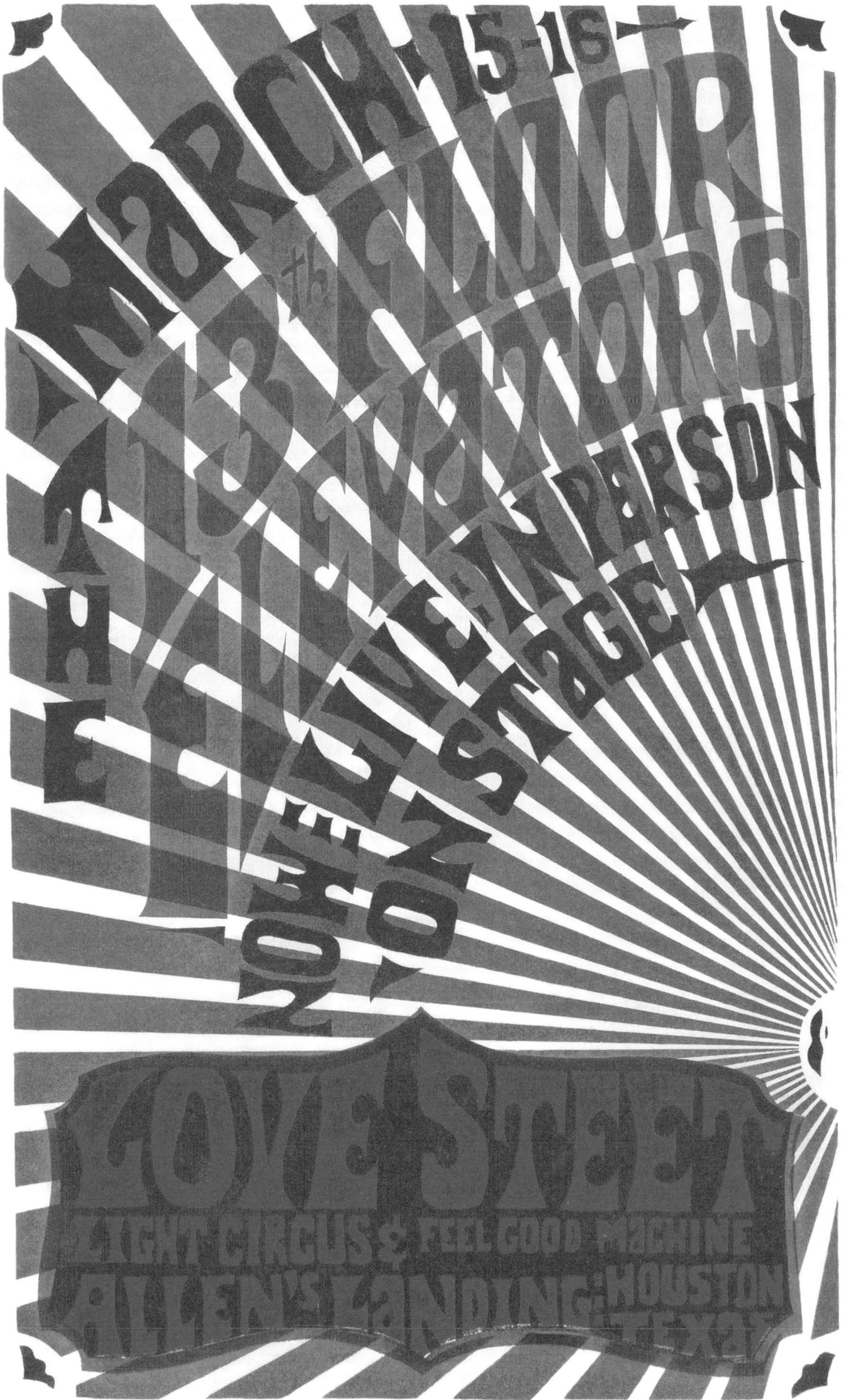
MARCH 15-16
THE 13th FLOOR ELEVATORS
LIVE IN PERSON
ON THE STAGE
LOVE STREET
LIGHT CIRCUS & FEEL GOOD MACHINE
ALLEN'S LANDING · HOUSTON
TEXAS

Opposite: Blacklight poster for the band's March 15–16 shows at Love Street (rendered here as "Love Steet"). The last known poster from the Elevators' original run.

himself—lay down some ideas, and then later on we'd get together and work on them. The beautiful thing about the Elevators was that Stacy had the sound, Roky had the voice, and Tommy had the lyrics. And that chemistry changed, and once Tommy fell out of the mix, Stacy became the driving force. And I thought it was good, because by that point, he was battling the heroin addiction so bad, I thought this was a great positive thing for him, that it could really help his life—make him more creative and bring him out of his dark energies.

The 13th Floor Elevators performed one of their final shows on the same bill as legendary bluesman Lightnin' Hopkins at Rice University in April, and Lelan Rogers took the opportunity to record Hopkins from IA's new base at Gold Star Studios with the Elevators as his backing band, a session that would result in his album *Free Form Patterns*. Hopkins assented to playing with Danny T. and Duke Davis, but, unwilling to compete on lead guitar, he kept Stacy pacing the corridor, hoping to be invited in. Following the session, Lelan was unceremoniously sacked after an argument with IA boss Noble Ginther, who had arrived at the studios drunk.

With Lelan gone, Stacy started work on the new LP totally unsupervised, on February 7, 1968. By the twenty-second, he had laid down enough backing tracks to invite Roky and Tommy to add their contributions, but when Roky showed up at the studio at midday, he found it empty. Still, rather than waste studio time, IA put him to work immediately. He laid down several takes of "May the Circle Remain Unbroken," the first song he'd written entirely on his own since "You're Gonna Miss Me." The rest of the band arrived at midnight and blasted out "Livin' On," a Hall-Sutherland masterpiece of self-realization that perfectly captured the band's defiant mood and the reality that they were still a musical force to be reckoned with. It would turn out to be their swan song.

DUKE DAVIS: "Livin' On" was a magical moment. Because there was so much dissension going on creatively, and trying to get Stacy involved, and Tommy back in—[get] everybody on the same page. The feelings were pretty good that night, and I think that one reason the track "Livin' On" was a real special moment [was] . . . it was "turn the tape on and go."

Next, the band switched attention to Roky's "May the Circle Remain Unbroken." Stacy got Johndavid Bartlett to clink a large glass ashtray while he manipulated the sound through a series of Echoplex units daisy-chained together, creating a haunting effect. Following this, on March 2, it was Tommy's turn in the studio to overdub jug parts, and the next day Roky added his final vocal overdubs and rhythm guitar to "Never Another" and "Livin' On."

In the meantime, the band played a few live shows: the concert with Lightnin' Hopkins (which Danny Thomas recalls as being one of their best gigs), and two nights at Love Street in Houston on the fifteenth and sixteenth. By this point, the Elevators' reputation as pioneers had been cemented outside of Texas—despite their being landlocked inside the state—and, as Danny recalls, their Love Street shows were attended not only by local musicians such as Billy Gibbons and Johnny Winter, but also by touring musicians like Grace Slick, other members of the Jefferson Airplane, and Iron Butterfly.

While Stacy worked in the studio, Tommy formulated material for his next project, *The Beauty and the Beast*. The only new composition anyone can recall from this was the unrecorded "Jerusalem," which was performed live.

Advertisement in *The Rag* for an April 1, 1968, show in Houston.

JOHNDAVID BARTLETT: "Jerusalem"? It wasn't much like other Elevators tunes. I saw Tommy sing it: the lyrics were "Jerusalem," wailed, moaned, screamed, and cried. It was almost a mantra—a song cycle and a glass bead game. One of the most pleasant memories I have of their live performances . . . Tommy wasn't driving me nuts, [but] I could see where people would lose interest in what he was saying pretty quick.

DUKE DAVIS: Oh yeah, "Jerusalem" [*laughs*], I remember that. It was so weird. One concert, Tommy went into that and even the audience went, "What the heck's he doing?" It was just so crazy, it really didn't make any sense. It was almost a discomfort.

JERRY LIGHTFOOT: Tommy came up with the idea that Houston was Jerusalem and Austin was Damascus, so he wrote a song called "Jerusalem"... There's a philosophy rule of thumb that if you come up with an idea, you should be able to explain it from a couple of points of view, and Tommy had always done that—and then when he got into this Jerusalem thing, he started to say, "Well, you've just got to believe me." Tommy was one of these guys who would initiate a project, and if you didn't do that—and Stacy got tired of doing *that*—then fuck you. And Roky was having these terrible mental spells that were never dealt with properly. The spell broke. That's when [Tommy] gave up on the project, and gave up on everybody, and started having a very patronizing attitude to everybody. Because if you didn't see it Tommy's way, you just didn't get it.

▲ **SIBYL SUTHERLAND**: [The Elevators] got a chance that year to play at HemisFair [the 1968 World's Fair], which was quite an honor. They had dozens and dozens of stages with different things happening on them all the time.

Starting April 6 and set to run through the ensuing six months, HemisFair '68 promised—in numerous newspaper ads under headlines proclaiming "Happiness Is HemisFair"—the opportunity to "visit the pavilions of

Top: Cover mock-up by Bill Narum for a proposed 1969 reissue of *Easter Everywhere*.

Bottom: Cover mock-up by Bill Narum for the projected album *The Beauty and the Beast*.

American Industry, browse the wares of foreign countries, then thrill to the view atop the Tower of the Americas, 622 feet above the pageantry of the Southwest's first World's Fair."

The local music industry had seen their World's Fair as a chance to rival Monterey Pop. Phil Krumm, who knew the Elevators via Love Street, ran the fair's "Y Project" youth tent and booked them to play HemisFair on April 8, during their concurrent showcase residency at the Love Street location in San Antonio. The band disintegrated, however, before they set foot inside the fair.

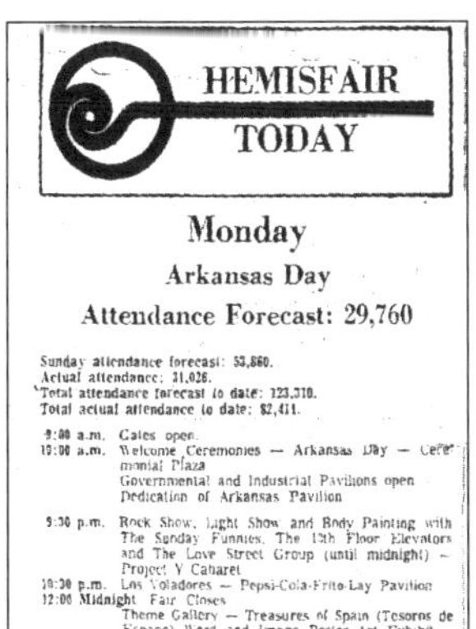

HEMISFAIR TODAY

Monday

Arkansas Day

Attendance Forecast: 29,760

Sunday attendance forecast: 53,860.
Actual attendance: 31,026.
Total attendance forecast to date: 123,310.
Total actual attendance to date: 82,411.

9:00 a.m. Gates open.
10:00 a.m. Welcome Ceremonies — Arkansas Day — Ceremonial Plaza
Governmental and Industrial Pavilions open
Dedication of Arkansas Pavilion
9:30 p.m. Rock Show, Light Show and Body Painting with The Sunday Funnies, The 13th Floor Elevators and The Love Street Group (until midnight) — Project Y Cabaret
10:30 p.m. Los Voladores — Pepsi-Cola-Frito-Lay Pavilion
12:00 Midnight Fair Closes
Theme Gallery — Treasures of Spain (Tesoros de España) Word and Image Poster Art Exhibit

Listing for the band's planned—but unrealized—appearance at the 1968 San Antonio HemisFair.

PHIL KRUMM: April 8, two days after the opening of the fair: it had to be right then that everything that was the Elevators blew apart. [It] happened at Love Street. And Sebastian [who ran the club] was chewing Tommy out and excoriating him, calling the Elevators washed-up losers. So, I regarded the non-concert at Love Street as the last event for them and the final gig of the Elevators.

DANNY THOMAS: The San Antonio Love Street was a great idea; it was right across the street from HemisFair. A great venue with a balcony [and a] great sound system. That's when Roky would not go up onstage; I wouldn't even call [it] a full gig—I think our equipment was set up, and we got up there and messed around a little bit, but we never did a full show. He didn't freeze; he just wouldn't go out.

SIBYL SUTHERLAND: Anyway, they were playing, and Roky just walked off the bandstand. He was very paranoiac; he thought they were out to get him. He said, "They're after us," whoever "they" were, and he wouldn't come back. So they had to dismiss them and finally get someone else. Stacy was very annoyed.

THE SAN ANTONIO LIGHT, *APRIL 27, 1968:*
The 13th Floor Elevators no longer appear at Love Street Light Circus. During a show last week lead singer Rocky [sic] *Erickson walked off stage after the second tune. A couple of nights he didn't show up. Rumors have been flying around for a year about the group splitting up. Some of the Elevators are getting fed up with the other members. It's the public's loss because they are one of, it not the best, acid rock bands on [sic] the state. San Antonio's newest group, The Bubble Puppy, will tour with the Grateful Dead, the Electric Flag and the Vanilla Fudge throughout Florida in May.*

Bubble Puppy were San Antonio's answer to the psychedelic sound developed by the Elevators, and they would soon sign to IA. When their first single—"Hot Smoke and Sassafras," released in January 1969—began to take off nationally, the Elevators were history at the label.

EVELYN ERICKSON: When Roky came home from the HemisFair—I had taken Ben and Sumner to see the band—he

Opposite: Portraits of Roky, Tommy, and Stacy taken at Love Street.

> looked really tired, and I asked him, "Do you want to go home tonight?" And he didn't come home then, but he came home the next day. And he was just . . . exhausted, and I could tell something was wrong. [Roky] slept all week, [and] friends took him out and got him high. This went on about three weeks. [His breakdown] was in the middle of the night. He started talking gibberish, out by the swimming pool, and it scared me to death. And I called the emergency hospital and said, "I have to get an emergency psychiatrist." [In] the morning I got him to the car and got him over to the Holy Cross Hospital, and [they] knocked him out with drugs.

Roky was released from Holy Cross into Evelyn's care on May 4; when she called the hospital to get a repeat prescription of Roky's medication, however, their previous doctor—a man named Kerr—was unavailable, and the doctor to whom she spoke was furious that Roky had been released in such a heavily-medicated condition.

> EVELYN ERICKSON: I got really upset with Kerr, because he said [Roky]'d be a vegetable the rest of his life—no hope at all. And I said, "Well, who would you recommend that thinks completely differently from you?" He said, "Well, there's a Dr. Hermon in town—came from Europe." So I went to him, and he was kind—able to talk normally to me, a lowly patient's mother—and he took Roky off most of the medication, gave him a very low dosage, and he improved so much it was amazing. He had a nurse, Robert Williams, who had heard Roky's music and was a fan, so he said, "I'll help you take care of him." He took him for about a week and let him live over there with him, but Roky walked away from them and was gone again.

In fact, Dr. Harry Hermon—known to the Austin authorities as "Crazy Harry"—had already assisted Roky with his draft-board plight. A thirty-eight-year-old Austrian research psychologist with a federal license to prescribe LSD and marijuana, Hermon was eventually run out of town by Captain Gann of the vice squad. Hermon then joined Arthur Kleps's Neo-American Church in upstate New York, which had a membership of more than 10,000 and regularly used hallucinogens as a religious sacrament.

Amid the chaos, it was left to Stacy to keep the Elevators going in hopes they'd regroup. The band played a couple of shows without Roky that were—as Duke recalls—"truly atrocious," and Stacy continued to report to Gold Star Studios, where he endlessly overdubbed or rerecorded the backing tracks for the new album, waiting for Roky's vocals to be added. In June, he even overdubbed "Never Another" and "Livin' On" (the only two tracks complete with Roky's vocals) with a brass section. The two trombonists and one trumpeter from the Houston Symphony Orchestra arrived at the studio around 1:00 a.m. one evening, fully tuxedoed after a performance conducted by André Previn; taking their cue from Tommy's jug runs, they added their parts and left.

Above: Tommy, Roky, and Stacy at Love Street. Warner: "The color portraits of Roky and Tommy were taken at Love Street, in the upstairs office behind the light booth, and Stacy outside on Allen's Landing, March, 1968."

DUKE DAVIS: I think the band had pretty much dissolved. There were no more gigs because Roky was in the hospital, and Tommy had been out of the picture for some time. We were finishing *Bull of the Woods* with just Stacy, Danny, and I. I didn't want it to break up; that wasn't my choice. Stacy—he could have been the saving grace of the band, but there was so much dark energy around him.

By June, IA was done waiting for the undelivered album and finally revisited the "Bynum tapes" from the winter and spring of 1966. For a pre-album "teaser" single, the label released "May the Circle Remain Unbroken" backed with the band's cover of Buddy Holly's "I'm Gonna Love You Too" from the Bynum sessions. The message was clear: IA wanted an album's worth of material (complete with Roky Erickson vocals) or they would issue the unreleased Bynum material. Though the A-side was unlike any other Elevators tune—no drums, an effects-laden, ethereal soundscape—the label hoped it might be destined for FM underground radio, while the B-side was targeted for AM radio play. Despite IA's plans, the single—after receiving a small amount of airplay in Houston—died a death nationally. Still, the label wouldn't settle for anything less than a full album, and after reviewing every unissued recording they had, they scrapped together a full-length and overdubbed applause to create an unconvincing "live" album.

In July, after a three-month hiatus, IA succeeded in convincing Evelyn to allow Roky to return to performing, and the core band triumvirate reconvened for a show in nearby Baytown. The label came prepared, with an RV fitted with child locks to "protect" Roky. They had also brought Steve Webb (drummer with the band the Lost and Found, also signed to IA) along to act as Roky's understudy and backup.

LELAN ROGERS (*JS*): People in Texas were not ready for drugs at all. At all! Once, I took them to Baytown to do a show. We used to go and do the dances. The kids enjoyed the music—just music. Charge two dollars to get in at the door, rent a hall, make a little money . . . but down there, we got nailed in the parking lot by Texas Rangers, the sheriff, the police chief, all but the FBI. They took all our equipment out of the back of the van. They had screwdrivers and pliers—they took every amplifier apart, tubes out, and had them scattered all over the parking lot. We got there at seven o'clock, and at ten, the kids were all on the inside waiting for the Elevators. They knew we were getting busted . . . I kept them clean. The law used to vacuum the cars. They carried hand vacuum cleaners and they'd vacuum our cars looking for seeds. So, you can bet your ass I vacuumed before we left. I had them turn their pockets inside out, "And if you've got a trace, get rid of it or we'll all go to jail." So the kids at the place that night went and got other equipment and set it up for us. We just picked up the pieces and threw them in the van, and went in and played.

↓Houston↓ ↑Austin↑

Univ. of Houston - Bergan Exhibit - 2nd Floor - UC. Vietnam Scene - Lobby of UC - Photographic study of Vietnam- what little there is is good.

Univ. of St. Thomas - Look Back - Jones Hall.

PRESERVATION HALL - Chenevert -Jazz sets every sunday - Some people still want to preserve big band jazz.

SAM HOUSTON COLISEUM -Jimi Hendrix Experience - Aug 4 -8:30 PM only - tickets on July 20 only--if you miss this you are out of it.

CINDER CLUB - The Young Americans and the Swinging Rivieras - soul sounds.

IMAGE - Rhythm Rockers; liteshow included.

LOVE STREET - The 13th Floor Elevators may be there. Why don't you go & see?

James "Smokestack" Tisdom and John Lomax in concert at 2020 Herman Drive, Jewish Community Center - 8 PM - Sunday,Go if you can, it will be good.

SAND MOUNTAIN - Richmond Ave. - they always have some good folk there -even protest if you like.

KFMK - 98 FM - they play the good albums.

HISTORY OF THE NEGRO PEOPLE - 8 PM - Friday -Ch 8.

WHAT'S HAPPENING TO AMERICA - 9 PM - Friday - Ch 9- Let's see what has happened now!

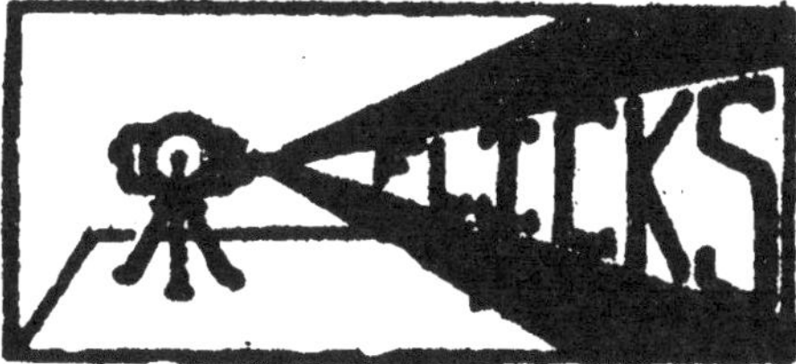

2001: a space odessey - Windsor Cinerama - the story's kind of a bummer but the photography and liteshow are mind-blowers.

PATHER PANCHALI - Jewish Synagogue at TSU - City Film Festival - it's free, so go.

ELVIRA MADIGAN - Delman - tragic love affair; the military is even knocked; it is pretty wild.

THE UMBRELLAS OF CHERBOURG - 8 PM Sunday - 2020 Herman Drive - operetta-onto-film.

THE CRACK IN THE TRUMPET - 8:30 PM -Thursday, Friday, & Saturday - Theater Suburbia - 1410 W 43rd. Original play about a fake tent revivalist - all God's children got shoes.

Above: Listing in July's issue of *The Rag*, featuring what had become an all-too-typical concert blurb: "The 13th Floor Elevators may be there. Why don't you go & see?"

JOHN LEWALLEN (Houston friend): The Baytown show was where I was arrested for US federal drug charges, along with the drummer. I had taken LSD. Baytown was the result of Roky's mom's concern about the band providing drugs to Roky. The record company reps had a recreational vehicle, and overheard me offering to provide DMT to band members. During the break, the drummer [Danny Thomas] left with me, and the Baytown police followed us and took us down.

DANNY THOMAS (*1977*): [The cops] sat there and listened to the rest of the set. They were polite enough to stand there by the edge of the stage, which I thought was a gas, because I was worried about them coming up there and taking me off in the middle of a song: "We're from the state of Texas and we've got news for you, sir. Come on down."

Evelyn's diary records that Danny Thomas gave Roky drugs after his return to Houston, which served as pretext for his being "voluntarily" admitted to a private rehabilitation center—Hedgecroft Hospital in Houston—on July 11.

ROGER ERICKSON: Hospital with bars on the window . . . It wasn't advertised as having guards, but there were obviously guards around. Yep, I remember visiting there.

EVELYN ERICKSON: International Artists said they had a big van with sleeping facilities and a bodyguard for Roky to keep him away from drugs. I protested vehemently, saying we were doing so good in Austin; with another month I thought he might be ready to go back with the band. [IA] convinced him he should go to their psychiatrist in Houston. I thought they meant just to talk to him, but they wanted him to commit himself under Dr. Howard Crow. But I wasn't sure [that was] God's plan. Dr. Crow looks at me and says I'm the cause of all of Roky's problems, that I'm too religious. I get angry and fire back, "Don't you have any faith?" It's all very dramatic and charged with hostility. I ask Dr. Crow if I may call my husband to tell him what is happening—or Reverend Sumner, whose prayers for Roky were so helpful—but he screams at me, "Don't you dare use my phone, get out of my office! This boy is twenty-one years old and can sign himself in." I reply, "He won't be twenty-one until July 15."

ROKY (*NFA*): She was like a straitjacket—that's the best description I can give of my mother at that time. She was, like, the wrong person to tell about anything.

On his twenty-first birthday, Roky was administered electroshock therapy.

TOMMY: They had given him shock treatments, and that really brought me down. I was trying to help him, so I thought, "We'll get him out and get him in the open air, and maybe he'll clear up." He didn't.

FRED HYDE: I'd never met Roky, [but] I'd known Tommy for quite a while, so we went down to visit [Roky]. He was just this weird guy, long hair and a real spaced-out look, and he was walking around smoking a cigarette—walking, walking, walking. He got these shock treatments when he was in the hospital. He was so drugged up. He and Tommy talked, and we talked about how to get him out. The plan was, we were going to come up the back stairs; but as I opened the door, there was a guard standing there, and he ran me right out of the place. I don't really remember how Roky got out of the hospital . . .

ROKY: Tommy took the door off the hinges with a screwdriver, and snook me out of the hospital, and left some money to pay for the damage.

Tommy's idea was to hide out at a safehouse until his parole ended on August 9. Then, as soon as he could freely leave the state of Texas, he did, fleeing to San Francisco—without informing Stacy—and taking a new band lineup with him.

FRED HYDE: "How's Roky; is he alright?" That's all you ever heard. Go to a bar, go to a club, everybody's just taking care of Roky. Tommy and Stacy seemed at odds with each other during that time. My first trip out [to San Francisco] was in a VW bus—myself, Tommy, Roky, David [Green], and Jack Scarborough and Harry Buckholts [Roky's friend from Travis High]. Jack was supposed to be the new drummer and Harry the bass player, I suppose, in the Elevators; nobody believed it was going away. But the bus exploded—in Big Spring, Texas, just the armpit of the world. We didn't have a prayer of getting out of there [until] we met the only hippie in Big Spring, and he took us back to his little shack, and we got high. [We decided] we'd have to hitchhike, but nobody's going to pick up seven hitchers, so we split up: Jack and Harry went together, Tommy and David went together, and I got stuck with Roky. I was riding with Roky and he was just a basket case. He was just this wide-eyed guy—he'd look at you weird like you were flirting with him. By the time we finally got to El Paso, I was just irate, freaked. A guy stopped in a sports car going all the way to San Francisco with room for one guy, so I put Roky in that car and said, "Here, call this number—Clementine." [Eventually] we got to Clementine's house in San Francisco, and Roky still wasn't there! 'Cuz he'd freaked [the driver] out; the guy had let him out in Los Angeles. Somehow, Tommy got Roky picked up.

Following Tommy and Roky's departure, IA wasted no time, issuing the fake live album in August 1968. Ronnie rejoined what was left of the band—now just Stacy and Danny Thomas. The label sent them on a brief promotional tour in the new RV, playing the beachfront in Corpus Christi before moving on to San Antonio and back to Houston. The only documented show was August 3 at the Municipal Auditorium in San Antonio supporting the Hombres, who'd scored a novelty hit in 1967 with the Dylan pastiche "Let It Out (Let It All Hang Out)"—produced by the "Crazy Cajun," Huey P. Meaux. The band thought it was "hokum."

JERRY LIGHTFOOT: IA had a house on Old Galveston Road [in Houston] and they let Stacy stay out there. Ended up being a horrible drug den—speed freaks. I used to go in [to IA] with Stacy, and beg for twenty dollars—he went down there and he argued with them, "I've honored every bit of all of this, I'm the only one out of everyone, and all I want is a Barney Kessel Gibson guitar and I don't think it's too much to ask at this fucking point." And anyway, they finally relented and got him one, and the first night he had it, some speed freak knocked it down the stairs and knocked the head off it—broke his heart. That's when he got real disgusted with everything, and he had every right to be.

During this period, Stacy met Bunni—his future wife.

RONNIE: He first met her when we were out there on the Old Galveston Road, at the house . . . and we'd had a bunch of people over and they'd all left and it got to, "Where's Bunni?" Anyway, Stacy went back in his room and opened up the closet door—she was drawing blood out of one arm and shooting it in the other because she didn't have anything to shoot up. She just liked the needle. And he ran her off, and then he started dating her—and I was going, "Stacy! Why are you dating that girl?!" And they got into heroin, after speed, and that's when it really went downhill.

The situation in San Francisco was no less bleak.

TOMMY: We took Roky to this Indian mystic [who] we hoped would help him, but he didn't. I was so confused. I didn't know what to do, or what my responsibilities were to him, and it was all really a mess.

CLEMENTINE: They brought Roky to me. That was an incredible experience. I kept him in my house [on Shrader Street], and I treated him very much like I did my own son, except that he was more fragile. He was saying things like, "I'm picking up transmissions from the Russians in my tooth, and they're telling me to kill Jacqueline Kennedy, and I don't want to do it." And then he'd turn to me and he'd go, "You look like Jacqueline Kennedy, Clementine." Whenever he'd get really distressed, we would drive to the beach and stand him in the water and let the waves pound on him; that was the best therapy, and we'd put him back and dry him off, put him to bed, and he'd be talking normal for a few days.

Tommy returned to Texas to find Stacy. The nearest anyone can remember to a rehearsal with Roky, Jack, and Harry—Tommy's San Francisco Elevators lineup—was prior to a Sir Douglas Quintet show between August 23 and 25, 1968, at the Avalon. And though Roky reported, in a letter to his mother, that he was "safe and sound and healthy and happy"—highlighting, in green felt-tip marker, "God it's good to be out of the hospital"—Evelyn was still wary; she responded by wiring $25 to the Superbar Food Market on Haight, requesting they only give him food, "no cash."

TOMMY: I came back [to Texas] because I'd been given this money by this lawyer out here [in San Francisco]—Brian Rohans, who handled the Airplane—and I was supposed to get Stacy, but then he was shooting smack! At that time, I didn't know enough about smack, and what that has to do with your responsibility, but smack—intellectually, it's shortening your life. Same with coke and speed. So I was just sitting around trying to figure what to do. We were like a self-destructive group. Although Stacy and Roky were good musicians, we were amateurish in what happened to us—the whole situation.

FRED HYDE: Tommy was pissed; he didn't like [Stacy continuing the band] at all. He was writing stuff like "Jerusalem," and he had new stuff, and as far as he was concerned it was still all happening: Roky was going to get on top of his game, Stacy was going to come out to California, they were going to be billed at the Avalon. But Stacy wasn't coming back. I don't remember how we all split up. Tommy had this girl with him [whom he] moved in with. I asked Tommy, "What's the deal? Gay [Jones, Tommy's then-girlfriend] is your other half—what are you doing sleeping with this other girl?" That's when I started realizing he started justifying this kind of stuff—which is OK, but it didn't fit the rest of the scheme, so I started seeing holes in the whole philosophy. The whole time I was with Tommy he was in love with Gay—but Gay was just a little girl.

Gilbert Shelton's "Delightsome Demonical Grackle Debacle," scheduled for August 29, 30, and 31, was to be Stacy (or "Stacey," as the poster read) and the Elevators' final show at the Vulcan. The band performed a few old Elevators tunes, some of Stacy's new material, and some blues jams, and the general consensus was that though they were good, it was a disappointment because "it wasn't the boys." The exact lineup remains a mystery: Steve Webb, IA's backup for Roky, managed to excuse himself from vocal duties, and he was reluctantly replaced by James Harrell, the Lost and Found's singer/songwriter. Most likely, the band consisted of Stacy, Danny Thomas, James Harrell on vocals, and a stand-in bassist—Ronnie does not recall playing the show.

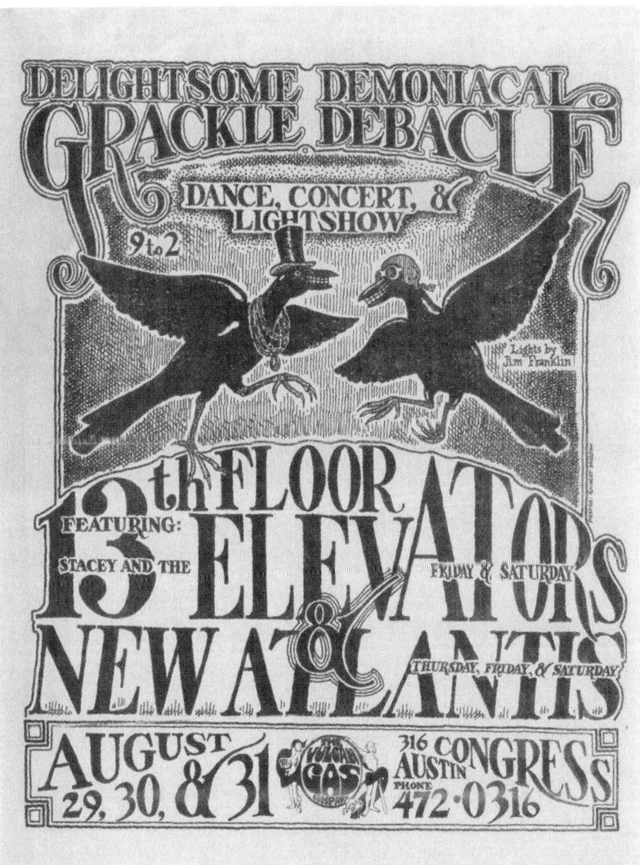

DELIGHTSOME DEMONIACAL
GRACKLE DEBACLE
DANCE, CONCERT, & LIGHTSHOW
9 to 2
Lights by Jim Franklin
FEATURING:
13th FLOOR ELEVATORS
STACEY AND THE
FRIDAY & SATURDAY
& NEW ATLANTIS
THURSDAY, FRIDAY, & SATURDAY
AUGUST 29, 30, & 31
316 CONGRESS AUSTIN
PHONE 472-0316

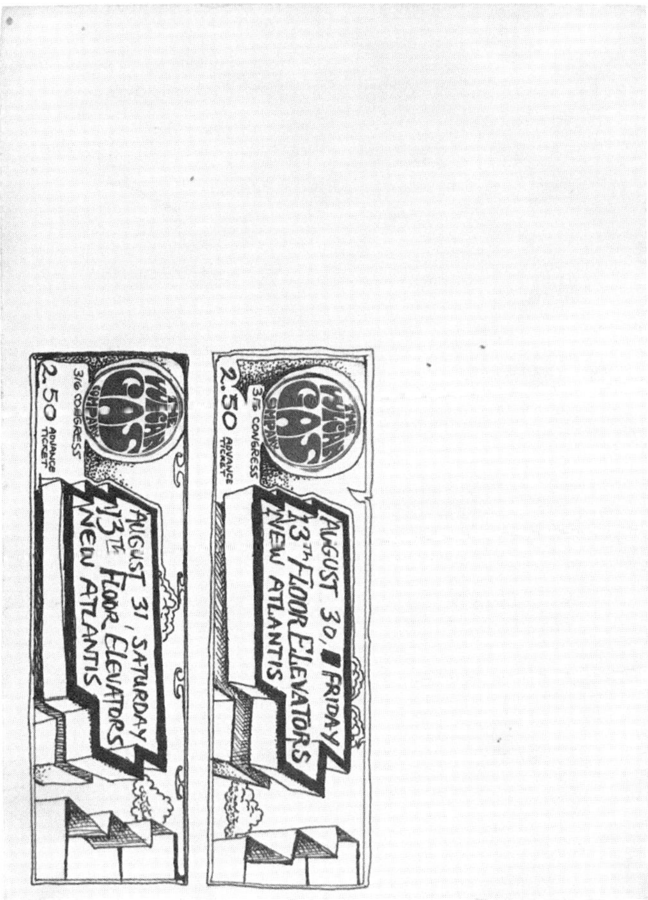

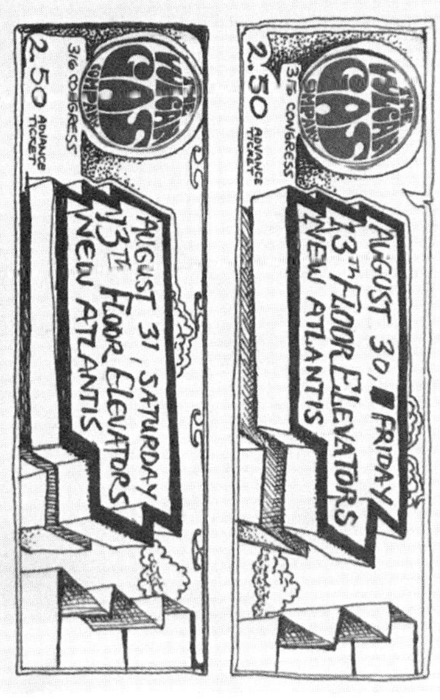

316 CONGRESS
2.50 ADVANCE TICKET
AUGUST 31, SATURDAY
13TH FLOOR ELEVATORS
NEW ATLANTIS
316 CONGRESS
2.50 ADVANCE TICKET
AUGUST 30, FRIDAY
13TH FLOOR ELEVATORS
NEW ATLANTIS

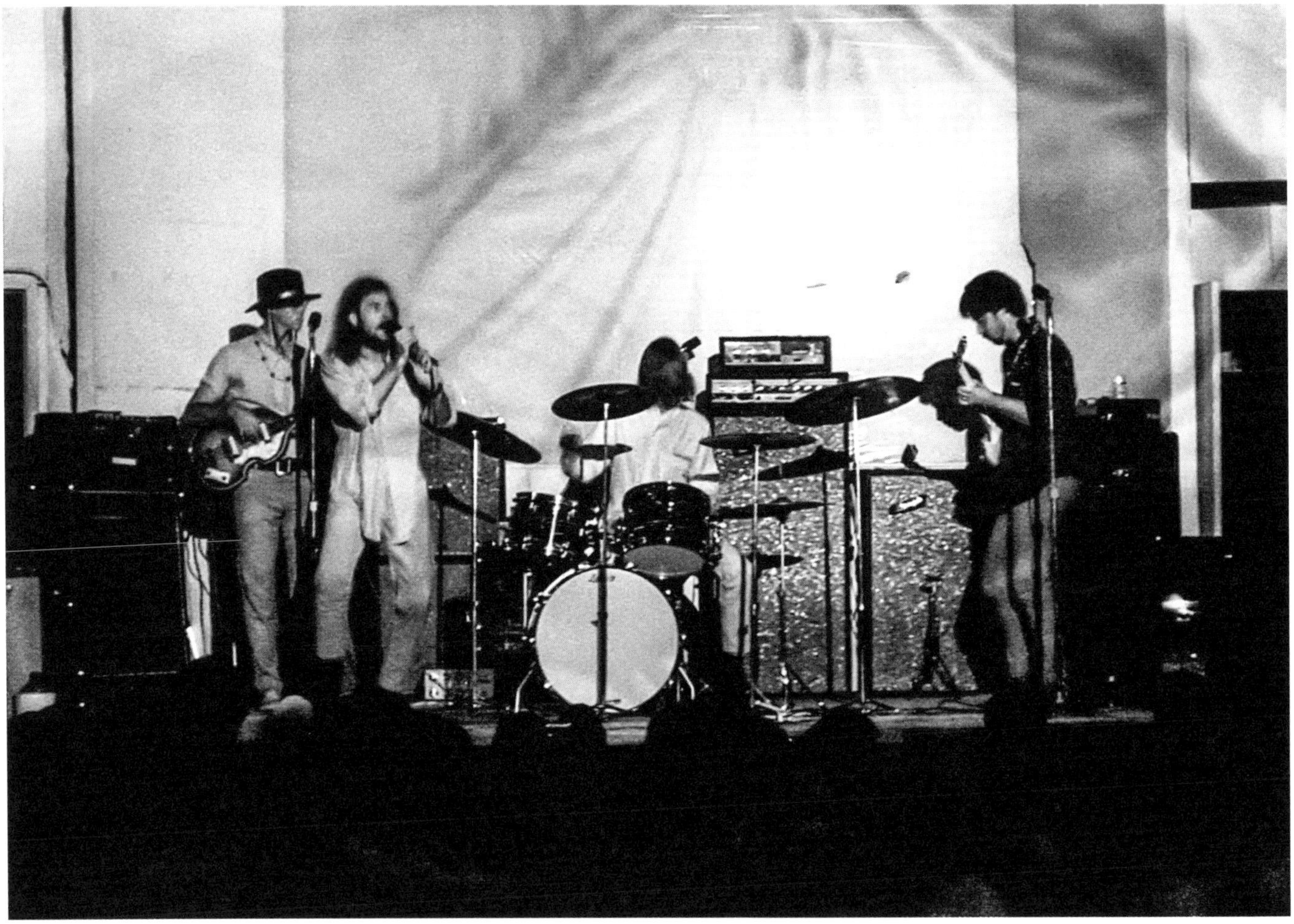

Austin Statesman advertisement for the "Grackle Debacle" concert at the Vulcan Gas Company, August 1968.

JAMES HARRELL: We were still under contract from International Artists, and still had to do what they said. I didn't feel comfortable about taking Roky's place, and playing rhythm and singing and remembering all them words, but that's the job they gave me—being Roky Erickson. Yep, it was terrible for me. That was under extreme pressure—under protest, under contract. Stacy was out [of] the picture for quite a while—after his overdose, heroin I believe. He didn't say much about it. We were doing psychedelics and he wanted to do the big heavy stuff.

Tommy soon drifted down the coast from San Francisco, living for a period in a cave commune run by the Brotherhood of Eternal Love, on Laguna Beach. The Brotherhood had been started in 1966 as a registered nonprofit religious outfit that viewed marijuana and LSD as religious sacraments; by the late sixties, *Rolling Stone* had branded them the hippie mafia. Eventually, Tommy got caught walking into a festival with controlled substances on him and spent a brief spell in jail. From there, he was assimilated into the growing community of sixties refuges in the Bay Area, eventually taking up residency in the mid-seventies in a slum hotel in the Tenderloin, where he still lives in a one-room apartment.

JOHN LEWALLEN: Tommy was living in the basement of the Chinese Communist newspaper in Chinatown; that was the last time I saw him. I went to the Old Galveston Road house [in Houston]—I remember Stacy sitting in a chair on the front porch without moving for an entire day. He rarely ever spoke a word. His guitar did all the talking for him. Galveston Road was dead—like "H" is dead, and the band was dead. That was the last time I saw Stacy.

Despite advertisements in *The Rag* for further shows at the Vulcan on October 11 and 12—the listing optimistically reading "13th Floor Elevators (with Rocky [*sic*] maybe) and New Atlantis"—Johnny Winter performed instead. A band called the 13th Floor Elevators did, however, continue to perform without any original members—not even Stacy, who was still recovering from his overdose.

Opposite top left: Gilbert Shelton's full poster for "Stacey [*sic*] and the 13th Floor Elevators" at the "Delightsome Demoniacal Grackle Debacle." Per Shelton: "The Vulcan Gas Company's budget for posters shrank considerably. I produced one or two posters using a crude silk-screen technique, in which we used the light of the sun to expose the screens and the hot water in the shower in the bathroom to develop them. After I had finished the Grackle Debacle design, Sandy Lockett told me that the word 'grackle' didn't rhyme with the word 'debacle,' and I was abashed. Later, I found that there is more than one correct pronunciation for 'debacle,' and I felt vindicated."

Opposite top right: Shelton's original ticket artwork for the "Grackle Debacle" set of shows at the Vulcan, August 1968.

Opposite bottom: Ronnie, an unknown guest singer, Danny Thomas, and Stacy at Love Street. Warner: "The guest singer was part of some other band that was doing something there that weekend. Part of the reason the Elevators were playing at Love Street so much was that IA was buying the club. As a business at the time, [they wanted] to have a club, promote concerts, management, cover all the bases." Ronnie: "Stacy and Danny and I played every week at Love Street . . . but we were only a trio. That was how they made money to live on while we finished the recording . . . We were doing some of Stacy's new stuff. We didn't really sing much."

316 CONGRESS
9 TIL 2
VULCAN GAS CO.
COMING ATTRACTIONS
OCT 11-12 13TH FLOOR ELEVATORS + NEW ATLANTIS
OCT 18-19 SHIVA'S HEADBAND
NOV 1-2 SHIVA'S HEADBAND
TENTATIVE BOOKINGS:
B.B. KING QUICKSILVER BOBBY "BLUE" BLAND
LITTLE MILTON STEVE MILLER BO DIDDLEY

Above: Advertisement in *The Rag* for October shows at the Vulcan Gas Company. Johnny Winter would ultimately perform instead of the Elevators.

Opposite: November 26 review in Boston's *Mass Media* underground paper for IA's long-threatened "live" album cash-in release.

STACY: I didn't do any more [speed] for about a year and a half, and then I got back into it and I got on a really bad rib with it for two years. Witches and goblins . . . I lived in a haunted house in Houston, with spirits walking around.

On September 26, Stacy had gone into the studio to review recordings and overdub the old sessions one last time. New material was recorded between October 21 and November 18, and the endless sessions for the Elevators' third LP finally wrapped.

MASS MEDIA Page 7

NY SCENE

"Elevators" Rising

by Rich Hanson

They come on stage to the shattering applause of an audience that sounds like a remnant of the 1955 Ebbetts Field crowd. Then they are introduced as "THE original psychedelic group in the land," and The 13th Floor Elevators proceed to put down some very heavy and very funky sounds. This is the group that has held top billings on the same tickets as The Grateful Dead, Moby Grape and Quicksilver Messenger Service, yet they are virtually unknown on the East Coast. Their latest release, "13th Floor Elevators Live" (International Artists) should help spread the Word known mostly to a small but fanatical "Elevators" cult in the Southwest and West Coast areas.

This particular album cannot be considered "psychedelic," if such music exists in itself. Moreover, it can't even be called progressive. Instead, The Elevators interpret many rock traditionals and, with a clean and simple style, actually outdo the originals. Despite the overdubbing of crowd-reactions and the Stone Age recording techniques of International Artists, "Live" must stand out as one of the finest releases of the year. They have combined incredible versatility with a flair for tasteful renditions of other artists' materials. Their version of Dylan's "Baby Blue" on their last album is an outstanding example.

If I'm not inclined to think that their music is psychedelic, I should say that their lyrics are very much so. Thus The Elevators may have the most succinct definition of psychedelic music yet advanced, lyrical psychedelicism. "Everybody Needs Somebody to Love" takes the listener to the wonderful world of The Rolling Stones and beyond, to "Levitation," where the guitar work was apparently scraped right off the pavement of Jagger's "Route 66." "Before You Accuse Me" is a tribute to the genius of Bo Diddley, while "I'm Gonna Love You Too" sounds more like Buddy Holly. Highlighting the originals on the album are "You Can't Hurt Me Anymore," "Roller Coaster," "She Lives In a Time of Her Own," and their only known genuine hit, "You're Gonna Miss Me."

Although it isn't exactly background music for a formal tea, "Live" might raise sagging spirits on a dull, rainy night. They're meant to be loud, and fast, and free, so if you can find a copy, you'll find that they don't lay their meaning between the cuffs. Turn on to The Elevators, it beats the tube!

Top: Cover of the so-called *Live* LP.

Bottom: The last known handbill from the Elevators' original run: October 26, 1968, at Love Street.

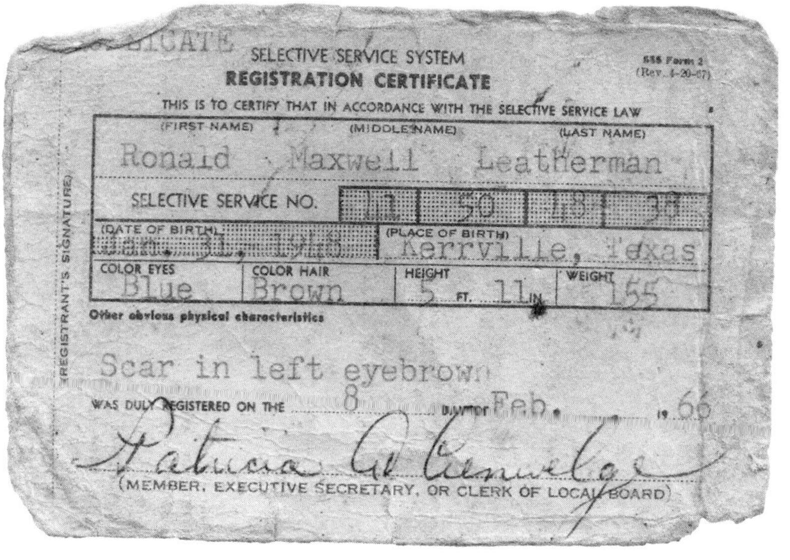

ICATE

SELECTIVE SERVICE SYSTEM
REGISTRATION CERTIFICATE

SSS Form 2
(Rev. 4-20-67)

THIS IS TO CERTIFY THAT IN ACCORDANCE WITH THE SELECTIVE SERVICE LAW

(FIRST NAME)	(MIDDLE NAME)	(LAST NAME)
Ronald	Maxwell	Leatherman

SELECTIVE SERVICE NO. 11 50 48 38

(DATE OF BIRTH)	(PLACE OF BIRTH)
Jan. 31, 1948	Kerrville, Texas

COLOR EYES	COLOR HAIR	HEIGHT	WEIGHT
Blue	Brown	5 FT. 11 IN.	155

Other obvious physical characteristics

Scar in left eyebrow

WAS DULY REGISTERED ON THE 8 DAY OF Feb. 19 66

(MEMBER, EXECUTIVE SECRETARY, OR CLERK OF LOCAL BOARD)

(REGISTRANT'S SIGNATURE)

Top and center: Ronnie's draft card, photos in uniform, and dog tag.

Bottom right: Ronnie in Kerrville as part of his then-current project Killer Chicken and the Dumplings; he'd soon be finally sent to Vietnam.

Top: James Harrell, Danny Thomas, Ronnie, and Stacy.

Bottom: Stacy and James Harrell at IA's new home at Gold Star Studios for the *Bull of the Woods* sessions, circa October 1968.

VII

LIVIN' ON

The Reformations

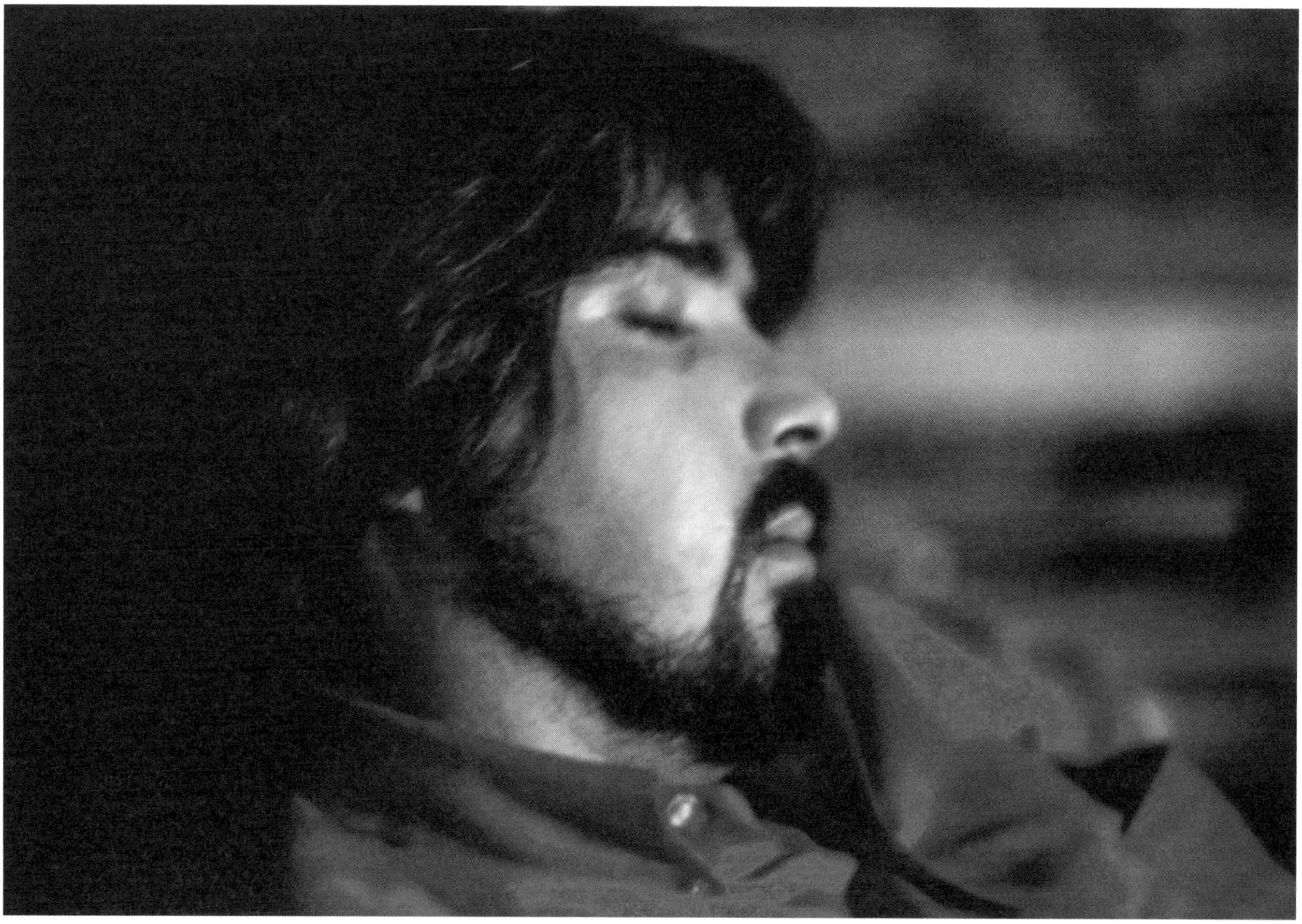

CHET HELMS (*K*): The last time I saw Roky, I was stoned on acid at a party and I got scared, wanted to run away, so I stumbled out on the street, and sort of realized I was near his apartment. I ducked in his door. He was really spaced out, and there was a meth-freak chick in there with him who was sort of supporting his trip. Actually, being in there for a while made me realize that I was actually more together than I thought. After a while he was sort of getting into my head, so I split.

TERRY MOORE: [San Francisco] was like paradise when we got out there; we scored our acid, and you could go hear a different psychedelic band every night. Everyone spoke of Roky in reverent tones, almost like the Second Coming, his kinetic energy; he could open a door without touching it, and levitate, and on and on and on. George Kinney and Tom Ramsey [ex–Golden Dawn] were both wanted in Texas on drug charges. George said, "Hey, Roky's really in a bad way. We need to get him back to Austin; can we ride back with you?" This was the height of Tommy and Roky being in the same house, but they wouldn't be in the same room together . . . When I finally saw him, he didn't look good; his lips were all dry and cracked and caked and he really looked wasted. This was the first time I'd seen Roky since Austin, when he was bright and articulate. Just a different person—he didn't even recognize me; he was babbling and incoherent, withdrawn. The next day there were six of us riding back in my little VW Bug and I got pulled over for going too slow on the highway. The highway patrol got us all out of the car, and Roky was barefoot, and Roky couldn't even tell them his name. We said he's sick and [that we were] taking him back to Texas. George had a fake ID, so did Tom Ramsey—they were just shaking their heads . . . We made a pit stop in San Jose, and Roky and George were in the bathroom for a real long time. George came out and admitted that Roky had been strung out on speed for the last three weeks, and he took him in there and hit him up with his last hit. That just appalled me—to think Roky, who was preaching the psychedelics and the right way, was doing hard drugs, really set me back. I was indignant with George for allowing him to do it . . . So we got into Arizona at dusk—beautiful sunset, looked like a good time for a trip. I reached to break out the acid that we'd scored and gave everybody one. I had reservations about Roky, who was sitting shotgun on the side of me; I could feel his eyes burning in the back of my head. So I turned and said, "Roky, would you like one?" He reaches in the bag and takes a

Opposite: Danny Thomas, Ronnie Leatherman, and Stacy during the final *Bull of the Woods* sessions at Gold Star Studios, October 1968. Warner: "IA moved their offices from Gold Star to a little building on Richmond Avenue behind a Black Angus steakhouse. At the back of that was this little garage, shed-type thing. For a while, Stacy was crashing there, living in the back of the office."

handful and stuffs them in his mouth—at least ten. These were 1,000 micrograms; each one you could split in half and have a good trip. He really went into a bad way, hugging himself and holding his arm until we got to El Paso. He was hitting on his arm and telling the demons to get out of his body. George made a call to this girl Ginger Pane we went to high school with, to take care of him—she was doing heroin. When they got him in a more stable state, they took him on to Austin.

EVELYN'S DIARY, JANUARY 2, 1969:
Some friends come in from California, bringing in Roky. He's covered in sores and he mumbled something about having a venereal disease. I put him in the tub with lots of Tide, getting him to take off all the scabs very gently—then I'll doctor him with ammoniated mercury. I think the sores are impetigo and if I'm right, this will cure them. He keeps saying, "Don't touch me, I'm unclean." The next day I take him for a blood test. It's OK. Thank goodness, and thank God!

JERRY LIGHTFOOT: The next time I saw Roky after [Hedgecroft Hospital], he was walking around Houston barefoot, when it was cold. I remember, it was in the Montrose area, and he was walking around in white pants, shirt, and a vest—no shoes or socks—and he had a syringe of speed sticking out of his pocket without a point on it, and he was wanting someone to give him an injection.

THE AUSTIN AMERICAN, *FEBRUARY 23, 1969:*
"Austin Pair Arrested on Drug Charge"—A small plastic vial reflected a little too much light early Saturday morning and resulted in the arrest of two twenty-one-year-old Austin men in connection with possession of marijuana. Roger Erickson of 2002 Arthur Lane and John S. Kennedy of 611 Wood Lane were charged with illegal possession of marijuana in Justice of the Peace Bob Kuhn's court Saturday morning. Kuhn set a $3,000 bond on Erickson and a $1,000 bond on Kennedy. Both remained in Travis County Jail on Saturday in lieu of bond. Patrolman Vernon Sigler said that he drove to the top of Mt. Bonnell at about 2:50 a.m. to investigate a parked small foreign car. While following the car north on Mt. Bonnell Blvd., Sigler saw one of the occupants of the car toss something light-colored out of the window and into the grass, the officer said. After stopping the two men in the auto, Sigler said he went back to the spot he had seen the object tossed and located a small, plastic vial containing what he believed to be marijuana. The contents of the bottle were sent to the Department of Public Safety for analysis, he said.

ROKY: I was arrested for marijuana when the policeman said he found the vial. I think I was set up for that. It doesn't seem right that I would throw out a vial of grass into the weeds, and a policeman would stop and set his flashlight on it and get it.

JOHN KEARNEY: I would see Roky periodically at people's houses, while we were smoking. Roky was totally uncool all the time; if he saw a uniformed policeman, he'd freak out. Not the way to be—you'd be cool all the time, and not throw stuff out the window.

ROKY: Stacy was always worried we were going to get busted. We would say if you're gonna worry about being busted, you're gonna get busted. And they would point at Stacy and say that's what he was doing.

DANA MORRIS: I'm in San Francisco, healed from hepatitis. Roky's gone, I met this beautiful Leo man, Jerry—he wants to take care of me. I still loved Roky, but I was grateful. One day, I come home and there's a message from Western Union: "You've got a message from Texas, it'll cost you . . ." I said, "I don't have any money!" and they said, "OK, we'll read it to you." It was from Roky; it said, "Dana, I have been busted, come home." That's all I needed to hear, so I packed up and Jerry goes and sells his flute to buy me a ticket to get back to Texas. So I go out to see Roky; I drive up, it's raining, and I don't know where to park, and I see this fence, and then I notice Roky's walking round in this courtyard in circles. So I get out, he jumps the fence and jumps in my car!

MIKEL ERICKSON: Roky's in the State Hospital and [his] friends, supposedly his friends, they go out there and talk him into leaving the hospital. So my father would get me—"He's gone again"—and so of course Mike would have to go and get Roky, right? It was a strange trip for me to get into with my older brother, who I never would ever mess with. I mean, Dana and all those people wouldn't leave him alone and if they had, he probably could have got out of that little pot bust, that little matchbox of pot from Mt. Bonnell. I had to physically get Roky and take him back. But he was so screwed up from the State Hospital popping him full of whatever drugs they'd give him, when he got out. And then I'd feel real stupid when I got there, because the State Hospital gave him all this other crap to bring him down. He was like a guinea pig for all this stuff: up and down, up and down. They would never leave him alone.

SUMNER ERICKSON: Mom told me that they would say, "Well, you know, if your boy keeps leaving here, then we're going to have to put him in some place he can't leave."

Meanwhile, the final Elevators single, "Livin' On" b/w "Scarlet and Gold," was released in January along with the final LP, *Bull of the Woods*. The releases leaked out without a traceable mention in *Billboard*; in fact, the only discernible evidence of the album's release was a review in *Record World* and a Bay Area radio spot. The cover concept, like the majority of the record itself, came from Stacy; his idea had been to portray the band's Texas heritage as the silhouette of a longhorn, similar to the proud Spanish bull. Instead Dillard swiped a menu from the steakhouse adjacent to the IA offices and told the art department to lift the image for the cover.

In mid-January, Stacy booked into Gold Star under the 13th Floor Elevators name and recorded a lost song called "Uptown Woman." On March 24, 1969, he was back as "Stacy Southerland" to demo a new song, the records for which indicate, *"Tape copy taken by Stacy. Original tracks made on scrap ½" ERASED."*

Stacy's house on Old Galveston Road was nicknamed Funky Mansions. There were rigs hidden in the walls; Stacy even let two friends from Dallas who'd robbed a bank hide out for a week, which ended in a gun battle in the house. He still hadn't given up on the dream of the Elevators, and was still performing occasionally up through mid-1969; with a core band of himself and Danny Thomas, he'd cobble together new lineups, sometimes even including former roadie Cecil Morris for one-off gigs. One last attempt at saving the band came when Stacy met and recruited a young guitarist from Houston, Paul Tennison (aka Paul Vivano).

> PAUL TENNISON: Actually, I borrowed a guitar from Stacy. I'd broken mine and needed a guitar, and this friend said, "I know this guy" . . . So he loaned me the guitar and I had to take it back, and we sat there and just played for thirty minutes—didn't say anything. I knew the Elevators. Later, Stacy called me and asked me if I wanted to play in the Elevators, and I said OK. We went to their record company, International Artists, and they had to sign me. I think I was twenty; I was underage when I signed their contract, anyway, and they moved us into the Old Galveston House. Oh man, I used to have nightmares there. I felt like a very young kid—I was still living at home when I moved there . . . Once, I was asleep and I woke up to the glass shattering: someone had shot a shotgun. I never put my head up—in fact, I crawled under my mattress. There were all kinds of other things that went on there: weeklong parties—it was very much a drug den. Then there was one real big drug raid. Somebody had come over in the morning [and] before that had robbed a drugstore and had a shoebox full of pharmaceutical drugs, and there were underage girls. Everybody was asleep, and I woke up first and I walked down the stairs and I got to the front door. I put my hand on the doorknob and the door flew open—they'd kicked the door in and there was a .45 in my face. And the irony of that was we were in jail exactly forty-five minutes and they let us all loose; they had no warrants, and it was illegal . . . Horrible event. That was pretty much the last straw—after that we were gone.

DANA MORRIS: I called the DA, and said [Roky] didn't want to wait at the Austin State Hospital for trial; wanted to get his head together, and if he'll tell us the date of the trial, we'll be there. And they said, "Well, we're not going to tell you the day, and you're gonna miss it," and they would file a fugitive charge, which was a second federal offense, but then they said, "If you turn yourself in to a psychiatrist, we won't do it." So we went to Houston and got with Bill Dillard and Noble Ginther, and called Dr. Crow up.

ROKY: They said Hedgecroft would be the best way to get out of it—yet it was really an insane asylum. You'd be sure to call it an asylum. It's a positive way of looking at a word that would scare you into a straitjacket. And then they did drop their charge of "fugitive." And from there everything got real vague.

At International Artists, everything had become localized. In January 1969, the label bought into the local club scene, purchasing Love Street. They set up a booking agency called Artists Management Company Incorporated (AMCI) and started promoting shows. Roky was immediately booked for a series of solo shows starting at Love Street on July 18, backed by Endle St. Cloud in the Rain—the new band consisting of Peter Black and James Harrell from the Lost and Found. Harrell was relieved to be backing Roky up this time, rather than imitating him. Roky's persona for the shows was that of a disheveled Abe Lincoln: tailcoat, bare feet, top hat, and full beard.

The only old Elevators material that suited Paul Tennison's voice remained in the setlist for Stacy's new lineup: "You're Gonna Miss Me," "Fire Engine," and "Slide Machine." The rest consisted of Stacy's new material and cover songs; as Paul recalls, "Basically, it was a rock 'n' roll lineup." One of Paul's first shows as lead vocalist was at the Jade Room on August 14. During the second song, the stage was invaded by Roky, who bounded up, plugged in a guitar, cranked the volume to ten, and proceeded to let rip with furious distortion and feedback before setting the howling guitar down in front of the amp and disappearing through the front doors. As usual, Roky's actions spoke louder than words: he was in town to perform his Austin comeback show the following night at the Action Club, and he and Stacy met after the Elevators show to discuss the possibility of them working together on Roky's new material in a new band.

ROKY (*1975*): Noble [Ginther] said, "Don't go back; they'll get you." So I flew to Austin. At the Action Club, the police were waiting for me. This policeman says, "Hi man, I used to be a good friend of your father's—you used to ride horses on my land. All we want to do is ask you some questions; just come down and answer the questions." Soon as I got down [to the police station] they put me in a cell. And I didn't hear from them for a week, and the club didn't know where I was. They said, "Listen, if you get arrested, make sure you make your phone call to the club." And I wasn't able to make that connection. So I was just shafted—I was just run over.

Above and opposite:
The final *Bull of the Woods* artwork, circa January 1969. Stacy's wish to depict a proud Texan bull was realized instead with an image lifted from a menu Dillard swiped from the Black Angus steakhouse in front of IA's office, 2049 Richmond Avenue, Houston.

BULL OF THE WOODS

IA-LP 9 STEREO

SIDE ONE

1. LIVIN ON
(Sutherland-Hall)
2. BARNYARD BLUES
(Sutherland)
3. TILL THEN
(Sutherland-Hall)
4. NEVER ANOTHER
(Erickson-Hall)
5. ROSE AND THE THORN
(Sutherland)
6. DOWN BY THE RIVER
(Sutherland)

SIDE TWO

1. SCARLET AND GOLD
(Sutherland)
2. STREET SONG
(Sutherland)
3. DR. DOOM
(Sutherland-Hall)
4. WITH YOU
(Leatherman)
5. MAY THE CIRCLE REMAIN UNBROKEN
(Erickson)

CREDITS:

Produced by: RAY RUSH
Engineers: HANK POOLE, JIM DUFF and FRED CARROLL
Cover: LLOYD SEPULVEDA
Publisher: TAPIER MUSIC-B.M.I.

13th FLOOR ELEVATORS

On October 8, Roky returned to the 147th District Court of Travis County, where the band's fate had hung in the balance three years prior. Roky was advised—poorly—by his state-appointed attorney to act crazy and plead insanity. This plan backfired with disastrous consequences: in spite of one report stating that "Mr. Erickson is a character disorder who is faking paranoid schizophrenia . . . His talented display of the symptoms suffers mainly from exaggeration," the jury declared him guilty of three counts. He was declared insane and hospitalized for his own welfare.

August 15 *Austin Statesman* advertisement for Roky's projected return to Austin.

MIKEL ERICKSON: The strategy was "You know, Roky, if you plead insanity, then everything's cool. You'll be in for a little bit, then they'll let you out." But no, they stuck him in Rusk—and you don't get people out of Rusk State Hospital at all.

ROKY (*1975*): They get me in there—[*heavy Texas accent*] "Son, we looked at your head, and you've taken over 300 trips—trips, I say—trips of LSD, and you may have a regression where you're seeing things again. They call them flashbacks" . . . "Why, he may have a flashback and might go crazy again" . . . And then they'd put their arm on my shoulder and say, "Son, then we'd have to put you back in here again."

Rusk State Hospital was referred to as a slave colony for good reason: inmates were often poor and black, and once committed, they rarely left.

ROKY (*1973*): When I got [to Rusk] I had long hair and a beard, and I was wearing that top hat, so they didn't know what to think. I looked like Abe Lincoln. They had a slave colony there. They shaved me and cut my hair so I looked like a girl from the Kremlin, then they led me down dark hallways and up long stairs.

The town of Rusk's economy was boosted by the construction of a penitentiary in 1877, and a railroad connected an iron foundry to the prison work camps. The two stated requirements for prison staff were "brawn and bravery," as the inmates were dangerous murderers, rapists, and psychopaths. And then, there was Roky.

ROKY: It was too severe. When I first got there, I put my clothes underneath my bed and one of the attendants, Dan Ball, came by and pushed me down and started kicking me and said, "Don't ever put your clothes underneath your bed." That was the Rusk thing.

The drug regimen at Rusk was as severe as the physical mistreatment.

ROKY: They were giving me Navane, which made my tongue go to the top of my head and my eyes roll back.

MIKEL ERICKSON: Of course, I was one of the only people left on his guest list—me and Mom . . . They'd busted pretty much all the other people for trying to sneak stuff in.

Top: Handbill for the Roky benefit concert at Jubilee Hall (formerly La Maison) in Houston on June 17, 1969, organized by George Banks—who, as "Flash Graphics," had been the cover artist for *Easter Everywhere* as well as for the Golden Dawn, the Red Crayola, and others.

Bottom: Handbill for Roky's solo Love Street comeback, July 18, 1969.

P.O. Box 14130 – Houston, Texas 77021
Code 1-713,
~~Phone 926-1795~~
923-2286

ARTISTS MANAGEMENT

POP CLIENT LIST

*BUBBLE PUPPY ✓

*SHAYDE ✓

*TREEKS ✓

DAVE ALLEN BLUES BAND

**BIG SWEET

ENDEL ST. CLOUD IN THE RAIN (~~Featuring Rock Erickson of the 13th Floor Elevators~~)

*GINGER VALLEY

JOHN BARTLETT

~~HAPPY~~

~~THE LEFT BANK~~

~~BANGO FLYING CIRCUS~~

~~ZZ TOP~~

SHIVA'S HEAD BAND

Roky Erikson

Nazz

P.O. Box 14130 – Houston, Texas 77021
Code 1-713,
Phone 926-1795

KRIO PRESENTS THE SHOW OF THE YEAR

Date: August 23, 1969.
Time: 8:00 PM to 12:00 Midnite
Groups: NAZZ, Bubble Puppy, and Roky Ericson.
Flat Price: $2700.00
Deposit of: $1350.00
Balance of $1350.00 to be paid in full at end of performance.
or $2000.00 + Motel Rooms and meals.

Holiday Inn: Nazz - 3 rooms 2 double beds in each.
Bubble Puppy - same as Nazz.
Roky - 2 rooms, 2 double beds in each.

or
make what you consider a reasonable offer.

Rocky Erickson + Endle St. Cloud in the rain.

date: Friday 15 Aug. 69 Sat. 16 Aug. 69

place: Action Club, Austin, Texas

Time: Friday 15 Aug. 69 - Total of 4 - 45 min Sets between hours of 8 & 12 P.m.
Saturday 16 Aug. 69 - Total of 4 - 45 min Sets between hours of 9 + 1 P.m.

Money. 600.00 guarantee against 50% of gross gate receipts.

advance: $300.00/nt to be paid to performer or their representative before First Performance

mail to: Robert A. Hatcher
P.O. Box 4949
Austin, Texas 78751

DAVE ALLEN BLUES BAND

ALBUM SOON TO BE RELEASED "THE MAN"

NAZZ

WELL ESTABLISHED NATIONAL GROUP WITH 2 ALBUMS (NAZZ, NAZZ NAZZ) ON SGC LABEL. ALSO 2 SINGLES "OPEN MY EYES" & NEWEST RELEASE "SOME PEOPLE" A PICK IN BILLBOARD.

ROKY ERIKSON –

THERE IS LITTLE EXPLANATION NECESSARY ON ROKY. HE WAS THE FORMER LEADER OF THE NATIONALLY RENOWN "13th FLOOR ELEVATORS", AND IS AT HIS BEST WITH A NEW BACK-UP GROUP.

GINGER VALLEY

FUN LOVING GROUP FROM CORPUS CHRISTI THAT CARRIES HAPPINESS WHEREVER THEY PLAY.

BIG SWEET

THIS GROUP IS THE LEADER IN THE SOUTH WEST IN THE WORLD OF HARD ROCK. THEY

I didn't know any of the technical words for the stuff they were giving Roky [besides] Thorazine—they'd go in one ear out the other—but I do know they'd give him one drug and it'd stiffen up his neck, and then they'd give him another drug to loosen him up. He was screwed up; he was like a walking zombie.

ROKY: When they asked me to talk to get things out of my system at Rusk, I wouldn't do it. One bad word in there keeps you there another year.

Meanwhile, the case against John Kennedy—the other person who'd been in the car with Roky—was dismissed, because there was no evidence that the marijuana thrown from the car by Roky had been in Kennedy's possession.

With Roky incarcerated, the dream of getting the original Elevators back together passed, and with Paul as vocalist, it became apparent that the band could no longer use the name. Reluctantly, Stacy declared the 13th Floor Elevators defunct and started a new project, Ice, which featured the Lingsmen's old singer Max Range on vocals. Although Ice entered the studio twice, no material was ever completed and any recordings are lost. In September of '69, Stacy was busted again, and IA bailed him out for $6,000. But on January 28, 1970—exactly four years and a day after the first pot bust of January 27, 1966—Stacy was arrested for violating parole and sentenced to two years in Huntsville Prison, the very place Roky had pleaded insanity to avoid. Despite a regime of hard fieldwork, Stacy fared well in comparison to Roky, and his two-year sentence was reduced to eight months for good behavior.

IA, having realized that they'd under-promoted the Elevators, poured everything available into Bubble Puppy, which they saw as their second chance. But Bubble Puppy didn't have the Elevators' talent, and their rush-released cash-in album failed to chart, making them another one-hit wonder. In early 1970, IA poached Dale Hawkins from Bell Records (who'd worked with the Elevators in Dallas in 1966) in a desperate attempt to reinvigorate the label. He organized a promotional campaign spearheaded by a remastered "You're Gonna Miss Me" that was heavily promoted in the Midwest.

DALE HAWKINS: IA hired me as a consultant when they were in deep trouble. I wanted to help them there as much as I could, but IA had too many owners, and were too deep in trouble for me to save.

Opposite top left: List of bands signed to IA's new AMCI artist management company, mid-1969.

Opposite top right: Handwritten listing for the projected KRLD Radio–sponsored "Show of the Year" in Dallas, on AMCI letterhead.

Opposite bottom left: Handwritten AMCI sheet listing Roky's planned solo engagements.

Opposite bottom right: AMCI blurb copy meant to hype Roky's anticipated solo outings.

IA had been abusing credit deals for years, and by 1970, everyone—from Columbia Mastering to Sumet Studios (whose October 1966 invoice for the recording of the first Elevators LP remained unpaid), printers, industry magazine subscriptions, and hotels—had had enough and withdrew their services. Dillard wrote his letter of resignation as president on April 28, 1970, and IA folded soon after.

▲ *INMATE 208574 STACY SUTHERLAND, EASTHAM UNIT, LETTER TO PAROLE BOARD:*

> *Gentlemen, I have been playing music for a living for the past five years. During this time I enjoyed a short termed amount of minor national success in recording. I had been using narcotics only slightly prior to this period and somehow connected it to what success the band I was with had. When our short-lived popularity ended and our band fell apart for financial reasons I was deeply disheartened as the vision of security faded from my grasp. After this I used drugs for comfort, similar to the reasons of an alcoholic.*

ON AUGUST 27, Stacy reported that it nearly "blew his mind" when he was in his cell listening to the radio and heard Dylan's "It's All Over Now, Baby Blue" followed by "You're Gonna Miss Me." Later that night, he was woken at 3:30 a.m. by the prison guard beating on his bars to inform him that he had been granted parole; on September 23, 1970, he was freed.

Upon his return to Kerrville, he and Ronnie began rehearsing a new band called Raincrow at their friend Robert Eggar's ranch—an old Elevators haunting ground. This was not the turnaround in lifestyle he had promised the parole board:

> STACY (*K*): I went to Kerrville, started drinking, and didn't get a job like I should have. I was so happy to be out.

Raincrow was Obie Holdeman on vocals, Stacy on guitar, Ronnie on bass, Bobby Rector on drums, and the Elevators' old roadie Cecil Morris on harmonica. There was an unspoken conformity to the band's material—their only ambition was to earn a living performing honest blues-based music, and their repertoire consisted of a mixture of covers: blues, R&B, rock 'n' roll, Dylan, and current Stones numbers.

> OBIE HOLDEMAN: I was the only black dude in the band. The blues I kind of picked up on my own, and the talent I have to give to God.

> STACY (*K*): Like Tommy, I didn't go and see Roky at Rusk—but believe me, it wasn't because I didn't love him. It was just a different world then, and I was in a different place. I remember for years that I almost didn't want to see him; I didn't feel

Current Groups of IA

Fred
Big Sweet
John Scott Thompson
Thomas George
Richard Malone
Tommy Null

The Blox
Jared Sattiewhite
Robert Turner
Tim Oliver
Rick Barnes

Bubble Puppy
David Fore
Roy Cox JR
Todd Potter
Rod Prince

Categorical Imperative
Jerry Cook

Coastliners
Ricky Dowden
Bob Williamson
Charles Hart
John Kulbeth

Fred
Endle St. Cloud in the Rain
Pete Black
David Potter
Alan Melinger
James Harrell

Chris
Ginger Valley
Robert Donaho
David Garing
Richard Mauch
Hulen Edward Clifton III
John Kenney

Happy
Stephen Ross Chaxe
Clifford Doror
Richard Morris Jr

Ice
Stacy Sutherland
Max Range
David Browne
Michael Marschell
Paul Vivian

Lost & Found
Pete Black
Jim Frost
Steve Webb

Love Army
Alberto Isordia
Salvador Martinez
Jaime Valle
Fernando Buhauks
Fernando Castaneda

Pattern
Ron Towery
Bill York
Rich Watson
Tony Taboada

The Red Crayola
Mayo Thompson

Shayde
Bob Bailey
Stewart Bailey
Donnie Butler
Joe Ryan

Stonewall
Mike Bruce
Duke Davis
Richard Sterd

St. Laufren
Michael Barton
John McCrow
Jim Weaver
Lee Parmeter
Curtis Voelkel

Toby
Steven Dane Gibson
Micheal Seibel
Harvey Martin
John Garza
Randy Lindsey
Gary Powers

The Treeks
David Carbonneau
Eugene Mathew
Kenneth Mathew

True Notes
Arthur Burrell
Whitcomb Ray Greene
Joe Kyle
John Terry
Otis Pochia

Ice
BAND MEMBERS

MAX Range
425 Emerson

Stacy Sutherlan
PO Box 864
Kerrville

Paul Viviano

David Brown
220 Fresno
SA

Michal Marschell

Top: 1969 listing of "Current Groups of IA," featuring Stacy's new band Ice.

Bottom: Ice's lineup, which featured Max Range (previous singer for the Traditions, Signatures, and Lingsmen) back on vocals.

RAINCROW
Marshall
Marshall
Marshall
ALWAYS

RAINCROW
Center

Opposite top: Raincrow playing in Kerrville, circa 1971: Ronnie Leatherman, Bobby Rector (ex–Golden Dawn, playing John Ike's old kit), and Stacy.

Opposite bottom: Raincrow as a full band: Ronnie, Cecil Morris (the Elevators' former roadie), Bobby Rector, Stacy, and Obie Holdeman.

like it would do either of us much good. We were all flipped to some degree about what had happened to us.

ROKY (*1975*): Roky's in Rusk Concentration Camp—"Roky, what's today?" Why do I have a need for knowing the date? I'm never going to get out. So I would just forget. I'd say, "Roky, you're in here forever, you might as well not remember any kind of success you've had or anything. *You're a talented rock 'n' roll singer*? Forget it!"

Q: What prompted you to become a reverend?

ROKY: I just did. It would make you feel real religious to be in a place like that. All you would have would be your religion. You'd want God and Jesus with you at all times to help you through.

On February 28, Evelyn was allowed to take her tape recorder into Rusk and record Roky. The first known recording was typical of the material he was writing to appease the authorities.

EVELYN ERICKSON: He wrote one called "I Pledge Allegiance to the Flag" . . . everybody questioned your loyalty to the United States if you were a hippie or were the mother of a hippie. It [was] just a weird time. He had a band called the Missing Links while he was in there, and the doctor was very proud of him and took him out [to] play around the town.

ROKY (*1975*): A couple of groovy guys managed to get me out to be in a rock 'n' roll band with some of the patients, and we called it the Missing Links. We performed, but you know I couldn't perform. I'd be under so much tension that I couldn't scream while I was there. I wouldn't do my own material in this band—I'd do others'. Because you were in with people that were there for murder; I mean, vicious murders. "Well, alright, here's the guy with the vicious murder, and here's Roky." They're crazy. It's like "The Lonesome Death of Hattie Carol"—there's injustice in injustice.

EVELYN ERICKSON: I just wanted him to stay in his music. I thought that was his salvation.

ROKY (*1973*): Our band at Rusk was even on television three times, but we sang an antiwar song and about a million straights called up and said "That's a bunch of shit, we believe in war so let's not have any of that peaceful shit on TV."

Meanwhile, George Kinney was busy smuggling manuscripts out in his boots for a book of Roky's songs and poems that would be published in 1972 as *Openers*.

ROKY: I wrote *Openers* in Rusk because everyone was telling me that I was crazy, and I had to have something to tell them I wasn't.

By then, Mikel was earning enough money working for the Teamsters' Union in San Francisco to be able to appoint a firm of lawyers—Simons, Cunningham, and Coleman—to review Roky's case. John Howard, a junior partner, studied law at UT with an internship at Rusk, and while touring the wards, he had been amazed to recognize Roky Erickson. He determined that virtually none of the inmates had any form of legal representation and that nobody reviewed their cases; during the summer of 1971, he noted that only two lawyers visited clients at Rusk.

Roky's trial was set for November 27, 1972, and lawyer Jim Simons requested a motion of discovery to obtain the medical charts at Rusk and details of all laboratory work performed on Roky, including any brainwave tests or tests for brain damage or malfunctioning. Roky's defense team was also busy organizing for outside psychiatrists to examine him—the doctors at Rusk couldn't agree as to whether Roky suffered from simple or chronic schizophrenia, and thus whether he was a hopeless case or not. Howard decided that since there was only one actual psychiatrist on the staff, outside opinions should be put on the record to help determine the current status of Roky's sanity, and he brought Dr. Richard Alexander in to privately diagnose Roky's condition.

> DR. RICHARD ALEXANDER: *He is not out of contact with reality and is not given to false beliefs or delusions as was the case on his admission to Rusk. His condition is a stable one at this time, and I do not feel he is apt to change in the near future. I feel an attempt should be made to bring him back into the community, he should remain on medication and under the supervision of a physician.*

Dr. John Rollyson, who visited Roky and also interviewed Dr. Hunter, concluded that "Mr. Erickson now meets the legal requirements of sanity, namely he doesn't have a mental condition requiring hospitalization either for the welfare and protection of himself or others. This is not to say," he added, "that Mr. Erickson is completely free of emotional problems, but rather that the psychological difficulties he suffers are not sufficient to justify considering him insane."

In short, the new evaluation found that Roky was suffering from a hysterical personality disorder, usually found in women and commonly misdiagnosed as simple schizophrenia in men; that Evelyn being overly involved with Roky had caused him to be a dependent man-child; and that

Opposite top: Roky at Rusk, 1971, being recorded as a means of documenting his new songs and poetry for their inclusion in *Openers*, his prison book published in 1972.

Opposite bottom left: Donnie Erickson with Roky in the Rusk recreation area, Christmas 1969.

Opposite bottom right: The Missing Links (Roky's band at Rusk), as seen in the *Rusk Cherokeean* newspaper performing at the "East Texas Indian Summer Festival," November 6–7, 1970. Left to right: unknown (deaf tambourine player), Charles Hefey (bass), John Walcott, and Roky.

Top: Roky outside Rusk's chapel, September 1972.

Bottom: Roky and Donnie Erickson in the Rusk cafeteria and at the visitor's entrance, September 1972.

Opposite: Roky performs in his cell for Joseph Kahn and John Howard, September 1972.

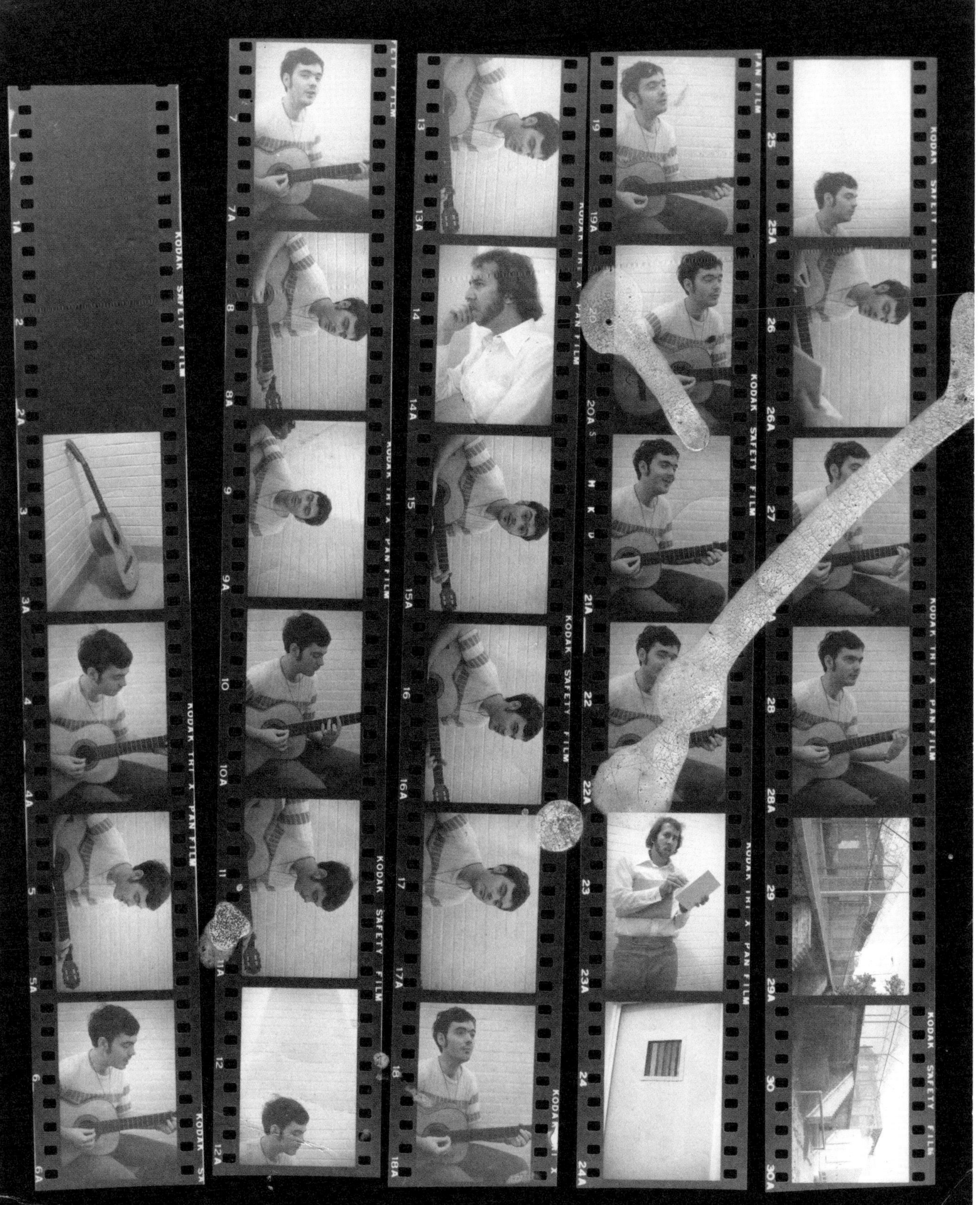

Roky had a dislike of the mundane, and was playing the role of a schizophrenic to placate what others expected from him. Rollyson also brought in a friend for a second opinion: Dr. Joseph Rickard, who concluded that Roky was below average in judgment, lacked self-control, and was impulsive. However, he found that Roky was not grossly psychotic but only mildly schizophrenic, and that he was above average in nonverbal communication. He recommended that Roky be discharged and placed in an outpatient program.

EVELYN ERICKSON: Well, [Rusk] had their own psychiatrists saying that he'd OD the minute he left. I was so tense. I thought they should have a halfway house for him to go into. I thought it was just really bad—I could see their point of view, putting him back on the streets right away.

CHRISTINE GAY (jury foreperson): *Verdict of the Jury, 1:52 p.m.: We, the Jury return into open court the following answer to the question submitted to us and the same is our verdict in this case: We, the jury, find that the defendant at the present time is sane.*

JOHN HOWARD (*K*): We got him out, free and clear. It was beautiful. Jim [Simons] said that in his ten years of practicing, there had never been a more exciting moment than when he escorted Roky up to the judge and the judge declared Roky sane. He is now home living with his mother, who is watching him like a dog—she got upset the other day when I was visiting him and we walked out of her sight. She won't even let him have cigarettes.

Q: So was Roky effectively a free man as soon as the trial ended?

EVELYN ERICKSON: Oh, it was with the knowledge that he would be in my care . . . he was, what, [twenty-five]? I mean, there was no way . . . [But] Dana came over and took him off right away.

JERRY LIGHTFOOT: He was staying at Evelyn's, and I would call him and he would sneak out, and we'd drive around and smoke a joint. It was a sad scene.

Opposite: Joseph Kahn's contact sheet of Roky performing in his cell at Rusk, also featuring two photos of Roky's attorney John Howard, spring 1972. Kahn: "Two of my roommates while attending Harvard were big Elevators fans from Houston. I was introduced to their music in 1967. Through them, the band developed a kind of cult following among Harvard students. After graduating from college in 1971, I began wondering what had happened to the band; to my mind, these guys were far more innovative—not to mention 'out there'—than many of the bands that had become more nationally famous and commercially successful. On and off over the next five years, I did my best to track down all the band members and dozens of people who'd been close to them. My ultimate aim was to chronicle the band's story from beginning to bitter end. I became friends with attorney John Howard, whose law firm was representing Roky during his incarceration at Rusk. John—one of the true unsung heroes in the Roky Erickson story—arranged for the two of us to pay Roky a visit in the spring of 1972. There, I interviewed Roky for a couple of hours, during which time he picked up his guitar and played several songs he'd written while in Rusk. These photos are from that session—the only time I'm aware of when a journalist spent time with him prior to his release from Rusk later that year."

Dear Stacy - just a line to keep in touch. I receitently got out of the Maximum Security Unit at Rusk where I spent two years with Roky Erickson. I played Rhythm guitar ~~with~~ him in the M.S.U. band. He wants to get ~~in~~ for touch with you and reform the Elevators. Rokys address is

ROKY ERICKSON Wd-8
P.O. BOX 318
RUSK, TEXAS 75785

please drop him a line as he would like to hear from you. as a matter of fack I would also.

George Richie
(Randy St. Michaels)

TO
FROM
ROKY

Top: Telegram to Stacy from Rusk inmate George Richie, June 26, 1972. *"Dear Stacy, just a line to keep in touch. I recently got out of the maximum security unit at Rusk, where I spent two years with Roky Erickson. I played rhythm guitar in the M.S.U. band. He wants to get in touch with you and reform the Elevators. Roky's address is P.O. Box 318 Rusk Texas 75785. Please drop him a line as he would like to hear from you. George Richie (Randy St Michaels)."*

Bottom: Signed copy of *Openers*, Roky's book of lyrics and poems, published in 1972 while he was still at Rusk.

DANA MORRIS: He told me while he was in Rusk never to take drugs again. That's when we found Christ and our lives started healing. And then one day, after he'd got out of Rusk, I went over to see him and it was obvious he'd been up all night, and I said, "What are you doing? You're going back." He said, "Well, you have, too . . ." Like we were blaming each other for taking drugs.

▲ **IN 1973**, in the wake of the inclusion of "You're Gonna Miss Me" on the *Nuggets* garage rock compilation, *Rolling Stone* reassessed the band's legacy—as "mystic punks" and "one of the strangest groups in the history of rock 'n' roll"—and suggested a full-scale reissue of the band's albums.

John Ike—for whom the dream of the Elevators had never really faded—felt irked by the amount of press the *Nuggets* compilation was attracting, and so when he ran into Roky at the Armadillo World Headquarters club in Austin, he suggested resurrecting the Elevators. Roky had, at the time, slipped Evelyn's leash and was living in a hippie house on 37th Street.

ROKY: [About reforming the Elevators] I just felt there was something I hadn't said, and wanted to get together and say it.

Q: Why wasn't Stacy in the band?

ROKY: Oh, by that time, they had figured the things they were thinking about being busted were real. They didn't want to chance it.

John Ike flat-out vetoed Tommy's involvement, and was hesitant about Stacy, who was back using heroin. Since Stacy had always been an idol of Roky's brother Donnie, they drafted the latter to play lead guitar. Donnie brought John McGiver, a jazz bass player, on with him. Instead of a jug player, Roky elected to ask a young piano player with whom he'd jammed—Johnny Mac (for McAshan), who also lived with him—to join in on keyboard.

DONNIE ERICKSON: John Ike Walton was the chief on getting that together I guess. And they said Stacy would be a bad influence . . . Well, they were successful. I wasn't very comfortable up there onstage.

STACY (*K*): I hadn't been out two months before I was shooting dope again. I got strung out and my parole officer said, "Look, we know what you're doing. I don't care if you ruin your life, but you better leave town or we're gonna send you right back." Anyway, I split—went down to San Antonio. My parole officer down there was real groovy; he used to come to all our shows, smoke weed, had all our albums.

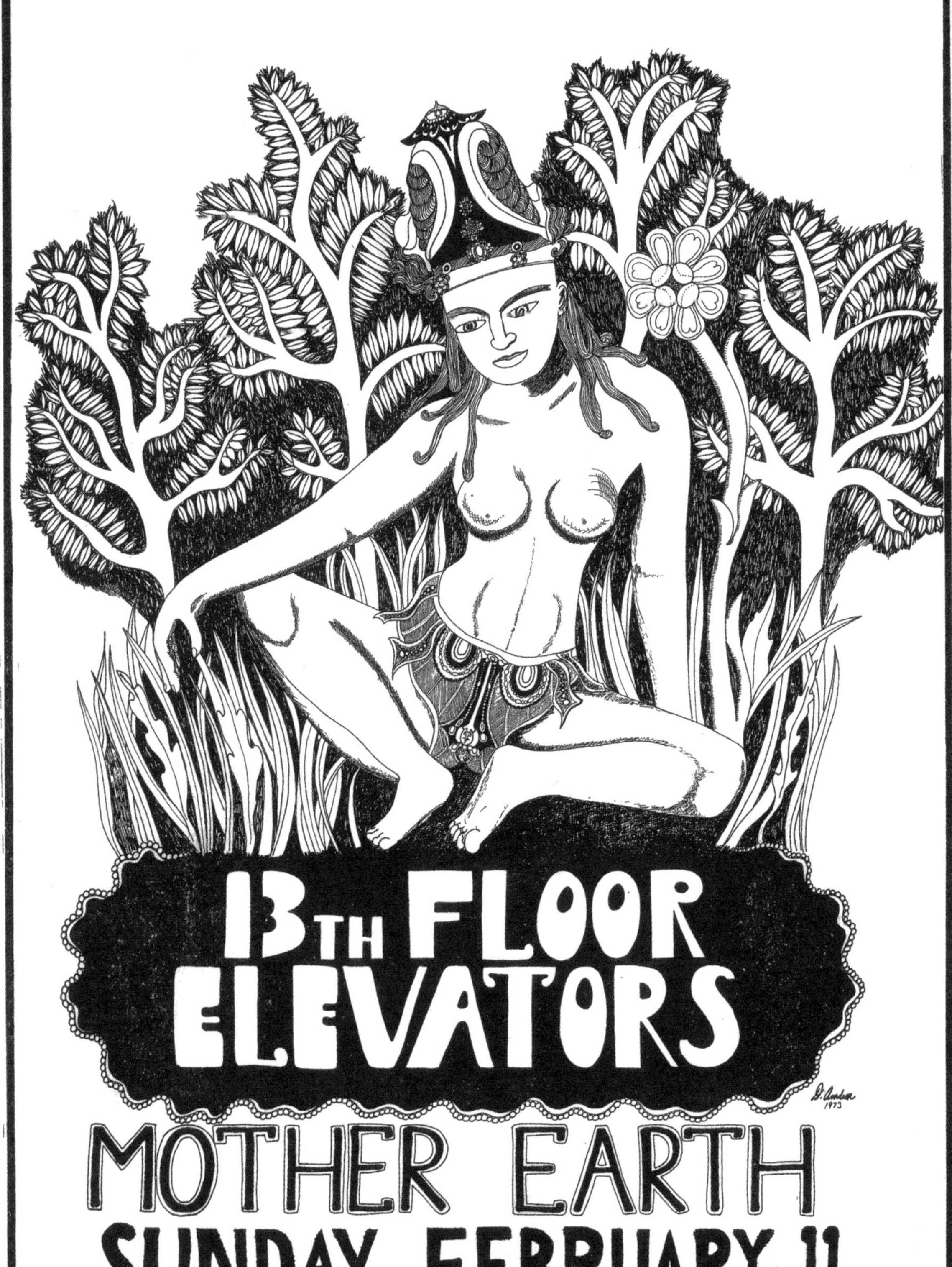
13TH FLOOR
ELEVATORS
MOTHER EARTH
SUNDAY FEBRUARY 11
ALSO MATEUS

Opposite: Poster for the Elevators reunion at Mother Earth, Austin, February 11, 1973.

Top: The band performs at the Mother Earth reunion. Left to right: Roky, John McGiver, Donnie Erickson (John Ike and Johnny McAshan don't appear in photo).

Bottom: John McGiver, John Ike, Roky, Donnie Erickson at the Mother Earth show.

In less than a month, the reformed Elevators were booked to play their first show, on February 11, 1973, at the Mother Earth club in Austin. They played "You're Gonna Miss Me," "Splash 1," "She Lives (In a Time of Her Own)," and "Levitation"; the rest of the set consisted of Roky's new material and Dylan covers. The demand for the band proved overwhelming, and they rebooked the club again for another sellout performance.

Over the following weeks, the band performed at least two undocumented gigs, including one at Armadillo World Headquarters. *Rolling Stone* picked up on the reunion, calling the band "true rock psychedelic crazies." Unhappy with their bass player, John Ike called Ronnie to let him know that the group had three nights booked at La Bastille in Houston for $3,000, and asked whether he wanted to reconsider joining. Ronnie played a final show with his band Savage, and then was back in the Elevators. Impressed by the strength of Roky's new material, Ronnie had a clear vision of what they needed to do: get Stacy back in the band, spend two months practicing at Stacy's parents' ranch, and then go directly into the studio to record.

The band's next known show was March 18 at "The Last Bash on the Hill," a massive festival organized by Roger Collins of the One Knite club in Austin. Approximately 15,000 people showed up at the "Hill on the Moon" to witness what turned out to be the last stand of sixties Austin's counterculture. In the intervening years, however, a new subculture had been born: the "cosmic cowboys," rednecks who smoked weed, listened to Willy Nelson, and frequented venues like Armadillo World Headquarters.

> JOHNNY McASHAN: The Hill on the Moon concert was the biggest thing we played in Austin, and we were the headliners. Willie Nelson was playing and nobody had heard of this guy. It was a unique mixture of cowboys and hippies—all these poor hippies in their blankets, and then we see RVs rolling down, and everyone's moving their blankets out of the way, like everyone had seen a spaceship. It was Willie's people.

The band went on so late that most people had fallen asleep, but when they struck up, everyone was awoken by their loud electric set. The old Elevators material was performed with a new urgency and drive, and the band's rendition of Slim Harpo's "Shake Your Hips" tore up the Stones' version. Following the show, the band made an attempt at recording, at Sonobeat Studios. The studio's cofounder Bill Josey (also of KAZZ-FM) had been funded by Columbia to make test recordings in quadraphonic stereo, or "Sonoquad," as he called it. This was primitive stuff—still made using a four-track deck—but the idea of experimenting with new sound techniques suited the Elevators perfectly. Unfortunately, the one song recorded, "Maxine," doesn't appear to have survived.

> DONNIE ERICKSON: Roky and I got in an argument onstage. I thought Roky was the singer and I was the guitar player and

Above: Handbill for the March 16, 1973, "Last Bash on the Hill" reunion show.

he started [telling me], "You are outta tune." I thought his voice was enough, but he wanted to be lead player too.

The squabbling led to yet another lineup change: when the La Bastille comeback took place on April 1 through 3, John Ike sacked Donnie at Roky's request and switched guitarists, hiring Terry Penney at a moment's notice. Terry was part of Ronnie's triumvirate; along with ex–Golden Dawn drummer Bobby Rector, the three had performed in countless trios in Kerrville, and even in a late version of the Golden Dawn with George Kinney in January 1968.

JOHNNY McASHAN: Roky would just take his finger and run it on the top of the knobs on his guitar so every single one was on ten. John Ike installed a secret volume knob after the first gig and we were sailing great, and then, at the Bastille gig, Terry Penny went and fooled with it, and Roky caught him and gave it away.

Stacy, who was standing in the audience watching a 13th Floor Elevators show, was overjoyed to be invited up the following night for a twenty-minute guest appearance. It was the first time he and Roky had seen each other since August 1969. KAUM, a local radio station, broadcast a thirty-minute retrospective of the band and caught the madness in an interview with Roky backstage.

ROKY (KAUM broadcast): Hi, I'm criminal Roky, we're interviewing—what radio station is this? K-A-U-M, we're the 13th Floor Alleviators and we're interviewing KAUM.

KAUM: What do you think of the future of the band?

ROKY: We're all going to be turning into road lizards.

JOHNNY McASHAN: Roky was [facedown on the] carpet, conducting the interview. It was sad. The last thing Roky needed was for people to give him drugs, and everywhere we went, people gave him drugs.

Joseph Kahn, a young writer from Boston, had come to Texas in search of the Elevators and, in 1973, he interviewed Stacy while the band was negotiating a possible reunion with him at Robert Eggar's ranch. Stacy's thoughts from the time reveal his hopes and misgivings about a reunited Elevators:

STACY (*K*): [Roky] seemed more like the Roky that I'd known when I first met him. Then I got scared because he's still an impressionable kid. Somebody has to take care of him. I know now there are times when he's completely normal, and other times when he's just gone. If he doesn't quit messing around with whatever he's taking, one of these days he's going to go lulu and that'll be it. They told him in the hospital that if he kept taking acid, one time he'd get so far-out that they wouldn't be able to help him. Roky told me that himself. Hell, after

LING KONG PRESENTS
13th Floor Elevators
+
Rapunzil from Ft. Worth
Guys—$2.00 Girls—$1.00

STONE CITY ATTRACTIONS
PRESENT
Sun. April 15, 1973 5:30-11:30 P.M
ROKY ERICKSON and the
13th FLOOR ELEVATORS
SUNKEN GARDENS AMPHITHEATER
SAN ANTONIO, TEXAS
$2.00 Advance $3.00 Door
No. 3207 No. 3207

Top left: Roky, John Ike, and George Banks at the La Bastille Club in Houston, April 3, 1973.

Top right: Roky accepts a cigarette from Renee Bayer at the La Bastille show. She would give birth to his first child, Spring.

Center: John Ike's home-made poster—referencing the Lingsmen—for the last gig of the 1973 reunion, April 22 in Port Aransas.

Bottom right: Ticket to the April 15, 1973, reunion show at San Antonio's Sunken Gardens Amphitheater.

Roky Erickson and
13th floor Elevators
A STONE CITY ATTRACTION
The Rebirth of
Roky Erickson and the
13th Floor Elevators
-International Recording Artists-
Arthur Gee
-tumbleweed Recording Artist.-
Bump-Bump
Banshee
-From Austin-
A Happy Sunday in the Park
Beer food
Light Show
Tickets:
Mr. Naturals 1&2
Flip-Side
Green Earth
Side Issue
Saturn Lighthouse
Sunken Gardens
5:30-11:30
2.00 advance
3.00 gate
Richard Contreras
Steve Miller Band May 18th

Opposite: Poster for the Sunken Gardens reunion show.

Top: Tommy Hall in San Francisco, April 1974.
Kahn: "I spent three months living in SF. Having managed to track down Tommy Hall, I visited him two or three times at his apartment. These photos are dated April '74."

Bottom: Stacy's final Austin Police Department mugshot, circa 1973.

three years of that shit, he oughta believe it himself. It's really gonna break my heart if this band doesn't work. It would really be pathetic after all these years to have a second chance to get back together and then go out and blow it all again. I see problems right away. John Ike and Roky have a real bad communication problem, for one thing. When Roky played me one of his new songs, it rocked; I was climbing the wall it was so fine. A little bit later we were over at John Ike's and I asked him to play the song again; God, it didn't even sound like the same song. But Roky can get that way around John Ike.

JOSEPH KAHN: I guess the logical question is, what if Tommy gets back in touch with you guys now?

STACY (K): Well, I love ol' Tommy deeply; I mean, he's one of the closest friends in my life. We would have to learn to know each other again, that's how I feel about it. 'Cuz, like, the place Roky's in, a lot of how I feel about that would depend on the personalities, because of the control Tommy had on Roky. And Tommy was stirring Roky, a really heavy drug thing; my biggest fear about this whole thing is that it's going to be a reproduction . . . He'd have to change his ideas about drugs; otherwise it's really obvious where it's heading.

ROKY: What I feel with Tommy is, walking up to him and saying, "Tommy, I need my home back. I've been on every drug in the world, every place but home."

But the reunion Stacy sought was not to be: the day after the San Antonio show, a summons was issued for him to face drug charges on April 30. He'd been caught red-handed with a used rig in his pocket.

John Ike had always gauged the band's success by the amount for which he could book them. After a good start with the new lineup, he had to concede that "Everything else we did was twenty-five dollars apiece." Hoping to capitalize on potential spring break audiences, he booked the band to play in Port Aransas on April 22. The Elevators were supported by Rapunzil, a band from Fort Worth, billed on the homemade poster as "Ling Kong Presents" in homage to their former incarnation as the Lingsmen, some eight years prior. The Elevators ended at Easter, the supposed time of rebirth, where Roky had first taken the stage with them in 1965.

Opposite top: Flyer designed by Bunni for Stacy's wedding and birthday reunion bash at the Ol' Dog Saloon (run by Cecil Morris) in Old Ingram, Texas, May 28, 1977.

Opposite bottom left: Stacy and Bunni, circa 1977.

Opposite bottom right: Stacy performing at the Watering Hole, Kerrville, 1976.

Cecil Morris Presents:

THE ORIGINAL 13TH FLOOR ELEVATORS

WITH DANNY THOMAS and BENNY THURMON

ROKY - STACY - TOMMY - RONNIE - JOHN IKE

ONE TIME ONLY

Saturday, May 28th 8:00 and 10:00

OL' DOG SALOON in the heart of

Old Ingram 6 mi. N.W. of Kerrville, Hwy. 27

TEXAS HILL COUNTRY MUSIC

2 am - 2 pm

FREE ADMISSION and FREE KEG BEER

B-B-Q available

▲ **THERE WOULD BE** a few more attempted reunions, if they can be called that. Stacy tried to reform the band to play at his wedding to Bunni in 1977 in Old Ingram. Roky was unavailable—busy touring the West Coast—so the show turned into a half-hearted Elevators/Raincrow setlist. The lineup was Stacy, John Ike, Ronnie, Obie Hardeman, and Cecil, and the band never came back for their second set.

Then, on August 24, 1978, Stacy died under tragic and somewhat mysterious circumstances. He and Bunni had been drunkenly arguing all day when Bunni's son came to her defense and Stacy moved to "discipline him." Bunni, who wrote a harrowing account to Sibyl explaining the event, reportedly stood in her son's bedroom doorway holding a .22 rifle toward Stacy, who advanced on the gun and was shot. With the bitterness surrounding his death, there have been other allegations. He has been sadly missed by all who knew him and plenty who didn't.

The early 1980s saw another massive resurgence of interest in psychedelia, with new bands being touted as "neo-psychedelia," or part of the "Paisley Underground." Once again, John Ike decided to react against the tidal wave of 13th Floor Elevators bootlegs by approaching Roky to reform the band. On June 16, 1984, a lineup consisting of Roky, John Ike, Ronnie, and Stacy's friend Greg Forest on lead guitar performed as the 13th Floor Elevators at Liberty Lunch in Austin.

> GREG FOREST: John Ike—he kinda dropped out for years, and then when he did come back, when we played the Elevators show, we thought we were going to kill him. He was out of shape; he hadn't played hard rock—probably fifteen years since he'd picked up sticks. But he was a metronomic powerhouse; never fancy, he always kept the groove.

> JOHN IKE: Tracy Cluck calls me up in '84 to do the reunion thing with Roky; he was going to be Roky's manager. Well, [Roky's] guitar playin' is so horrible, he's out of key and he's out of meter. He's playin' the same licks on every song, no matter what key it's in. His guitar playing is pathetic. I'm sure it wasn't very good, because we rehearsed for four or five days and then got up there and did it.

A second reunion gig was booked at the Consolidated Arts Warehouse in Houston on August 11, but the band was introduced this time as Roky's new band, Evil Hook Wildlife. However they were billed, they certainly weren't the 13th Floor Elevators: Ronnie having opted out, the band consisted of Roky, John Ike, Brian Beach on bass, and Stan Morris on guitar. After the show, John Ike found Roky passed out on the dressing room floor and resuscitated him by kicking him in the ribs before walking out in disgust.

Then, in 1987, John Ike and Ronnie visited Roky and sounded him out about a further reunion.

JOHN IKE: After the Houston reunion, I hadn't seen Roky for a while, and I went over to his house. They said, "Roky's doing OK," but he was in pretty bad shape. He was listening to all these TVs and radios that were all tuned to different stations. It was madness, and we could hardly talk, and we cut out and took off early.

Beyond a couple of guest appearances in the early nineties, Roky wouldn't make a significant return to the stage for nearly another twenty years, after his youngest brother, Sumner, realized that Roky's care was bordering on life-threatening neglect and intervened. On March 19, 2005, Roky made a tentative return at the Ice Cream Social, an annual fundraiser benefiting his family trust, where he blasted through three songs supported by the Explosives, his late-seventies backing band. Slowly, with the right people around him, Roky began touring internationally, and the response was ecstatic: fans couldn't believe that the reclusive Roky Erickson had returned and was performing in their town. The only Elevators material in his 2000s setlists, however, were his songs "You're Gonna Miss Me" and "Splash 1," prompting the natural question of whether he'd ever perform a full 13th Floor Elevators set again.

In the mid-2000s, a new wave of local musicians had begun engaging with Austin's sixties musical heritage. The Austin Psych Fest, founded by Roky's former backing band the Black Angels, sought to host as many of the original musicians from that period as possible: the Golden Dawn, the Moving Sidewalks, and others. The Elevators themselves seemed an impossible dream: Roky had systematically refused to perform pretty much any of the band's material beyond what he considered his songs, and Tommy Hall had in recent decades taken a dim view of his past, dismissing his work in the band as youthful folly. Most dubious was the question of whether John Ike would set foot on the same stage as Tommy, even for money. But despite the obvious obstacles, the decision was made in 2014 to attempt a full-band reunion. It was this or time travel.

When I called Tommy (whom I considered the least likely participant) to ask whether he'd be involved, he said yes. It turned out that after successful treatments for a stretch of ill health, he'd entered a period of renewed positivity, and with it had begun to reengage with his past. I called the rest of the surviving members and was thrilled to hear that they were all onboard—apart from Danny Thomas, who'd put down his sticks for good. Since Benny Thurman and Danny Galindo had both sadly passed, this left a reunion of the classic *Psychedelic Sounds* lineup.

The show was scheduled for the band's fiftieth anniversary, in 2015, and after a full year of starts, stops, and outright chaos, the day finally came when Austin Psych Fest—now renamed Levitation, after the Elevators song—achieved the impossible and brought to the stage a lineup consisting of Roky, Tommy, Ronnie, and John Ike. Eli Southard, from Roky's backing band, fulfilled Stacy's role, with Fred Mitchim on guitar and vocals and Roky's son, Jegar, on harmonica, rounding out the sound. The show was a massive success, with the festival reporting a record-breaking sellout crowd of more than 10,000: not bad for a band that hadn't played together in over forty years.

The day after the show, the heavens opened, the weather turned biblical, and the festival site flooded. Promoters from all around the world had already begun mounting frantic inquiries as to whether they could book the band for international tours. But despite the possibility that the Elevators might finally be able to clean up financially, history repeated itself: further engagements were not to be. As ever, the band's internal politics were at the heart of it, and, as the band's biographer, it soon became all too apparent to me why the East Coast tour in early 1967 had never happened. When I interviewed Roky immediately after the festival, he was resolute that he wanted to continue performing with Jegar's band the Hounds of Baskerville—no more Elevators shows, in other words. Ronnie and Tommy, for their part, were willing to play more shows, but John Ike proved difficult as ever. Tommy was invited to join Roky on a Hounds of Baskerville tour performing Elevators music but declined, saying that without the Hill Country boys—Ronnie and John Ike—it wasn't the 13th Floor Elevators.

R.I.P. Roky Erickson, Stacy Sutherland, Benny Thurman, and Danny Galindo. Goodbye 13th Floor Elevators.

BENNY: Roky, they say he stole his voice from an angel—and they tried to steal it back [*laughs*]. We had the pyramid and the eye up there, and we were trying to get to God; it was close to God, the feeling of God.

RONNIE: It's still positive to me. That's what I liked about the Elevators: everyone was looking for a future. Such a short period of being out in public, [but] I can't believe how well it's lasted.

TOMMY: We were able to objectively and scientifically approach acid, where other groups couldn't do that.

STACY (*K*): I would guess it was a form of religious madness. I look back on it as expansion. There was definitely a mystical element. They believed in God the source, I believe in God the being. But I studied these messages to get myself higher. I studied to get myself higher to the light.

ROKY: What I was thinking was that the songs were kinda like prayers . . . if you said a prayer, you would have good luck. And I wanted to add that. Our songs could have been like prayers too.

Opposite and following pages: Roky Erickson and the 13th Floor Elevators at the final reunion: Levitation Festival (previously the Austin Psych Fest) at Carson Creek Ranch, Austin, May 10, 2015—the first time Tommy, Roky, and Ronnie had shared the stage in decades.

CREDITS AND ACKNOWLEDGMENTS

AUTHOR ACKNOWLEDGMENTS

Walt Andrus (R.I.P.)
Pam Bailey (R.I.P.)
George Banks
Johndavid Bartlett
Andrew Brown
Peter Buesnel
Gordon Bynum
Stephanie Chernikowski
Scott Conn
David Craig (R.I.P.)
Stephen Curran
Duke Davis
Diana Driver
The Erickson family (special thanks to Sumner, for all his ongoing help over twenty years)
Dana Erickson
Donnie Erickson (R.I.P.)
Evelyn Erickson
Jegar Erickson
Mikel Erickson
Roger Erickson (R.I.P.)
Greg Forest
Jim Franklin
Max Fredrikson
Danny and Robert Galindo
Johnny Gathings
Tommy Hall
Carolyn Hall Lawrence
James Harrell
Dale Hawkins (R.I.P.)
Chet Helms (R.I.P.)
Liz Henry
Dennis Hickey
Don Hyde
Fred Hyde
Jack Jackson (R.I.P.)
Simon Jameson
Gay Jones
Bill Josey, Jr.
Joseph Kahn
John Kearney (R.I.P.)
Jim Langdon
Ronnie and Amy Leatherman
John Lewallen
Colleen Lightfoot
Jerry Lightfoot (R.I.P.)
Sandy Lockett (R.I.P.)
Patrick Lundborg (R.I.P.)
Johnny McAshan
Adam McCoy (R.I.P.)
Billy Miller
Terry Moore
Tary Owens (R.I.P.)
Charlie Prichard (R.I.P.)
Bobby Rector (R.I.P.)
George and Priscilla Ripley
Lelan Rogers (R.I.P.)
Powell and Toby St. John
Bob Snider
Bob Sullivan
Beau and Vicki Sutherland
Heather Sutherland
Sibyl and G. C. Sutherland (R.I.P.)
Paul Tennison
Danny Thomas
Benny and Jennifer Thurman
Steve Tolin
Allan Vorda
John Ike and Alice Walton
Houston White

PUBLISHER ACKNOWLEDGMENTS

Keith Abrahamsson
Phoebe Allen
Amy Buckley
Tom Clapp
Michael P. Daley
Jesper Eklow
Maggie Lyn Eklow
Sarah Evans
Sam Kilroy
Sofia Kugelberg
Paul Major
Dominic Masi, Jr.
Daylon Orr
Jesse Pollock
Beth Rudig
Andres Santo Domingo
Wesley Stokes
Spencer Sweeney
Ben Swift
Casey Whalen
Dr. Lila Wolfe

PHOTOGRAPH AND IMAGE CONTRIBUTORS

Photography and artwork: Collection of Paul Drummond

Additional images courtesy of:

The Art Institute of Chicago (229 right)
The Austin American-Statesman (33 top left, 35–37, 43, 61 left, 64, 85 top and center right, 86, 90 top, 92, 145 center left and right, 147 top, 150 right, 151 top, 216, 255, 270)
Austin History Center (68 top)
Austin Police Department (55–58, 61 right, 293 bottom)
Vicki Welch Ayo (237 bottom left)
Bellaire Historical Society (151 bottom)
Peter Buesnel (103 bottom left, 243 bottom)
Charly Records (132–133, 186, 212–213, 258 top, 268–269)
Guy Clark (178 bottom, 195–197, 207 top right, 218–219)
Scott Conn (25 top)
David Craig (148 top and center)
George L. Craig (xii, 140)
Stephen Curran (178 bottom)
Dick Clark Productions (106, 127)
Neal Douglas (xx [Copyright © Neal Douglas])
Diana Driver (71)
Erickson family (4, 11 top left and center right, 12, 14, 44, 137, 280, 287)
Mikel Erickson (237 bottom right)
Robert Galindo (189 bottom)
Carolyn Hall-Lawrence (7)
Clementine Hall (23 center right, 48 top, 189 top)
Dennis Hickey (85 bottom, 89 top left, 102, 117 bottom, 128 bottom, 177 top right, 208 bottom, 228 top, 271 top, 292)
Mitchell Howell (11 center left)
Richard Morton Jack (97 top left, 229 right)
Sam Angus Jackson (25 bottom)
Gay Jones (226, 232 bottom)
Bill Josey, Jr. (38, 65 left, 128 top left)
Joseph Kahn (281–282, 291 top, 293 top)
Ronnie Leatherman (11 top middle, 152–153, 259)
Jerry Lightfoot (169)
The Mass Media (257)
Ralph Y. Michaels (74, 75 left, 76, 77 top and center, 82–83, 148 bottom [Copyright © Ralph Y. Michaels. Used with permission])
New Journalism Project (125 bottom, 135 top left, 138–139, 146 top left, 222 top, 228 bottom, 242, 249, 256 top)
Glenn Pitts (75 right)
Record World magazine (89 top right, 128 top right, 145 top left, 167 bottom)
Rhino Entertainment Company (100 [Artwork by Stanley Mouse and Alton Kelley; © 1967, 1984, 19??. Rhino Entertainment Company. Used with permission. All rights reserved], 112–113 [Artwork by Stanley Mouse and Alton Kelley: © 1966, 1984, 1994. Rhino Entertainment Company. Used with permission. All rights reserved], 134 [Artwork by Steve Renick; © 1967, 1984, 1995. Rhino Entertainment Company. Used with permission. All rights reserved], 184 bottom [Artwork by Rick Griffin; © 1967, 1984, 1995 Rhino Entertainment Company. Used with permission. All rights reserved], 239 [Artwork by Victor Moscoso; © 1968, 1984, 1996. Rhino Entertainment Company. Used with permission. All rights reserved], www.familydog.com)
Larry Sepulvado (177 top left, 222 bottom, 223–225)
Gilbert Shelton (230, 254 top [Copyright © Gilbert Shelton. Used with permission])
Gilbert Shelton and Lieuen Adkins (215 top and bottom right [Copyright © Gilbert Shelton and Lieuen Adkins. Used with permission])
Betty Shumate (182–183)
Bob Simmons (cover, 23 top left, top right, center left, bottom left, bottom right, 40 top, 50, 68 bottom, 69 top and bottom left, 70 center left and bottom left, 72–73, 78, 81, 299–301)
Bob Snider (viii, x, 154–155)
Sutherland family (8, 276, 295 bottom)
Texas Student Media/*The Daily Texan* (147 bottom, 150 left)
Benny and Jennifer Thurman (11 bottom right, 17 bottom, 29 bottom)
TV Guide magazine (104, 126 top)
John Ike Walton (11 top right, 17 center right)
William Warner (160–165, 173 top and bottom left, 177 top left, 178 top, 180–181, 208 top, 210, 220–221, 234, 244, 247, 254 bottom, 260, 262 [Photographs by William Warner. Used with permission])
Russell Wheelock (173 bottom right, 174, 198, 200, 202–204, 206, 207 top left and bottom right [Photographs by Russell Wheelock. Used with permission])
Mark Weakley (146 top right and bottom left, 149)
Wes Wilson (94)